THE
RadioTimes
1993
YEARBOOK

THE
RadioTimes
1993
YEARBOOK

Edited by
Alison Wear

RAVETTE BOOKS

First published by Ravette Books Limited 1993

Printed and bound for Ravette Books Limited
8 Clifford Street, London W1X 1RB
An Egmont Company
by Bath Press Colourbooks

ISBN: 1 85304 341 9

Contents

Introduction

Unlike the gardening year, a year in broadcasting is rich in surprises. Of course there are the hardy annuals, the new seasons that herald the return of favourite programmes as faithfully as the cuckoo, but a feature of television and radio is the need to change – to woo and keep a huge audience on the edge of its armchairs.

So, welcome to the first *Radio Times Yearbook*. We hope that, with this book beside you, the year's highlights – and novelties – will become a matter of historical record. No more of those infuriating family rows about which year *Desert Island Discs* celebrated its 50th birthday. It was 1992.

In fact, 1992 was a year of anniversaries. The Queen celebrated the 40th anniversary of her accession to the throne. Radio 1 notched up 25 years. Paul McCartney turned 50. And Patrick Moore was still shining and sparkling – 35 years on with *The Sky at Night*.

It was the year of Spain, too. Barcelona hosted the Olympics. Spanish pride overflowed in a celebration of Christopher Columbus's historic voyage. And even the wandering gourmet, Keith Floyd, got in on the act.

All this and much more is recorded in the *Radio Times Yearbook* and, as you would expect from this country's best-selling magazine and most complete guide to broadcasting, the book is easy to use and comprehensive.

We've included some of our greatest hits. You'll find Brian James's moving interview with Falklands hero Simon Weston on his confrontation with the Argentine pilot who left him disfigured. Libby Purves's encounter with Gielgud and Branagh – the master and the young pretender – is included, too, as is Sue Arnold's hilarious review of *Going Live!*

But the bulk of the *Yearbook* is new material, generated by our stable of talented writers.

1992 was a great year. It was also the year that we wore the badge of excellence. I hope after reading this book you'll see why the judges named us *Magazine of the Year*.

Nicholas Brett
Editor of *Radio Times*

Drama and Comedy

With such a wealth of drama and comedy programmes broadcast during the year, it has been difficult deciding which of the many series and plays to feature. However, a combination of established favourites, such as *Lovejoy*, *London's Burning* and *Inspector Morse*, and innovative new drama programmes including *The Camomile Lawn* and *Screen Two's Truly Madly Deeply*, give the chapter a wide appeal.

The production with the most star-studded cast of 1992 was Radio 3's *Hamlet*, and the most stunning costumes appeared in *The House of Eliott*, BBC1's period drama series.

Find out about behind the scenes expertise on *Casualty*, and how the 'injuries' are made to look so realistic in a fascinating feature by William Greaves. Spend a day with *The Archers*, Britain's longest-running radio series, and say goodbye to *'Allo 'Allo!* which came to an end in December.

A profusion of TV detectives kept viewers entertained, and in the year of Spain, we were introduced to *Eldorado*, BBC1's new soap.

The most popular of the sitcoms featured older characters, with Richard Wilson as Victor Meldrew in *One Foot in the Grave* heading the ratings.

In December, the Radio Times Comedy and Drama Awards honoured the achievements of writers and performers, with awards for both newcomers and established names in radio and television.

Drama and Comedy

THE HOUSE OF ELIOTT

BBC1's lavish drama series set in the world of *haute couture* in the 20s returned in the autumn. Nicki Household meets Stella Gonet and Louise Lombard, otherwise known to viewers as sisters Beatrice and Evie Eliott

When Beatrice (Stella Gonet) and Evangeline (Louise Lombard) Eliott, looking stunningly chic, set sail for America – where they were to show their latest collection – at the end of the last series of *The House of Eliott*, they took with them the hopes and fears of around 10 million viewers – if not of the dashing Jack and Alexander, neither of whom deserves to be loved by so wonderful a woman!

Beatrice and Jack did, of course, have a brief reconciliation before they parted, although poor Bea was disappointed in the expectation that her handsome husband might stride up the gangplank at the last moment. But Evie vowed bravely never to see Alexander again, after he had demonstrated so clearly that his social standing and political career meant more to him than she did.

So what can we expect when the series returns in 1993? 'Everything's been left nicely up in the air, although I think Beatrice and Jack have realised that the old flame is still burning,' says Stella Gonet, who went straight into a starring role, opposite Robert Lindsay, in the West End production of *Cyrano de Bergerac* when the series ended.

She confesses that she has become 'very, very fond' of Beatrice over the 24 episodes, and can't wait to start playing her again. 'It's been

Jack (Aden Gillett) and Beatrice (Stella Gonet) with Evie (Louise Lombard)

Chris Capstick

lovely to be able to create and develop a character so fully. Beatrice has come a very long way since she and Evie were left penniless by their father. But her defences are still up. I think that's why she is so obsessed with the business. She doesn't ever want to be dependent on a man again, not even her husband – which is very unusual for a woman of that era.'

One of the chief fascinations of the series is that it is set in a decade when things were changing very fast for women. Says Gonet: 'Although she's become an emancipated woman of the 20s, Beatrice would have had a strict Edwardian upbringing, so when she bobbed her hair and shortened her skirts, she was making a very definite statement – whereas Evie, being 12 years younger, took all the changes for granted.'

Another great strength of the show is the bond between the two sisters who, despite their contrasting natures – Beatrice, mature and caring; Evie, headstrong and passionate – are utterly devoted to each other.'They're almost more than sisters,' explains Gonet, 'because their mother died in childbirth and Beatrice brought Evangeline up. Now that she's grown into a beautiful and intelligent woman, I think Beatrice is really proud of her – although she realises that she can't protect her anymore and that Evie's got to make her own mistakes.'

Louise Lombard feels she has been 'uniquely fortunate' to have taken her character from the age of 18 to 24 during a period of such exciting social change. 'She was quite shy and insecure at first, because she'd led a very sheltered life. But now that she's found recognition as a designer, I think she's really come into her own. She's creative, instinctive, impulsive and naturally unconventional. She couldn't care less what people think. At 24, she should really be married, but that's not a priority for her. She's learnt to enjoy the freedom of thought and action that having her own money brings.'

Not surprisingly, the two actresses quickly became firm friends outside work, and when, early in the first series, their characters abandoned their long Edwardian locks for a fashionably short bob, they went hand in hand to the hairdresser to give each other moral support. 'We both had really long hair, so it was quite traumatic having it all snipped off,' recalls Gonet. 'But once it had gone, we felt the same liberation that Beatrice and Evie did. Short hair gave us different personalities, and we had to go out and buy different clothes to go with them!'

The most unexpected thing about Stella Gonet is her Scottish accent. Now 32, she grew up in Greenock near Glasgow (where her Polish father and Scottish mother still live) and is one of 12 brothers and sisters. Rather than change her accent to become an actress, she decided to arrive at auditions speaking exactly as she thought the character would speak. 'It worked brilliantly,' she laughs, 'and it was great fun seeing the producers' faces when I relaxed into my normal speech after they'd given me the

Stella Gonet (left) and Louise Lombard as the Eliott sisters

Chris Capstick

part!' But now that she's well known, she doesn't have to resort to such tactics.

She decided to act because, as a middle child in a very large family, 'it was the only way to get people to listen to me'. She went straight from school to the Royal Scottish Academy of Music and Drama and, after a couple of years in the Scottish theatre (in Ayr, Dundee and Glasgow), she was invited to join the company for a young writers' festival at London's Royal Court Theatre.

Then followed leading roles at the National Theatre – Ophelia in *Hamlet* and Frances Purnell in *Racing Demon* – and the part of Irina in Chekhov's *The Three Sisters* with the Royal Shakespeare Company. Then came the first series of *The House of Eliott*, followed by a trip to Moscow to co-star with Robert Duval in an American film about Stalin. 'It's been ten years of solid work,' she says happily. 'Mostly theatre, with bits of telly in between.'

Unlike Beatrice, Stella is happy in a settled relationship with her partner of four years, the actor Nicholas Farrell, whom she met at the RSC. 'Having a steady relationship is very important for me, because I need a good anchor,' she says. 'At home, my family were my anchor.' The couple share a house in south London, where Stella says she loves cooking 'and being homely and cosy'.

At 22, Louise Lombard, who has a flat in Richmond, Surrey, leads a less settled life, although she too comes from a big family. She's the fifth of seven children and, like Stella Gonet, the only one to have become an actor. 'But I'm nothing special in my family, in fact I'm quite overshadowed, because both my sisters are lawyers and my younger brother Declan has been chosen to play for the Irish national football team!'

Although her parents are Irish – they came to England in the 50s – she grew up in Woodford, Essex, leaving Trinity Roman Catholic School at 16, with nine O' Levels. 'I was quite into school and was expected to stay on for A's and go on to read English at university,' she says. But she'd wanted to act since her early teens, so when an agent offered to take her on at 16, she abandoned all ideas of higher education or even drama school, and went professional. She quickly found roles in TV staples like *Casualty*, *The Bill*, and *Bergerac*, and at 17, appeared in an Aids warning commercial, as a girl who was tempted to try drugs at a party. 'My parents were very doubtful about that, but in a funny sort of way it clinched my career, because immediately afterwards I was offered the role of Anna in *Chancer*.'

Neither she nor Stella Gonet knew much about *The House of Eliott* when they were chosen for their roles in January 1991. Says Lombard 'Only the first two episodes had been written, so we had no idea where anything was going. But as far as I was concerned, just the fact that it was a two-girl story set in such an interesting period was reason enough to take the part.'

She has done endless research on the 20s since then, amassing a large personal collection of books, 'so that whenever there's a reference in the script to something that I don't know much about – like, say, the General Strike, I can go straight to a shelf and look it up'. She also immersed herself in the 'feel' of the period, by visiting the 20s costume department of the Victoria and Albert Museum, which recently displayed an exhibition of Joan Wadge's BAFTA Award-winning designs from the first series of *The House of Eliott*, alongside its permanent exhibition of 20s couture garments.

Despite having had 'considerable qualms' about stepping into Joan Wadge's shoes, the series' second costume designer, James Keast, has succeeded in creating a range of outfits that are just as authentic, stylish and sumptuous as his predecessor's. Working in a vast, cluttered subterranean studio in the basement of Television Centre, he has designed and supervised the making-up (by outside theatrical dressmakers) of all the clothes, hats, shoes and accessories worn by Beatrice, Evie and all the other principal characters in the show.

His research – from books, original magazines and the British library has been never-ending – although he makes a point of never actually copying illustrations 'unless I come across something absolutely brilliant'. Using the script as his starting point, 'because it gives me a feel for the story and what the characters would be likely to wear,' he sets about creating costumes which are as close as possible to what people really wore at the time. The only constraints are practical. For example, wide-brimmed hats are out, because they cast a shadow

Louise Lombard (seated left) and Stella Gonet with some of the stunning costumes from *The House of Eliott*

under studio and location lighting.

Wherever possible he used real period fabrics, which he obtains by scouring Bermondsey, Camden and Brixton markets or, in the last resort, from a specialist supplier. Occasionally he gets unexpected help from a viewer. For example, the black and gold beaded bodice of an evening dress which he created for the collection that the sisters took to America, was made from five yards of material that was offered to him by a retired dressmaker in Essex.

'I base a lot of Beatrice – both what she wears and how she designs – on Coco Chanel,' he explains, 'whereas I saw Evie, who's younger and artier, as more like the painter Sonia Delauney'. Costs are high, but nothing is wasted. All the costumes in the sisters' recent collections will re-appear in the next series on characters who will theoretically have 'bought' them. Hats – James Keast's favourite items – are re-trimmed to be used again, and much of the jewellery comes from his own collection.

The techniques used to make the clothes are very similar to ones used in the 20s. 'We now have labour-saving devices like overlockers to stop fabric fraying at the edges, but if a seam is going to be seen on camera, it's always oversewn by hand,' explains Keast. Viewers sometimes request the patterns of costumes they've seen in the series, but none exist. The dressmakers work straight from James's drawings, making a calico version on a stand, for his approval or alteration, before the fabric is cut.

Leading ladies Gonet and Lombard are highly appreciative of his designs. 'You can't beat the combination of exquisite fabrics and flattering lines,' says Louise Lombard, 'and they're really comfortable to wear.

'Twenties fashions must have given women a real sense of freedom after the corsets that characters like Aunt Lydia and Lady Haycock wore in the first series. They also allowed women to show their figure – hemlines have been rising higher and higher as the series goes along.' Wearing such beautiful outfits has heightened Lombard's own awareness of clothes. Having stuck mainly to leotard tops with jeans or long skirts in the past, she says she's now developed a taste for 'rather sumptuous classic suits and long dresses'.

The lavishness seems almost sinful to Stella Gonet, who got used to borrowing or adapting her sisters' hand-me-downs as a teenager – 'We got very good at finding odd things to make an outfit look completely different for a special occasion. It taught you to use your imagination. But it's been wonderful to be able to wear so many glorious, flattering creations in *The House of Eliott* – and to have such a good relationship with James Keast, who made allowances for all our likes and dislikes.'

Of course, authenticity in *The House of Eliott* goes far beyond the costumes. The outside scenes are all shot in Bristol, which can be transformed into 20s London more easily than the capital itself. 'What you see on screen is as close to 20s London as possible,' says producer Jeremy Gwilt. 'We go to enormous lengths to achieve that.' The exterior of *The House of Eliott*'s design studio is in Bristol's Berkeley Square, where most of the buildings are Georgian or Edwardian. Although London's Chelsea might have been just as suitable architecturally, it would have been impossible to find space there for the production's huge make-up and catering trailers. Even in the quieter streets of Bristol, outdoor filming is restricted to Sundays, to minimise local disruption.

It takes the BBC design team around three hours to send Berke-

Evening dress – *House of Eliott* style

Chris Capstick

ley Square back to the 20s. Lamp-posts are 'antiqued', yellow lines temporarily hidden with latex paint, special 'cobblestone' mats put down, and parking meters disguised with glass fibre posts which look like cast iron. Then more period atmosphere is piled on with news-paper boys, flower sellers, horses and carriages and vintage cars. 'Old photographs of 20s London show that the streets were packed with cars and activity, so we do our best to reproduce that,' says Jeremy Gwilt.

'We do at least provide a little entertainment for people who have to put up with our presence on a summer Sunday,' says Stella Gonet. 'When the weather's nice, the public come and sit on the grass in the middle of Berkeley Square and watch all the goings on.' She's become very attached to Bristol over the two series, although when asked to pick a favourite scene or episode, she plumps, without hesi-tation, for Paris, where Beatrice and Jack fell in love. 'It was wonderful to film such a totally romantic episode in the world's most roman-tic setting,' she says. 'It epitomised what *The House of Eliott* is all about.'

Nicki Household

TRULY MADLY DEEPLY

Screen Two's Truly Madly Deeply, **already a cinema success, brought the combined talents of Juliet Stevenson and Alan Rickman to the small screen in March. Julie Allan looks at the success of Anthony Minghella's play and the careers of Stevenson and Rickman**

Truly, madly, deeply they were in love – Nina and Jamie. So in love that when Jamie died, still young, and Nina could find no life without him, he came back to be with her, to hold her, to laugh with her, to annoy her with his strange habits and stranger friends, and finally to fade away when Nina was able to face their parting.

Truly Madly Deeply starring Juliet Stevenson and Alan Rickman, and written with Stevenson in mind by her long-time friend Anthony

Minghella, did well at the UK box office before its screening on BBC2 in March last year. It was also one of the few British films to do well in the USA and it won *Evening Stan-dard* Awards for Stevenson (best actress), Rickman (best actor for this and other roles) and Minghella (best newcomer).

The success of the film meant that both Stevenson and Rickman were introduced to a wide audience. Both were experienced actors, with many favourably received or acclaimed roles to their credit, but this film seemed to touch many hearts. 'It is not a film about bereavement specif-ically,' says Stevenson, echoing writer Minghella's view, 'it is a film about being stuck, being unable to progress. I know what it is to lose someone and to think that without

them you won't ever again be complete. I've had experience of that, and it has taken all my skin off.'

Truly Madly Deeply was indeed based on aspects of Stevenson's own life, including her living alone in a muddle in a London flat and having to get someone in to rid her of rats. 'It was initially a very private thing,' she says of the film, 'so when it was released and the world said it liked it, it was fab.' Her willingness to lay herself completely open for a role prompted Minghella to com-ment, 'it's like there's nothing between you and her soul'. Steven-son admits, 'I do ruthless daylight raids on my own life. There is noth-ing, however private, I will not use. I appal myself sometimes.'

And where her real life isn't

Alan Rickman and Juliet Stevenson in *Truly Madly Deeply*

BBC Photograph Library

enough, she is meticulous in her research. To play Isabella in *Measure for Measure*, who flees to a convent, she stayed in a convent herself to help her assess Isabella's motivations. But her Olivier Award-winning performance in the harrowing *Death and the Maiden* early last year challenged her resources enough to frighten her.

She portrays a woman raped, humiliated and tortured at the hands of a fascist regime in South America, who gets the chance to exact revenge on the man she believes was responsible. Stevenson contacted Chilean exiles and met

Helen Bamber, who runs the Medical Foundation for the Victims of Torture.

'It was like meeting a saint or Ghandi,' she says. 'It was arrogance to believe I could ever imagine being tortured. I wondered "How could anyone live with this memory and with the rage which hasn't found any outlet?" But then I thought, "I must give myself permission to do this" and I called upon everything I had.'

The play went to Broadway; Stevenson did not. It was all to do with how many Americans had been acting over here and how many Brits had acted over there,

and the actors' union Equity wouldn't allow her the role. Instead Glenn Close got it. On this issue the intense but usually equable actress bristles with irritation. 'I was very disappointed, but more than that it's a point of principle. It seems crazy, when there is no language barrier, not to encourage cross-fertilisation in the theatre. You don't stop French painters from exhibiting in Germany or German musicians from playing here.'

Stevenson herself has spent plenty of time in various countries – all at a young age. The family went wherever her brigadier father (who died last summer) was posted. When she was 9, Juliet Stevens (Stevenson was a later change imposed by Equity) went to boarding school in Berkshire (Hurst Lodge, and yes she was there at the same time as the Duchess of York). It was run by the elderly sister of actor Leslie Howard and the arts were considered important. She enjoyed it, winning prizes for ballet, verse-speaking and drama.

Then came training at RADA, followed by the RSC for eight years and roles including the Laurence Olivier Award-nominated Isabella in *Measure for Measure*, Cressida in *Troilus and Cressida* and the title-role in *Yerma*. At the National Theatre in London, her performance of Hedda Gabler was particularly acclaimed.

She likes variety, wants to try new things and recent involvements have included a 'quasi-erotic' role in a film version of Kafka's *The Trial*, a BBC TV production of *The Doll's House*, and credit-spotting viewers may also have noted her name as narrator on various television programmes, including last autumn's *Doctors to Be* series, and a December *Horizon* special called *The Truth About Sex*. 'I do things that interest me. It gives me the chance to come in contact with a wider range of subjects than through simply acting. Sometimes I learn things I can draw on for performances,' she explains.

Her wish to learn about new fields, however, didn't stop her narrating *Army Lives* a couple of years ago, which interested her because of her connection with the

Juliet Stevenson as Nina

BBC Photograph Library

real thing and it was the knowledge she gained from *Death and the Maiden* that led to her December television appearance presenting BBC2's *Prisoners of Conscience*: 'You become aware of an appalling human rights violation and you realise that you can help to stop it.'

It was at the RSC that she met up with her *Truly Madly Deeply* co-star Alan Rickman, and their long-standing friendship, together with other performances together, was useful to both in creating the sweet and sometimes sadness-tinged intimacy between their characters Nina and Jamie. Earlier they had played opposite each other on the West End stage in *Les Liaisons Dangereuses*, she as Mme de Tourvel, he as the dedicated seducer Vicomte de Valmont. 'People allow the Valmonts of this world,' said Rickman at the time. 'It was fascinating to watch that kind of evil being so entertaining and erotic.'

His early life and career progression were not perhaps as clear-cut an advance toward the theatre as were Stevenson's. One of four children, he was brought up on a council estate in Acton, west London, and his father died while he was still young. He won a scholarship to Latymer direct grant school, from where he went to art school, training in graphic design at Chelsea and the Royal College of Art.

At 26, he gave up his design business in London's Soho and odd-jobbed his way through RADA. He was at the RSC for three years, although immediate acclaim was not to be his: the story goes that one season a directors' meeting was called to discuss his awfulness. Fortunately he quickly made good and has never looked back. 'I also spent seven years doing plays at the Bush, at Hampstead and the Royal Court, which I regard as my spiritual home as much as the RSC,' says Rickman.

Apart from his *Evening Standard* best actor award for his roles in *Truly Madly Deeply*, *Robin Hood, Prince of Thieves* (in which as the hilariously over-the-top Sheriff of Nottingham he rather stole the show from Kevin Costner) and

Close My Eyes (as a wealthy husband who discovers his wife to be having an affair with her brother), he won a BAFTA for best actor in a supporting role (*Robin Hood*) and a BAFTA best actor in a leading role nomination for *Truly Madly Deeply*. He was also Tony nominated for his performance in *Les Liaisons Dangereuses* on Broadway.

Recent stage roles include a tour of *Hamlet*, despite the fact that in 1991 he apparently told a reviewer that this was a role he was now too old to play, and the lead in *Tango at the End of Winter*, as a Japanese actor nearing the end of his career. Rickman's slight concern about the accessibility of the play to a British audience also highlights his annoyance at the lack of investment Britain puts behind its acting talent. '*Tango at the End of Winter* is from a culture which puts its actors on pedestals...this is not true of Britain, where actors spend a lot of time working on rubbish tips, standing in dole queues and on whatever the opposite of a pedestal is.'

Of the state of British theatre, particularly with regard to funding outside London, he has said: 'When I left drama school you could go to a repertory theatre and be in a Shakespeare play or something large where you could go and make ghastly mistakes. The only places you can do that now are the RSC and the National. Everyone's

Alan Rickman as Jamie

BBC Photograph Library

making their mistakes in great big places.'

When his peeved Sheriff of Nottingham cried 'no more merciful beheadings' you feel sure that Rickman would have been happy to confine to the dungeons anyone who asked about his private life or commented on his bad-guy roles. He's a wary interviewee but a dry sense of humour emerges when he's talking about craft. 'I've worked very closely with Juliet on many productions,' he volunteers. 'In fact I think that we performed the first radio oral sex in another of Anthony Minghella's plays. It was appropriately titled *A Little Like Drowning*.'

Juliet Stevenson is not so guarded on matters personal, although one mystery certainly remains: where on earth does she conjure up the energy that she appears to put in to her every waking moment. She will speak about the ended love affair that she drew on for *Truly Madly Deeply*, will say that she has found and lost several soulmates, declare that she doesn't see quite how she could ever be married and state that she'd really love to have children: 'It's so constructive to give a human being the space to grow, to learn from it.' Her concern on that front is that she might not have sufficient energy. It is a touching characteristic that, for all her relentless openness, Juliet Stevenson still wonders about herself.

Julie Allan

THE CAMOMILE LAWN

Mary Wesley's saga, *The Camomile Lawn*, starring Felicity Kendal and Paul Eddington, also introduced viewers to several talented newcomers. Richard Johnson looks back on Channel 4's starry production directed by Sir Peter Hall

Actors are trained in the art of the grand entrance – but for the young cast members of period drama *The Camomile Lawn*, it has been a grander entrance than most. Tara Fitzgerald, Jennifer Ehle, Toby Stephens – out of drama school less than two years – have become established faces over the past year,

Ehle winning the Radio Times Comedy and Drama Award for best TV newcomer at the end of 1992. In the words of Paul Eddington, who played Uncle Richard in *The Camomile Lawn*, 'It's very moving to think that the future of my profession is in such good hands.'

Paul Eddington and Jennifer Ehle

The Camomile Lawn captured the atmosphere of the war for the young – the frivolity and the fear. But inevitably the tabloids were more interested in the frivolity. Felicity Kendal certainly got a sex scene the like of which she'd never had on *The Good Life*, but to an audience reared on *The Men's Room* and *A Time To Dance*, it was all quite tame. What was odd was that *The Camomile Lawn* was written by a woman who had her first novel published at the age of 72.

Despite its grim wartime backdrop, *The Camomile Lawn* also qualified as a high-quality five-hour soap opera. But then that seemed to be the way Wesley had lived her war. 'There were impromptu parties all the time in London because people were always passing through, and if you speak to anyone of my generation, you'll find we had a very good time, compounded by the real horror of people getting killed and losing one's friends, and the terror.'

During the war, Wesley worked in various jobs, including decoding radio signals. 'We weren't allowed to tell our husbands or anyone where we worked or what we did. I remember lunching with an ex-boyfriend in the Ritz one day and it was pouring with rain. He offered me a lift and I told him I wasn't allowed to say where I worked, so we went our separate ways. We met in the lift going up to my office. He worked on the floor above me.'

Filmed in Cornwall, Oxfordshire and Pinewood, *The Camomile Lawn* took 13 weeks to shoot. Using over 100 sets, the look of the film was always important. Director Sir Peter Hall remembered the war as 'black and white, with all the windows blacked out, grey buses, and streets very empty of cars.' It was a memory which set the visual tone of the series, and distinguished the different time periods. The pre-war scenes in Cornwall were brightly lit and colourful, the war years more monochromatic.

Mary Wesley did not believe that the house she had written about – with a camomile lawn running down to the sea – could exist. It was, after all, purely a figment of her imagination. But the location manager scoured the south-west, with Wesley's description in mind, and proved her wrong. A National Trust house overlooking a bay in Veryan, Cornwall, was perfect in every detail – apart from one. There

was no tree from which Sophy could eavesdrop on the family. One was transplanted for the duration of the filming, with six tons of concrete as temporary roots.

Another requirement for filming was the camomile lawn itself. For close-up shots, real camomile, which looks like moss, was planted on the lawn, but for longer shots the crew made do with turf. In an effort to maintain the lawn's pristine appearance, despite the trampling feet of a crew of 130, grass seed was strewn over the lawn every night. The habit was abandoned because of the continuous rain throughout the shoot. But then coping with what was laughingly called the British summer in 1991 was all part of Hall's job.

For Hall, founder of the Royal Shakespeare Company, artistic director at Glyndebourne and erstwhile master of the National Theatre, it was to prove the least of his problems. He had to bring to life a plot which involved 20 major characters across four generations – 'And every character had to age through 40 years' says Hall. 'Now, one actor or actress can go from early 40s to early 80s without much difficulty, but to make the transformation from 20 to 60 is simply not on.' So his great casting search began.

'Thankfully Sophie and Glenn

Felicity Kendal (as Helena) and Paul Eddington (as Richard)

(co-producers Balhetchet and Wilhide) and Channel 4 did not say, "You've got to cast Barbra Streisand or we can't make it". They said, "How can we cast this as well as possible?" I think it's because of that we ended up with a very heavy-weight, starry cast.' *The Camomile Lawn* was certainly the year's most well-heeled drama, starring Felicity Kendal and Paul Eddington, Virginia McKenna, Claire Bloom and Richard Johnson.

Their ageing was down to layers of liquid latex – comparable, according to Felicity Kendal, to having a plastic bag over the face. To make her mouth look shrivelled, Kendal had artificial dentures clipped onto her own front teeth. Together with wigs and a false bosom, Kendal's silhouette was considerably altered. Blue eyes fade as people get older, and she wore bright blue contact lenses as the young Helena, and paler ones as the 80-year-old Helena.

The young cast of *The Camomile Lawn*

Felicity Kendal

The Camomile Lawn's key characters were a group of teenagers who were emotionally and sexually awakened by the war. They were cast before their older counterparts and allowed the freedom to establish their roles first. 'It was less important that the actors looked alike, but they needed to be similar in some way,' says Balhetchet. 'For

example, Virginia McKenna and Tara Fitzgerald, playing Polly, have very much the same qualities of stillness and reserve.'

The Camomile Lawn gave new meaning to the term family saga. Toby Stephens, who played the young Oliver, was the son of Maggie Smith and Robert Stephens. His character was drawn to Calypso, played by Jennifer Ehle. Hall cast Ehle without realising that she was the daughter of Rosemary Harris. The 21-year-old had kept her family background a secret during auditions, not knowing that Hall had jotted down in his notebook, 'Sounds like Rosemary Harris'. Once Jennifer was cast it seemed natural to cast Rosemary Harris as the older Calypso.

Then came the matter of casting the pivotal role of the 10-year-old orphan Sophy. Balhetchet and casting director Ann Fielden saw

hundreds of girls for the part, and Hall himself interviewed 30. Two weeks before shooting, Balhetchet suggested Hall's 9-year-old daughter Rebecca. She was a natural. Wesley herself admitted, 'She's exactly as I imagined Sophy to be.' She learnt her lines two days before each shoot, but according to her father, 'Directing her was no different from directing Felicity Kendal'.

The older actors varied in their approach to the drama. McKenna (who had to wear brown contact lenses to match Fitzgerald's darker complexion) studied Fitzgerald's scenes to see if there were any particular vowel sounds, intonations or movements she should incorporate. Johnson, however, didn't look at the rushes of Toby Stephens. 'He's a good actor,' says Johnson, 'and we will interpret the part between us. Oliver would have changed anyway as there are 40 years between the two parts.'

The Camomile Lawn was Stephens' first professional assignment after graduating from the London Academy of Music and Dramatic Art. Since then he has gone to Stratford to join the Royal Shakespeare Company for *Antony and Cleopatra* (with Richard Johnson), and *All's Well That Ends Well*. Jennifer Ehle left the Central School of Speech and Drama before the final term in 1991 to appear as Calypso, and has gone on to tour with Derek Jacobi in *Breaking the Code*. Hall cast both in his recent production of *Tartuffe* at the London Playhouse.

Tara Fitzgerald was in her last term at The Drama Centre when she was chosen to star as the romantic lead in the film *Hear My Song*. After *The Camomile Lawn*,

Tara Fitzgerald

she went on to ITV's *Anglo Saxon Attitudes* and *Our Song* in the West End. Her next TV project is a return to Mary Wesley with *Harnessing Peacocks*, where she plays an upper-class waif, down on her luck, forced to become a call-girl. 'It is better to arrive with a bang than a whimper' says Fitzgerald. 'But now I can't fall too far. When I make mistakes I'm doing it in front of millions of people instead of three people in a rep theatre in Outer Mongolia.'

Richard Johnson

FAY WELDON'S THE CLONING OF JOANNA MAY AND GROWING RICH

1992 saw even more of novelist Fay Weldon's work make the successful transition to innovative television drama – *The Cloning of Joanna May*, starring Patricia Hodge and *Growing Rich*, with Martin Kemp and John Stride. Richard Johnson meets the stars and the author

For Fay Weldon (MA, DLit, Fellow of the Royal Society of Literature) the year's television work, in the shape of *Growing Rich* and *The Cloning of Joanna May*, came as welcome relief from the rarefied world of books. 'Accessible is a dirty word in certain circles of the literary world. There is a great tradition that if you are likeable and people in any number respond to your work, you must be cheating. You're no good, in other words, if you are not hard work. This is where television scores – you cannot be obscure.'

Fay Weldon was christened Franklin Birkinshaw. Her mother was a writer, her father a doctor. She was born in England, raised in New Zealand in an all female household of sister, mother and grandmother, and educated in Scotland, where she read Economics and Psychology at St Andrew's University. She then went into advertising, and became famous as the copywriter who coined the slogan, 'Go to work on an egg'.

After a decade of odd jobs (including answering letters for the *Daily Mirror* problem pages, clerking in the Foreign Office, and market research in the street), she started writing 'out of sheer irritation'. Her first book was *The Fat Woman's Joke*, published in 1967. She has four sons of varying ages ('I could only wipe one face at a time') and works as a novelist, playwright and critic out of her home in north London.

Weldon's first major adaptation for television was Jane Austen's *Pride and Prejudice*, but by the 80s producers were turning to her for original material, including *Heart of the Country* and *The Life and*

Loves of a She-Devil. And 1992, with *Growing Rich* and *The Cloning of Joanna May*, offered her another chance to indulge her appetite. 'Television is such enormous fun,' she says. 'You communicate with enormous numbers of people on an everyday level. It's very exhilarating making the fantastic real, reshaping real life.'

Growing Rich tells the story of three bright Fenland girls (played by Rosalind Bennett, Caroline Harker and Claire Hackett) who fail their A' Levels and fall into the adult world, determined to escape a life of pram pushing and Tupperware parties. Looking to bring about their fall are local raff and entrepreneur Sir Bernard Bellamy (John Stride), and the Devil (Martin Kemp), disguised as Sir Bernard's suave chauffeur.

The girls start their professional lives outside the Job Centre. There they meet a market researcher with a clipboard who tells them they have an 82 per cent chance of falling pregnant within the year. 'The three girls are trying to live honourable lives in a world which makes it very difficult', says Weldon. 'When you're thinking about whether it's possible for somebody to sell their soul to the Devil, it's difficult, because everyone's done it. So the Devil has a hard time providing anything that anybody can't have anyway.'

Weldon has a knack of putting the woman's point of view first. Her characters live in a woman's world and, as The *Independent* put it, 'The women are on top even when downtrodden.' But if Weldon's novels – most notably *The Life and Loves of a She-Devil* – are principally about women, it's because they are what she understands. 'My characters get pregnant, are betrayed, are victims of their biology, of each other and of ill-chosen males. It's this thing of the erotic and the maternal always being in a sort of conflict.'

The men in *Growing Rich* certainly have to work hard to make amends for the sins of their gender. According to Weldon, they get off lightly. 'If you look at the statistics, the reality of men is far worse than the version I produce. And the women characters aren't much to boast about. They've just got bigger parts. If you look at most traditional drama, men act and women react. Men make statements, the women ask questions. If you reverse that, it comes over as if the men are really weak. In fact, they're behaving as people behave rather than as somebody of a certain gender.'

For Martin Kemp, playing the Devil was an education. 'Good you can take to the limits in everyday life – and who notices these days? But to be asked to explore evil, and pass that barrier you set up for yourself in everyday life, is exciting. There are new types of adrenalin that only exist when you cross the barrier. And if you're given the opportunity to look at that and put it back in its box, you'll know more about yourself. I can almost feel why people who've committed a certain crime once want to do it again – it's the only way they can get back in touch with that adrenalin.'

Kemp was born in a large house in Islington with aunts living upstairs and cousins downstairs. The family had no bathroom, an outside loo, and an air-raid shelter in the yard. His bedroom overhung a pub, and he was sung to sleep by *Roll out the Barrel.* But he always craved glamour. When he was in the local football team, he painted his boots sky blue and lined them with fur. And at the age of nine he went across the road with his brother Gary to the Anna Scher Drama School. But he turned his back on acting to join the band Spandau Ballet in 1979.

Being a rock star helped his exposure, but it didn't help his credibility when he returned to acting. 'At the beginning of *The Krays* it was like trying to make the film with one arm tied behind your back. You weren't really allowed to let loose because people were still saying, "Spandau Ballet". Even today trailers for the film say "Spandau Ballet star Martin Kemp". It's not fair. At one point the producers were asking us to do an end-out song. But that was the problem with *Buster.* One minute Phil Collins was acting, the next he was singing. As soon as he started singing he

lost complete credibility – he was Phil Collins again.'

To prove his comedic talent Kemp recently took the ham role of Baron Frankenstein in horror spoof *Lost In Time* – no gangland violence, although the monster does crush his head and send his brains flying across the laboratory. And in another effort to escape the criminal underworld, he is starring with Patsy Kensit in a remake of *The Innocents*, the thriller based on Henry James's *The Turn of the Screw.* 'I play the ghost who's possessing the young boy – another nice role. I'm doing all these films, and *Growing Rich*, but there's nothing I can show my daughter until she's 18. She's going to wonder where I get my money from.'

Kemp's Devil busies himself by bringing gargoyles to life, putrefying fruit on supermarket shelves, and having cathedrals disappear and reappear on dual carriageways.

Martin Kemp in *Growing Rich*

Rex Features

Special effects on the £3 million serial were supervised by production designer Spencer Chapman, the man responsible for *Tales of the Unexpected.* Weldon's favourite of the 30 different electronic effect shots was the Devil's stab at genetic engineering. 'He makes a girl's legs longer, waist smaller and her bust bigger. She calls him terribly old fashioned,' says Weldon, 'because the Devil's obviously a tit man.'

Not every effect could be created electronically, and the people of Norfolk won't forget the day the Devil (and the entire *Growing Rich* camera crew) came to town. The script required a motorway construction-site, so Anglia Television bought up a pea field and moved in the mechanical diggers. Locals were convinced it wasn't a film shoot at all, but that they were getting their own six-lane bypass. Bar talk reached its peak when the Norfolk police discovered bones on newly-turned soil. The area only avoided a murder hunt when set designers revealed that 'the motorway' was being built on an 'Anglo-Saxon burial site', and the bones were plastic.

One special effect beloved of budget-conscious television companies is the art of turning one country into another. On the ITV drama series *Making News*, the budget wouldn't stretch to filming in Australia, so the part was played by Snowdonia in North Wales. But *Growing Rich*'s producer Roger Gregory, had allocated money for filming in New Zealand early on. 'If we shot it in Wales we could paint in mountains with snow onto the back of certain static shots. But then we could only shoot in one direction. And we wanted to continue the fluid shooting style we've got. We were there in shearing season, with snow right down the mountains. The lakes and light are a different colour from any in the world.'

In the adaptation of *The Cloning of Joanna May*, Joanna (Patricia Hodge) discovers that Carl (Brian Cox) her villainous partner of 20 years has run off – not with another woman – but with three clones of her younger self. Carl is convinced that the clones are naturally destined to love him with Joanna's unwavering devotion. But he is bewildered to find that Alice, Gina and Jane are modern young women with ideas of their own, and unimpressed by his power and money. Determined to free Joanna, the three clones turn on the man who brought them life.

The stuff of medieval witchcraft? Science fiction run riot? The inspiration for Weldon's novel, published in 1989, was rooted in fact. 'I read a small piece which said that it is now possible to clone a human being, but it would never happen because there was no call for it. I thought, "Why isn't there a call for it?" If you wanted to make a clone for purely physical reasons, then there's no reason why not. I went to see an Egyptologist in Sweden who was working on cloning a mummy. He reckoned he had got 90 per cent towards it but then the government intervened.'

Weldon insists there is nothing wrong with cloning, and for her it is more than just fantasy. 'Officially the Egyptologist is supposed to have stopped his research, but I believe it's still going on. Of course it will happen, and may have happened already. And I don't think it's such an awful thing. I don't see why people shouldn't breed for brains and beauty. People are much happier if they are bright and beautiful.' Not that Weldon is quite such a She-Devil – she enjoys mixing her narrator's voice with the author's.

If *The Life And Loves of a She-Devil* was the woman's revenge, then *The Cloning of Joanna May*, a modern fairy tale, is definitely the man's last laugh. *Joanna May* angered some feminists because, in the end, the heroine stands by her man. But, as producer Gub Neal points out, 'Ultimately Fay's work is also a celebration of feminine intuition and values – because Joanna May ultimately rejects the ignoble aspects of Carl's machismo and all the bad things that he represents.'

The production (which Weldon described as a 'tale of technology, lust and undying love') reunited Ted Whitehead, director Philip Saville and executive producer Sally Head, the team which produced *She-Devil*, with Patricia Hodge, who

Patricia Hodge, who starred in *The Cloning of Joanna May*

played the manipulating mistress in the award-winning drama serial. Commenting on her reaction to the role of Joanna May, Hodge said, 'I know this is an incredibly disturbing storyline, but I am not frightened of growing older. I believe women who allow themselves to age gracefully have a certain beauty all of their own.'

The mid-life crisis passed Hodge by. 'The sort of women who are hit by it are the women who were terribly dominant in the swinging 60s, all those leggy blondes and models who came out of the woodwork. Interestingly, they haven't aged very well, and although they had a fabulous time in their 20s, they have retained that look, but now they are older and haven't done much with their lives. People like me were not at all fashionable at that time – and I had to find my own way; it's happened over a number of years. My growth has been more organic, if you see what I mean.'

Weldon meanwhile continues to grow methodically and organically. She has been busy with a radio play for Walter Matthau, and *Eclipse*, her new novel. There's talk of her adapting the romantic historical novelist, Georgette Heyer, for television, and her name has even been linked with the team behind a new soap opera – 'although I can't talk about that until they pay me the acceptance fee'. As usual in the world of Weldon, all things are possible.

Richard Johnson

RADIO 3'S HAMLET

Kenneth Branagh plays Prince to John Gielgud's Ghost in Radio 3's all-star production of *Hamlet*. Libby Purves meets the two stars of Shakespeare's tragedy

Kenneth Branagh at Kronborg Castle, Elsinore, Denmark. Known as 'Hamlet's Castle', it has been the setting for film and stage productions of the play, though the tragic prince himself never slept nor saw a ghost here

Sixty years ago last summer, on those grand old coffin-shaped BBC microphones, *Hamlet* was performed on radio. The Prince of Denmark was played by young John Gielgud, great-nephew of Ellen Terry, who was Sir Henry Irving's leading lady. In the spring of 1992, Shakespeare's birthday was honoured by an uncut four-hour stereo production of *Hamlet* on Radio 3. And Gielgud is still there.

This time he is the ghost of Hamlet's father, freezing our blood and harrowing our souls up on the battlements of Elsinore. Last time he played the part it was to Richard Burton's Hamlet. Now his son is Kenneth Branagh, with Derek Jacobi as uncle Claudius; and the first *Hamlet* that Branagh ever saw as a boy starred Jacobi. And then – Mark me! as the Ghost would say – who but Derek Jacobi directed Branagh on stage as Hamlet?

Meanwhile they all remember Olivier and argue about his Hamlet, and Ian McKellen's, and wish they had seen Gielgud's. And Richard Briers (who was Kenneth Branagh's

Malvolio in *Twelfth Night*) is now Polonius; and Judi Dench is Queen Gertrude, passing on hints to young Sophie Thompson (Branagh's sister-in-law) from her past experience as Ophelia. Sir Michael Hordern, another Shakespearean knight, takes a modest part as the Player King; and the Player Queen, the original lady who 'doth protest too much' is Branagh's wife Emma Thompson (a former Ophelia and no doubt a future Gertrude), happy to take a humble 30 lines in such august company.

And Sir John Gielgud beams upon them all. His being there, doom'd for a certain term to walk the night in the cellarage of the BBC, provides the magic and tan-

gible link across a century of Shakespearean actors that stretches all the way back to Irving.

You have to understand this to feel the full thrill of the occasion. Any map of Shakespearean connections among British actors rapidly takes on the appearance of a demented spider's web. There is something even more intense about *Hamlet* connections, because the play is so tormentingly difficult to do – an actor's Everest. This cast is almost an embarrassment of riches: a radio production can concentrate talent better than anything else because, let us be practical, it only takes eight working days and costs peanuts. Actors both fear and enjoy radio: free from costumes and sets, it amplifies the meaning and sets up new, exciting resonances.

And in-jokes. Paradoxically, this fleshless Radio 3 *Hamlet* is a very theatrical event. When Hamlet lectures the Players on acting – 'Speak the speech, I pray you...trippingly on the tongue...Nor do not saw the air too much with your hand, thus' – a good part of the joke lies in the fact that this is the rather schoolmasterly, boy-wonder Branagh telling Sir Michael Hordern how to suck eggs. When the Ghost lays his chilling burden on his son, the thrill is more solemn: this is Sir John Gielgud, two years off his 90th birthday, handing a torch to the self-same cocksure, ambitious Branagh and departing with 'Adieu, adieu, Hamlet. Remember me'.

When he spoke the lines, sitting in plain clothes on a BBC chair, Kenneth Branagh recalls that the

(From left): Sophie Thompson, Judi Dench, Richard Briers, Derek Jacobi and Kenneth Branagh

rest of the cast were virtually 'hanging from the rafters, craning out to see him'. The frisson was tremendous. On the air, it still is.

So it was these two actors, with nearly 60 years between them, who were pictured together to celebrate the event. Branagh is inured to baddish personal publicity by his meteoric rise: since he left the RSC to form the Renaissance Theatre Company, starred in and directed his own film of *Henry V* in an echo of Laurence Olivier, took to directing far senior actors with unsettling self-assurance and wrote his autobiography at 29, almost everything written about him has carried a fierce subtext of 'Who does he think he is?'

'I'm an actor. I love plays. I enjoy work and I love to play in the First Division,' he says. 'It is honestly not a power trip. Perhaps in 40 years people will look back and see that I was straight about that. I don't want to buy 16 film companies and ten theatres. I want to end up playing the Ghost in someone else's *Hamlet*.'

It was Glyn Dearman of Radio 3 who asked Branagh to co-direct this production, and he was pleased but nervous. 'I didn't know much about radio, but it was educative and inspiring. There is a freedom about it,' he says. 'It is wonderful not to have an audience reciting "To be or not to be" and "Alas poor Yorick" under its breath.' It helped him think about Hamlet for his RSC part in the autumn of 1992. 'Because you don't have to project the soliloquies across a whole theatre, but can do them very privately with a close microphone, you really go from thought to thought, not trying to act up or be beautiful. You just serve Hamlet's intelligence.'

Another advantage, he thinks, was that this production is uncut. 'Keeping every word gives us a new view of Elsinore: an echoing, uneasy place with Gertrude and Ophelia isolated and everything overshadowed by politics.'

Had Branagh felt competent to give directions to his oldest star, Sir John Gielgud? 'Er, no. Not remotely.' Had he liked him? 'He is marvellous. Incredibly up-to-date, very well-informed about new things. I'm sure that's why he's

Gielgud (left) and Branagh discuss the production

lasted so long, his mind never stops.'

On cue, elegant and slightly smiling, Gielgud arrives. 'Oh dear, I'm going deaf suddenly. I have to get to Harley Street by 12. I sat between the Princess Royal and Audrey Hepburn the other night and couldn't hear a word. This won't do.' It is a most beautiful voice. He and Branagh chat about current jobs. 'You're doing *Coriolanus*? I hate the play. At Chichester? Nasty theatre.' says Gielgud cheerfully. It is palpably true about his mind: even hampered by the new deafness, he picks up everything, nips between topics, dissects the Oscars. They pose for a photograph with a BBC property skull and I notice that they are exactly the same height. Yet the older man towers, his refined face an ancient ivory carving beside the smooth-cheeked, pugnacious Branagh. Everyone calls him 'Sir' and Branagh 'Ken'.

We talk about *Hamlet*, and again that acuteness shows: he does not want to reminisce but to concentrate on the current job. 'The Ghost is very difficult. You have to be very strong and commanding and at the same time ghostly and insubstantial.' He remembers with relish a 1991 experimental film role in Peter Greenaway's *Prospero's Books*. 'This terrible cloak, four people had to lower it on to me and I was supposed to walk around. Either that or I was stark naked in an icy pool.' I press him

to reminisce: when was his best Hamlet? 'I enjoyed New York most. In 1937. I was on my mettle, and Leslie Howard was doing his out there at the same time. We tried to be gentlemanly, but the papers called it the "Battle of the Hamlets".' Did he win? 'Yes.' Has he improved since? 'Yes, I hope so. I used to sing the lines too much. I have had to learn to be less fond of my own voice.'

He snaps back to the present. 'It's good to see young actors so happy to do Shakespeare. And Richard Briers, who's connected to modern work so much, now turning into such a very fine Shakespearean actor. And I did like Kenneth Branagh's *Twelfth Night*, it had great tenderness and romance, which is rare now. I sometimes think there are too many productions, though, all competing. And I do not like Theatre in the Round, or modern dress.'

He feels his age, not in himself so much as in the loss of friends. 'It's awful to be the only one left – Ralph Richardson, Olivier, Peggy Ashcroft, Gwen (Ffrangcon-Davis) all gone. I'm suddenly on a peak in Darien, alone. Nobody is as old as I am. But I can still work.' Like the Queen Mother, I murmur. He catches that joyfully. 'Ah yes, I sometimes go and read poetry for her in her house at Windsor. She enjoys that.'

Who would not?

Libby Purves

TV DETECTIVES

1992 was the year of the television detective. With an abundance of crimes to solve, Inspectors Wexford, Morse and Taggart kept viewers entertained throughout the year. Richard Johnson investigates

Television detectives have come a long way from the age of Agatha Christie and Ngaio Marsh, when upper-class sleuths (as a diversion from a glass of darned good port) strode into drawing rooms and stroked their moustaches while looking for clues. Nowadays our screens are full of lateral thinkers with complicated home lives who don't always get their men – or women. They occupy a more recognisably human world, scored by violence and riddled with greed and desire. Theirs is a difficult job, and 1992 saw its fair share of casualties.

The most venerable representative of the old school was Joan Hickson's Miss Marple. Hickson bowed out at Christmas (or Christie-mas to judge by the schedulers' penchant for the writer) with *The Mirror Crack'd from Side to Side*, where everyone had a motive – and well-worn tweeds. 'I can't do with too much gore, it's so bad for the children,' says Hickson. 'Miss Marple is much gentler. It's been a remarkable series, but it's so much better for us to end now, when everybody wants more. One is getting on a bit.'

The year also saw the death of Ruth Rendell's Inspector Wexford. 'George Baker is wonderful in the role, and naturally I'm pleased he has been so successful,' says Rendell. 'But I really don't know if I'll write more of him.' That said, she couldn't bring herself to kill him off. 'I used to think I might do so in a book to be published posthumously, but unfortunately I have a weakness for seeing my own work published. The reader never gets tired of series characters, but the writer does. They leave very little opportunity for explanation.'

Although ITV viewers may have seen the last of Wexford, the Ruth Rendell industry shows no sign of suffering from recession. Her television films and series will continue

George Baker

into 1993 and beyond on the ITV network. And with the BBC screening *Gallowglass*, the second Barbara Vine novel to be adapted for television, and Spanish film director Pedro Almodovar bringing *Live Flesh* to the big screen, interest in the writer doesn't look like flagging.

And then there's always Hollywood. Three years ago movie moguls wanted to make a cinema film of *A Fatal Inversion*, a deeply English tale of dark and dangerous deeds in a Georgian country house. The BBC adapted it very success-

fully last year. 'But Hollywood wanted to put it into a Louisiana setting, a derelict plantation house with Spanish moss and all those American Gothic trimmings,' says Rendell. 'I turned them down for obvious reasons.'

Earlier this year came the end of *Inspector Morse*. 'I'm very fond of the old bugger, and I'll miss him,' says the man behind the mask, John Thaw. 'I will also miss working with the crew, and the routine of coming into make-up and wardrobe and seeing the same faces. One thing I can promise is that there will be no more series of Morse. But who knows whether he might rear his morose little head again in a few years' time. There's that old variety saying – you can be good, but you can be on too long.'

Central Films Managing Director Ted Childs, who has been executive producer of all the films, admits Morse was a calculated risk when the series first began. 'Central wanted a classy detective series made on a location within the region,' says Childs. 'Producer Kenny McBain had read the Morse books and thought they could be turned into quality films. Because they were quite complicated they needed two hours rather than the traditional one hour.'

Childs persuaded Thaw to take the lead role, and McBain brought in Kevin Whately to play Morse's

John Thaw as Inspector Morse

side-kick, Lewis. 'I'd just finished *Auf Wiedersehen Pet* and took a part in a play in the theatre which was eventually supposed to transfer to the West End,' says Whately. 'When Kenny McBain first approached me to play Sergeant Lewis I told him I wouldn't be available because it was going into London. Fortunately for me the play didn't bring them in and didn't transfer and Kenny was still interested in me.'

Writer Colin Dexter first created the Inspector in 1972, but handed over the work of adapting the books to scriptwriters. He retains the power of veto over what they do to his creation but there were major changes to begin with. In the nine original books, Morse drove a Lancia instead of a burgundy Jaguar 2.4. Lewis was Welsh, a contemporary of Morse, and a grandfather. Television moved his origins to the Northeast, cut his age and gave him two young children.

It's a mark of Morse's success that the series has shaken off fiction. People talk about Morse as if he were real. When a young woman was murdered in Oxford, newspapers rang up Dexter to find out what Morse's view of the case might be. And a leader in The *Guardian* recently asked whether Morse wasn't creating a dangerously false impression of Oxford as a criminal, corpse-strewn city. The City Council is unlikely to mourn Morse's passing away as keenly as the rest of us.

Exteriors have always been a Morse hallmark – they make for more interesting viewing than the formica tables of police interview rooms. The footage of Oxford was never made up of bog standard library shots of dreaming spires, but was always specially shot. And given that international sales are so important to British television, it made common sense for the Inspector to make occasional jaunts abroad. It gave the production team a chance to film some new architecture.

Despite the luxurious feel of a finished Morse, the pace on set was always far from leisurely. 'We don't have the option to sit on the bus all day and say we'll come back tomor-

row,' says producer Deirdre Keir. 'We have to shoot a 103 minute film in 25 days, and if that means changing the script, that's what we do.' A crew couldn't shoot outside in the English winter and expect the weather to be uniformly clement. So to keep on schedule, and within each programme budget of around £1 million, every exterior location had an interior alternative.

The final series was as full of in-jokes and party games as ever. The theme music began with Morse's name tapped out in dots and dashes (although one keen-eared telegraphist wrote to The *Guardian* to point out that it actually spells t.t.o.r.s.e. – the writer of Morse's signature tune, Barrington Pheloung, had slightly lengthened the dots on the M). Pheloung regularly entertains himself by spelling out the killer's name with notes in the episode's score.

Viewers without perfect pitch could have busied themselves by trying to spot Dexter in one of his

Hitchcockian cameo appearances. The writer appeared in every episode since Morse began in 1987. In previous series he appeared downing pints, crossing quads, singing in choirs, and reading in a launderette, but in the final series he managed to creep into shot sitting next to Sir John Gielgud – 'so I was happy. It's a bit of an in-joke now, me being in every episode. I'm almost like a good luck mascot in the series.'

And then there was the unresolved matter of Morse's christian name. In the first series, in *Service of all the Dead*, we discovered that Morse took the initial E – but Dexter never revealed what it stood for. He intends to leave it that way. 'Morse is embarrassed by his name. I don't think I'll ever say what Morse's christian name is – it's not Elvis. Even my wife doesn't know what it is. I think John Thaw knows what his name is – I think I told him once.'

When all the constituent parts of

Thaw (left) and Whatley at Brasenose College, Oxford

Terry O'Neill/Central TV

a *Morse* are put together, you are left with the televisual equivalent of a good read. Edgar Wallace wrote rattling good plots ('there's so much nastiness in modern literature that I write stories containing nothing worse than a little harmless murdering'), and it's a formula that has been adapted successfully for *Inspector Morse*.

After nearly 30 episodes in five years, the series could have started to look staid. But according to Whately, the problem never arose. 'John (Thaw) has a philosophy that you should surprise people,' he says. 'He always comes out of a different corner. It's different for me because Lewis doesn't get so emotionally involved. One of the things John does, if a scene is quite bland, is lose his temper. He'll bark a line. He doesn't let the film lollop along too easily.'

Thaw is keeping quiet about his camera technique. 'I ain't going to tell them to you because we'll get imitations of John Thaw all over the place. Those techniques will go with me to my grave.'

Thaw didn't have a traditional theatrical upbringing. 'Coming from my background in Manchester, a talent for acting was just like being able to write with your left hand if you're right handed – you know, so what? It certainly wasn't something you made a career of.' He left school to be a porter on the fruit market at Covent Garden – but didn't like getting up at 3am. 'Eventually I met a friend of a friend who was an elocution teacher, and she coached me for RADA.'

After graduating, he went on to make his name as Jack Regan, the villain-hating hero of *The Sweeney*. 'In lots of ways it was harder to make than *Inspector Morse*. In *Morse* there's no action, just talk, so I've got a lot of learning to do every night – maybe five or six pages. Whereas some days on *The Sweeney* we could say, "No learning tonight because tomorrow's all car chases and punch ups".'

Considering that the series has been sold to more than 50 countries, and watched by more than 750 million people, and that last year's films attracted a record average of more than 16 million

viewers, Thaw and Whately have their feet firmly on the ground. 'Acting for me has always been a job,' says Whately. I don't see film acting as an art form. It's very technical and methodical. Apart from anything else, I think people would be surprised how plodding it all is on location. John and I don't have lengthy plot discussions. We're not great analytical actors. We're not method actors.'

Despite playing Lewis for six years, Whately was challenged by the part right to the end. 'It's all acting. I can see quite easily how someone like William Roache can do *Coronation Street* for 30 years.

Mark McManus

For all the character being second nature to you, you're still having to play different situations every day, and different lines. It starts to feel like a factory by the end of the shoot, but you'll see the finished product and you'll think, "Yes, that's what we were doing".'

Whately will be as sad as Thaw to leave *Inspector Morse* behind. 'Well, I think it's wise to believe in the old theatre adage – leave them wanting more. It's not a soap – you can't go on with these things forever. Obviously I've had the time of my life playing Lewis and I'll be sorry to let him go. I'll be even sorrier to stop acting with John, who is a really close friend. We

won't do any more series, but there is always the possibility of one-off specials some time in the future.'

Inspector Morse was never too bloody. 'We've got to show a murder, but we start transmission at 8pm' says Keir, 'so we can't be gory about it.'

But there are detectives who work on the other side of the tracks. For Detective Chief Inspector Taggart, the cases can never be too bloody. Victims have been despatched with everything from linoleum cutters to poisonous frog's spittle, and it's a formula that has caught the imagination of the public. The movie- length 1992 New Year's Day special, *Violent Delights*, was seen by an audience of 18.3 million.

Created by Glenn Chandler, Taggart is street-tough and cynical – the perfect part for Mark McManus. Son of a miner, McManus earned his living boxing in Australia until he was mismatched with an Aborigine giant. 'I suppose I can be tough in real life', says McManus. 'I wouldn't take a step back from anybody, put it that way. In Glasgow, if you don't show front, you're not regarded. I wouldn't go up to anybody and say, "D'you want a fight?" But if it comes, well...'

The realism of today's television detectives is light years away from the cosy world of policing populated by *Dixon of Dock Green*, where life was one long cup of rosy with the desk sergeant. Now there are feisty investigators like Anna Lee, played by Imogen Stubbs. And according to Nick Elliott, controller of drama at London Weekend Television, she is the first of a new breed. 'We want to create new stars who are not creaking old men like John Thaw, David Jason, George Cole and George Baker.

'We are not going to attract new, younger audiences with actors like that. Inspector Morse never has sex, but Anna Lee does – although it does create complications for her.' It remains to be seen whether British audiences in 1993 want reality in their television detectives ('Anna Lee has split ends and dirty hair just like any other woman', says Stubbs), or just a little harmless murdering.

Richard Johnson

OFFBEAT DETECTIVES

The popularity of the television detective soared in 1992 and two of the less conventional series – *Lovejoy* and *Boon* – have continued to entertain viewers. Anne-Marie Sapsted takes a look at what makes these two characters so successful

Neither *Lovejoy* nor *Boon* could be described as conventional heart-throb material, but both have more than their fair share of female admirers and fan mail. Both are shortish, plumpish, favour leather jackets and the scruffy look, are unlucky in love and sometimes have difficulty staying on the right side of the law. Their methods certainly wouldn't win the approval of other TV detectives such as Wexford, Morse or Taggart.

Actors Ian McShane, who's played Lovejoy, the antiques dealer since 1985, and Michael Elphick as Boon, the security man, now in his seventh series, share similar experiences in real life. Both have lived hard, played hard and have had to face up to problems with booze. Both are now reformed, and confess to making efforts to keep fit and trim. Both are dedicated when it comes to their work and have created characters which have captured the public's imagination.

Lovejoy was originally based on the books by Jonathan Gash, though the character is nothing like the one featured in the books. The witty scripts are by that well-known BBC comedy team Dick Clement and Ian La Frenais, and part of Lovejoy's charm is that he doesn't win all the time. He takes the knocks that life doles out, including a prison sentence for something he didn't do, picks himself up and cheerfully starts all over again. It's a game of snakes and ladders for the lovable rogue with the soft heart.

Ian McShane owns the rights to the series, having bought the Gash book rights some years ago. In fact his own company co-produces *Lovejoy* for the BBC. He is also involved in planning and directs one of the programmes in each series.

Shot entirely on location in East Anglia, the team employs a full-time researcher to ensure that details about any facet of the antiques trade are accurate. In the 1992 Christmas special, filmed in Czechoslovakia, a spectacular replica of the religious icon, the Prague Sun – a monstrance used to carry the Host in procession round the church – was made up specially for the programme. The original is housed in the National Treasury in Prague and the replica was eventually presented to the embassy of the Czech and Slovak Federal Republic in London just before Christmas.

This year has seen Lovejoy comparatively settled in a converted barn which doubles as a home and a base for the business he runs with his 'associates': the innocent boy-biker Eric, and Tinker the antiques academic, specialist in obscure subjects, who has a weakness for good whisky. Lady Jane Felsham, played by Phyllis Logan, close friend and partner in the long-running will they/won't they romance is leaving the series next year after 50 episodes.

This year saw real romance for

(From left): Ian McShane (as Lovejoy), Phyllis Logan (as Lady Jane) and Dudley Sutton (as Tinker) outside Lovejoy Antiques

Lovejoy when Joanna Lumley appeared, introduced by Lady Jane as a friend of long-standing. But yet again, Lovejoy proved unlucky in love. Now former *Chancer* actress Caroline Langrishe has been chosen as his new co-star and will appear in the fifth series as a Sotheby's executive and highly motivated career woman. There is, though, the promise of romance.

The first series of the programme

Ian McShane (as Lovejoy) with Joanna Lumley (as Victoria Cavero)

was broadcast in 1986 and there was then a gap of five years. During that time McShane had a spell in Hollywood which included a part in *Dallas*. Settled in England with his well-documented wilder years of women and booze in Hollywood behind him, McShane faced personal tragedy in 1992 when his American actress wife of 12 years Gwen Humble found she had breast cancer. Doctors have now given her the all-clear.

At 50, McShane doesn't share Lovejoy's passion for antiques, but he looks remarkably like the character he plays. Both have the same black curly hair, mischievous twinkle in the eyes, and wear black jeans, black polo neck, blue denim jacket and cowboy boots. Apart from the boots, McShane wears his own clothes for the part. 'It helps me to feel comfortable,' he says.

'The longer you play a character, the more you inject of your own personality.'

The third series last year attracted average audiences of 12 million and McShane puts the series' success down to good scripts, an interesting mix of characters, and never doing the same thing twice.

Michael Elphick as Boon has built up a devoted following, too. One TV critic wrote about the programme: 'It's a team that has become as much a part of autumn as Bonfire Night and the nights drawing in.'

In some ways the programme is an unlikely success. From the beginning Elphick was determined to create a hero who didn't rely on fist fights or shoot outs for his wide appeal and as Boon is supposed to be a security man, that has taken some doing. But with his heart of gold and his ageing motorbike, better known as White Lightning, Ken Boon has become a family favourite.

The set-up still has Boon as the dogged workhorse while his partner Harry Crawford (David Daker) dreams about hitting the big time. Neil Morrissey is there as heart-throb biker Rocky. But with secretary Laura Marsh (Liz Carling)

Michel Elphick as Ken Boon

(From left): David Daker (as Harry), Michael Elphick (as Boon), Neil Morrissey (as Rocky) and Saskia Wickham (as Alex)

Tony Smith/Central TV

moving north, a replacement was needed. She appeared in the stunning shape of Saskia Wickham, best known for her part in *Clarissa*, the harrowing BBC period romance. She plays Alex, a girl of dubious past and unsavoury connections, and quickly becomes part of the team.

The 13-part seventh series featured a host of special guest stars including John Nettles, Martin Jarvis, Barbara Ewing, David Troughton, Christine Kavanagh and Sean Gallagher. And of course, that wonderful BSA bike. Though Elphick does get to do some of the riding himself – he says he's never fallen off yet – most of the real bike riding is done by his look-alike and stunt man Scott Hammond.

The trouble is that Elphick has been a little accident-prone, a fact which led his Central TV bosses to insure him for £1 million two years ago. In the past he's been thrown from a horse while filming his other hit TV series, *Three Up, Two Down*, almost suffocated in a coffin on stage and was treated for smoke inhalation after his jacket caught fire while filming *Boon*.

It was during work on an earlier series of the programme that Elphick decided his boozing had got out of hand. It was threatening to destroy his career as the problem began to interfere with filming. He checked into a private clinic and joined

Alcoholics Anonymous. Central rescheduled filming and since that time four years ago, he hasn't touched a drink.

'I used to be completely drunk by 9pm each night,' he said. 'Since I've stopped, life is much busier and much better. My relationships with people are more solid. I can see through the phoneys more easily and I don't tolerate the hangers-on as I used to. Going on the wagon has made me a bit grumpy, but I'm a wiser man for it.'

Filming the series means working 12-hour days for months at a time. But on Saturdays, he gets away to spend a day at his country hotel in Henley-in-Ardwick, Warwickshire, though he says he now spends more time in the restaurant than in the bar. Elphick has a wife and daughter living in London.

His popularity as Boon does have its drawbacks. He took a role in the recent film about the Kray brothers, appearing in just one scene. But it brought angry letters from some of his fans who didn't believe that it fit in with his lovable, easy-going Boon image.

Still, while other TV characters come and go, the lovable rascal Boon, who ranks alongside Lovejoy, Arthur Daley and Del Boy in popular television, is watched by millions in the confident expectation of another happy ending.

Anne-Marie Sapsted

THE BILL

Julie Allan goes behind the scenes of *The Bill* to meet the cast and find out if the programme really does reflect real-life police work in the Met

Could it be, with so many people staying in to watch ITV's *The Bill*, that Sun Hill, the country's most popular nick, might actually be keeping crime off the streets? Pity the on-duty police who can't stay home and watch – *The Bill* is a known favourite of the boys and girls in blue and with an extra weekly episode to catch this year, the video recorders of real-life police officers are having to serve above and beyond the usual call of duty. The Met, the London service on which the programme is loosely based, occasionally complains about some things in the programme, but the real-life and fictitious forces get along pretty well. As a senior police officer wisely said when *The Bill* first began, 'if we don't help them get it right, we can hardly complain when they get it wrong'.

Both sides recognise that the balance is a delicate one. Explains executive producer Michael Chapman, 'they don't expect us to do a PR job for them. Sometimes we have differences. I think it's important to say that although the police often applaud the reality of what we show, we're certainly not writing what we're told and there's no question that they veto our script ideas. They wouldn't want to – their job is to be police, not make television drama. At the same time, we have ex-police advisers to the programme and the Met helps us by allowing actors, writers and directors to spend time with them as necessary'.

Trevor Hames and Brian Hart are the current advisers. Hart, a former Chief Inspector, joined *The Bill* in 1989 when he retired from the Met after $31^{1}/_{2}$ years of service. 'I get to look at all the story ideas and scripts as they progress towards filming,' he says, 'and I point out if anything doesn't ring true or if I can see particular problems. One thing I have realised is that the day you leave the police service is the day

Christopher Ellison as DI Burnside

Tony Scannell as DS Roach

Nula Conwell as WDC Martella

Eric Richard as Sgt Cryer

you become out of date. It's a constant process of change and occasionally writers will come up with information I have to make a few phone calls to check out.'

One of the advisers' roles can be to tone things down a bit. However realistic, *The Bill* is a drama series, not a documentary. 'New writers can get particularly enthusiastic,' comments Brian Hart. 'Sometimes I need to remind them that the essence of good police work is that it is not dramatic. It is quiet and efficient. The aim is to keep the

programme truthful while realising that it is, of course, a fiction.' But with last autumn's request from the Met for recognition of the extra difficulty of their position – it is in London that most of the UK's violent crimes take place, for example – could *The Bill* actually be a bit soft in some ways? Brian Hart thinks that may be so. 'Because we have an 8pm time slot,' he comments, 'the real Met may be considerably more dramatic and violent than we show on *The Bill*. It is a potentially dangerous job.'

Michael Chapman believes that the greatest secret of *The Bill*'s success is that it's really about 'the small currency, rather than the stabbings and shootings. It's about the relationships between characters and their reactions to events. After all, there are only so many criminal situations and we'd soon run out of episodes if that was what we based the programme on. Instead we can look at different events through the eyes of different people.'

This approach, of course, relies on the characters being utterly real and human. It also pre-supposes that you take for granted the reality of what is around them – like Sun Hill police station. There are no three-walled rooms or sets held up with scaffolding at Sun Hill – it's the real thing, with real offices and real corridors. 'Even the furniture's authentic,' comments Brian Hart. 'All the London police stations have exactly the same type of desks and chairs, so *The Bill* buys them second hand. I can tell you, when I first walked in to Sun Hill, it was eerie. I felt like I was in a real station.'

But surely it can't all be for real? What about all those CID filing cabinets, for example? 'Full,' says Michael Chapman. 'Each drawer of the CID's entire battery of filing cabinets has in it exactly what it should have for Sun Hill as a real station – and on the correct forms. Even the books in the offices are the ones you'd find in any police station. Apart from anything else, it helps the authority of the actors.'

The current Sun Hill is actually the third version. The first was in Wapping, behind the News International plant, and during the printers' strikes, more than one uniformed actor almost got involved in scenes that were nothing to do with their script for *The Bill*. Eventually, the problems of filming while the dispute continued to rage prompted Sun Hill's first move to North Kensington and then when that site was no longer available, to the current location – a converted wine warehouse in Merton, south London. It isn't especially sunny or hilly (the name came from a street in creator Geoff McQueen's home town of Royston in Hertfordshire), but clever and extremely accurate design and construction work have ensured that the station has remained unchanged throughout.

Just as a police station has a life of its own, so has *The Bill* set. The team eats in the Sun Hill canteen when it's not in use for filming. They relax in Sun Hill's recreation room. They sit on police chairs in police offices reviewing their notes, or should that be scripts?

The realism of the set and series leads to security problems of its own. 'It's a huge responsibility that we take very seriously,' says Chapman. 'Our uniforms are the real thing, so they're stored under lock and key. And you'll never find a complete uniform in one place. Then there's the warrant cards, which are checked out, checked in, and carefully guarded. The squad cars are a bit tricky too – they're not real but they look it, with the Met logo on the side and the blue light on top. All that gets covered up through the rehearsals until we're actually ready for a take.'

The actors are justifiably proud of the illusion they create but, partly because it is so real, are eager to point out that it is an acting job. They don't really feel like police, although the research they put in to the roles is extensive.

Kevin Lloyd, who plays DC Alfred 'Tosh' Lines, reckons he's the lucky one in the cast when it comes to knowing what police work is about. 'My father was a real policeman in Derby,' he says. 'He was a detective and later a station sergeant so we lived in the police house on the council estate. Until I was 21, when he died, I was surrounded by the police life, and my uncle and grandfather were also policemen.' So does *The Bill* feel like the real thing? 'I was amazed when I first joined to find out how realistic it was,' says Lloyd. 'Now when I see my father's friends they joke that they wish they had Tosh working for them because he always solves the case. They say the series is the best thing since sliced bread and sometimes they'll ring me up and say, "I was watching you on TV last night and it was just as if Taffy was back." Taffy was my Dad. He used to love *Z Cars* because he thought it was the nearest a drama series had got to the truth and I know that he'd love *The Bill*.'

Eric Richard (Sergeant Bob Cryer) happened to live next door to a real sergeant in the Thames Valley police when he got his part and had long conversations with him about the philosophy of it all. 'The nearest thing I got to a surprise was in finding that it was even more difficult in real life than I'd thought. After all my years as a fictional sergeant, I still can't think of anything I'd less want to be. The Met are such a front line – the government dismantles society and then expects the police to hold it together. It's not that I want to make out the police are heroes, but they are sometimes put in impossible situations.

'The sergeant got promoted to inspector and I asked him again what was so good about the job. Eventually he said, "I think I just like being the man on the white horse", meaning that he liked the idea of the police being there to help people when they need it. One thing I think must be depressing about being in the police is that you usually see people in negative situations. You rarely join them for the good times.'

This is a thought echoed by Trudie Goodwin, who plays WPC June Ackland. 'I'm a lot more sympathetic towards the police than I used to be,' she says. 'They deal with things every day that most people choose to pretend don't exist. And, just like actors, there's this question of how to draw the line between work and home. Personally, I usually manage to leave work behind at the end of the day, although I don't always manage to leave the family behind when it comes to work. The police have the same dilemma because they have to deal with people all the time.'

Like other cast members, she's used to being treated as if she were in the police when 'off duty'. 'After so long in the role, you even have to remind yourself it's only acting sometimes,' she says. 'There you are on a street, in uniform, and the camera so far away you don't see it. The whole point is that as far as you can, you are being what you're pretending to be. It can feel very real.'

But there is not a member of the cast who would volunteer to be in the police. 'I'd go mad', Peter Ellis (Chief Superintendent Charles Brownlow) admits. 'I wouldn't last five minutes. Actually, I reckon I'd probably get away with it for about four hours. I do remember being at a Met dinner once and realising they had forgotten I was an actor. I caught myself about to join in the conversation and shut up just in time.'

His greatest surprise was finding out that real chief superintendents are not as out of touch as he had expected. 'I think they can be more radical than those down on the deck,' he says. 'They've seen it all to get where they are. The one where I live in London's East End is quite active in saying what he thinks, like, "If you want me to sort this out you need to sort out the housing conditions on this estate".'

As in real police life, *The Bill* is changing with the times. Officers come, and officers go, and with the arrival of new female characters early in 1993, *The Bill* will continue to reflect what is happening in the real world of the Met. CID Trainee Investigator (TI) Suzi Croft, played by Kerrie Peers recently arrived in February and new WDC Jo Morgan, soon to arrive in April, are among several new female roles which will give the programme a fresh perspective. The current series will mean everyone working flat out to meet increased demands on limited resources ('three episodes a week means three crews filming three different stories, all needing access to the same Sun Hill and cast,' says Michael Chapman of the continuing logistical nightmare).

But there is hope, in one quarter at least, that some things will never change: 'Hollis,' says series adviser Brian Hart. 'I love Hollis (Jeff Stewart), he's a natural comedian. I'm told that in police stations across the country, if someone's being a complete prat, they'll get told, "Don't be a Hollis". There are Hollises everywhere.'

Who says the laughing policeman is a thing of the past?

Julie Allan

LONDON'S BURNING

After five successful series, and with a sixth in the pipeline, Angela Thomas reviews LWT's *London's Burning* conceived from Jack Rosenthal's original idea in 1986

In 1986 Paul Knight, the producer of hits like *Robin of Sherwood* and *Black Beauty* was asked by LWT drama controller Linda Agran to oversee production of a single film written by award-winning Jack Rosenthal. The film was inspired by Rosenthal's long-time friendship with a local fireman and triggered by the horrifying events at Broadwater Farm in London during which firemen were attacked and PC Keith Blakelock was killed. Over six years later that single film has developed into *London's Burning,* one of the most successful home-grown drama series on British TV today.

An award-winning producer with an eye for the commercial, Knight still remembers the first time he set eyes on Rosenthal's script: 'I had talked to people in the past about making a fire brigade series and when Linda brought Jack's script to me, I thought Jack had found a way of making it work dramatically by including the humour which is so much a part of the way they deal with the stresses of the job.'

Although Rosenthal's writing contribution ended with the first, highly acclaimed film, Knight has stayed with the series. Determined to retain the spirit of the original, while sustaining interest through a series, Knight hand-picked writers whom he felt could develop the existing characters and introduce new ones. 'I had been in America when LWT decided to commission the series, so when I came back there were already some scripts written, but there was only one which I think captured the spirit of the original film. That was written by Tony Hoare and I used him and a writer called Anita Bronson for the first season.

'We made the decision from the start that it would be a serial rather than a series. Initially LWT wanted a series of one-off films, but it became clear that treating it as a serial would be a much better proposition. To sustain interest we knew we had to develop the characters and include something of their home life. Also there had to be something more that just a series of spectacular shouts [incidents] because that would make the series just too costly.'

There was also a suggestion at one point that *London's Burning* should be made into a twice weekly

The cast of *London's Burning*

LWT

serial similar to the popular long-running police series *The Bill*. 'It just wouldn't have worked,' explains Knight. '*The Bill* is a series which uses limited special effects and there are only the occasional major incidents. *London's Burning* however, has a very strong special effects content and you couldn't do those sort of stunts twice a week.'

Although the major stunts have kept the series in the news, it's the changing cast lists and a few shock departures which have ensured interest in the series has been sustained. 'Because we have actors and actresses facing danger every week something has to happen to one of them at some point,' says Knight. 'I made a decision at the end of the second series to kill off a main member of the cast so it would give the audience a kick and a start.' The unlucky character was one of the most popular, the womanising Vaseline played by Mark Arden. 'He was such a popular character the audience couldn't believe it at first that we'd actually kill him off. It was exactly the reaction we wanted and it gave the series the edge we needed.'

Vaseline was the first of a number of characters to leave the cast over the years, but each has been replaced, usually by a relatively unknown actor. 'Apart from James Hazeldine (Bayleaf), the actors have usually been fairly new to TV; we deliberately wanted new faces because we didn't want them too closely associated with any parts they'd played in the past,' explains Knight.

As well as the freshness of the faces, the production team has prided itself on the authenticity of the content of the series. Every incident, no matter how bizarre or dramatic, is based on actual events taken from fire service reports. Says Knight: 'Our writers have worked closely with the fire service and we have access to their archive material. At the beginning of each series we decide what major shouts we are going to be doing, and how we're going to cope with them.' On hand to ensure everything looks totally authentic is Fire Brigade Liaison Officer, Brian 'Nobby' Clarke. Like Knight he has also been involved

with *London's Burning* from the very beginning.

This attention to detail has helped *London's Burning* maintain its position as one of the most popular drama series currently on British TV. The first film attracted an audience of 12.5 million and the series really hit the heights with the dramatic final episode in the fourth series which was seen by an incredible 18.9 million viewers. The last series which ran on Sunday nights at the end of 1992 attracted average audiences of 14 million and the team is currently back in south London working on the sixth series which introduces viewers to two new key characters whom Knight hopes will become as popular with his audience as Bayleaf and Co.

Angela Thomas

CASUALTY

William Greaves goes behind the scenes of BBC1's *Casualty* to find out how the frighteningly real accident and emergency scenes are re-created

Viewed from outside, the street is about as animated as you would expect from a Bristol trading estate on a drizzly Sunday morning. Only the emotive scent of sizzling bacon emanating from a catering van on the forecourt gives any suggestion

that there might be life behind the grim warehouse walls.

But once through the narrow portals of Unit B6 the scene is instantly transformed into the kind of calculated chaos more usually associated with a hospital accident and emergency department. Which is exactly what it is pretending to be.

Oh yes, there is life within all right – except that not much of it seems to belong just now to the man on the bed, whose blood-encrusted face is contorting in perfect time with each agonised scream as Dr Julian Chapman's fingers explore his naked abdomen.

The fingers are probing all the right places, of course, because Dr David Williams has just demonstrated in precise detail how you set about locating a fractured pelvis. And it is easy to tell which of the two men is the professional medic because Chapman (actor Nigel Le Vaillant) is in regulation white coat, whereas Williams's jeans and open-necked blue shirt could only belong to a kidney specialist on his weekend off.

This is just another working day on the set of *Casualty*, BBC1's massively popular weekly insight into the blood, sweat and toil of a major NHS accident unit.

And, as ever, the real doctors and nurses are keeping an eagle eye on their television counterparts to

The team create a 'patient's injuries' for an episode of *Casualty*

Bill Robinson

ensure that no innocent departure from absolute accuracy would give rise to amused or outraged censure from either their own hospital colleagues or the professional cognoscenti among a weekly audience of around 16 million viewers.

'I wasn't too happy with the way Rob (newly arrived Dr Rob Khalefa, played by Jason Riddington) removed the needle after taking blood from the cannula in the arm vein,' says Williams, lifting his gaze from the monitor screen. 'It looked a bit like someone doing it for the first time in his life, whereas he would actually be doing it every day.'

holding the head, one with a hand on shoulder and waist, another holding hip and just above the knee and the fourth with one hand under the knee and the other under the ankle. You are the senior nurse, Charlie (clinical nurse manager Charlie Fairhead, played by Derek Thompson), so I think you should be holding the head and dictating the pace.'

'Quite right,' agrees Dr Williams. 'After all, we don't know that the poor chap hasn't also broken his neck, so one mistake with the head could cut the spinal cord and he would end up a quadriplegic.' Michael Morris takes careful note.

fictional alter ego, Charlie Fairhead. And during that time Derek Thompson and his professional mentor have developed a remarkable carbon-copy relationship which has proved to be the prime contribution to *Casualty*'s much acclaimed realism.

'We've come to understand each other's jobs over the years,' says Peter Salt. 'Nursing involves quite a bit of acting – talking and moving in a way to calm patients down and reassure them – and both jobs require a lot of thinking on your feet. And, of course, there have been changes in the NHS which Derek and I talk about, and because of the time it takes to make each series we have to try to keep about a year and a half ahead of likely developments.

'We have to remember, too, that there are positive sides as well as negative. It would be an easy cop-out just to carp about hospitals all the time, which wouldn't give a true picture.'

'It seems to work pretty well, too,' agrees Derek Thompson. 'I keep having conversations on trains, particularly with nurses, who talk to me as though I really am one of them and understand their problems. In fact, the only criticism I get is about Charlie's tendency to put his hands in his pockets. Pillars of the RCN (Royal College of Nursing) regard that as a terrible habit.'

Peter Salt smiles approval: 'That's a conscious choice that tells you something about this creature and how he deals with authority. It all adds to the authenticity.'

Meanwhile, back on set, the plot thickens. The log roll having been concluded to the satisfaction of both director and professional consultants, Dr Chapman decides on an emergency pelvis operation. The whole army of technicians, actors and equipment move down the road to Bristol Royal Infirmary, whose sixth-floor Heygroves Theatre, unused at weekends, has been put at their disposal. Despite the fact that the warehouse's 'resuscitation room' contains every manner of ECG and defibrillating machinery, drip feeds and cardiac monitoring equipment, a full-blown operating theatre set is beyond its resources.

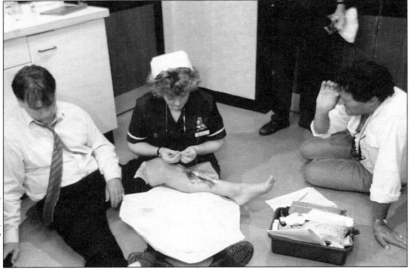

BBC Photograph Library

Another case for the *Casualty* staff

'Right then, once more,' says director Michael Morris. And a few minutes later: 'How was that, David?'

'Much better.'

'OK, print that. Well done everyone. Take a break.'

One false step has been successfully averted but director and cast are not yet out of the minefield. To be absolutely sure of his diagnosis, Dr Chapman has still to examine the patient's lower back – and this means turning him over in what is known in the trade as a 'log roll'. It is the moment for Sister Helen Stratton of Bristol Royal Infirmary to take over.

'We need four people on the same side of the bed,' she says, 'with one

'OK then, Derek, you go up to the end and Nigel, you'd better slip in a line asking Rob to go over the other side to help. Let's rehearse that ...'

Casualty charge-hand Simon Andrews moves in to fit the 'patient' with cardiac monitors, drips, cervical collar, naso-gastric tube, sandbags to either side of his head, blood-pressure cuff and all the other necessary trappings. 'He's really got the hang of all this,' says Dr Williams. 'If ever he's out of a job in the film business...'

Peter Salt looks on approvingly. Over the past six years his career at Bristol Royal Infirmary has gone from charge nurse to clinical nurse manager for the accident services – a progress matched precisely by his

At the infirmary a new team of medical expertise awaits. 'Just look at the poor man's face,' exclaims theatre sister Dina Plowes. 'It's so realistic I keep wanting to clean him up a bit.'

'Don't do that,' says make-up designer Sue Bide with mock horror and a glance towards sundry pots marked 'congealed blood' and 'raw flesh'. 'It's taken a lot of time and effort to get him like that!'

Once again the victim lays himself down on the bed, while *Casualty*'s own prosthetician, Simon Tytherleigh, arranges a lower torso made of gelatine over him, complete with injury scars and pubic hair, and Sister Plowes goes about her well-practised drill of laying out the instrument trolley. Mr George Langkamer, lecturer in orthopaedic surgery at the BRI, steps forward to administer two stitches to one of the scars and to feel for the spot where a 'blood vessel' has been inserted under the surface. Later Mr Langkamer's own hands – supposedly those of Dr Chapman – will be seen on camera making the slit along this line, thus releasing a positive fountain of Simon Tytherleigh's pre-positioned gore. In the true tradition of the operating theatre, this is no place for faint hearts.

'How long will you need?' asks Michael Morris of lighting director Cedric Rich. 'Four minutes,' comes the precise reply.

'Right,' says the director. 'And don't forget, everyone, that we have an actor lying here in a very uncomfortable position.'

It was just the sort of compassion you would expect to hear when theatre moves into the theatre.

William Greaves

A DAY WITH THE ARCHERS

Nicki Household visits Ambridge to spend a day with *The Archers*, and discovers the secrets of Britain's longest-running radio series

An awful thought occurs, as I head towards the BBC's Pebble Mill Studios in Birmingham to spend a day with the Archers. Will this visit turn me into a non-believer? Will coming face to face with the actors

and going into the studio to witness all the little tricks and deceptions that go into the making of radio's longest-running and most popular serial, make Ambridge and its inhabitants seem less real? But it's too late to turn back.

They're recording three episodes – two in the morning, one in the afternoon. Sometimes a fourth has to be fitted in because now that there are only six studio days a month (compared with 12 in the past), ten episodes must be completed in three days. The actors, who come from far and wide, spend Wednesday, Thursday and Friday of two consecutive weeks at Pebble Mill, and then don't meet again until the following month. The arrangement suits them. It means they don't get a chance to become sick of each other, and it enables the ones who have been lucky enough to be offered other work to go away and do it. As even the most stalwart characters only get paid for the episodes that they are in, other work can be very necessary.

The first episode has a cast of eight – Norman Painting (Phil Archer), Patricia Greene (Jill Archer), Angela Piper (Jennifer Aldridge), Sara Coward (Caroline Bone), Margot Boyd (Marjorie Antrobus), Tim Meats (Robin Stokes), Susie Riddell (Kate Aldridge) and Tamsin Grieg (Debbie Aldridge). They're sitting in the Green Room when I arrive – waiting, scripts in hand, to go into the rehearsal room for a read-through. Slouched comfortably in their chairs, sipping coffee (surely it should be *tea*) and swapping British Rail horror stories, they don't look or sound at all like the Archers.

The Archers editor Vanessa Whitburn, who is directing the episode, arrives looking businesslike, and everyone moves into the tiny, windowless rehearsal room, just big enough to hold a small circle of ten chairs. The actors are already familiar with the script, because they receive it a few days in advance, so once Vanessa has announced some cuts and changes, they launch straight into the read-through. And suddenly, smoothly, miraculously, they become the familiar characters who are known and loved (or

hated) by seven million listeners.

There's just one difference between this preliminary rehearsal and the one that takes place 20 minutes later in the studio, just before the 'take'. The giggles. Later on, the cast will be 100 per cent 'in

Vanessa Whitburn, editor of *The Archers* since June 1991

character', but the read-through is punctuated by loud bursts of laughter, usually because a character is being so hilariously true-to-type. First it's Marjorie who prompts an outburst, when she tells the vicar that she suspects everyone thinks she's dotty. Later on, Robin has everyone in stitches because he can't keep his mind off the parish magazine when he's meant to be kissing Caroline.

Next door in Studio 3, they're getting ready for the recording. The episode requires lots of sound effects – a horse approaching at a canter, then stamping restlessly on gravel, a Land Rover reversing through a gate, a crackling fire, a dog making contented noises, the sound of knitting needles, the voice of little Alice Aldridge, a doorbell. These are the responsibility of Lynne Taylerson on 'grams', and they must all be spot on. When in doubt, she consults a document which lists the make of each car, the breed of every dog and cat and the age of every child in Ambridge.

Even so, some noises (today it's little Kylie burbling happily) have to be specially recorded. 'We can't be too careful,' says Lynne, 'because there are dozens of experts out there just waiting to tell us we got it wrong – that the bird they heard tweeting would actually be in Africa at that time of year!'

Certain sounds, like the pouring of tea, the opening and closing of doors and the clatter of cups and saucers are produced 'live', by a 'spot effects' man in the studio, who hovers around the actors poised to do whatever's necessary. So when the vicar asks Mrs Antrobus: 'Will you pour or shall I?' – it's Liall the 'spot effects' man who picks up a rather plain-looking blue teapot and pours water into two distinctly ugly pottery mugs. And there was I, thinking that Marjorie Antrobus had a really pretty tea set!

Borchester and Felpersham!

The read-through over, the actors take up their positions behind the relevant screens, and the director joins the rest of the production team in the control room. A big glass window lets them see what's going on in the studio, but they can only communicate with the actors by microphone. The main purpose of the studio rehearsal is to get all the sound-effects perfectly timed and exactly right. Too loud, and they drown the dialogue, too soft and they're undetectable. Sometimes, even though the noise is technically correct, it *sounds* wrong, and has to be changed. Jill's knitting needles (she's knitting for

the parish magazine and Caroline and Robin don't make love), goes straight onto tape without a single hitch. But, even if the odd hiccup occurs – an actor fluffing a line, a sound effect lasting too long or not long enough, a mysterious twitter (called a 'gremlin') suddenly appearing on the tape – it's not a disaster, because sections can easily be repeated and edited in.

When Whitburn took over as *The Archers*' fifth editor just two years ago, she says it felt like 'coming home'. She had worked as a producer on the series in 1979-80, and was responsible for casting Sara Coward as Caroline and Trevor Harrison as Eddie Grundy. One of the things she enjoys most about the job is being able to develop storylines over a long period: 'In a single play, time is short, so you only see things from a single character's point of view,' she explains. 'But as we operate in "real" time, we can look at an issue like, say, Elizabeth's pregnancy and abortion, from the point of view of lots of people – Phil, Jill, David and Shula, as well as Elizabeth.'

She's currently enjoying getting to grips with the issues raised by Caroline's relationship with Robin – especially the conflict between traditional Christian morality and the modern acceptance of unmarried sex. 'We honestly haven't decided where that relationship is going,' she insists. 'We debate and argue a great deal about storylines. The two main criteria are that whatever happens has to be true to character – and it has to be a good story.'

Big storylines, like births, deaths and marriages, are decided at a twice-yearly meeting between Whitburn, her two fellow producers, Joanna Toye and Keri Davies, and the eight regular Archers writers. 'That gives us a state of affairs to aim towards,' she explains. 'Then we have a lot of fun at our three-monthly planning meeting and our monthly story meeting, deciding how we're going to let it happen.'

Individual episodes are planned three months ahead, written two months ahead and recorded one month ahead. So how do up-to-the-minute topical comments (about

BBC

During 1992 in *The Archers* friendship has slowly blossomed between Caroline Bone (played by Sara Coward) and Robin Stokes (played by Tim Meats)

The studio is divided by screens into three separate areas. One, containing a sink and cooker, is for pub and kitchen scenes. Another, with table, chairs, teapot and mugs (and, just today, a piano for Phil) is anybody's living room, and the third, containing nothing, is the great outdoors. It's very difficult to believe that this relatively small space, measuring less than 20 feet square, is not only Brookfield, Home Farm, Bridge Farm, Grange Farm, The Bull and every other building in and around Ambridge, but in addition Lower Loxley,

Ruth's baby, of course) are a case in point. The sound on disc, of someone really knitting, is odd and unrecognisable – so the spot effects man comes to the rescue, making a much more convincing sound with a couple of metal rulers.

Not until she's satisfied that everything is exactly as it should be, does Vanessa Whitburn say 'OK, let's go for a take'. And, with any luck, the episode (in which Phil and Jill manage not to quarrel about Rickyard Cottage, Debbie and Kate fall out and later have a heart-to-heart, Marjorie comes clean about

Britt Ekland joined a long line of stars who have guested in *The Archers* when she recorded a scene with Eddie Grundy (played by Trevor Harrison) and his wife Clarrie (played by Rosalind Adams). The episode was broadcast on 23 December 1992 when the Grundy family won tickets to see Britt perform in panto at the Birmingham Hippodrome and met her backstage afterwards

the French lorry drivers demonstration, just when Clarrie and Eddie were going to France, Terry Waite's release and the result of the General Election) find their way into the script? Answer: by editing them on to the tape at the last moment. It is not unknown for a topical insert to be recorded at 6.00pm, edited in half an hour later and taken by hand to the continuity suite in time for the 7.05pm broadcast.

The actors themselves don't have any 'official' influence over what their characters get up to, but some of them – especially those who've been around a long time – will speak up if they feel something is out of character. And they're listened to. For example, when Phil Archer reached 60, Norman Painting (who has played him since *The Archers* began 42 years ago, and wrote 1,200 episodes himself between 1967 and 1982) didn't agree with the way he was made to 'slow down'. 'I don't think people's personalities change just because they've reached a certain age,' he says, 'so I staged a little one-man revolt. Phil was such a tearaway in his youth that, even though he's

obviously settled down and stopped chasing girls, I felt he would never go all calm and passive.' But Norman is happy with Phil as he is today. 'He's gone back to being the person I played as a young man.'

Phil's relationship with Jill is another aspect of the show on which he keeps a keen weather eye. 'It's important that we should hang on to the idea of the Archers being an "ideal family". It's one of the reasons the series has survived. Obviously Phil and Jill have arguments, but both Paddy [Patricia Greene] and I feel they should never disagree too glibly because we've worked at creating the impression of a couple who've been married for 30 years. Even if one of them storms out of the house and slams the door, it's all forgotten soon afterwards.'

Now 68 – two years younger than Phil – Norman feels he's been 'extremely lucky' to have worked in the series for so long. 'It's part of me – I really look forward to studio days and I can't imagine my life without them.' Although he underwent major heart surgery recently, (his absence from the series was

explained by Phil's hip operation) and is under strict instructions to take life easily, he regards retirement as out of the question. 'Fortunately I can work without exhausting myself because I don't live very far from Birmingham and they send a car for me on the days I'm needed.'

He doesn't mind not being able to take part in quite as many 'extramural' Archers activities as some of the other actors, and he is not totally happy with the idea of, as he puts it, 'masquerading' as Phil Archer outside the studio. 'I'm happy to be introduced as Norman Painting, who's played Philip Archer from the beginning, but I've never really looked how Phil would look – especially in the days when he was bronzed, handsome and every woman's fantasy! So I do find it embarrassing to stand at the door of someone else's farmhouse and say: "Welcome to Brookfield"!'

But some members of the cast really enjoy the increasing number of events (conventions, seminars, specially written plays that tour the country and now, 'Archers' holidays to Spain and Scandinavia) that are organised by *The Archers* fan club, 'Archers Addicts'. Not that they necessarily *like* the characters they spend so much time pretending to be! Carole Boyd, for example, absolutely loathes Lynda Snell. 'The only time I let her character take me over is when I've got to make a complaint to someone like the Gas Board because she's so wonderfully insensitive. But it's quite cathartic to play her, as I've often been treated the way she treats people and it's quite fun to get my own back.'

Sara Coward, on the other hand, has become very fond of Caroline Bone – and has definite views about her future. 'I don't want her to settle down and get married because I don't think she would in real life. Who would a woman like her really meet in a place like Ambridge? And Judy Bennett (married, in real life, to Charles Collingwood, who plays Brian Aldridge), feels tremendous sympathy for Shula Hebden (née Archer), whom she's played for 21 years. 'She's not like me, but I'm fond of her and I do feel very sorry for her over the baby business. You know what you'd like for the character, and having a baby would change Shula's whole life. But that doesn't mean she's going to! I often wonder what *will* happen to her.'

After 35 years as Jill Archer, Patricia Greene says she slips into the character almost without noticing it. 'To a certain extent, she has taken me over – for example, I think I *am* her at garden fetes! It probably helps that we look alike now. She's not me, of course, but she's had an influence on me – a good influence because she's such a nice person. She's even got me making jams, jellies and chutneys!'

She has witnessed many changes over the years. The village has got bigger, the cast has increased and the show has become less agricultural. 'In the beginning it was almost like facts-for-farmers in a sugar-coated pill,' she says. She's particularly pleased at the way women characters have come to the fore in recent years. 'When I first joined, the men were the ones who did things, and the women were just there to be wooed or chained to the kitchen sink. That's been changing slowly over the years, but having Vanessa in the hot seat has made a huge difference. Whether it's Elizabeth's abortion, or Caroline's love-life or Clarrie's town-twinning, we get the women's point of view far more now. The women have become three-dimensional.'

Like Norman Painting, she can't imagine life without the camaraderie of *The Archers*. 'One of the nicest things was that my life here didn't change when I was widowed. At home, people tend to withdraw from you, but here at the studio everything carried on the same. I could go on just being myself, giggling in the Green Room and going out for a steak and a glass of wine. We all get on tremendously well. There are no bad apples in the barrel.'

Driving home in the car, I flick on Radio 4 at 7.05pm and there's the familiar tune, followed by Jennifer voicing terrible concern about Kate. I needn't have worried. Going behind the scenes has only increased my addiction.

Nicki Household

SOAPS

With the introduction of *Eldorado*, and strong storylines in *Brookside*, *Coronation Street* and *EastEnders*, soap addicts were kept entertained throughout the year. Daniela Soave recalls some of the plots which kept audiences hooked

The cast of *Eldorado* at the launch of the new soap

1992 saw a major television event occur with the birth of a new soap opera, *Eldorado*. That the thrice-weekly show was up and running within months of the go-ahead was one thing, but the very fact that an entire working village had to be constructed from scratch, never mind built in a foreign country, was nothing short of a major feat.

The concept of *Eldorado* is one of the most ambitious projects in British television history. The series is shot entirely on location in Spain in a production village which has been built within 25 acres of land. Construction work started at the very beginning of 1992 and five months later it was ready for filming. There are no studios: each house, apartment, hotel or shop is complete, with running water and electricity in most.

The village was designed by Keith Harris, who also created Albert Square for *EastEnders*. But this was a far greater challenge which involved clearing part of a hillside and building an entire village complete with old town, newer buildings and a shopping plaza.

Eldorado was created by Tony Holland from an idea by Verity

***Eldorado* is filmed entirely in the specially built production village in Spain**

BBC Photograph Library

Lambert and John Dark. Using a cast made up of British, Spanish, Scandinavian, German and French actors, the action focused on ex-pat characters living in southern Spain, where they had carved a new life for themselves. Producer Julia Smith, who also created *EastEnders* with

Ross Kemp (left) and Steve McFadden who play brothers Grant and Phil in *EastEnders*

Holland said, 'I want to give people blue skies, brown bodies, greenery and sea. This is going to be something that is a pleasure to look at.'

The advent of a new soap – the first since *EastEnders* burst onto the scene seven years previously – had a marked effect on the existing three major soaps *Brookside*, *Coronation Street* and *EastEnders*, as script writers leapt into a flurry of activity.

Like *Eldorado*, the 10-year-old *Brookside* is filmed within a real housing complex, although creator Phil Redmond simply bought a chunk of a new housing estate and adapted it accordingly rather than designing and supervising the building of an entire village completely from scratch.

But while *Eldorado* reflects the lighter side of life, *Brookside* remains studiously gritty. Themes running through the Liverpool soap during last year included child abduction, post-natal depression, debt, illiteracy, shop-lifting, racism and arson. In October, the subject of date rape reared its ugly head when Peter Harrison attacked Diana Corkhill, recently estranged from her husband Rod, with the case coming to trial in December.

But the major conflict involved Barry Grant, who disappeared from view in May when Terry confronted him over the murder of his wife Sue and baby son Danny. The confrontation ended with the blast of a shotgun, and viewers were left wondering if Terry had got his revenge by murdering his former friend...until the middle of October, that is, when Barry returned to Brookside Close as owner of a new local nightclub. The emergence of Grant as an arch-villain was compounded when he spurned his pregnant girlfriend Fran, in May, but it was obvious that this was a storyline that would run and run.

Although the main highlight of the *Coronation Street* year had to be three weddings within three weeks, the script had a sharper edge, with Emily Bishop suffering from clinical depression; the break-up of Ivy and Don Brennan's marriage and his subsequent car crash, which resulted in the amputation of one of his legs; alcoholism as experienced by Ivy when she couldn't cope with such traumatic events; death, when Ted Sullivan succumbed to a brain tumour.

Even two of the three weddings were tinged with grief. When Terry Duckworth married his pregnant girlfriend Lisa on 27 May, he was handcuffed to a prison officer as he was on remand for assault. On 5 June, Rita Fairclough married Ted Sullivan, knowing full well that he had not long to live. And the happy event of the birth of Lisa Duckworth's baby on 9 September was clouded by Ted's death. Only the marriage of Mike Baldwin and Alma Sedgewick on 19 June seemed to be free of upset. The year ended with two of the soap's strongest female characters, Bet Gilroy and Rita Sullivan, facing life alone: the former due to the break-up of her marriage to Alec, the latter because of Ted's untimely demise.

But it was surely *EastEnders* which held all the trump cards. The year began with Willmott-Brown attempting to return to Albert Square. Having served his sentence for raping Kathy Beale in 1988, he tried to buy a house in the Square. The emotional meeting between Willmott-Brown and his victim and her ex-husband lured in 22.52 million viewers.

When Mark married Gill, viewers were aware that he had been diagnosed as HIV positive and his new wife was dying from full-blown Aids. On 23 June they were married but a week later, Gill was moved first to a hospice and then to hospital, where she died. The first Aids death in a popular TV soap was very well received by viewers and critically acclaimed by the press, with letters pouring in by the sackload. With an audience figure of 16.3 million, this was a particularly impressive result for the height of summer.

EastEnders was the first popular TV soap to show a death from Aids, when Gill (played by Susanna Dawson) died in June

Do tragedies make for higher viewing figures? Certainly, the ongoing affair between Sharon and her brother-in-law, Phil, stirred up fervent interest and the arson attack on the Queen Vic by her husband, Grant, in which Sharon was nearly killed, notched up greater numbers, as did the bubbling flirtation and eventual affair between Arthur and Mrs Hewitt. But one of the highest viewing figures of the *EastEnders* year turned out to be Michelle and Sharon's night out in November, in which 22.58 viewers tuned in to witness Michelle embarking on a one-night stand. Which goes to show: happiness triumphs every time.

Daniela Soave

CHILDREN'S DRAMA

The combination of a young cast in a contemporary setting tackling real issues has proved to be a winning formula in children's drama. Julie Allan looks at some of the most successful series

Teenage boys and girls, coming to terms with what love and sex are about, discuss who went 'how far' with who else; some of them get pregnant. Youngsters get involved in ugly gang rivalry, theft, racist attacks. Words are used in playgrounds that cannot appear on this page. Children are sexually abused by their parents.

This is some of the stuff that makes up life. No wonder many a caring adult wishes their children inhabited that good old *Watch With Mother* world they are certain used to exist, where innocence was preserved and children could stay children for the proper length of time. But reality intrudes and the dilemmas begin, and joining those who tread the line are the producers of contemporary drama for children.

The pioneering and oft-debated *Grange Hill* (BBC1), a teenager itself; the younger *Byker Grove* (BBC1); BAFTA award-winning *Press Gang* (ITV); Manchester's *Children's Ward* (ITV); and for those who like good looks and sunshine with their thorny issues, ITV's American import, *Beverly Hills 90210*, each explores what life is like for today's youngsters. They face both bouquets and brickbats for doing so, but the miracle is that they do it at all. Some things are simply not allowed to be shown on children's television, and, more than that, programme-makers are well aware that even what is allowable may not be advisable in view of the wide age-range of the audience.

Explains *Byker Grove* producer Matthew Robinson, 'we know that there are 8-year-olds in our audience even though we are directing the programme for young teens. I'd say that you could split *Byker Grove* viewers into three groups, say 8-10, 10-12 and 13+, and what appeals to one group won't interest the others so much. We try not to

offend, embarrass or distress but we can't completely fudge difficult issues or patronise youngsters, and this means that although some stuff that has meaning for teenagers will go over the head of an 8-year-old, it might prompt curiosity and a few awkward questions. I do think it's then down to the parent to deal with the curiosity.'

Debbie (Nicola Bell) and PJ (Anthony McPartlin) of *Byker Grove*

Among the storylines of *Byker Grove* have been teenage romance, child abuse, involvement with a strange cult, the effects of bankruptcy on a family and joy-riding. It was a storyline involving the characters PJ and Debbie sleeping with each other (it wasn't shown on screen but PJ buying condoms from a vending machine was) that attracted the widest comment – and a complaint to the Broadcasting Standards Council. Letters to the programme asked if the 'aim of so-called children's television was to rob our children of innocent childhood' and stated, 'it is still wrong to have sex before marriage and to encourage this shows complete lack of responsibility'. Other viewers were 'distressed', 'appalled', 'disgusted' and 'shocked'.

The complaint was in fact not upheld, with the Council considering the offending scenes not inappropriate in the context of the story, 'nor did it think that the scenes would have given rise to widespread concern, having regard to the well-known reputation of this

long-running series for tackling important issues confronting teenage children'.

All did not end well for Debbie, it has to be said. PJ turned out to be a rat and there was upset all round. Teenagers wrote in to thank the series for its honesty and for showing what can happen. 'We had 40 complaints altogether,' says Matthew Robinson. 'But I think what we showed was a very moral tale, as all our stories are in the end. PJ was acting in a predatory manner, whatever his sweet-talk, so the programme was in fact a warning.'

When *Grange Hill* tackled teenage pregnancy through the story of one of its characters, Chrissy Mainwaring, there were those who considered it an unsuitable subject for children's television. Interestingly, the tale, which followed Chrissy as she had her baby and faced a much-changed future, came at a time when surveys were showing an alarming increase in teenage pregnancy and there were calls from the Health Education Council for more effective sex education. BBC Social Affairs Editor Polly Toynbee wrote in *Radio Times*: 'The average number of pregnancies in girls under 16 in Britain now runs at four per school a year...many parents and teachers may be glad children are getting a realistic presentation of such an important problem.' Perhaps not so well received by teachers was the storyline about a

Filming an episode of *Grange Hill*

school uniform revolt at Grange Hill, which had children across Britain turning their blazers inside out in copycat fashion.

But to concentrate on the complaints of the few, however deeply felt, is to ignore the often critically-acclaimed quality of such contemporary drama and fosters the belief that its makers are hard bent on covering the issues of the day, no matter what. The truth is more basic: the appeal of these series to their young audience lies in their honest look at changing relationships. Sometimes the relationships are between the young cast members, but they also look at those between adults and children, often through the eyes of the child – a moving and highly-praised *Children's Ward* story followed the fortunes of a runaway teenage couple and the abuse of the boy by his father.

Sandra Hastie is the producer of ITV's *Press Gang*, a fictional group of schoolchildren who run their own newspaper. It won a BAFTA in 1991 for a two-episode treatment of child sexual abuse, a theme that, both thankfully and sadly, has been taken up at some point by most of the 'teen soaps'.

'All our stories are about relationships,' says Hastie. 'We have the continuing on-off romance of Gazette reporter Spike and Linda the editor, for example. Perhaps one of our most important stories in 1992 was about Spike's father dying but that wasn't so much about bereavement in itself as about how Spike and his father got along together. The way people treat each other and the attitudes they have in *Press Gang* are always shifting, as they are in life. After all, people learn about themselves from the relationships they have with other people.' A touching postscript to the bereavement story was a letter Sandra Hastie received from a young Australian girl who had hated her father for leaving her mother and had now been able to get in touch with him and talk it all through.

Hastie also thinks that quality writing is important to the success of any drama series and that in *Press Gang*, the humour in the scripts means that emotional issues and moral tales don't preclude laughter and entertainment. *Byker Grove* producer Matthew Robinson is equally sure of the importance of the scripts and looks for talented newcomers as well as having used pens of experience from such series as *Casualty, EastEnders, Coronation Street* and *Rockliffe's Babies*. Robinson himself is a former director of *EastEnders, Bergerac* and *Howard's Way*, among others.

'I go for stories first,' he says. 'I don't say, "let's do an issue" and then try and find a story. We put the characters through a series of emotions – they get squeezed by circumstances or other people and emerge better or worse. That's what makes us human beings. And we can't let the baddies win – that would give quite the wrong message.'

Moral with a vengeance is *Beverly Hills 90210*. Fewer episodes have been seen here than in

Julia Sawalha and Dexter Fletcher, stars of *Press Gang*

America, its country of origin, since in the States it has a 9pm time slot. Forget Newcastle youth clubs, Manchester hospitals, London comprehensive schools and the like, the students of Beverly Hills High have perfect tans, perfect teeth and gallons of glamour. Like anybody, they do not have perfect lives, but viewers find that Doing the Right Thing brings rewards.

The cast of *Beverly Hills 90210*

Beverly Hills characters have discovered that the commitment of a sexual relationship needs mature consideration and preferably avoidance while young; drinking and gambling do nobody any good; you shouldn't have an affair if you're married; and adventures in the great outdoors build character. It's American, yes, but it's still boy-meets-girl-meets-the-world stuff, even if the beach plays a larger role than it would in Britain. And the characters have to do the decent thing or get their comeuppance because, apart from anything else, they are pin-up gorgeous and have adoring teen fans hanging on their every glance.

The debate about what is acceptable viewing for children will continue, and properly so. No programme maker would have it any other way, and nor would many young viewers, who are frequently keen to join the debate themselves. As one 12-year-old *Byker Grove* viewer wrote, 'BG deals with issues which are embarrassing for children to talk about. It helps me open up to my parents.' Perhaps those nostalgic for *Watch With Mother* might find watching with their children today an education and an opportunity.

Julie Allan

THE DARLING BUDS OF MAY

Based on the books about the fictional Larkin family by HE Bates, *The Darling Buds of May* returned for a new series early in 1992. By Anne-Marie Sapsted

That Britain's best-loved comedy *The Darling Buds of May* ever made it to our television screens, was pure chance. It was the result of an encounter between Richard Bates, son of the late HE Bates who created the stories, and a failed monk. It is an unusual story in itself.

Vernon Lawrence was a novice in the late 50s studying with the Anglican Society of the Sacred Mission when his mother died. He left so that he could spend time with his father, learned about comedy firstly on the radio with *Take it from Here* and *Round the Horne*, then moving to television. There he worked in both variety and comedy at the BBC, moving to independent television and eventually becoming Yorkshire TV's controller of entertainment. It was in this role that he met Richard Bates on Yorkshire TV's stand at the annual Cannes television sales fair.

Bates confided that he was looking for someone to turn his father's books into a suitable series. The two came to a gentleman's agreement, sealed with a handshake, and scarcely had the first episodes appeared than Yorkshire had a hit on their hands of such proportions that it even managed to knock *Coronation Street* off the top of the ratings.

Lawrence sums up *Darling Buds'* appeal: 'It's got nostalgia, something we all love. It's wonderfully English. Better still, it's rural English. It's about a family who live the way we secretly all long to live, never paying the income tax; never bothering about modern fads, like dieting.

'It's about a little man who pits himself against bureaucracy and wins, and who breaks through all the class barriers of his period – he deals in junk but hobnobs with brigadiers and the lord of the manor. It's escapism at its best. And above all, it's good, clean fun, without being saccharine.'

The creator of Ma and Pa Larkin and their enormous family was a Kent man himself who lived only a few miles from Pluckley, the Weald village which was chosen as the setting for Yorkshire TV's £3 million series.

Keen to stay as close to the books as possible, it took a week and a team of producers and researchers to find the ideal Kent farm which would be turned into the main setting. With a lot of careful planning and the attentions of a team of carpenters and painters, the farmhouse began to take on the right sort of dilapidated look.

But the farmyard was the biggest headache because it had to be filled with 50s junk. Finally the show's prop buyer took a large van and roamed the Kent countryside stopping at farms and junk shops collecting anything and everything. They ended up with tons of apple boxes, apple picking equipment, tyres, oil drums, old farm machinery and a load of scrap metal. Swathed in yards of dead vine and plastic ivy – though sadly the nettles mentioned several times in Bates's books couldn't be grown in time – the set was suitably run-down and ready for filming.

In the middle of all this was the 'perfick' Larkin family in the shape of Britain's undisputed king of comedy David Jason as Pa, Pam Ferris as the ample Ma, unknown – though not for long – Catherine Zeta Jones as their devastatingly beautiful daughter Mariette and Phillip Franks as Charley the tax man who later became Mariette's husband. There was also a host of other children and eventually a grandchild glorying in the name of John Blenheim, but in fact Daisy May Bates, the real-life great granddaughter of HE Bates.

When it first appeared *The Darling Buds of May* created television history when it shot to number one in the ratings and stayed there ahead of *Coronation Street* and *EastEnders* with regular viewing figures of around 18 million. The second series was not quite so popular, attracted a lot of poor reviews from the critics, and eventually the show's stars said they were willing to continue as long as the ratings did not fall below 11

David Jason as Pop Larkin

Rex Features

million, considered the make or break mark for drama.

As four of the five Larkin books had already been adapted for the first two series and the other was shelved because Pa Larkin had a heart attack in it, Yorkshire TV decided to strengthen its writing team. They brought in David Nobbs, author of the vintage BBC success *The Fall and Rise of Reginald Perrin*, who had written scripts for David Jason's other Yorkshire TV hit *A Bit of a Do*.

Catherine Zeta Jones as Mariette

The success of the series has also been good news for the villagers of Pluckley – previously infamous as the most haunted village in England – now regularly visited by *Darling Buds* fans. Even the farm set's owners, Ashford ironmonger Raymond Holmes and his wife Gladys, can see the funny side of the invasion. And this despite the fact that one weekend they had to have a security guard at the gate to stop visitors marching up to take photographs and now have a brand new 'Private Property, Keep Out' sign donated by Yorkshire TV.

The vicar is absolutely delighted by the interest. A routine survey of St Nicholas, the parish church, found that it was badly in need of repair and payment for the church's use in filming and donations from visitors have swelled the restoration fund. Ma's pantry, an idea from a mother with children at the village school, has proved a roaring success, too, and is raising money for the school and the village hall.

The series itself pulled off a financial coup late last year when Tetley Tea signed a £1.2 million sponsorship deal. The company plans to use the Larkin family on packets, in supermarkets and in competitions. Yorkshire has already sold the programme in 15 countries, plus video cassettes at £20 a time and a host of other spin-offs. All this for what David Jason describes as 'great escapism. It lets people get away from their troubles. I don't think life was quite like that back in the 50s but people like to think it was.' Pa Larkin would undoubtedly have approved on all counts.

Anne-Marie Sapsted

'ALLO 'ALLO!

We had to say 'goodbye goodbye' to *'Allo 'Allo!* as the final series drew to a close in December. But, 'leesen vairy cairefullee, I shall say zees only wernce', the programme was an unlikely success. Anne-Marie Sapsted reports

When the pilot for *'Allo 'Allo!* was first shown ten years ago, it stirred up a great controversy with some critics suggesting that the French Resistance was definitely not a fitting subject for comedy. In the end, it lasted four years longer than the war itself!

Over the years it has gathered a huge following and some unlikely fans. On his appointment as Chairman of the Broadcasting Standards Council, Lord Rees-Mogg, the champion of politically correct broadcasting, surprised everyone when he confided that *'Allo 'Allo!* was his favourite programme. The Queen Mother is also believed to be an enthusiastic viewer.

Not only has the programme been a huge success here, it has also been sold to more than 50 countries including America, Yugoslavia, Greece and Switzerland, and even finally to the Germans. A significant victory was won in 1989 when the French finally gave in and bought two series.

The series was created by writers Jeremy Lloyd and David Croft, who also used the same background for other BBC comedy classics like *Dad's Army* and *It Ain't Half Hot Mum*. Croft and Lloyd made sure that their scripts made fun of every nationality, including the British, and Arthur Bostrom's gendarme Crabtree and his tortured vowels became one of the mainstays of the series.

The last series was set in 1943 – unlike the previous ones set in 1941 – and the ending ensured that the idea cannot be resurrected. So we will no longer hear Gorden Kaye as the lecherous, put-upon cafe proprietor trying to keep his business going while not offending the Germans and trying to co-operate with the Resistance, utter the words 'You stupid woman' to his long-suffering wife Edith, played by Carmen Silvera. He will no longer have to divide his passion between lustful waitresses Yvette and Mimi and fend off the amorous Lt Gruber, played by Guy Siner.

Much of the action was set in René's bar and more than two thirds of *'Allo 'Allo!* was filmed in the studio in front of an audience.

René (Gorden Kaye) and Yvette (Vicki Michelle) get to grips in *'Allo 'Allo!*

René (Gorden Kaye) and Edith (Carmen Silvera) outside the Cafe René

Shots of the town square and other exteriors were created from plywood in the courtyard of a country hall near the village of Swaffham in Norfolk.

The costume designer was Jill Taylor and she made sure that all the clothes were genuine 40s style by combing market stalls and the BBC wardrobe for examples. These were then copied in larger sizes because it was found that people in general are now bigger than they were in wartime, even down to the size of shoes. The German uniforms were hired, the hats were made according to designs of the day and the jewellery, copies from original pieces.

One of the biggest costume challenges in the last series was an amazing scene where the whole cast had to dress up as sea creatures. René was dressed as King Neptune and there was a crab, a prawn, an octopus and two mermaids. They had to look homemade, but convincing at the same time.

Special effects have also featured throughout the series, including a memorable scene where a hot air balloon became untethered and sailed away, though machine gunfire and explosions of various sorts were routine.

The series also generated a highly successful stage show which saw the *'Allo 'Allo!* team through four West End seasons and several nationwide tours, as well as to Australia and New Zealand. And the characters made regular celebrity appearances on a host of other television shows.

Back in 1990 the show's star, Gorden Kaye, was involved in a freak accident when a plank smashed through the windscreen of his car during hurricane-force winds and embedded itself in his head. Five and a half hours of brain surgery followed, and he hovered between life and death before pulling through. He was hit by depression after the accident, but returned to work in a remarkably short time. Then 18 months ago he collapsed from exhaustion and doctors told him he had to slow down.

He already had plenty of work planned after the series, though, starting with a tour in an Alan Bennett play and the BBC is hoping to find a new comedy vehicle for him. Kaye once met the man who dubs the voice of René into French and found they shared the same sense of humour. 'He told me he had to keep stopping because he kept getting the giggles,' said Kaye. 'It only proved to me that the French *do* have a sense of humour.'

For those of us who miss the complex plots and strangled vowels, we can pass on a bit of news, so... leesen vairy cairefullee, I shall say zees only wernce, the BBC has sold the show to its own new satellite channel UK Gold.

Anne-Marie Sapsted

'THE OLDIES'

The established formula for sitcoms featuring families with teenage children has recently made way for the older generation. Christopher Middleton reviews the success of grey-haired comedy

Once upon a time, TV appearances by people over 60 were limited to documentaries chronicling the 'problem' posed by a rising elderly population. Grey hair was something newsreaders and director-generals might be allowed to have, but in light entertainment, when winter came to your hair, so too did the cold shoulder.

Today the situation has totally changed, thanks in large part to the tremendous popularity of three BBC sitcoms featuring older characters – *One Foot in the Grave*, *Waiting For God* and *Keeping Up Appearances*. Each is currently embarking on its fourth series, and each regularly attracts audiences of more than 10 million (16 million in the case of *One Foot in the Grave*).

With two other 'oldie' sitcoms also running (*Last of the Summer Wine* and *As Time Goes By*), you might think the BBC was operating a deliberate pro-elderly policy. Not so, says Gareth Gwenlan, who as head of comedy commissioned both *Waiting For God* (which he now directs and produces) and *One Foot in the Grave*.

'Thank God we haven't yet taken up the American idea of making shows like products – specifically marketed at A and B sectors of the population', he says. 'We rely on writers to come up with new ideas and new themes, and it often happens, as it has done with these older sitcoms, that independently of each other, writers all round the country start writing on the same theme.

'And frankly, if you get six scripts on the same theme and five of them are good, you make those five shows, because there aren't that many good scripts around.'

Despite the similarities between the three senior-citizen sitcoms, Jenny Secombe, the BBC's light entertainment publicity officer, rejects any suggestion that they are all tackling the same topics.

'It's really only *Waiting For God*, being set in a retirement home, that is specifically about old age', she says. '*Keeping Up Appearances*' (starring Patricia Routledge as Hyacinth Bucket, pronounced 'Bouquet') is more about class. And in *One Foot in the Grave*, although Victor Meldrew has had retirement thrust upon him, the comedy has more to do with his personality than his age.'

And it is that personality – stubborn, cantankerous but somehow still lovable – which has endeared the show – and Victor Meldrew – to millions. 'He's a spokesman for the nation', says *One Foot in the Grave*'s producer-director Susan Belbin. 'Victor is irritated by the things that irritate all of us – difficult neighbours, delivery men who don't turn up when they say they will. It's just that his irritation is magnified because having been forced to retire early, he has only these little things to focus on.'

Quite the reverse is true for Richard Wilson, the actor who plays Victor. After nearly a quarter of a century of being a face to which people couldn't quite put a name, he is now established, thanks to *One Foot in the Grave*, as one of the country's best-known and most sought-after comedy performers.

He was born 56 years ago in Renfrewshire, whence he derives his distinctive Scottish lilt. He began his working life as a medical researcher, but at the age of 30 gave up his daily bus journey to and from Paddington General Hospital, and set out down a less well-signposted career path as an actor.

Richard Wilson as Victor Meldrew in *One Foot in the Grave*

BBC Photograph Library

His first television roles were character parts in programmes such as *Dr Finlay's Casebook* and *Crown Court*. His talent for sitcom began to shine in the late 70s, when he played snooty Dr Thorpe in the hospital sitcom *Only When I Laugh* (James Bolam and Peter Bowles were his patients). And as quirky rock-band manager Eddie Clockerty, in *Tutti Frutti*, and tough-talking newspaper executive Richard Lipton, in *Hot Metal*, he invested his performances with a

Annette Crosbie and Richard Wilson as Margaret and Victor Meldrew

BBC Photograph Library

certain manic-yet-comic quality.

Those hints were enough to convince *One Foot in the Grave* writer David Renwick that Richard Wilson was the actor to play Victor Meldrew. At first, the naturally cheerful Wilson had misgivings about playing a crotchety old codger. 'I could understand why, having been thrown on the scrapheap, Victor was so irascible; but I did feel he lost his temper rather too much.'

However, as the ratings rose, and Victor's character developed, the doubts disappeared. 'I think what people like about him now is that he says the things they would like to say, but never do.'

Like Victor Meldrew, the central figure of *Keeping Up Appearances* is also something of a monster. Hyacinth Bucket (Patricia Routledge) is a pretentious, snobbish, be-hatted bungalow owner, with airs and graces that are comically, and often tragically, at variance with her real station in life. A less than upper-crust family, most notably her idle sister Daisy (Judy Cornwell) and uncouth brother-in-law Onslow (played by former *Coronation Street* star Geoffrey Hughes), provide her with constant rude awakenings from what are otherwise contented delusions of grandeur.

Patricia Routledge herself admits to being surprised at the affection in which Hyacinth is held by viewers. How, she wonders, can such a dreadful woman arouse such sympathies? The show's postbag provides the answer.

'We get hundreds of letters from people saying they know someone just like Hyacinth,' says producer-director Harold Snoad. 'Usually, it's daughters saying she reminds them of their mothers, but we also get quite a lot of people writing in to say that Hyacinth is just like them.'

Unlike much of writer Roy Clarke's other work (*Last of the Summer Wine, Open All Hours*), *Keeping Up Appearances* is not set in an identifiably northern location. Indeed, both Hyacinth's bungalow (in the real-life suburbs of Leamington Spa) and her sister's house (on a Coventry council estate) were chosen for their could-be-anywhere-in-Britain look.

Patricia Routledge as Hyacinth Bucket in *Keeping Up Appearances*

BBC Photograph Library

The same quality attaches to the old people's home which is the setting for *Waiting For God*. It is, in fact, a genuine retirement home, at Oakenholt, just outside Oxford, although the conservatory in which much of the action happens is a bolt-on, bolt-off addition. 'We fix it onto the home when we are filming there, and then we dismantle it and bring it back to London for the studio scenes', says Gareth Gwenlan.

In fact, *Waiting For God* began life several thousand miles away from Oxfordshire. The show's writer Michael Aitkens originally set it in a retirement village in Australia, with the two main characters – Tom and Diana – meeting each other on their adjoining balconies. 'There was no way you could do this in a British climate, though', says Gareth Gwenlan. 'Hence the conservatory.'

Although it's the show which relates most specifically to old age, *Waiting For God* has, in Stephanie Cole, a star who at 51 still has nearly a decade till she gets her bus pass.

'I've always played older than myself,' says north London-based Stephanie. 'Most actresses keep quiet about their age because they don't want people to know how old they are, but I don't want people to know how young I am!'

There is certainly no shortage of youthful vigour about the way in which her character Diana, a former photo-journalist now stricken with arthritis, fights against the just-waiting-to-die mentality that afflicts many of her fellow residents at the Bayview Retirement Home. Her biggest ally is the trusty Tom (Graham Crowden), who shares her dislike of the home's shifty manager Harvey Bains (Daniel Hill).

But for both Cole and Crowden, the interest in matters of age does not stop when they leave the *Waiting For God* set. Along with *One Foot in the Grave*'s Richard Wilson and his screen wife Annette Crosbie, they both belong to the celebrity committee of the charity Age Concern, lending their face and fame wherever it will help attract publicity for the organisation's activities.

Not surprisingly, both Age Con-

Stephanie Cole as Diana and Graham Crowden as Tom in *Waiting for God*

cern and Help The Aged are delighted that sitcoms featuring older characters have become so popular.

'We think they're a marvellous thing,' says Margaret McClellan, publicity officer for Age Concern. 'What pleases us in particular is that the shows present life as it really is. Sometimes people say the characters come across as rather grumpy; if they are, it's only because they're fighting to get a better deal for older people.'

Age Concern's input to *Waiting For God* goes beyond mere congratulation, however. The organisation keeps writer Michael Aitkens supplied with a continual flow of suggestions for issues he might like to incorporate into an episode.

'Michael's writing doesn't set out to be overtly crusading', says Gareth Gwenlan. 'What it does do, though, is to demonstrate repeatedly that old people cannot be shuffled off into a corner and forgotten about – that they have just as much right as anyone else to enjoy their lives to the full.'

Perhaps the most controversial manifestation of that philosophy came with the broadcast of the episode in which Diana and Tom ended up in bed together. When discovered and chided by tut-tutting Bayview staff, Diana produced from under the sheets a copy of Age Concern's book *Living, Loving and Ageing*. 'You should read this', she told them, brandishing it defiantly.

The results of this single programme were dramatic, says Margaret McClellan.

'I think it fair to say that up until *Waiting For God*, the subject of sex between people over 60 had never been discussed other than in a negative way. In many respects, it was seen as a kind of taboo area. The day after the programme went out, however, we had hundreds and hundreds of calls from older people, all asking where they could get hold of a copy of the book, and all saying how grateful they were that someone had actually raised the issue on television.

'We had for some years been trying – without great success – to get people at least to acknowledge that older people do have sex. Overnight, it seemed, simply because it had been in a sitcom, the subject had become instantly acceptable.

'It made us realise the immense influence television – and particularly television comedy – has over people. One popular half-hour programme can completely change an entire country's attitudes.'

Christopher Middleton

THE 1992 RADIO TIMES COMEDY AND DRAMA AWARDS

Nicki Household reviews the 1992 Radio Times Comedy and Drama Awards – an event which honours the achievements of writers and performers, with awards for newcomers and established names

Attended by HRH Prince Edward and a host of celebrities and VIPs from the broadcasting and entertainment worlds, the 1992 Radio Times Comedy and Drama Awards, held at London's Mayfair Theatre on 1 December 1992, was a glittering occasion. Angus Deayton of *Have I Got News For You* fame, fulfilled his role as chief presenter with characteristic wit and aplomb, aided and abetted by a galaxy of guest stars – including Richard Jobson, Jenny Seagrove, Ian Hislop, Emma Freud, Peter Barkworth, Alison Dowling of *The Archers*, writer Lynda La Plante, Danny Baker and Jenny Agutter – who announced the winners of the individual categories.

In his welcoming address from the stage, *Radio Times* editor Nicholas Brett declared that this year's awards were 'bigger and better than ever', as they had been broadened to honour the achievements of both established and up-and-coming writers and performers, as well as to encourage and reward the talent of new and first-time scriptwriters.

There were 20 awards in all; four for new writing (New Comedy Script for Radio, New Comedy Script for Television, New Drama Script for Radio, New Drama Script for Television) and four for already-broadcast scripts (Best Comedy Script Radio, Best Comedy Script Television, Best Drama Script Radio, Best Drama Script Television).

The other 12 awards were for performers; Best New Performers in Radio and Television Comedy, Best New Radio Actor and Actress, Best New Television Actor and Actress, Best New Actor and Actress in Radio Comedy, the Radio and Television Comedy Performances of the Year and, finally, the Radio and Television

Drama Performances of the Year.

These new-style awards, as Brett explained, built on the considerable success of the Radio Times Drama Awards, which began in 1973 and were joined by the Comedy Awards in 1985. More than 16,000 scripts have been submitted to the two competitions over the years. This year's writing competition (with cash prizes totalling £20,000) attracted more than 1,000 entries, and the final short list was judged by writer Fay Weldon, actors Jimmy

HRH Prince Edward at the Awards ceremony

Mark Harrison

Guy was shown in the 1991 *Screenplay* season on BBC2. And more than 50 past entries to the radio section have been broadcast on BBC Radio.

Although most of the press attention focused on the famous actors and actresses who had won (or were presenting) awards, it was nevertheless the winners of the writing competition who, being unused to such accolades, were the most surprised and delighted award-winners of the day.

Mulville and Leslie Phillips and comedienne Helen Lederer as well as the heads of BBC Drama, Comedy and Light Entertainment.

Many winners and runners-up of past competitions – including the authors of ITV's *Second Thoughts* Jan Etherington and Gavin Petrie, multi-award-winning radio dramatist Shirley Gee and *Kinsey* author Peter Gibb – have gone on to great things. Three recent winners of the television section have seen their scripts speedily reach the screen. Yorkshireman Ron Pearson, who took up writing as a retirement hobby, won in 1986 with *Harry's Kingdom*, which starred Timothy West. A young actor, Martyn Hesford (who now divides his time between acting and writing) won in 1988 with his black comedy *A Small Mourning*. John Random's winning 1990 drama *The Fallout*

'I was stunned. I felt it proved that I hadn't been talking through my hat to my students for all these years,' says Frances Gray, a 45-year-old drama lecturer at Sheffield University, whose entry *Sally Jo and Harris of the Yard* won the New Comedy Script for Radio award. A part-time writer for ten years, Gray was a runner-up in the 1985 Drama Awards, had a play performed at the Soho Poly in 1980 and has just completed a book about women in comedy called *Women and Laughter*. Also the mother of an 8-year-old son, she wrote her winning script in just four weeks. 'The competition provided a wonderful deadline. Without it, my script might never have got written,' she says.

The judges described her play – a comedy about two old school friends who meet again by chance

Editor of *Private Eye* and TV personality Ian Hislop

Mark Harrison

when both are going through a mid-life crisis – as 'original, funny and touching, with a good twist at the end'. Winning the competition has fuelled Gray's determination to become 'a writer who teaches a bit instead of vice versa. Awards give you something to aim for,' she says. 'You're not writing in a vacuum, because you *know* your script will be read.'

Surprisingly, perhaps, in a competition for *new* writers (but very encouragingly, for the more mature scribbler!), three of the four main winners were aged over 45. The exception was 18-year-old Daniel Peak, whose script *Where There's a Will* – written in the fortnight after he'd taken his A' Levels – won the New Comedy Script for Television award.

Peak, who comes from near Manchester and is now reading Psychology and Philosophy at Oxford, says he was 'amazed' to hear his name read out as winner. His past writing experience has been restricted to school revues and entertainments, an unsuccessful entry to last year's Radio Times Awards 'and various things I sent to *Spitting Image* which were always sent back'. But now he has set his sights on becoming a professional writer.

According to the judges, his winning comedy, which follows the increasingly surreal train of events following an eccentric suicide, 'was

bizarre and imaginative, used excellent parody devices and showed amazing talent'. The £3,000 prize money, said Peak, would make him 'quite a lot richer', and he planned to spend a substantial chunk of it on records over the Christmas holidays.

Robin Lloyd-Jones, winner of the award for New Drama Script for Radio with *Ice in Wonderland*, took early retirement from Strathclyde Education Authority in 1989, to concentrate fully on writing. Now 58, and originally a Londoner, although he's lived in Glasgow for

Chief presenter Angus Deayton

30 years, Robin Lloyd-Jones has published two novels, a children's book and a collection of short stories, but *Ice in Wonderland*, adapted from his own novel *The Dreamhouse*, was his first attempt at writing for radio. Set in 19th century Alaska, at the time of the gold rush, it tells the story of an ex-actor and con-man who arrives in a corrupt, chaotic mining town, determined to make his fortune.

The judges described it as 'a most accomplished and extraordinary work of the imagination'. But it would never have been written, if Lloyd-Jones hadn't read about the Comedy and Drama Awards. 'I was brought up on radio, so it's engrained in me, but it had never occurred to me to *write* for radio until I saw the competition advertised,' he explains. 'But as soon as I started work on my script, I felt completely at home in the medium.' He's now hooked and is already writing his second radio play.

Fifty-two-year-old Sean Damer, whose screenplay *Payment with Interest* won the New Drama Script for Television award, says he used the competition 'as a target to discipline myself', and that winning it has been 'a fantastic fillip to my self-confidence'. After years of part-time, dilettante writing, Damer decided to become a full-time professional writer in 1991, bringing to an end a long career as a social

Mark Harrison

historian at Glasgow University. He has since had short stories published in the *Glasgow Herald* and broadcast on Radio Scotland. Winning the award has, he says, reinforced his commitment to creative writing, 'about which I am deadly serious'.

Set in present-day Glasgow, his play, which he describes as 'a moral tale for our times', involves a violent money lender, Mo, and his debtors Frank and his wife Carol, who was once Mo's lover. The judges said it displayed 'very powerful writing, a very good ear for dialogue and an individual voice'.

The other prize-winners in the new writing section were:

New Comedy Script for Radio – 2nd, Mary Stewart Davies for *Casey's Crises*; 3rd, Russ Spencer for *Song of the Mad Prince*.

New Comedy Script for Television – 2nd, John Garner for *Why do Winos Sing?*; 3rd, Annie Hayes and Peter Waddington for *Hearts and Flowers*.

New Drama Script for Radio – 2nd, Caroline Forbes for *Michelle and the Landlady*; 3rd, Chris Giles for *Shadow Play*.

New Drama Script for Television – 2nd, Alex Summers for *Yam! Bang! Wham!*; 3rd, Bob Gallagher for *Foreign Powers*.

The highest accolades of the day, the awards for the Radio and Television Performances of the Year, were presented by HRH Prince Edward. Nigel Anthony won the radio award for his role in the BBC World Service drama *Lost for Words* (which also won the Best Radio Drama Script for its writer Ken Blakeson) and Sue Johnston (known to millions as the long-suffering Sheila Grant from *Brookside*), received the television award for her performance in BBC2's powerful three-part drama serial *Goodbye Cruel World* by Adrian Shergold.

By an extraordinary coincidence, both dramas centre on a character who is afflicted with a fatal wasting disease. Anthony played Adam Lowell, an MP in his mid-40s, whose brilliant career is cut short by the onset of motor neuron disease. The panel of judges – which included actress Penelope Keith

and broadcasters Ned Sherrin and Barry Took, alongside distinguished writers, journalists and producers – described Anthony's performance as 'absolutely remarkable, extremely involving and technically extraordinary'.

'It was exhausting and gruelling, trying to convey the feelings of a man whose speech is intelligible only to his wife,' admits the actor, 'and yet, even though the subject was so sad, it was a tremendously rewarding production. Ken Blakeson's dialogue cut through to the real human dilemmas of the situation in a very brave and uncompromising way.'

In *Goodbye Cruel World*, Sue Johnston played courageous wife and mother Barbara Grade, who, after the shock of finding out that she is suffering from a rare and fatal muscle-wasting disease, decides to set up a self-help group for other sufferers. 'It was an extraordinary piece to work on,' says Johnston, (also seen recently in *Caribbean Story* and the comedy series *Full Stretch*). 'Some moments were bad, because of the realisation that for some people the situation is real and they can't just get up and walk away. But it was really exceptional material and a great, great part.'

It was no surprise that the award for Best Drama Script Television went to Anthony Minghella for his international screen success *Truly Madly Deeply* (starring Juliet Stevenson and Alan Rickman), which he also directed. Already the winner of *Evening Standard*, Writers' Guild and BAFTA awards, the former university teacher was nevertheless delighted to add the Radio Times Award to his collection. 'It's very gratifying to get this endorsement and encouragement from one's peer group,' he commented. 'I have much to thank the BBC for. Both for having faith in me as a writer and for being instrumental in launching my career as a director.'

Thirty-year-old Charles Simpson, who won the Best New Radio Actor award for his performance as the youngest of three invalid First World War soldiers in *The Lavender Song* by Patricia Wood, said he was proud to be carrying on the

tradition of his grandfather Ronald Simpson. 'I never met him, but he was one of the founders of radio drama and played Soames in the first radio *Forsyte Saga*. It's a great thrill to win the award and I feel that somewhere upstairs my grandfather is a happy guy.'

The other Radio Times Comedy and Drama Awards were as follows:

Best Radio Comedy Script – Andy Hamilton and Nick Revell for *The Million Pound Radio Show – Election Special'*, BBC Radio 4.

Best Television Comedy Script – Andy Hamilton and Guy Jenkin for *Drop the Dead Donkey*, Hat Trick Productions for Channel 4.

Best New Performer Radio Comedy – Nick Hancock for *Room 101*, BBC Radio 5.

Best New Performer Television Comedy – Rob Newman and David Baddiel for *The Mary Whitehouse Experience*, A Spitting Image Production and BBC2 co–production.

Best New Radio Actress – Siriol Jenkins in *Unreasonable Behaviour*, BBC Radio 4.

Best New Television Actor – Mark Rylance in *The Grass Arena*, BBC2.

Best New Television Actress – Jennifer Ehle in *The Camomile Lawn*, Channel 4.

Best New Actor Radio Comedy – John Forgeham in *Accidental Death of an Anarchist*, BBC Radio 5.

Best New Actress Radio Comedy – Doon Mackichan in *The Nick Revell Show*, BBC Radio 4.

Radio Comedy Performance of the Year – Sally Grace in *Week Ending*, BBC Radio 4.

Television Comedy Performance of the Year – Lenny Henry in *Bernard and the Genie*, Talkback Productions for BBC1.

'Remember, it's not the winning, but who you beat,' commented a wry Angus Deayton, resolutely refusing to let the occasion take itself too seriously as the star–studded presentation ceremony drew to a close and the Prince, the Awards Committee, the judges, winners, runners–up and their guests moved towards the Crystal Dining Room and lunch.

Nicki Household

Music

It was a year of anniversaries with *Desert Island Discs* broadcasting in its 50th year, Radio 1 reaching the age of 25, and living legend Paul McCartney celebrating his 50th birthday.

During the past 12 months, Radio 3 has experienced the most dramatic changes of all the radio networks and the station's new style is reviewed.

The 98th season of the BBC Henry Wood Promenade Concerts produced a feast of music during the summer months, with all 66 concerts relayed live on Radio 3, and Frederick Kempf became the BBC's *Young Musician of the Year.*

We said farewell to Fab 208 with the demise of Radio Luxembourg, and Marc Bolan, star of the 70s, was remembered 15 years after his untimely death.

2 Music

DESERT ISLAND DISCS' 50TH ANNIVERSARY

The longest-running record programme on radio celebrated its golden anniversary in January 1992. William Greaves met Sue Lawley to find out what magic ingredient has kept the discs spinning for 50 years

The world's most exclusive hideaway appears in no travel agent's brochure. It boasts not a single hotel and its beaches have never been photographed – largely because no one knows where they are. It doesn't even have a name. Yet the resident population of this uncharted island is made up of as distinguished a band of do-it-yourselfers as you could find anywhere on earth. And to celebrate the 50th anniversary of the programme on Sunday, 26 January, the Prime Minister John Major joined them with a special edition and documentary on Radio 4.

Over the years 2,000 castaways have been dispatched by Roy Plomley, founding father of the BBC Home Service's *Desert Island Discs*, and his Radio 4 successors Michael Parkinson and Sue Lawley.

Each settler is, of course, the proud owner of eight records, a book and one luxury. In an outburst of generosity three Christmases ago, Dirk Bogarde (now Sir Dirk) was allowed to take with him an entire whisky distillery – so the island's golden jubilee party seems destined to be something of a wow.

The first hundred castaways were allowed no such luxury at all and the programme was 400 editions old before they were granted a book to while away their mythical years of solitude. But throughout all this gentle evolution, the formula has remained the same – an ultimately sympathetic amalgam of words and music. Not once in 50 years has the listener been lurched out of his or her eaves-dropping ecstasy by that most irritating of intrusions, 'We're going to break now for some music,

Sue Lawley and Prime Minister John Major, on the 50th anniversary programme in January 1992

BBC

Presenters Roy Plomley and Sue Lawley with famous 'castaway' guests. (Left to right): Noel Coward in *Desert Island Discs* 21st anniversary programme – January 1963; Paul McCartney; Vivienne Westwood; Roy Plomley, holding gramophone, surrounded by some of the guests who have appeared on *Desert Island Discs*, when the programme celebrated its 40th anniversary in January 1982; Terry Waite; Frankie Howerd; Julie Andrews; The Duchess of Kent; Pamela Stephenson; Norman Tebbit.

but don't go away' – because each record choice is as much a part of the celebrity guest's character as the talk that surrounds it.

Desert Island Discs has never sought to shock or expose – merely to reveal. What tears have been shed over the years come far more often from the castaway's nostalgia than from any more tangible form of distress. Yet as a top people's personality peepshow, it became so quickly a broadcasting institution that, long before its first year was out, willing victims knew that they had received an invitation far more prestigious than the promise of an entry in *Who's Who*.

The range of those volunteers is illustrated by the milestones along the way: the 500th programme featured Eddie Calvert; the 1,000th, Viscount Montgomery of Alamein; the 1,500th, Bulgarian bass Boris Christoff and the 2,000th, actor John Thaw. In between have been royals such as the Princess Royal and Princess Grace; several leaders of the Opposition – including Margaret Thatcher in 1978 – and former Prime Ministers Lord Home, Sir James Callaghan and Edward Heath; at least one archbishop of Canterbury; cinema greats like Stewart Granger, Bing Crosby and Deborah Kerr; and opera singers, pop stars, academics, writers, explorers – and in 1988 Salman Rushdie was given an ironic foretaste of hideaway existence.

So what is the magic ingredient that has kept *Desert Island Discs* alive for half a century? 'I believe it adds a dimension to a listener's mental picture of a well-known person, giving the same insight he would receive from visiting the celebrity's home and seeing the books, pictures and furniture with which he surrounds himself,' wrote Roy Plomley some years before his death in 1985.

Sue Lawley who has been dishing out one-way tickets to the ultimate in away-from-it-all holidays since taking over from Michael Parkinson in March 1988, has a more succinct theory. 'It's simple and it's terrific radio,' she says. 'There have been various simple ideas, like *Top of the Pops* and *This Is Your Life*, for instance, but someone has to think

of them first – and in this case it was Roy Plomley. The beauty is that you're able to ask any questions you want, and the one particular one which is so often revealing – how do you think you will cope on your own? Except perhaps for something very private, like the breakdown of a marriage, there are no forbidden territories and the interviewee can't say, "I don't think that's relevant" or refuse to answer on the grounds that the subject was not on the previously agreed agenda. So everything is there, from what the Chancellor looked like in short trousers to what he thinks of the Prime Minister – both of which I find equally interesting!'

THE DESERT ISLAND DISCS TOP TEN

The most requested discs over the past 50 years are:

1. Beethoven's Ninth Symphony, the 'Choral'
2. Debussy's *Clair de Lune*
3. Elgar's *Pomp and Circumstance*
4. 'Liebestod' from Wagner's *Tristan und Isolde*
5. Gershwin's *Rhapsody in Blue*
6. *Ave Maria* sung by Gracie Fields
7. Mendelssohn's 'Nocturne' from *A Midsummer Night's Dream*
8. Beethoven's 'Pastoral'
9. Handel's 'Hallelujah Chorus'
10. Verdi's 'Dies Irae'

These rules of absolute candour have been broken only once during the Lawley years – when Ken Dodd refused to speak about his relations with the Inland Revenue. 'In the end we went on the air with no mention of income tax,' she recalls. 'But in retrospect, I think we should either have scrapped the programme altogether or at least told the listeners why that topic was left out.'

Although most guests appreciate the honour and enjoy the age-old game of picking their eight favourite sounds (the choice doesn't have to be music; Anthony Hopkins picked a recording of D-Type Jaguars) not everyone has found the prospect irresistible. Lord Olivier repeatedly

declined and George Bernard Shaw returned Plomley's letter with 'No. Too busy with more important things. GBS' scribbled in the margin. In recent years Albert Finney, Rupert Murdoch, Elizabeth Taylor and Michael Caine have also proved uncatchable.

Sue Lawley readily admits that she and her producers, Olivia Seligman and Janet Lee, have not always seen eye-to-eye over whom to invite. 'I have bees in my bonnet about encouraging certain people to think even more of themselves than they do already!' she says with a rather unsaintly grin. 'And there are others whom I believe to be simply too young or have not achieved enough to sustain 28 minutes of interview. I mean, Michael Parkinson invited me on to one of his programmes and I certainly wouldn't have chosen me. On the other hand, I do tend to argue for more down-market people being included. Popular soap opera stars, for instance, have got just as much place as men of wisdom and academe.'

And her most memorable castaways? Sir Claus Moser, 'for choosing such wonderful pieces and being able to talk about them with love'; Lord Hailsham, for his somewhat unlikely inclusion of *I Do Like to Be beside the Seaside*; Alan Bleasdale ('a real rat-a-tat interview') and John Schlesinger – 'a good example of the programme at its very best'. But after due consideration, two names come out on top of the pile. 'AS Byatt was tremendously good, because she knew what she wanted to say and she said it as well as you would expect her to. Everything was there, from her difficult early life, to her relationship with her sister Margaret Drabble, winning the Booker Prize and the death of her young son in a road accident.

'And Sarah Miles was just zany and wonderful. She bubbled on merrily and we had to cut out one bit about how she lost her virginity because she blurted out the name of the rather well-known man to whom she lost it. And she then went on to reveal how she once fell in love with an elephant!'

William Greaves

25 YEARS OF RADIO 1

On 30 September 1967 Radio 1 was born. After 25 years with the station, John Peel recalls its greatest hits

A few months ago I was involved in BBC2's night of those-we-have-not-loved-very-much, *TV Hell*, (I was the glum chap in the Bill Shankly T-shirt). I observed, in the course of one of the complex sentences I had written for myself to read from Autocue, that the apparently second-rate often catches the spirit of an age more nearly than the apparently first-rate.

Twenty-five years ago, as I crouched on the steps of All Souls, Langham Place, London, waiting for the photographer to immortalise the DJs who were to bring Radio 1 to life, I would have been mortified to have heard such heresy. The John Peel of September 1967 was, in addition to being a slimmer citizen with rather more hair than the 1992 model, a pretty earnest soul, gripped by the belief that the flower-power philosophies he so fervently espoused would, in a day or so, lead to the world's armies laying down their arms and lying down to listen to Country Joe and the Fish's *Electric Music for the Mind and Body* LP.

I had reached All Souls from the pirate ship Radio London. Before that I had been making the night air hideous from KMEN, San Bernardino, California, where it had occurred to me that the music I was hearing in the Los Angeles clubs was more interesting than the records I was compelled to play on air, and I suggested to my boss that perhaps we could devote some airtime to, say, the Doors, Love, even the Velvet Underground.

Astonished, he asked me what I thought the advertisers would make of such a hare-brained scheme. Having no civil answer for him, I bided my time until I came home and was able to put these deviant notions into some sort of practice on Radio London.

At the BBC I found that producer Bernie Andrews was thinking along the same lines, believing, as I did, that the music was more important than the disc jockey. (I still believe this, as a matter of fact.) As a consequence, records played on our programme, *Top Gear*, were allowed to finish and fade away before I chipped in with such profundities as 'The clouds are poems written in the sky'. On the other hand, the station's stars, such as Tony Blackburn and the wonderful Emperor Rosko, missed no opportunity to talk over the beginnings and endings of every record.

The first DJs to feature on Radio 1 and Radio 2 line up on the steps of All Souls, Langham Place, London in September 1967. Front row (from left): Pete Murray, Ed Stewart, Pete Drummond, Mike Raven, Mike Ahern and John Peel. Middle row: Bob Holness, Terry Wogan, Barry Alldis, Mike Lennox, Keith Skues, Chris Denning, Johnny Moran and Pete Myers. Back row: Tony Blackburn, Jimmy Young, Kenny Everett, Duncan Johnson, Robin Scott (Controller of the Light Programme), David Ryder, Dave Cash, Pete Brady and David Symonds

Emperor Rosko during his weekly show *Midday Spin* – November 1968

It is difficult to imagine now, at a time when 1FM is more obviously involved in music than at any other time in its history, how much the fledgling station was personality-based. Blackburn was a major national figure. When he appeared in public, huge crowds gathered and Tony often required police protection when he was called upon to, for example, open a shop. On the only occasion on which I was asked to open a shop, a record dealer's in London, I ended up

Tony Blackburn – the first DJ to broadcast on Radio 1

earning my modest fee by holding the door open for would-be customers. In fact, my lack of celebrity status was such that I was once refused admission, on account of my long hair and air of decay, to one of my own gigs.

From the start, Radio 1 gave employment not only to a horde of DJs but also to substantial numbers of musicians, from the Northern Dance Orchestra to Tyrannosaurus Rex. *Top Gear* featured two or three groups in session each weekend and, as Bernie Andrews gave way to John Walters in the producer's chair, the search for snappy new bands intensified. This search took me from a night at the Hobbits' Garden, Wimbledon, where Roxy Music played for the first time in public supporting a scarcely better known Genesis, to

The Radio 1 Roadshow

an encounter in Bethnal Green with a man who assured me that he was the Small Faces. Not one of the Small Faces, you understand, but all of them. I tried to persuade Walters we should put him in the studio. Walters rejected this scheme, although he did book Roxy Music and Genesis.

Mind you, I do not want to give you the impression that my involvement with Radio 1 has been all musical. I went with the rest of the staff for what were styled Fun Weeks in our major cities. On one

of these, in Birmingham, my previously doctrinaire view of Tony Blackburn was substantially adjusted in his favour when, with a Radio 1 producer at the piano, he treated a bar filled with resentful salesmen to a half-hour of popular song in his inimitable light baritone. The fact that the salesmen had no wish to be so entertained deterred Tony not at all.

There was also the football. The Radio 1 team, awe-inspiringly inept despite the management skills of Teddy Warrick, the Bill Shankly of pop, played at several notable grounds, including Elland Road. Here, our team, despite including the toothsome Noel Edmonds, was upstaged by a fund-raising Jimmy Savile who jogged round and round the pitch as we played. A five-a-side team twice played Wembley stadium. I scored on both occasions. Just thought I'd drop that in.

And the Radio 1 funsters motorraced as well. In our races at Brands Hatch and Mallory Park, Noel Edmonds played Nigel Mansell to drummer Cozy Powell's Ayrton Senna. The rest of us, incompetent and ego-maddened, wrecked cars behind them. A meeting at Mallory at which the Bay City Rollers were helicoptered on to a small island, protected against fans by men in wetsuits and flippers, while Blackburn sped to and fro in a boat piloted by a womble, is something poker-worked into my memory for all eternity.

Steve Wright

The 1FM of 1992 is a very different critter from the Radio 1 of 1967: leaner, fitter and, as I hinted before, in the shows of Andy Kershaw, Mark Radcliffe, Mark Goodier, Pete Tong, Alan Freeman, Tommy Vance, the Man Ezeke and others, more music-based than ever before. Not perfect yet – but then, apart from the Liverpool team of the 77/78 season, what is? As for me, I'm pretty much counting on being around for the 50th anniversary celebrations in 2017.

John Peel

FAREWELL RADIO LUXEMBOURG

After nearly six decades, Radio Luxembourg is no more. John Collis reports on the rise and fall of Fab 208

In 1992, nearly 60 years after it was founded, Radio Luxembourg could only be heard under limited and unlikely conditions, as part of the menu available to those subscribing to the Astra satellite. It is a tribute to its remarkable stamina that it survived at 208 on the medium wave for so long, decades after its uniqueness had been compromised, and in the face of relentlessly growing odds.

My children can walk down the road with Michael Jackson plumbed directly into their ears. Pop music is available to them on an ever-growing range of radio stations, from national Radio 1 to Old Kent Road pirates. We can be swamped with the sound and images of MTV, and whether we choose it or not are surrounded by pop, from shop doorways and passing cars, in hotel lobbies, pubs and supermarkets. It would be difficult for a child of the 90s to imagine a world without this constant soundtrack.

My generation, on the other hand, had Radio Luxembourg. The BBC maintained a lofty disdain towards youth music. The sops it granted as the 50s wore on were welcome, but remained somewhat avuncular. America had invented the teenager, and with it a rock'n'roll world of cars, drive-in movies and soda joints, whatever they might be. *Our* musical world resembled more that of a youth club in the church hall, whether it styled itself *6.5 Special* on television, *Saturday Club* or *Easy Beat* on radio.

Occasionally vulgar Americans, heroes like Gene Vincent and his chum Eddie Cochran, were allowed to gate-crash, but order would soon be restored with another popular melody from Bob Miller and the Millermen, a traditional jazz-band number or some amiable trombone tomfoolery from Don Lang and his Frantic Five.

Soon the young, brash, irreverent producer Jack Good was allowed to shake things up with such shows as *Oh Boy!*, which offered wall-to-wall pop stars, uninterrupted by fashion tips and trendy vicars. But he was still confined to a weekly 30-minute ghetto. In this atmosphere, Radio Luxembourg and its sponsored record shows flourished.

A musical revolution had happened in America, with such dangerously exciting artists as Little Richard, Fats Domino and Chuck Berry crossing racial barriers, and Elvis Presley inviting us to *Have a Party*. For us the party took place on Radio Luxembourg, not the BBC's Light Programme.

But Luxembourg had long pre-dated rock'n'roll. It was not, of course, conceived as a music station pure and simple, but as a way of breaking that other British broadcasting taboo, advertising, using popular music as its main vehicle. Its vast transmitter first beamed the words 'This is Radio Luxembourg' in 1933, intoned by the English announcer Stephen Williams. The station pitched itself, as Williams has put it, 'slightly lighter than the BBC Light Programme'. In the stern days of Lord Reith, this field was wide open.

The pre-war growth of Radio Luxembourg was grimly matched by the rise of Nazi Germany, and when the Germans marched into the Grand Duchy they inevitably seized a valuable propaganda weapon, the Radio Luxembourg transmitter. It was from here that the British traitor Lord Haw Haw broadcast to the United Kingdom, with the aim of sapping morale and resistance by hammering home his message of the Führer's inevitable victory.

In the 50s the station entered its most successful period. Early in the decade the concept of a hit parade based on record sales rather than sheet music was introduced, and was published weekly. This, the rock'n'roll revolution, and the Reithian dictate that Sunday evenings on the wireless should reflect all the gaiety of a strict Calvinist household in mourning, gave Radio Luxembourg an opportunity too good to miss – the broad-

BBC Photograph Library

Tony 'Your Royal Ruler' Prince (left), Muriel Young and David Jacobs in the BBC *40 Minutes* tribute *Farewell, Fab 208*

casting of the brand new Top 20 in its entirety on Sunday evenings. This simple idea, together with other American-style innovations such as game shows, delivered an audience in millions. *Take Your Pick* could offer far more attractive prizes than the half-a-crown and black pudding of Wilfred Pickles' homely *Have a Go!*.

Luxembourg retained a family feel amid the youth music, however, with *Family Favourites*-style request programmes; barbershop gospel from the Deep River Boys; the Ovaltineys and Dan Dare, Pilot of the Future. When Ovaltine revived their infuriatingly cosy Ovaltiney song for a television campaign in the 80s, replete with pipe-and-pullover dad and fretwork wireless, it was obviously Radio Luxembourg that the happy family were listening to. After all, a proprietary brand of malted beverage had no place on the BBC.

And though *Journey into Space* was one of the Light Programme's 50s triumphs, with its cliff-hanging pre-Sputnik adventures one of the few guaranteed radio topics of conversation in the burgeoning tele-

vision age, over on Luxembourg the hero from page one of *The Eagle* comic, Dan Dare, had one advantage – you could listen to his exploits while sipping the bedtime cocoa from an authentic spaceship-style Dan Dare mug.

Cocoa, shampoo, football pools – it was the advertisements, Radio Luxembourg's *raison d'être*, that added to the fascination in the 50s and early 60s. Most famous of all was the ponderous West-Country burr of Horace Batchelor, inventor of the infra-draw pools method for spotting next weekend's football draws, who lived in K-E-Y-N-S-H-A-M, Bristol. One wondered, naturally, why he found it necessary to go on flogging his secrets year after year instead of retiring to the sun. Years later, the Bonzo Dog Doodah Band named an album in tribute to an unassuming suburb that had enjoyed a decade of international fame, thanks to Radio Luxembourg's most faithful advertiser. And when Luxembourg began that Sunday-night Top 20 show, which took the station triumphantly into the 60s, Batchelor was inevitably one of its sponsors.

The most familiar image of Luxembourg to my generation is that of listening to its fade-and-boom signal under the bedclothes. Although the airwaves are democratically available to all, and Radio Luxembourg was legally operating from the Grand Duchy, it always retained an air of illicitness – it went on late at night, when we should have been slumbering before another school day, and the mention of brand names, let alone brazen advertising, was scrupulously avoided on the BBC and therefore must be somehow naughty.

Jimmy Savile recognised the fact that a sizeable proportion of his audience were listening surreptitiously to his show *The Teen and Twenty Disc Club*, and on the BBC2 *40 Minutes* tribute *Farewell, Fab 208* shown in March last year he recalled: 'I struck a deal with prefects in boarding schools that for the period of my show there was an amnesty, where you could listen to the radio provided you had your trannie under the bedclothes. So I formed the Under the Bedclothes Club.'

In the mid-60s, however, came

the first nail in the coffin of 208. Radio Caroline set sail in 1964, Radio London, Radio City et al – from reconditioned boats and derelict forts the growing band of pirates beamed unadulterated advertising-supported pop to Britain. Radio Luxembourg had a head start but had lost its monopoly, and soon its variable signal and more mixed programming began to seem rather quaint.

It still had a part to play, within the industry as well as among its faithful listeners – Noel Edmonds and Kid Jensen were among the younger generation who, like Pete Murray and Jimmy Savile before them, cut their broadcasting teeth in the Grand Duchy.

Edmonds was a typical 18-year-

Noel Edmonds, who began his career with Radio Luxembourg

old hopeful, brought up on 60s pop music, who 'bombarded Luxembourg with audition tapes'. Though most pop addicts of his age would be forming a band and trying to interest record companies, another route into the music business had been opened up, thanks to Radio Luxembourg. 'They got me out there to read the news,' he recalled at the time of the BBC2 programme. 'But unfortunately I used to find the bulletins funny, so they moved me on to disc jockeying. It was a young man's dream. I'd been listening to 208 all through my teens, and suddenly there I was hob-nobbing

with John Lennon and Paul Mc-Cartney.'

Then in 1967 came another blow. The Marine Offences Act couldn't touch them, of course – it was designed to deal with the ever more cluttered North Sea – but Radio 1 was launched as the BBC's belated response to the style of broadcasting pioneered in Luxembourg and continued at sea. And in 1973 the cruellest blow of all – land-based, legal, local commercial radio.

Radio 208 battled on against these gathering forces – and a similar growth of competition on the continent – for almost 20 years, until at midnight on 29 December 1991 it succumbed to the inevitable, and ceased broadcasting on 208 metres. A year later, on 30 December 1992, after a year of unpublicised obscurity broadcasting on the Astra Satellite, Radio Luxembourg ceased completely. Its powerful role in piping rock'n'roll beneath the bedclothes of a generation had become an honourable part of broadcasting history.

John Collis

McCARTNEY AT 50

One of the world's most successful songwriters, and one of Britain's richest men, living legend Paul McCartney celebrated his 50th birthday in June 1992. Author Ray Coleman remembers the star he first met in 1962

Liverpool – autumn 1962: the Beatles gathered in a cramped office to sign a management contract with Brian Epstein. As they queued to reach his desk to sign in turn, the silence was broken by a nasal voice from the back: 'Well, I hope we're going to make it big as a group, I really do. But I'll tell you what – whether we do or not, I'm going to be a star.' Those were the words of James Paul McCartney, aged 20, of 20 Forthlin Road, Allerton.

Thirty years later, Paul McCartney, MBE, is beyond stardom. A legend, a multi-millionaire leader of the aristocracy of popular music, the world's most successful songwriter, he has written himself into the history books with a multitude

of awards. But he did not make a jamboree out of his 50th birthday last June, for the key to McCartney's happiness doesn't include too much dwelling on the past. A boyish craving for taking risks with new challenges keeps him looking ahead, not back.

Despite three decades of heady achievements, he remains a man of extraordinary paradoxes and elusive spirit. Gregarious, amusing and charming in company, he tends to distrust people outside his family, perhaps understandable after his battles inside and outside the Beatles. He likes control, although there is still something of the old hippy in his fundamental outlook. He cherishes his position in the hierarchy of entertainment but prefers to present himself as one of the lads. He wants to be viewed as equally acceptable to high society and a shop assistant. He can be alternately bombastic and insecure; thoughtful and mercurial; compassionate and unforgiving; open and impenetrable.

His public image as a cheery, thumbs-up, lightweight, man-of-the-people pop star has irritated him as much as his critics, who taunt him for his alleged superficiality. Friends who have known him since his earliest Beatles years have noticed a new aura of sophistication and self-assuredness about him lately. The sharp-eyed youthful enthusiasm, laced with caution, remains, now joined by the personality of an elder statesman, a diplomat.

In the Beatles years, marking this 50th birthday would have seemed inconceivable. Historic though the group was, pop stars were not expected to assume any significance, still less join the Establishment. McCartney, however, was always somewhere outside the general scrum of rock'n'roll. He had a vision of his music beyond its function as a totem of youth; he wrote classics such as *Yesterday*, *Michelle* and *Here, There and Everywhere* to indicate the strong romanticism beating inside a rock 'n'roller's heart. To understand why he will not regard reaching 50 as a hazardous milestone or time to retire, it's important to recognise that he is something of a driven man, still the conventional and

Rex Features

McCartney in 1992

victims. And when the rebellious Lennon loosened his tie and shirt button, McCartney would smarten him up again using a persuasiveness only he could get away with. The good name of the Beatles mattered more to him than to anyone except Epstein, and he applied himself diligently to protecting their public image around the world. His critics have always found that concern with public relations unpalatable. In truth, he has always embraced orthodox show business more than the alternative culture of rock'n' roll. When they reached London from Liverpool, it was McCartney who was the socially mobile talk-of-the-town, while the other three sought domestic refuge in the Surrey countryside.

At work, too, he seemed to absorb more varied musical influences. While some 60s figures saw rock'n'roll itself as their stepping stone to fame and fortune, the ambitious McCartney was more scientific. His musical palette has always had a broader range, stimulated by his jazz piano-playing father, and he knew from the start he was entering the show business arena as a career – and that would require stamina.

His partnership with John Lennon produced epic pop music but it was destined to fall apart. The two men had mutual affection and admiration during the Beatles' heyday, but after Brian Epstein's death in 1967, when they launched their own company Apple, things turned sour. By then, John and Yoko were artistic, as well as romantic partners. In an interview with me, Lennon said Apple was in dire financial danger 'and if it carries on like this we'll be broke in six months'.

'BEATLES GOING BROKE' headlines flashed around the world – and McCartney was livid. When I met him at Apple he reprimanded me for merely reporting Lennon's remarks. 'This is only a small company and you're trying to wreck it,' he said. 'You know John shoots his mouth off and doesn't mean it.'

Lennon and McCartney were polar opposites who proved right to bounce off each other, but only for a while. Their backgrounds and

respectful son of a cotton salesman and a midwife (the 'mother Mary' he sang of in *Let It Be*).

As he was when we first met in 1962. I was a reporter with *Melody Maker*, an elitist music paper that looked disdainfully at the vapid British pop scene. My phone rang one day and a quiet, cultured voice announced himself as Brian Epstein. He was calling from Liverpool where, he said, he managed an 'outstanding' group called the Beatles. The name alone was funny and nothing in pop came from Liverpool. The press, he continued, was 'very late' in realising that Liverpool had thriving pop groups. Cynical but intrigued, I made the 200-mile

journey to see 'the boys', as Epstein always paternally described them. Meeting them for the first time in his office, I found them cocky and witty, confident about their first single, *Love Me Do*. The songwriters were clearly the leaders: Lennon arty, waspish, quizzical; McCartney eager, personable, exceptionally alert. As the Beatles story gained speed, I wrote that Paul had more sense of destiny than the others.

Cast as 'the prettiest Beatle', he played the cherubic soothsayer to John Lennon's loudmouth. When Lennon landed the Beatles in trouble, an embarrassed McCartney would collaborate with Brian Epstein to find a way to placate any

The Beatles

Paul and Linda McCartney performing with Wings in the 70s

McCartney in the 70s and 80s

aspirations carried the clue: John had drifted into art at Liverpool Art College while the academic Paul, next door at the 'posh grammar school', the Liverpool Institute, seemed to be heading for a career as a teacher or an accountant. Secure with his Beatles millions, Lennon met Yoko Ono, said the Beatles were finished, and reverted to his love of art and the life style that went with it. McCartney, dumbfounded and frustrated, tried in vain to keep the Beatles together then went on to form a new band, Wings, in 1971.

When Lennon moved to New York that same year, never to return to Britain, his relationship with McCartney became strained. They had just about patched it up, talking by phone about their families, when Lennon was assassinated in 1980, aged 40. After some turbulence in the aftermath of the Beatles, his relationship with George Harrison and Ringo Starr is harmonious, with a rapport like that of brothers who do not need to meet regularly. Both Harrison and Starr have recently returned to the concert stage in their own right and McCartney is as immersed in music as he ever was.

Topping some of his old work will never be easy since, as he says, he and John Lennon were 'mining gold' in the 60s. But still he pushes on, and he has recently been in the recording studio working on a new album.

While his position in the pantheon of music greats is secure, McCartney faced flak for what some considered a loss of musical direction in the 80s. Accused of losing his muse, he shot back with examples of his curious, unending desire for street credibility by collaborating with Michael Jackson, Stevie Wonder and, later, Elvis Costello. He confessed that he missed the spark of Lennon's partnership, but such flirtations with artists whose pedigree was nowhere near his own was a mistake. It smacked of a temporary lack of self-esteem.

More realistic was his 1989-90 world tour to gigantic crowds. McCartney was at his best, giving stunning performances of Beatles classics amid the newer songs. Little had changed from the Beatles years in the three concerts I saw: he addressed the large crowds self-consciously with empty words, but his very presence evoked a majestic reminder of pop's halcyon years. He sent millions of people away happy, and for Paul McCartney such experiences are treasured. A rock'n' roller he might be, but he continues to be a show business trouper in the traditional sense, and that's what separates him from mainstream rock.

He tries not to let the fortune he's made out of the business change his life, working hard at living simply and keeping his feet on the ground. He loathes ostentatiousness: the striving artist side of him created the grandiose idea for *Sgt Pepper's Lonely Hearts Club Band* – but he took the bus to the Beatles office from his London home every day. This contrast was often to be seen: he would run the office with meticulous attention to detail, his bossiness enraging the staff, and then he would go off and write a touching song about his sheepdog, or a blackbird, or a human relationship.

Today he runs his own company, travelling to London most days from his country home. His homespun family life in a five-bedroomed Sussex farmhouse belies his position as one of Britain's richest men, worth an estimated £380 million. *Yesterday*, his anthem, is the world's most recorded song with 1,600 versions. In America, it has been broadcast on the radio five million times. Outside the Beatles, his album *Band on the Run* by Wings, sold six million copies, the most for any ex-Beatle before John Lennon's death sent sales of his final LP *Double Fantasy* soaring to seven million within seven months of his assassination. In all, McCartney has sold more than 100 million albums and more than 100 million singles, and is listed in the *Guinness Book of Records*.

Many entertainment figures amass fortunes, but McCartney has played a stupendous game of chess in assembling his investments. When he married Linda in 1969 her late father, the top New York lawyer

Lee Eastman, asked him how he wanted to invest. 'Well, not oil or industrial things,' he replied. 'I know about songs.' Eastman helped him with his shopping and he has collected a portfolio of precious song publishing catalogues that includes copyright to the collection of songs made famous by his early idol Buddy Holly, 10,000 golden standard songs including *Stormy Weather, One for My Baby* and *Sentimental Journey*, and the copyrights to the soundtracks of such Broadway musicals as *A Chorus Line, Hello Dolly, Grease, Mame, Annie*, and *La Cage aux Folles*. Each time these songs are played anywhere in the world, McCartney gets richer.

It remains important to him that his company owns songs because, for all his wealth and status, he remains above all else a musician. He is still striking out for new boundaries, as in his return to his native city during 1991 for his first classical work, *Paul McCartney's Liverpool Oratorio*, with the city's Philharmonic Orchestra.

The inevitable snipes from some quarters hurt him but he's wary of placing much trust in the judgment of critics. 'When you put your sentiment on the line in your work, as I do,' he said to me recently, 'you've got to expect some people to take pot shots at you.' Even so, his ego is often bruised.

He keeps close emotional links with Liverpool, which awarded him the Freedom of the City (he still owns a house on the Wirral) and he has been busy trying to raise more than £7 million from music industry sources to convert his old school, now closed, into a nursery for new talent called the Liverpool Institute for Performing Arts. Last year he toured the dilapidated building and, as he walked around the classrooms, he remembered every detail: his teachers' nicknames, tests that went awry in the science laboratory, stories of his bus journeys to school when he was taunted as 'college pudding'. Set against that deep sentimentality is an astute businessman who likes his company run tightly, even frugally. He would never allow money to be poured into any project on a whim. He

seeks proof that Liverpool needs it, deserves it.

The thought of resting on his laurels, of a pampered life of idleness, is anathema to him. After a few months of that, he says, he would have to pick up a guitar. In family life, as in music, he works for success. In a show business world littered with broken relationships Paul and Linda McCartney's marriage and life style symbolises what matters most to him. He was ridiculed for persuading her to play keyboards in his band, but to McCartney that was natural: they are kindred spirits as well as husband and wife. She is a gifted photographer who has published a collection of classic 60s portraits, as well as an expert cook. They are both militant vegetarians and support the cause of animal rights, even to the extent of buying land in Devon to ensure that stags are not hunted there. Their children – Heather, from Linda's first marriage, Mary, Stella and James – went to state schools, McCartney maintaining that what served him well was perfectly adequate for them.

A benign Beatle? For Paul McCartney at 50, it's only part of the passing show, just another turn of the page of his chameleon-like life story. Founder of the world's greatest pop group, exceptional songwriter, professional and proud Liverpudlian, 60s philosopher, artist, band-leader, businessman, silent supporter of charities, preacher of basic family values – he seems as energetic now as he was when he wrote his prophetically titled hit *Can't Buy Me Love* in 1964. While his old partner went off and wrote 'Imagine...no possessions' Paul palpably adopted the theme of that song to a degree that will always be difficult for a millionaire. What matters to him is that he can afford perhaps the most valuable elixir of all – a smile at his flecks of grey hair.

Ray Coleman

• Ray Coleman is the author of biographies of John Lennon, Beatles manager Brian Epstein, Eric Clapton, and co-author with Bill Wyman of *Stone Alone*. Coleman travelled with the Beatles, and was editor-in-chief of *Melody Maker*

MARC BOLAN – 70s SUPERSTAR

Channel 4's *Marc Bolan – the Legendary Years*, shown on 16 September – 15 years after he died in a car crash – paid tribute to the 70s star. John Collis looks back on Bolan's career

Marc Bolan, who died 15 years ago when his car crashed into a tree near Putney Common in south-west London, was a worthy star in an unworthy decade.

Pop music reached a low point in the 70s. The 50s saw the rock'n'roll revolution, with great black artists like Fats Domino, Chuck Berry and Little Richard forcing their way into the charts, inspiring such world-shaking talent as Elvis Presley and Buddy Holly.

The 60s gave rise to the Beatles and Bob Dylan, to the southern soul of Otis Redding and to the idea of 'rock' as something distinct from the deliberately short-lived trivia of 'pop'.

In the 70s, by and large, kids were peddled trivia once more. Such phenomena as Abba, the Carpenters and Boney M were more marketing strategies than intense musical experiences – the last of these didn't even exist as a group, but were simply a varying cast of human puppets fronting a record producer's confections.

Superstars like Elton John and Rod Stewart emerged, but something was clearly wrong. Mother and daughter could find themselves buying the same record. Without a rebellious generation gap, rock 'n'roll is dead. And the necessary late-70s corrective, punk rock, was so sterile as to leave nothing worthwhile behind it. Meanwhile entrepreneurs found groups of pretty boys, dressed them in bizarre clothes, made up their faces and pointed them at a gullible public.

Marc Bolan observed all this, and capitalised on it. Like the built-to-last David Bowie and the brilliant musical joke Gary Glitter, he invented and re-invented himself as a chameleon pop star.

A Londoner born in 1947, Bolan (Mark Feld) first invented himself as a precocious mid-60s 'face', a nebu-lous job made up of strenuous night-clubbing, male modelling, pop-music dabblings, and striking clothes. He released a couple of unsuccessful singles before arriving at the name Marc Bolan and joining the psychedelic rock band John's Children in 1967, best remembered for Bolan's suggestive (and widely banned) song *Desdemona*.

With percussionist Steve Peregrine Took, and the encouragement of disc jockey John Peel, Bolan next emerged as an acoustic hippy in the duo Tyrannosaurus Rex. As with John's Children, there was clearly talent here in the studied rock'n' roll posing and the manic vibrato voice. But the title of their first album says all that is necessary about the modish and fragile pretensions of the project. It was called *My People Were Fair and had Sky in their Hair but now*

BBC Photograph Library

Marc Bolan

They're Content to Wear Stars on their Brows. Most of us chuckled and put on Wilson Pickett's *Midnight Hour* at hippy-crunching volume.

In 1970 Bolan took the necessary steps to greater stardom. The band plugged into electricity and expanded its line-up (without Took) while contracting its name to T Rex. *Ride a White Swan* began a run of hit singles lasting almost three years when Bolan's records invariably made the Top Ten, usually as far as the first three. His music was far more interesting than his glitter rivals, in that he delved back past 'glam rock' and hippydom to the roots of rock'n'roll. He could rip off a Chicago blues or give an innovative twist to a 12-bar tune by adding a little 70s flash.

And yet his music somehow remained a knowing pastiche, nothing more. Unlike his friend David Bowie, with whom he shared a manager in Tony Visconti, Bolan was shrewd as a teenybop star but could find no further depths behind the glitter to promise longevity. He never became a 'rock musician'.

This barely mattered while there was a market for tiny 70s rock'n' roll masterpieces like *Get It On, Jeepster, Telegram Sam, Metal Guru, Children of the Revolution, 20th Century Boy* and *The Groover*. But without the move towards more lasting rock credibility he was dependent on a young public, attracted to the posing, the face make-up and the supposedly decadent image.

The quality of the music didn't really matter to many of them – they may well have bought *Chirpy Chirpy Cheep Cheep* as well. This audience hero-worships with intensity, but briefly. The manipulators will always have new instant stars to refresh the market.

In chart terms Bolan may have begun to fade – he didn't merit a Top Ten placing after mid-1973 – but he remained a star. Indeed, his brashness was one of the elements of punk rock, even if the glitter make-up and camp posing were decidedly not. A 1977 TV series hosted by Bolan introduced many of the London club punk bands to a wider audience, and that year he toured with proto-punks the Damned.

Later that year came the fatal car crash. In rock'n'roll, death has often proved a smart career move, and Bolan continued to appear in the lower reaches of the charts for a further decade. The tree he collided with became a shrine for his devotees. But is it symbolic of Bolan's lasting musical influence that, 15 years after his death, the tree was cut down? Maybe not – Eddie Cochran died in 1960 and his influence is still felt, long after the lamp-post that killed him was taken to the scrap yard. In musical terms Bolan was no Cochran, but in the 70s his cunning revival of rock 'n'roll was most welcome.

John Collis

THE BRIT AWARDS

The annual music industry celebration took place at the Hammersmith Odeon in February where Seal swept the board, winning three of the awards. Lauris Morgan-Griffiths reviews the event

Although many might prefer to think that The Rock and Pop Awards, the scourge of award ceremonies, had died and gone to a music heaven in the sky, they live on. Their present incarnation is The Brit Awards. In 1987 it was decided to give the British music industry awards a new identity with one name – The Brits – and a recognizable emblem – a statue of Britannia.

The name has stuck, but the statue has been streamlined from a bronze figure seated with trident protruding, to a standing figure. (There had been an accident with the previous figurine when the spike became caught in Tina Turner's fabulous designer dress.) The venue has also been a moveable feast from the Grosvenor House to the Royal Albert Hall and the Dominion Theatre, and in 1992 The Brit Awards were held at the Hammersmith Odeon.

It is a show business evening of glamour and glitz, a self-congratulatory affair to some extent, but with a serious side. The music industry is very strong in Britain and the performers and their music form part of a huge export business, with British artists generating 25 per cent of the world's record sales.

Not surprisingly this country has produced some of the world's greatest international rock stars – the Beatles, the Rolling Stones, Eric Clapton, Elton John, Rod Stewart, Eurythmics and George Michael to name a few.

The record industry is big business, deserving of an appropriate awards extravaganza. However, there was a slight divergence of opinion between the BPI (British Phonographic Industry) and Jonathan King, producer of the 1992 Brit Awards, in the emphasis of the event. The BPI is all for selling records, and the Brit Awards are very deliberately set in February

because it is a low time for record sales.

Jonathan King wanted to establish the event as more than just another awards ceremony. His intention was to make it a celebration of the music industry as a whole, giving exposure to new bands as well as including the music of the established names.

to the next award, or a live performance from one of a number of special guests such as Lisa Stansfield, Simply Red and Seal.

But the event has not always run so smoothly. Broadcast live from the Royal Albert Hall in 1988 and presented by Noel Edmonds, with all the variables that live television brings, the show over-ran. Just as

Rex Features

Lisa Stansfield, winner of Best Female Singer award at The Brits 92

The 1992 event had no single presenter, it was produced by Jonathan King who had hosted and written it in 1987 and has produced and written it for three years since 1990. It was a slick affair, with the voice of Simon Bates announcing each new presenter, followed by a medley of that person's music. The winner was declared, the acceptance speeches were short and to the point, and the show moved on

Rick Astley was announced winner of the Best Single category, the Who struck up the final number and poor Astley had to retreat ignominiously to his seat empty-handed.

Then there was the 1989 debacle with Mick Fleetwood and Samantha Fox. Excellent performers in their own right, but not the best live television presenters. Everything that could go wrong, did. As Annie Lennox said, 'In a subversive way

Seal – winner of three Brit awards in 1992

made to leave. Luckily he was intercepted in the foyer, and persuaded to stay for another ten minutes – just long enough to collect his award for the Best Classical Recording for *Otello*.

As he collected the trophy from Right Said Fred he had recovered some good humour to complain, in broken English, about the loudness of the music.

PM Dawn, winners of Best International Newcomer, were lost for words, but did manage to say: 'I can't believe I received my award from Boy George', who looked suitably coy and sauntered off.

Seventeen million Radio 1 listeners had voted for *The Days of Our Lives* by Queen as the Best Single. There were tributes to Freddie Mercury from Elton John and Roger Taylor as well as a film clip showing Mercury choreographing a Queen video. The record shops voted for the Best Newcomer, Beverley Craven, and *Going Live!* viewers voted for Seal's *Killer* as Best Music Video.

The Brit Awards 1992

Best Male Singer:
Seal
Best Female Singer:
Lisa Stansfield
Best Album:
Seal
Best Group:
KLF and Simply Red (joint)
Best Producer:
Trevor Horn
Best Newcomer:
Beverley Craven
Best Soundtrack:
The Commitments
Best Single:
The Days of Our Lives, Queen
Best International Artist:
Prince
Best International Group:
REM
Best International Newcomer:
PM Dawn
Best Music Video:
Killer, Seal
Best Classical Recording:
Verdi's *Otello*, Sir Georg Solti
Tribute Award:
Freddie Mercury

---

the 1989 show was the best TV I'd seen in ages – it was so bad it was brilliant'.

Jonathan King then moved the venue to the smaller, more intimate Dominion Theatre in London's West End. It was presented by Cathy McGowan, and this time the BBC were taking no chances – it did not go out live, nor has it since.

The Brit Awards 91 was a case of it was 'alright on the night'. Because of the Gulf War no American artists would fly over, Sinead O'Connor backed out, and George Michael accepted an award but deferred from performing.

Having survived that, The Brits 92 seemed plain sailing. However, Jonathan King only just managed to foil disaster by discovering, during the rehearsal, KLF's intended stunt of spraying the front row (music business grandees) of the Hammersmith Odeon with animal blood. Not apparently to make any political statement, just in the anarchic spirit of the band. King took them to one side and pointed out that although not normally opposed to the element of surprise their stunt 'would harm the show, harm the audience and harm some of the other performers who would be playing later'. Fortunately KLF saw reason.

KLF's performance did have repercussions of another kind. Conductor Sir Georg Solti, finding the music an assault on his hearing

Seal swept the board, also winning the Best Male Singer and Best Album categories. Not wanting to detract from the profusion of awards, Jonathan King was nevertheless concerned about too many honours bestowed on new talent. 'If Genesis had won three Brit Awards 15 years ago they would not be still around and growing in 1992. Instead they were nurtured and taught how to write and make any mistakes out of the spotlight.' Time will tell what the future holds for Seal.

Looking back at the winners in the 80s, there are few names that are not still substantial talents. Many of them are now firmly international – Trevor Horn and Dave Stewart, for instance, have each won three awards over the last ten years. Some, however, are fading memories – Adam and the Ants, Five Star, Rick Astley, Yazoo, Go West, and where are the blonde Bros brothers now?

Simply Red have had five nominations but only won once in 1992 sharing Best Group with KLF. U2 have won Best Group three years running, and Paul Young and Lisa Stansfield hold their own 'Brits records' by having won Best Newcomer award and going on the next year to win Best Male/Female Singer. Annie Lennox has had the most previous nominations – 11.

The money raised from the staging of the 1992 event went to three different charities: the Nordoff/Robbins Music Therapy which helps mentally and physically handicapped children to express themselves through music; the Performing Arts & Technology School which gives experience to potential performers and technicians, arts administrators, lawyers and accountants; and the Terrence Higgins Trust.

The Brit Awards 93 will take a different format, but still no-one is risking a live broadcast. And Jonathan King will not be the producer, having resigned after 1992. Although not a great supporter of award ceremonies, he is a staunch champion of the British music scene. 'That is what I love most about our music business. We help the young fulfil their dreams.'
Lauris Morgan-Griffiths

RADIO 3

Radio 3 has recently undergone the most dramatic changes of all the BBC radio networks. Controller of Radio 3 Nicholas Kenyon reflects on the past 12 months

Nicholas Kenyon

It has been an eventful year for Radio 3: a year of change which has aroused some strong passions in listeners and has demonstrated what a much-loved, much-valued service Radio 3 is and continues to be. There was rather more fear about possible change, however, than actually occurred; we finished the year stronger than ever, with a vastly increased visibility in the public eye, and with the idea that gradual change could be accepted on Radio 3 established as part of our strategy for the future.

Part of that visibility was due to the controversial marketing campaign masterminded during the year by Saatchi and Saatchi for the network – the first time Radio 3 had ever had a marketing presence. It focused on two key areas of output; live music, highlighted by the slogan 'The Great Composers Live on Radio 3', and the other suggesting that our new programmes in the early morning and early evening were especially suitable for car drivers. A further blast of publicity was given to us by the press, which leapt onto possible controversy with enthusiasm, and gave us more exposure than money could have bought.

I saw many images of myself in the press last year as the new, revolutionary controller, which I hardly recognized: cutting and ruthlessly reducing the role of Radio 3 in order to save money. In fact, we were not under financial threat during the year, and the fact that I seemed rather cheerful about the changes and the reactions they provoked puzzled some. I still treasure the article in the *Daily Mail* headlining 'The lure of the laughing axeman'! The *Oldie* denounced Radio 3 changes under the headline 'Who's running this country?', a role which I must say I never even dreamt I had.

Press attention, stirred up early on before any changes had been announced by a letter to *The Times* from Bamber Gascoigne and Lord Norwich, and increased by leaks of intended plans, led to a veritable ferment of speculation. It was only when I was able to lay out the rather modest plans for new programmes in the early summer that speculation cooled, only to be revived during the 'silly season' when it emerged that some people, notably Gerald Kaufman MP, had taken a determined dislike to new strands of our programming.

Listeners responded in droves, both for and against: one sent me the on-off switch of his radio, which he had permanently disabled in protest, while others wrote to thank us for opening up Radio 3 to them

Stephen Sondheim

for the first time. In all these moves, the aim was not crudely to go down-market in search of audiences, but simply to accept that in the past Radio 3 has sometimes been off-putting, that the audience for classical music has changed, and that we need to make ourselves available to that audience.

But in fact most of the public visibility that Radio 3 achieved during the year was the result of exactly those new programme strands. They reflected a newly vigorous approach by Radio 3's producers and presenters to the musical world outside. In our early morning programme *On Air*, we include topical news of musical events and the occasional interview with a leading figure or critic in the arts world, complemented by brief news, weather and traffic bulletins: many listeners told me in no uncertain terms that they preferred only music at that time of day, and we have since made strides to strengthen the music content of *On Air*. From the start of 1993 it will be presented by a single presenter each week, and will include strong thematic elements such as a cycle of Haydn symphonies.

In Tune, the early evening sequence which replaced the much-loved but by last year somewhat routine *Mainly for Pleasure*, also aimed to bring Radio 3 into more contact with the musical world by including extended interviews with leading performers and composers, ranging from Pierre Boulez to

Natalie Wheen, a regular presenter of *In Tune* (and the first person to present the programme in July)

Brian Kay of *Brian Kay's Sunday Morning*

Stephen Sondheim. Players talked about their work and introduced their own musical enthusiasms, and instead of the sometimes stiff and off-putting introductions to new music heard on Radio 3, a livelier and more approachable style was worked towards gradually.

Brian Kay's Sunday Morning, a new three-hour sequence presented by one of radio's most approachable broadcasters, has been a great success with our listeners, and has forged new links with the *BBC Music Magazine*, a new monthly title from BBC Publications which has featured a free CD of complete works and has been another dramatic success. There have been other new programmes in the areas of jazz (*Impressions*), early music (*Spirit of the Age*) and contemporary music (*Midnight Oil*), and new regular strands late-night each weekday for vocal, chamber and orchestral music.

The aim of all these developments has been to sharpen up the schedules and help listeners to know where to look for the music they like. Of course in all these areas we have a long way to go, for new ways of working do not arise overnight. In particular, we want to make the connection stronger between those who produce music programmes for Radio 3 and those who present

them on the air: the big difference about *On Air* and *In Tune* is not actually, as many have supposed, the amount of 'chat' in them, but the fact that the presenters do the programming themselves, and can talk about their choices with knowledge and enthusiasm.

This change of approach has led inevitably to some losses: in order to make room for more fresh, outside voices on the network, we lost two of our continuity announcers, Peter Barker and Tony Scotland, whose distinctive voices had been a valued feature of Radio 3 to many listeners in recent years. In order to strengthen the music content of the network we reduced its drama output by about a third, provoking strong complaints from writers and actors, but apparently causing few problems for listeners: on Sunday evenings during the autumn we were able to mount an unrivalled and strong season of drama old and new, with a series of new plays to come in 1993. Cultural talk has been strengthened with a new strand after the evening concert, and our new discussion programme *Night Waves*, replacing *Third Ear*, has flourished with live, up-to-the-minute reviewing and stimulating talk.

During 1992, too, the first commercial national radio station

Brian Morton, presenter of the new jazz programme *Impressions*

has come on the air. That might not be thought at first sight to affect Radio 3 much but, following a series of debacles with the tendering process, this turned out to be a classical music service, Classic FM.

From the first, Classic FM claimed it was not in competition with Radio 3, for in order to be viable with its advertisers it had to aim at a larger, pop-music audience. Its approach was that of the commercial pop stations, with everything reduced to bite-sized chunks of music, wilfully uninformed (and badly pronounced) links, and only easy listening with no challenges at all. It would, we thought, perform a huge service by drawing pop audiences towards classical music, and opening up a new market for Radio 3. By the end of the year it looked likely that Classic FM was drawing large audiences, but not taking listeners away from Radio 3 – the best solution of all for the classical music lover.

We were encouraged too, because our belief is that in the new world of broadcasting the BBC should be offering something that the commercial sector cannot. Radio 3 perfectly complements Classic FM in offering its listeners full works, the widest possible repertory of classical music, developing new work and new artists, and presenting music in a cultural context which helps it to make sense. Commercial activity in classical music broadcasting helps us to focus our ideas sharply, and to clarify in our minds our strategy for the future.

There is one other huge distinction between Radio 3 and Classic FM, which is the chief justification of what we rather pompously call the public service role of Radio 3 within the BBC. Almost half of our music output on Radio 3, around 2,500 hours a year, is live or specially recorded. Instead of relying on what is available through the commercial market-place of records and discs, we *originate* music by employing orchestras and soloists, conductors and chamber music players to create that repertory for us. Thus we direct our music programming editorially, running the BBC Proms and public concerts, we

help to push the art-form forward throughout the country, and we establish local links with our audiences wherever the BBC orchestras are heard or lunchtime concerts take place which are broadcast on Radio 3.

This is an extraordinary achievement, unmatched anywhere, and a massive contribution to the musical life of the country which goes beyond just broadcasting into the role of cultural patronage. This unique contribution to the lives of millions is something that Radio 3 must keep alive in the future so that it is able to continue to develop classical music and culture. That's why it is so reassuring to find, both in the Government's Green Paper on the future of the BBC, and in the BBC's own manifesto for the future *Extending Choice*, that the role of the BBC as a cultural patron is stressed very strongly. I have certainly found in debates and forums, most recently in one organised by the National Campaign for the Arts, that it is this aspect of the BBC's role which arouses deep commitment and enthusiasm on the part of the public and the professionals.

Looking forward to the future role of Radio 3 within the BBC, *Extending Choice* says that it is unique, 'truly distinctive and unlikely ever to be matched in the commercial marketplace'. It should continue the journey which we have begun this year to being 'more accessible and appealing to classical music listeners', and for those of us who love classical music that is a task to be approached with enthusiasm. But, and this is the key statement, the BBC says Radio 3 has 'a highly valued place' which 'should be sustained in the long term'. That is our mandate for a full, active future. We want to be able to say by the year 2001 what another generation has said, as have many previous generations: that they were educated, culturally and musically, by the Third Programme and Radio 3. To reinterpret the ideas we value most for a new broadcasting age is our first aim.

Nicholas Kenyon

Nicholas Kenyon became Controller of Radio 3 in March 1992

YOUNG MUSICIAN OF THE YEAR

David Gillard reports on the growing success of the *Young Musician of the Year* event, from it's inception in 1978 to the 1992 final shown on BBC2 on 11 April

When the prodigiously gifted 14-year-old pianist Frederick Kempf won the BBC *Young Musician of the Year* competition at the Concerto Final in Glasgow on 11 April 1992, it was not only a great climax to television's most popular and prestigious showcase for young musical talent but the culmination of many months of complex behind the scenes endeavour.

For finding Britain's brightest young classical virtuoso is a long nationwide haul. The 1992 contest began in the March of the previous year with local auditions at 11 centres throughout the UK. This time 521 young hopefuls – all fulfilling the obligation of being under the age of 19 and having reached the standard of Distinction at Grade VIII in the Royal Schools of Music examinations – turned up to be assessed during a 15-minute recital in one of the four sections – piano (and, for the first time this year, organ), strings, brass and woodwind.

By June 1991 just over 200 competitors – including a 10-year-old harpist – had been selected to go through to the Stage 2 regional finals in September and October. Those regional finals would then reduce the numbers to 47 semifinalists – 12 pianists in the piano/organ section, seven violinists and five cellists in the strings section, four trumpeters, three trombonists, two each on horn and tuba and one on euphonium in the brass category and, in the woodwind section, four oboists, five flautists, one bassoonist and one clarinettist.

Executive producer, Roy Tipping was already predicting a vintage year: 'There are really exciting new talents here and we are also delighted that some of our previous semi-finalists have also reappeared at this stage. The programmes look like being more imaginative and

The four finalists (from left): Thomas Carroll, Kevin Norbury, Frederick Kempf and Rachel Barnes

stylish than ever before.' Indeed, the semi-finalists had chosen to perform works by a much greater variety of composers. Alongside such standard repertory names as Rachmaninov, Beethoven, Mozart and Chopin were also late 20th century figures like Bourgeois, Hopkinson, Rabe and Carmichael. One confident young performer even chose to play his own composition on tenor horn!

From those semi-finals – screened on BBC2 between 30 March and 2 April – the top 20 talented young players were eventually selected to go through to the four class finals, shown on BBC2 between 6-9 April. The four class winners – pianist Frederick Kempf from Chestfield, Kent, bassoonist Rachel Barnes, 16, from Westcliffe-on-Sea, Essex, 16-year-old tuba player Kevin Norbury from Guilden Sutton, Chester and Thomas Carroll, a 16-year-old cellist from Kittle, Swansea – went

on to take their chance in the Concerto Final, accompanied by the National Youth Orchestra conducted by Christopher Seaman. The competition's climax was shown on BBC2 on 11 April.

The distinguished jury – chaired by Sir Denis Forman and including Alun Hoddinott, Cécile Ousset, Raphael Wallfisch, George Zuckerman, Patrick Harrild, Joan Rodgers and Christopher Seaman – concluded that Frederick's imaginative and dynamic account of Rachmaninov's romantic 'Rhapsody on a theme of Paganini' deserved to bring him the *Young Musician* title, the trophy, a Lloyds Bank Travel Award and a place in the Eurovision Young Musician of the Year competition in Brussels.

Each of the finalists had already received a cheque for £2,000 for winning their particular classes. The Duchess of Kent, patron of the competition, also presented the

Walter Todds Memorial Bursary, awarded by the BBC to the performer, or performers who do not get into the Concerto Final but who show great promise. This year it went to Dominique Starosta-Binnie, aged 18, a violinist from Glasgow and 15-year-old Daniel Bates, an oboist from Bickley, Kent.

For the first time, the competition had been presented in association with Lloyds Bank whose £1.3 million sponsorship (over a period of five years) had expanded both the range and the prize money. A new competition, the Lloyds Bank Young Composer Award, provided a top bursary prize of £2,000 with £250 for all other finalists. Philip Howard, 15, from Merseyside and James Webb, 18, from Gwent were the joint winners and some of their work was broadcast as part of the Concerto Final. And the value of the prizes for the *Young Musician* competition had trebled from

£10,000 in 1990 to £30,000 in 1992, with some 300 prizes in the form of Lloyds Bank bursaries or travel awards.

And for the first time, too, all the finalists made a unique fashion impression, wearing outfits specially designed for them by the finalists in the Lloyds Bank Fashion Challenge and made up by top British fashion designer Paul Smith.

For Roy Tipping – who had conceived the *Young Musician* event with his colleagues Walter Todds and Humphrey Burton, and masterminded it since its inception in 1978 – this was to be his last competition before taking early retirement. But he is sure that 1992 will be seen as a 'golden year', both for young talent and for the popularity of the competition itself. '*Young Musician* is the most popular programme coming out of the Music and Arts Department. This year we drew an audience of between one and a half million and two million viewers for each programme – that's more than the Proms get on BBC2. There are times when you do get golden years – the first competition in 1978 was one. Our first winner, Michael Hext, is now principal trombone with the Royal Opera House Orchestra at Covent Garden and all the section winners have gone on to major careers. Two of the pianists – Stephen Hough who won the piano class and Barry Douglas who was a piano finalist – are now at the top of their profession.

'The vast majority of all our winners and finalists – except, of course, those who are still studying – are now well respected within the profession. I think the winners of 1992 will prove exceptional. Freddie, of course, is something special. You simply don't come across that sort of talent very often. But the other finalists are fine musicians, too.' And Roy was able to assess the talents of all four finalists in performance before the Concerto Final. 'I was asked if they would like to give concerts in the Middle East as part of a chamber music series for the Sultan of Oman and we all flew out to the desert for ten days. They made great music but it also gave them the opportunity to have a wonderful time. I don't think they'll forget swimming in rock pools in the desert!'

Tipping himself, though an enthusiastic pianist and organist, studied physics and electronics before joining the BBC and working in a number of areas (including the rough and tumble of TV's *It's a Knockout* and recording the first hole-in-the-heart operation) until he moved to Music and Arts and came up with the idea of *Young Musician of the Year*. It was accepted as a 'one-off' for a 16-programme series but was destined to become a respected part of the national music agenda and an established television favourite.

Frederick Kempf, the BBC *Young Musician of the Year* 1992

There have been criticisms along the way, mainly from those who believe that immature players should not be subjected to the sharp edge of competition or exposed to the pressures of publicity. Tipping does not agree. 'If somebody is going to find competition – and the results of winning a competition – difficult to cope with, then by goodness, they're going to find being a professional far more difficult. But we believe very much in aftercare. We make sure that there's professional help and guidance for our winners, advice on how to deal with things like repertoire, engagements and fees.

'I am confident that most of the young people who have taken part in the competition have found it positive and rewarding. And there is a need for a showcase for this age group – and for the public to see what's happening too. What we've done is bring chamber music to a very large public who knew very little about it. And we've encouraged people to view classical music not as middle class or esoteric but as something in which everybody and anybody can participate.'

Dennis Marks, former head of BBC Music Programmes – Television, was keen to use the security of long-term sponsorship to expand the range of the competition along a broader educational front. 'The *Young Musician* award has been criticised in the past for emphasising the competitive aspect of music-making amongst young people and I felt strongly that one of the ways the competition could be enhanced was in the direction of a festival created by young people. When the initial year with Lloyds turned into a three-year agreement we included travel scholarships and a young composers' competition. These are all ways of showing that not all the great range of talent and ability is reflected in the first, second and third prize structure. The contest has a broader scope than simply picking out winners.'

There was certainly a festival atmosphere at Glasgow's Royal Concert Hall for the Concerto Final. This was joyous music-making, not a night of nail-biting tension and hard-edged competitiveness. Conductor Christopher Seaman believes that the combination of young competitors playing with a youth orchestra (one of the orchestra's members, principal horn David Pyatt, was the BBC *Young Musician* of 1988) does a great deal to keep nerves at bay.

'A competition can give someone with enormous talent a chance to show their ability, which opens the door for other musical opportunities to present themselves,' he maintains. And what he aimed at on that exciting final night was, he insisted, 'a first rate concert with four gifted soloists.' That someone had to win was, in a way, less important.

Winning was certainly a hugely enjoyable experience for Frederick Kempf, an assured prodigy who seems destined for great things. 'It's transformed my life,' he admits. 'I'm enjoying it all tremendously. I'm not feeling any burden at all – it's my parents and teachers who are doing the worrying!'

The son of a hotel manager and a distant relative of the great German pianist, Wilhelm Kempff, he showed a precocious talent – 'I was 2-years-old when I learnt to work the record player!' At the age of 4 he was playing the piano and he gave his first public concert when he was 5. He currently goes to a public school in Canterbury, Kent, and attends the Royal Academy of Music in London one day a week. He practises for four hours every day, plays violin in the school orchestra and also finds time to compose, play in a jazz trio and ride his mountain bike round the cliffs and beaches near his home. In September 1993 he will go to the Academy as a full-time student, taking in composition, conducting and violin as well as piano.

'But a career as a concert pianist is what I'm aiming for,' he says. 'I've been offered more than 40 engagements since I won the title and I'm going to fit them in around my studies. And I'm hoping that I will be able to spend my travel award on a two week tour with Vladimir Ashkenazy, meeting people like Daniel Barenboim and Itzhak Perlman. That would be fantastic.'

One of his first engagements after becoming BBC *Young Musician of the Year* was to take part in the Eurovision Young Musician competition in Brussels (shown on BBC2 on 13 June). He limbered up for the contest with characteristic nonchalance by tackling the 'white knuckle' rides in a nearby pleasure park but admitted to some nervousness at the prospect of taking on Europe – 'I was representing the UK this time so there was more pressure.'

Again he won his way through to the final round, playing the 'Rhapsody on a theme of Paganini' with the Belgian National Orchestra

conducted by Ronald Zollman. But this time there were no glittering Euro-prizes to add to his tally, though the judges were full of praise for the poise and sensitivity of his playing. Well, you win some and you lose some – good training, says Frederick, for the sort of competition he's likely to meet as a professional in a tough world. Anyway, he had other things on his mind – like his GCSEs.

David Gillard

THE PROMS

The annual BBC Henry Wood Promenade Concerts produced a feast of music during the summer of 1992. David Gillard reviews the highlights

The BBC Symphony Orchestra conducted by Andrew Davis at the Last Night of the Proms

'This is the very model of a modern music festival,' sang conductor Andrew Davis at the Last Night of the Proms, launching into an hilarious pastiche of the Major General's patter song from *The Pirates of Penzance*. And who would deny it?

With 66 concerts in 58 days – all relayed live on Radio 3, ten of them seen on BBC television – the 98th season of the BBC Henry Wood Promenade Concerts lived up to its billing as 'The Greatest Music Festi-

val in the World'. For the first time, box office takings exceeded £2 million with attendances at the Royal Albert Hall averaging 81 per cent – a remarkable achievement in a time of recession.

It had certainly – on paper – looked as though it was going to be a great season. Announcing the programme back in May, the BBC Proms Director John Drummond had proclaimed: 'From first to last, this year's Proms have a truly international flavour, with no less than 11 foreign orchestras from Sydney to Toronto and a host of great conductors and soloists from around the world, all presented in the Proms' unique atmosphere of unrivalled accessibility. And where else in the world could you hear the Vienna Philharmonic for just over £1?

'The Proms continue to encourage new artists and composers: out of a total of 179, 54 conductors or soloists appear for the first time. There are 17 commissions and premieres – more than ever before. And at the heart of the Proms are the BBC orchestras, a vital resource and a crucial part of British musical life. In the coming season they will once again be carrying the commissions and much of the new music and also reaching out beyond the familiar.'

Indeed, 42 Proms appearances were made by the BBC's own orchestras and choirs. The BBC Symphony gave 15 concerts, five of them (including the First and Last Nights) with its chief conductor Andrew Davis; the BBC Philharmonic gave four concerts, the BBC Welsh and Scottish three each and the BBC Concert Orchestra – celebrating its 40th anniversary – gave two. The BBC Singers performed in seven Proms, the BBC Symphony Chorus in six and the BBC Welsh Chorus in two.

Though there were no themes this year, a number of the concerts commemorated important anniversaries including the 200th of the birth of Rossini, the centenaries of Honegger and Milhaud and the 500th anniversary of Columbus's discovery of America (this marked by the UK premiere of Walton's *Christopher Columbus* suite, arranged by Christopher Palmer, on

28 August in a programme given by the BBC Concert Orchestra). The 150th anniversary of the birth of Sir Arthur Sullivan found a better-late-than-never recognition from the ebullient Andrew Davis in joyful Major General mode on the Last Night, while living composers also celebrated birthdays at the Proms – Alexander Goehr (60) with his new work *The Death of Moses* (2 August) and Iain Hamilton (70) with his *Commedia* (1 September).

And the Last Night promised a special treat – New Zealand soprano Dame Kiri Te Kanawa celebrating the 21st anniversary of her Proms debut with her first Last Night appearance and a clutch of operatic arias plus the rousing *Rule, Britannia!*. 'I'm going to have a ball,' she told me in *Radio Times*. And she did.

But all that was to come. The season got off to a suitably stirring start on 17 July with Verdi's mighty Requiem with Andrew Davis and the BBC Symphony Orchestra once more at the helm. It is a festival close to his heart: 'The Prommers are actually the most attentive and quietest audience in the world, especially when you consider that there are sometimes 6,000 people jammed into that place. One can feel the intensity of their attention. And even on the Last Night we can do some very quiet, beautiful Delius piece and they will give you the silence of the grave. Even that manic bunch. Of course, once you get into the patriotic stuff, forget it.' But that was still a long way off.

The first BBC commission – Simon Holt's *walking with the river's roar* – received its world premiere under Yan Pascal Tortelier and the BBC Philharmonic on 21 July and the London premiere of John Tavener's *We shall see Him as He is* was given an enthusiastic reception with Richard Hickox and the BBC Welsh Symphony Orchestra two days later.

And the first foreign orchestra – the Cleveland from America with their principal conductor Christoph von Dohnányi – gave two virtuoso Proms on 24 and 25 July, followed by Glyndebourne Festival Opera's semi-staged version of Tchaikovsky's *The Queen of*

Spades. This gave the ubiquitous Andrew Davis the opportunity to don his other hat – that of Glyndebourne's musical director – and London the chance to savour the extraordinary gifts of the Russian tenor Yuri Marusin as the obsessive Hermann. It was a no-holds-barred performance – he even sent a pair of BBC microphones flying as he made one deranged exit! *The Times* called the occasion 'one of London's most compelling evenings of concentrated theatre'.

Andrew Davis, chief conductor of the BBC SO and Dame Kiri Te Kanawa at the Last Night of the Proms

The Budapest Festival Orchestra, under their founder-conductor Ivan Fischer, brought Bartók's brooding 20th century masterpiece *Duke Bluebeard's Castle* to the Royal Albert Hall on 28 July while early music buffs were rewarded with a reconstruction of *Music for a Venetian Coronation, 1595* from the Gabrieli Consort under Paul McCreesh two days later.

August began with another BBC commission – the world premiere of Richard Rodney Bennett's witty *Variations on a Nursery Tune* from the BBC Concert Orchestra under their principal conductor Barry Wordsworth. The following day another new work – Alexander Goehr's cantata *The Death of Moses* – received its British premiere from John Eliot Gardiner

and the Monteverdi Choir and Instrumentalists. Goehr used a sort of modernised Monteverdi orchestra – including bass guitar, saxophones and synthesizers – in a deliberate attempt to capture an ancient sound world in a modern idiom. The result, said The *Sunday Times*, was 'hugely striking'.

Simon Rattle brought his City of Birmingham Symphony Orchestra back on 7 August (they had already revived Roberto Gerhard's neglected ballet score *Don Quixote* on 19 July) and Lesley Garrett, rising star of the English National Opera, returned to the BBC Proms on 9 August to sing in Mahler's *Resurrection* Symphony with ENO colleague Jean Rigby and the National Youth Orchestra under Tadaaki Otaka.

Garrett had already won acclaim for her distinctive bare-all performance as Adele in ENO's *Die Fledermaus* but she had made her Proms bow two years before singing *Rule, Britannia!* on the Last Night. 'When I stepped on to the platform it was absolutely terrifying,' she said in *Radio Times*. 'Then I got a couple of wolf whistles and I thought: "This is a building site, really!". Everybody was beaming away so I relaxed and had fun, too.'

The following night saw a characteristically bravura display from another popular young woman – the profoundly deaf Scottish percussionist Evelyn Glennie. She premiered a new percussion concerto, *Veni, veni Emmanuel,* by her compatriot James MacMillan. At the end – in an ingenious and festive coda – the Scottish Chamber Orchestra discarded their instruments to take up hand bells and join Glennie in a wonderful, tinkling finale.

The Australian Chamber Orchestra made their BBC Proms debut on 12 August and the Danish National Radio Symphony Orchestra made their bow two days later. Two outstanding young Russians – violinist Dmitry Sitkovetsky and cellist Mischa Maisky – were the soloists in Brahms' *Double Concerto* with the Philharmonia under Claus Peter Flor on 16 August and, the following night, Christopher Hogwood conducted the Academy of Ancient Music in an all-Bach concert.

The Moscow Soloists added their Russian expertise on 19 August and conductor Klaus Tennstedt brought his Wagnerian authority to the Proms with the London Philharmonic on the following night. On 25 and 26 August the St Petersburg Philharmonic Orchestra gave admired programmes under their two principal conductors, Mariss Jansons and Yuri Temirkanov, and Mark Elder brought more Russian music on 27 August when he and the BBC Symphony Orchestra gave the London premiere of Shostakovich's recently discovered satirical suite *Hypothetically Murdered* (arranged by Gerard McBurney).

There was – in the best Proms tradition – something a little different on 30 August: *Big Band Rossini,* with the Mike Westbrook Orchestra jazzing up the likes of *William Tell* and *The Barber of Seville* to add a touch of classy swing to the Rossini bicentenary. This also made history as the first full jazz concert to be part of the main programme at the Proms. Kate Westbrook was the vocalist.

More overseas visitors – Tafelmusik, Canada's period instrument ensemble and the Royal Concertgebouw Orchestra from Holland under Riccardo Chailly – performed September's opening concerts and the young German violinist Anne-Sophie Mutter returned to play Berg's Violin Concerto in a memorable concert from the London Symphony Orchestra under Michael Tilson Thomas on 4 September.

That evening marked the start of a glorious Indian summer of music as the Proms moved into their last golden days. The next day saw what was, for many, *the* concert of the season – a mesmeric, inspired performance of Bruckner's Symphony No 8 by the BBC SO under their 80-year-old chief guest conductor Günter Wand. Hugh Canning in The *Sunday Times* asserted: 'If I never heard another performance of this great work I will be satisfied that I have experienced the essence of Bruckner's music through Wand.' And there was more powerhouse music-making to come in the final week. On 6 September, Vladimir Ashkenazy conducted the Berlin Radio Symphony Orchestra in a performance of Beethoven's *Choral* Symphony – with its adopted Euro anthem – that was part of the European Arts Festival which marked Britain's presidency of the European Community. The concert was attended by the Prime Minister, the President of the EC and the Arts and Culture Ministers of all the EC countries.

Another powerful, semi-staged opera was performed on 8 September when Opera North brought Musorgsky's epic *Boris Godunov,* with the British bass John Tomlinson – fresh from Wagner triumphs in Bayreuth – in the title role. The following night Claudio Abbado led the Vienna Philharmonic to the Proms for the first of two sell-out concerts, the second conducted by Pierre Boulez. The great orchestra – celebrating its 150th birthday – brought with it a varied repertoire of Haydn and Mahler in its first programme and a selection of 20th century masterworks (Stravinsky, Debussy, Boulez and Bartók) in its second.

And so to the traditional festivities of the Last Night. For Andrew Davis – who had already shown himself a natural master of ceremonies and revealed a particular fondness for what he calls 'a knees-up' – this was to be the fourth time that he had steered the great festival to its exuberant close. He said he saw the Last Night as a summing up of the whole season rather than merely a final fling of nationalistic jollity. 'I don't think it's all that chauvinistic. The words of *Rule, Britannia!* are the silliest gobbledygook you've ever heard – barely comprehensible and full of ridiculous phraseology. I don't think anyone really believes the sentiments.'

And the Dame who was charged with singing the 'gobbledygook' saw no harm in it or in the occasion. 'It's always such a wonderful night – the one and only time that British concert-goers feel liberated enough to get up and sing,' Dame Kiri told me. 'Well, it's the only time they're not told to shut up and listen! It's their night – they're the entertainment. They've been loyal throughout the season and they deserve it. All that glorious patriotism. Why not? Every other country in the world flies the flag. Why shouldn't Britain? I think it's good to be proud of your country. Don't damn others but certainly praise your own. The Last Night is a celebration of youth and the hope that the world will be a better place for them and because of them.'

And it was a great night. The veteran Russian pianist, Tatyana Nikolaeva played Shostakovich's Piano Concerto No 2, Dame Kiri, in celestial voice, sang arias by Massenet, Korngold, Catalani and Puccini – and bagpipes took to the Last Night stage for the first time when piper George McIlwham joined the orchestra for Sir Peter Maxwell Davies's *An Orkney Wedding with Sunrise.* Andrew Davis added a little extra zest to this particular piece by passing round a bottle of Scotch to the front desks of the BBC SO!

And then, after *Land of Hope and Glory* and *Rule, Britannia!,* it was left to Davis to remind us that he is the very model of a modern major maestro with the traditional final 'speech' turned into a brilliant G and S party piece.

David Gillard

'This is the very model of a modern music festival
Here's entertainment sonic, promenadable and aestival*
The Albert Hall consistently is full of teeming multitudes
Intent on lapping up an almost endless stream of pulchitrudes!
If for the great ambition of the season some should frown on us,
We just invoke our founder who is up there smiling down on us.
In Herculean labour none could beat Sir Henry Wood at it
John Drummond does the programmes and he's very, very good at it.
I think that one can say it without fear of being cavalier
These concerts simply wouldn't be the same without this rabble here.
Oh yes, in matters sonic, promenadable and aestival
This is the very model of a modern music festival.

'The programmes we can proudly say were plucky and adventury
Composers represented number well above a century.
We'd Adams, Bach and Berlioz, what music could be fruitier?
With Carter, Casken, Delius and not forgetting Dutilleux.
With Elgar and with Fauré, Gabrieli's sweet antiphony,
With Gershwin and Granados and Ives's strange polyphony.
For when it comes to relishing such treasures no one can enough
Of Liszt and Mahler, Mendelssohn, Prokofiev...Rachmaninuff!
And Rimsky-Korsakov, Rossini, Schubert, Schütz, Sibelius
Are brought to life like creatures of Jacques Offenbach's Coppélius.
In short in matters sonic, promenadable and aestival
This is the very model of a modern music festival.

'We'd 51 conductors, a variety remarkable
And thrice a dozen orchestras, all eminently harkable!
Of singers so amazing t'would be difficult t'invent a list
They totalled 83 with six and 40 instrumentalists.
Of choruses some 23 were heard in splendour glorious
And all these varied forces truly have emerged victorious.
But tho' into the future dim at best we can but feebly see
We know the Proms would not be here at all without the BBC.
So for now *auf Wiedersehen*, Goodbye, we have got to go
We really do sincerely hope that you have enjoyed the show
For still in matters sonic, promenadable and aestival
This is the very model of a modern music festival.'

*Pertaining to summer,' explained Davis.

3 Entertainment

Comedy, cookery, gardening, and nostalgia – just some of the varied topics which were broadcast over the year. From the light-hearted to the informative, radio and television entertainment has something for everyone.

Radio 4's *Woman's Hour* moved from its traditional afternoon slot to morning; the 2,000th edition of *Gardeners' Question Time* was broadcast; and after nearly eight years BBC1's *Wogan* show finally came to an end, though Wogan himself was soon to be back on our screens, as Libby Purves writes in her feature on the genial chat-show host.

One of Britain's most popular TV programmes, the comedy panel game *Have I Got News For You* entertained viewers with its unique, satirical look at the week's news, and in 'the year of Spain' we sampled a taste of that country courtesy of Keith Floyd's *Floyd on Spain*, and Maria José Sevilla's *Spain on a Plate*.

Entertainment

WOGAN

Friday, 3 July marked the end of an era. Terry Wogan, host of the chat-show that bore his name and became a national institution, presented his last early-evening programme. By Libby Purves

BBC Photograph Library

Terry Wogan

So, farewell then, *Wogan*. I can't believe it's going: after three doses a week for seven-and-a-half years and upward of 3,000 guests, the programme has entered the language. It has a status somewhere between a noun and a verb, as in 'doing *Wogan*', or the publicist's sad wail of, 'We're hoping for *Wogan* but they never rang'. A new-landed Martian would be puzzled: what is this *Wogan*? A sport? A religious ritual to be undergone after a major achievement – rather like a Roman triumph, or a service for the Churching of Women?

But the more you say a word – Wogan, Wogan, Wogan – the farther you get from its meaning. There has been a strange vacuum at the heart of all this whirling notoriety, and it seems to me that we have lost sight of the man who had the name first. He became the show: or perhaps the show became him. Certainly, whatever long-legged Sues and Selinas took it over, he had to leave half his name behind him to label them. The juggernaut show rolled on as *Wogan*, leaving him to go off on holiday as a mere Terry. Now the show is ending, and Terry can have his surname for his exclusive use again. It is like Peter Pan getting his lost shadow back: perhaps some kindly BBC Wendy will stick it on with soap. Michael Terence Wogan is back, as himself.

If I grow fantastical, blame memory. Eight years ago, and for 12 years before that, Terry Wogan was the dawn presenter for Radio 2 and fantasy was his trademark. He has always called his television programme 'chewing gum for the eyes, a mild narcotic', but on the radio he provided rarer pleasures. He was unlike any normal disc jockey, because he knew ten times more words, and presided over an original, funny, verbal realm. His trademark was an Irish delight in language and fantasy: serious critics said there was a bit of James Joyce in there, certainly of Myles na Gopaleen, the legendary 'Beachcomber' of the *Irish Times*. And it was all done on the wing, unscripted and unprompted except by increasingly demented letters from listeners. He used to sit in his windowless box pretending he could see the Director-General's teeth in a glass on the neighbouring windowsill, and the man himself on the roof: 'Look at him out there – he thinks he's the Duke of Devonshire, him in his soup-stained raincoat!'

There was the sacrificial procession of BBC Virgins, the Northampton Lighthouse, and, of course, the daily battle with Jimmy Young. 'Begone, you whey-faced hypocrite!' Wogan would cry. The Queen was a fan. Once the Queen Mother asked for a record. There is no show like it today. With its multi-coloured fantasy, comic abuse and uncontrived disrespect, he did not woo his listeners: he conspired with them.

When the TV show started, many

BBC Photograph Library

Wogan chats with Goldie Hawn and Kurt Russell

of us hoped for more of the same. Occasionally we got it, as when Jessye Norman left the set of the show to an enormous crash, and Wogan said, 'That's Jessye falling over' and got into trouble. There have been treasurable moments on the Eurovision Song Contest as he waffles about 'Malmö – jewel of the Skagerrak – or somewhere.' But by and large, we lost sight of our old Wogan. Then at the end of 1991, partly at his request, the show's knell was sounded and the news badly leaked, and it was made to seem as if *Wogan* was being accused of failing. It got through the armour, and he said at the time, most untypically, 'This is the first time I have felt slightly diminished.'

Sprawled on the sofa at his home near Maidenhead, he appears to have got over the feeling. 'Ah, I never expected life to be an ever-rising curve.' He offers me a drink before lunch, and I demur because I have a programme to prepare. 'Enough of that rubbish, you can't fool me. You're a Corinthian. You just go out and do it.' Terry Wogan has never admitted that what he, or any of us, does is hard. He makes a

refreshing change from broadcasters who talk about their jobs as if they were flying the space shuttle nightly to Mars.

Television has not turned him into a monster: he is still relaxed, still self-mocking. 'It's been, by the grace of God, seven-and-a-half years. They said it would collapse after six weeks. I think there's a law of diminishing returns. People get sick of the sight of you.'

He has enjoyed it, working in his idiosyncratic way, which involves arriving as late as possible at the office and refusing to conform with the nervy, showbiz atmosphere of the medium. 'I'm extremely lazy and I justify this by the Jesuitical reasoning that I work better if I come to it fresh. Besides, I'm a quick reader, I assimilate research easily and keep down the adrenaline. And another good argument is that you ought to be well enough read and full of general knowledge to interview most people without any research at all. Go on, have that drink.'

Wogan-bashers always dredge up incidents such as the Duke of Edinburgh's appalling rudeness over the 'idiot board' prompts that TV

interviewers routinely use; but the fact is, as *Wogan* producers will testify, he really can do it. You can sling anybody at this man and he will produce a conversation. Joan Collins, a sozzled George Best, Madonna, Simon Weston, Katie Boyle to discuss her breast reduction op – no problem, wheel 'em on, Wogan can cope.

Talking about a fellow chat-show hostess who goes on about her 'journalistic integrity', he says: 'I'm baffled. You don't have to be a journalist to conduct these interviews. The most successful ones are just fooling around.' Nor is he pompous like the radio host who said once, 'I'd rather play more records than do the wrong interview. I've nothing to say to Val Doonican.' Wogan wants to talk to everyone. That is his greatly underrated strength.

Another is that he is happy to go live. 'I like live TV, because I know I can go home and get my dinner. And I like the edges showing, the idea that things might go wrong. It isn't theatre, it isn't ego, it's letting other people shine. I loved June Allyson, and James Stewart, so frail – Gregory Peck, Bette Davis, such a nasty piece of work! – loved her – and Debbie Reynolds and Athene Seyler...' He goes into a brilliant impression of Athene Seyler, appearing asleep and gaga in her wheeled chair, but springing tigerishly into showbiz life when the lights came on. 'I love these old thespians, I do. Gwen Ffrangcon-Davies did me Juliet's speech when she was 100. And I did like Princess Anne the first time, so funny and jolly and unafraid.'

He regrets none of it, not even the tabloid attacks on him and his close, solid family. 'Haven't they got nasty? I suppose it's not unhealthy, though. Better than the awful American thing of total deification. We take the Armageddon view of stars. Chuck 'em away!'

Wogan in Hollywood with living legend George Burns

So what next for Terry Wogan? Another show, certainly – but at a different time and with a different style. 'Because of my optimism I've always taken chances with my career. There was no need to leave Ireland, or Radio 2, or *Come Dancing* or *Blankety-Blank*. Except this feeling of the law of diminishing returns.'

Not at all diminished, he was soon to return in a new late-night slot on Fridays. *Wogan* is dead. Long live Wogan.

Libby Purves

WOMAN'S HOUR

Anne-Marie Sapsted looks back on the changing face of Woman's Hour and its progressive coverage of controversial issues in the year in which the programme switched from its traditional afternoon slot to morning

It's been an exciting year for Woman's Hour. Not only has it been covering sensitive and controversial issues in its characteristic no-nonsense style, but the programme and its team have been making the headlines, too. Seldom since it started back in the 40s as a mirror of middle class Home Counties concerns, has the programme inspired such impassioned opinions.

Some writers suggest that little has changed in those 40-odd years, that it is still the same old-fashioned, cosy mix of recipes, cleaning tips and women's problems. Others suggest that it concentrates solely on radical feminist issues. But regular listeners, around a half million of them, know how far both these descriptions are from the truth. The daily diet of the topical, entertaining, intimate, sometimes campaigning or controversial, and often simply the useful, informative and fun has always kept pace with the times.

And that is the programme's great strength. 1992 has seen it settle comfortably into its morning slot, a move which caused a furore when first announced in 1991 when Michael Green, Radio 4's controller, saw *Woman's Hour* as the answer to the notorious R4 morning trough. With *Today* over, there had always been a steep decline in listeners and research suggested that *Woman's Hour* could be the answer to the problem. The move, in fact, was a complement to the programme.

It has long been known that men make up at least a third of regular listeners, a fact which the production team has always ignored. Women are its main sources and interpreters and regarded as its principal audience. When the programme made its move, Green's confidence paid off. The audience has grown and it's now reckoned that as many men as women tune in.

'The programme has a confident history,' explains Sally Feldman, co-editor, 'even at the beginning it was inspirational and it discussed controversial issues and was pioneering in many ways. I think it's comfortable and stimulating, practical and thought-provoking and it celebrates women's lives. It has managed to retain its distinctive tone.'

Woman's Hour is a programme which has a solid reputation for dealing fairly and sensibly with the

(From left): Hilda Whitlow, Olive Shapely, Christine Andrews, Marguerite Patten and Ruth Drew celebrate the 1,000th edition of *Woman's Hour* in April 1950

issues of the day and top people are prepared to interrupt their schedules to go to the studios for interview. Not surprisingly, women such as Alison Halford, Merseyside's former Assistant Chief Constable who had fought a long and bitter court battle against her bosses talked to *Woman's Hour* first.

Gillian Shephard, employment minister, was interviewed on the day her appointment to the Cabinet was announced. She stayed on after the programme and the *Woman's Hour* team were the first to use her new title 'Minister'. Margaret Beckett gave her first interview on the programme as new Labour deputy leader. And Margaret Thatcher gave her first major interview out of office. This was another broadcast which made radio history as this most experienced of politicians was left at a loss for words, unable to answer criticism of her government's lack of child care provision.

The programme's success has always been its skill in tackling all subjects from the trivial to the taboo ones of their time. Back in the 40s, discussion of divorce brought down the wrath of the BBC hierarchy. Homosexuality caused a fuss in the 50s, as did the contraceptive pill a decade later.

The subjects under discussion this year have also raised an eyebrow or two. Melvyn Bragg was invited on to discuss the controversial adaptation of his novel *A Time to Dance* about an obsessive love affair between a retired bank manager and a girl of 18. Also taking part in the discussion was Gloria Steinem, the feminist writer touring Britain to promote her new work, *The Revolution from Within, A Book of Self-Esteem*. The resulting debate was extremely lively, very good radio and attracted a lot of feedback from listeners, dividing almost equally between women offended by Bragg's book who had enjoyed his discomfort, and those who loved the series and felt he was given a dreadful time.

Salman Rushdie was heard live in the studio talking about why he wrote *Satanic Verses*. Unfortunately, he also chose the occasion to launch into an attack on his previous wife, comments which

were cut from the evening's repeat of the programme.

Woman's Hour made broadcasting history in May when it visited Holloway prison, in north London, to become the first live programme broadcast from a closed gaol.

But among these and other heavyweight subjects such as anti-pornography legislation in America, older women and environmental protests in Canada, there was also a rich diet of sauces, gravies and puddings, alongside a look at what makes a best-selling perfume, how to deal with chapped lips and advice on plucking eyebrows. Campaigning items played their part, too. There was the launch early in the year of a Breast Cancer Campaign, alongside which a helpline was set up which attracted 2,000 calls in one week. As a result of this, the subject was returned to later in the year, when listeners' concerns about how they were treated by doctors were discussed.

And there has been a lot of fun. The morning slot gave the team the opportunity to do a special April Fool's edition. This included items on the discovery of the gene which was responsible for nagging and a discussion on its repercussions for rowing husbands and wives, and a reading from a 'newly-discovered' Jane Austen novel. 'We got some

Jenni Murray, presenter of *Woman's Hour*

very strange letters from our listeners after that,' remembers Feldman. 'Really entering into the fun of it. And we got phone calls throughout the time the programme was on air as people guessed what we were doing.'

The serial has been one of the programme's little-recognised successes with a wide range of books chosen from classic literature, biographies, diaries, thrillers and little-known modern writers. Many of the readings are brought out later on cassette, and subsequently feature regularly on bestseller lists.

Celebrities, too, have their role to play, though men are never used in the traditional 'beefcake' interview. Michael Caine spoke particularly movingly about his experience when his premature baby daughter was born. He described how his hands were too big to put inside her tiny incubator, and about how the baby responded to his touch for the first time trying to grasp his finger. 'It was a most beautiful description,' remembers Feldman.

The *Woman's Hour* team is made up of ten producers, all with their own special area of interest, responsible for keeping up-to-date and suggesting ideas for the programme, and two co-editors. A great deal of care is taken to ensure that guests are made to feel relaxed and comfortable, especially those not used to broadcasting, and the hospitality room is a focal point of pre-programme activity .

Listeners, too, write in their hundreds every week and their suggestions and stories are regularly used. They might be serious or light-hearted like the one which made an amusing item when a listener wrote in to ask the team to find out why manufacturers of knickers had changed the placing of the cotton gusset.

The relationship between the programme and its listeners is one which is taken very seriously by the team. Letters are answered wherever possible and listeners' responses and views make a regular slot in the programme. Phone-ins, too, are now often used as a way of debating important issues. 'I hope our listeners see me as their friend and champion,' presenter Jenni

Murray said. 'I can only judge by the letters I receive but I think our listeners see me as someone who is on their side.'

Sally Feldman is not content to rest on the programme's laurels. Next year she hopes to have more broadcasts outside the studio and to travel the country more. There are already regular broadcasts from Manchester and Scotland, but there are plans to get away from the main broadcasting centres and out to more unusual locations.

Of course, it's very easy to poke fun at a programme called *Woman's Hour*. It's a sitting duck. But the proof of the pudding...as they say. And more people are listening to the programme now than there were a year ago.

Michael Green summed up the programme's enduring appeal: 'It covers a whole range of subjects and shies away from nothing. It's for all people. Its search for women broadcasters and contributors adds to its texture.'

Anne-Marie Sapsted

TV NOSTALGIA

Viewers were treated to a trip down memory lane with Channel 4's TV Heaven and BBC2's TV Hell, showing the best and worst of TV programmes from the past. As TV nostalgia became more and more popular – UK Gold, a new channel dedicated to the screening of repeats, was launched. By Daniela Soave

For an industry that is still in its relative infancy, television nostalgia has become surprisingly popular. Last year saw the birth of a new channel, UK Gold, dedicated entirely to repeats, and both BBC2 and Channel 4 launched their own foray into the archives with TV Hell and TV Heaven respectively.

We are the first generation to have grown up with television and to regard it as part of our culture. But until the beginning of this new decade, there has been a certain snobbery about repeated TV programmes which has denied viewers the chance to see their old favourites: whereas old films were

The comedy series *Porridge*, still as funny today as it was first time round

described as 'vintage' or 'classic', this deification did not cross over to anything that was specifically made for the small screen. Then, as a new generation experienced and enjoyed for the first time comedies such as *Dad's Army, Some Mothers Do 'Ave 'Em, Citizen Smith* and *Porridge*, it suddenly became permissible to grow rosy-eyed at our television past. And with good reason. The quality of many of these series has eclipsed the years and they are as funny – and pertinent – as they were first time around.

Although the National Film School Archive didn't begin collecting TV programmes until 1962, and the BBC wiped out many of their early series, Britain still has a rich heritage of used TV material. Although many of these programmes – especially comedies – have found a home on terrestrial television, there was a very obvious demand for a greater opportunity to relive the golden oldies of television, and so UK Gold was born.

Broadcasting continuous entertainment for 20 hours a day, the principal source of UK Gold's material comes from the libraries of the BBC and Thames Television. With the exception of *Dallas, Neighbours* and *Sons and Daughters*, the programmes are genuinely British with 120,000 classics available from the BBC, and 10,000 from Thames, including: *The Brothers, The*

Duchess of Duke Street, George and Mildred, The Onedin Line, Shoestring, The Bill, Tenko and *Miss Marple*. It has proved to be a winning formula.

Channel 4's sortie into the past lasted 13 weeks during the spring season. Attracting an average audience of 2.1 million viewers, *TV Heaven* picked a different year – or vintage, if you like – and showed a selection of comedy, drama, documentary and even advertisements over three hours of prime time Saturday night viewing. From 1963,

A scene from *Tenko*

for example, came the black and white images of a Harold Pinter drama entitled *The Lover*, which was made for Associated Rediffusion and was described at the time by Dennis Potter as 'a sizzling triumph'. (Pinter's play went on to win a Prix Italia award.)

Also on offer that evening was an edition of *This Week*, the current affairs show, discussing the satire movement made fashionable by Peter Cook and Richard Ingrams. How peculiar it was to watch Jonathan Miller and Michael Frayn dismiss this new movement as nothing more than a passing fad!

Although the series paid lip service to the 50s with one single programme, the remaining 12 weeks were given over to the 60s and 70s, and the absence of any BBC programmes was notable. Nevertheless, the series was critically acclaimed and well subscribed.

Just as recollections can be evoked by an old song, viewers discovered that a trip down television's memory lane also brought reminiscences flooding back. Saturday nights became a visual lucky bag of memories for thirty-something viewers upwards, while introducing the more youthful to entirely new delights.

Meanwhile, Alan Yentob's BBC2 brainchild, *TV Hell*, was the nadir of British television, but delightful nevertheless. The evening of 31

The 1981 drama series *The Borgias*, which featured in *TV Hell*. (From left): Anne Louise Lambert, Oliver Cotton and Adolfo Celi

August was given over to five hours of the very worst programmes ever made, and attracted two million viewers. But though the viewing figures vindicated Yentob's vision, it was an inspired and brave move. On the face of it, why would viewers want to watch programmes which were being paraded – and applauded – for being so dire?

The diversity of all that is truly bad was simply staggering. You could watch a man proudly displaying his talent for walking over eggs without breaking them – except all he did was simply hop over them, barely touching them, and still managing to crack them in the process. This happened on TV? You bet, on *Nationwide*, and that was only *one* of the embarrassing excerpts from the news magazine show.

Nul Points was a collection of losers from the *Eurovision Song Contest*, all of whom scored zilch on the old scoreboard – and yes, quite a few of the offending entries happened to be Norwegian. Then there was *Trading Places*, which showed doubtful antics by various celebrities and people in the public

Jonathan Ross, a possible contender for a future *TV Hell*?

eye. But perhaps the best compilation on offer was a truly unmerciful look at the worst moments in music, introduced by John Peel. Remember Jasper Carrott's *Funky Moped*? Or Father Abraham and the Smurfs (and was it really number one?) Peel's droll delivery was perfectly suited to such fodder.

If the exercise is repeated in the future, what could we offer from today's schedules? Definitely *The Word*, and large chunks of *The Big Breakfast*. Early episodes of *Eldorado*, and what about Jonathan

It's A Knockout with compere Stuart Hall (centre), provided some memorable moments of *TV Hell*

Ross? Like all of the programmes featured in *TV Hell*, every one of the aforementioned shows attract viewers in their droves because they are compulsive. And here lies the answer to why *TV Hell* won hands down over *TV Heaven*. This was television nostalgia with a wicked twist, compiled with a generous helping of the cringe factor. Watching old programmes is fun, but ultimately boring. Add plenty of toe-curling moments and, just as one does when groaning over old photographs, the room will soon be filled with squeals of laughter. More, please.

Daniela Soave

MASTERCHEF

Masterchef of Great Britain 1992, Vanessa Binns, recalls the trials and tribulations of winning this most prestigious amateur culinary award. How did she select the winning menu? Do disasters ever happen when the cameras are rolling? Has winning changed her life? Julie Allan finds out the answers and just what it takes to be the best

What am I doing here? That is the one question Vanessa Binns kept asking herself throughout her televised journey to becoming Masterchef of Great Britain 1992. The annual Sunday tea-time series that has five million or so eager viewers salivating at the screen each week, enthralled by what one reviewer described as 'hard core food porn', had Vanessa Binns driving up and down the motorway from her Cheshire home, between manic bouts of recipe practise and her job as a teacher.

Masterchef was the idea of British film director Franc Roddam who, while in California, got fed up of hearing British food criticised. He and the programme's producer, Richard Bryan, devised the 'cross between a food programme, competition and chat show' to explore the excellence and variety of cooking across Britain.

Vanessa Binns, a regular viewer of the 1990 series watched as genial host Loyd Grossman and guest judges 'yum-ed' (or *yerm*-ed) their way through perfectly presented plates nervously dished up by the amateur cook occupants of the red, blue and yellow kitchens. But it was

her husband Brian who sent off for the entry forms. 'I was never a particularly competitive person,' says Binns, 'and in any case, he was the cook of the family, not me. In 1977 he won the Sunday Times Amateur Cook of the Year award and he's been trying to teach me to cook ever since we got married.'

She was persuaded, however, to enter The *Sunday Times* competition in 1990, but was beaten by Sue Lawrence, who went on to become Masterchef 1991. 'I decided if she could do it, I could have a go,' says Vanessa, and she duly sent in her forms. 'They wanted to know a lot about you – hobbies, what you did for a living, what other people thought of you, and you had to suggest a three-course £30 menu, the same task they set for the actual competition.'

'The form is pretty daunting,' admits producer Richard Bryan, 'but this is a serious competition. The most important question is the menu – we're looking for balance and ingenuity. It seems that the mail arrives in the office around midday, so we're in the right frame of mind for spotting the good ones – we choose the ones that make us sali-

Vanessa Binns, the winner of *Masterchef* with Loyd Grossman

vate. Another good question is that we ask for a recipe for a local vegetable. You can tell a lot from that reply. Some people tend towards boiled potatoes while others really go to town.'

Vanessa Binns was among those whose forms made the grade for last year's competition. She and 15 others went to the preliminary heat in Liverpool – and heat was the operative word. 'I could hardly believe the temperature,' says Vanessa. 'We went eight at a time in a college in Liverpool, with eight industrial ovens going full blast. The chocolate decoration for my orange and Grand Marnier mousse was melting all over the place.' Two days later she was told she was one of the three selected for the first televised heat. 'That was the first time I thought, "this is serious",' she recalls.

'It is quite a challenge,' agrees Richard Bryan. 'We never compromise the food for the person but we have to see how the competitors do under pressure. We record the actual competition in just ten days, so a competitor could have the first round on a Friday, the second on the following Tuesday and the final on Wednesday. It would be tough even for a professional.'

In January, like all the other contestants, Vanessa Binns was given just three weeks to come up with the three menus she would cook in each of the rounds. 'They asked for all three so that you would be ready if you got through to the next round and the final,' she says. 'But it was a nightmare deciding. It would have been so easy to try and be a bit flash and impressive but in the end it just had to be what I liked and what I really thought I could do in the two and a half hours allowed.'

In February she and her husband were due for a long-awaited trip to Hong Kong, 'but we'd have been back only a week before I had to turn up and cook. I could never have enjoyed it, so we cancelled it. For the next few weeks I practised every recipe over and over. My friends all ate beyond the call of duty – we had them over four at a time because that's the quantity you have to make. One week we had

five lots round. My husband nearly had a breakdown because they all like their wine and we were going through it by the case. I don't know what the binmen thought.'

She recalls this tale of horror with much laughter and a slight air of disbelief. It was at this point that the television recording began, and the motorway journeys to London: a series of afternoon trips, sleeping (briefly) overnight in a hotel, into the television studio for the cooking, and back home ready for school the next morning. Not so much 'what am I doing here?' but 'where am I?'

By the time I knew I was in the final, I think I'd stopped feeling anything. I can't tell you how nerve-racking it was to be in a TV studio for the first time. I was up at five in the morning or earlier, writing out notes – we couldn't take recipes in – and we all had to practise sitting on the sofa, saying what we were making and walking to the kitchen. It really wasn't easy at all. And we wear body microphones while we're cooking. Mine stopped working once and somebody politely enquired if I was at a critical moment. I said not, was told just to continue and the next thing I know this sound man had his hand up my skirt. All I could think was, "I don't know what my husband would make of this".'

Her competition cooking was not without disaster, although viewers didn't see it on the screen. 'In the first heat I burnt something dreadfully,' she admits. 'I was peering in the oven distraught, trying to shoo

the camera away. I came so close to simply giving up but judge Michel Roux had arrived by this time and I thought I heard an adverse comment between him and Loyd about the balance of somebody else's menu. So I decided maybe I still had a chance and found time to make another batch.' In the final she managed to make a liquidiser fall apart with the sauce still in it. 'I said something extremely rude to the camera.'

After all she has been through and after all her success, she has one unanswered question. In common, no doubt, with many viewers

---

The menu which made a Masterchef:

Terrine of wild smoked salmon with smoked Buttermere eels

~~~

Lamb fillet with a garlic sauce
Shredded potato cakes
Tagliatelle of mangetout and carrots

~~~

Caramelised pancakes with raspberries and oranges
with a caramelised Grand Marnier sauce

---

she wants to know what the judges said that now lies on the cutting-room floor. 'They send us out for the judging,' she says, 'and they seem to edit it so that nothing particularly awful is said.' That, it would seem, remains one of the mysteries of the programme. The producer is not to be drawn: 'All the cooking is of an extremely high standard,' he says. 'The judges genuinely do have a hard time of it. And in any case, we don't want to show too much of what they say in case it gives the game away before the announcement.' Perhaps, then, nothing awful is said. In fact, given what it takes to be in the series, shame on the judge who is even a tad less than appreciative and constructive.

So, judged the best by Grossman and celebrity chefs alike (for the final he was joined by Sir Clement Freud and Richard Shepherd of Langan's Brasserie and other noted establishments), how did it feel to be told she had won? 'To be honest I was so tired I could hardly feel anything,' she admits, 'although later I got excited about it. I was presented with the trophy and then they take it back and you can't tell anyone – this was in March and the final wasn't actually broadcast until July.

'I remember being slightly disbelieving really. We sat at home and watched the semi-final because I wanted to see that they hadn't changed the ending.'

Vanessa Binns is not a teacher any more. 'I thought, well, I'm 45, I've got the opportunity to try something new, if it doesn't work there's still teaching, and the children don't need me around so much.'

She handed in her notice and is now doing all sorts of food and cookery-related projects that she is enjoying, 'although I think sometimes I'm going in too many different directions. I'm just feeling my way really.'

She denies she is truly a master chef – 'they're people like Michel Roux. It seems unnecessarily arrogant of me to think I could set up my own restaurant and become a professional chef.' Instead she's writing a book of her recipes – 'although I find working everything out to the last ounce is quite a discipline', does book reviews for newspapers, is in demand as an after-dinner speaker and demonstrator and has even made a film in Canada about the food there. 'I'd like to go into television,' she says. 'And I also feel there's a gap between the great chefs and the cook at home. I'd like to help link them in some way, show that great cookery doesn't need to be intimidating.'

She likes using her skills to help, such as being the 'celebrity canape supplier' at a fund-raiser for a local National Trust property. And she had a tremendous time at a local hotel where they served her winning *Masterchef* menu to a packed and appreciative dining room.

Are there any drawbacks to her new-found fame? 'I never go out without my make-up on. I get stopped in the street but actually I don't mind that. People are all so nice. I did once get caught and called a cheat buying ready-made meals in Marks & Spencer but I just said, "I have hungry teenagers at home. Doesn't everybody cheat sometimes?". And I do send my husband in if we buy fish and chips.

'But mostly it's lovely. I've met so many well-known chefs who I admire tremendously. And almost best of all I got to be the cover girl on the local glossy Cheshire magazine, which I don't think is bad at my age.'

Julie Allan

GOING LIVE!

Going Live! made a welcome return in the autumn, with ever-popular presenters Sarah Greene and Phillip Schofield. Like many parents, mother-of-six Sue Arnold has her own reasons to give thanks for its comeback

Hallelujah! Someone out there was listening. After months of tearing my hair out every Saturday morning as the children squabble, scream, scratch and slam their bedroom doors, peace was about to return to the world on the morning of the sixth day.

Going Live! began a welcome new series in September and – oh joy, oh bliss – I can once more go shopping by myself without a posse of children hanging off the side of my trolley like Gibraltar apes; I can lie up to my neck in scented bubbles, Ned Sherrin beside me (on Radio 4's *Loose Ends*, of course) without children demanding to borrow my shampoo; I can knock up a batch of gingerbread men without children arguing about who's licking the bowl. Why, I might even ask my friend Anthea over for a quiet cup of coffee and a chat about the new people at number 17.

All these simple Saturday morning

Going Live! presenters Phillip Schofield and Sarah Greene

BBC

pleasures that I used to look forward to so much throughout the frantic week's routine have gone to pot since the previous series of *Going Live!* went off the air last April.

It is not just because they keep the children entertained for three glorious hours that I approve of Sarah Greene, Phillip Schofield, Gordon the Gopher and their associates. It is because they seem to get so much more fun out of it than the mindless twaddle that most children's programmes have to offer.

In the good old days when television was a novelty and kids were so small-screen orientated you could stick them in front of the Hotpoint all day and let them switch programmes between non-fast colours and heavy-duty whites, it was so much simpler. Television on, kids comatose. Modern kids are much more discriminating, not alas, so discriminating that they actually turn the TV set off and practise their recorders or read *What Katy Did Next*, as I should prefer. But they are certainly discerning enough to switch channels if they are bored, and when you've got six children it is the channel-switching that leads to trauma. Eight-year-old James wants quizzes; Tom, 12, wants sport; the three teenage daughters don't really want *Open University* but they do if it winds up their kid brothers. As for Finlay, 2, he just wants cartoons.

Going Live! gives everyone a bit of everything. No, please don't suggest the obvious – why don't we have more than one TV? Because one is quite enough thanks. I still hold out hopes for those recorders and *What Katy Did Next*.

At this point I'd better come clean and confess that I have never actually sat down and watched the programme from beginning to end. I catch it on the hoof, glimpsing the odd item when I poke my head round the door to ask whose bath is overflowing into the dining room or to search for the Hoover, the car keys or the other half of the rabbit that the cat is eating on the stairs. Half the time I don't register what's on the screen, especially if it's cartoons. I loathe cartoons. And much of what I glimpse, anyway, is totally mystifying. Why, will some-

one tell me, is there a dog racing around a kitchen with a saucepan, catching tins of baked beans?

However, what makes me feel that the producer knows his onions when it comes to entertaining kids is that, like the best Punch and Judy shows, it caters to all tastes and ages. True, my teenage daughters tend to have only one eye on the box these days, the other being firmly focused on *Elle* magazine or the fourth coat of nail gloss they've just applied, but there's invariably something in the programme that arouses their interest or comment. Nellie, 15, the aspiring ballet dancer, once yelled as if she'd been shot because Darcey Bussell was being interviewed and the girls interviewing her were all from Nellie's school.

Earlier this year, a friend who has just started teaching at a Rudolf Steiner school came to stay. Her views on the evil influence that television has on children are, to say the least, disturbing. If she does not actually believe that a cloven-footed devil inhabits every television set, emitting sinister waves to undermine and corrupt the innocent minds of our little treasures, she isn't far off it.

We were discussing the eternal issue – box v books – over breakfast one Saturday, when she said, 'Come on, let's see what rubbish the children are looking at right now.' It was *Going Live!*, of course, and at the point we hit it, a bloke with a Worzel Gummidge haircut and bovver boots was singing a song which, if I remember correctly, went something like this: 'Eeny, meeny, makeraka, ping, pong, push; it's nice being horrid and it's horrid being nice'.

The culture slot over, we were now faced with some daft quiz, the winners of which would get either a sports bag, an electronic game or a cuddly penguin. My Steiner friend rolled her eyes heavenwards and if she didn't say, 'I told you so', she meant it.

But hang on: the merchandise slot was over and there was that nice wholesome Phillip Schofield talking to Tony Hart. At once – and as usual with the inimitable Mr Hart – eight pairs of eyes were glued

to the screen. They set great store by art at Rudolf Steiner schools and I could see my friend making mental notes about some of Tony Hart's tips for drawing posters.

That's the thing about the programme – you never quite know what's going to grab you. Speaking as a mother who spends most of her waking hours fending off requests for consumer durables, designer jeans and Japanese software, I could happily dispense with the glossy prizes *Going Live!* offers. Why not a few more educational ones? For instance, tickets for the Royal Festival Hall, a record token, or even a hardback copy of *What Katy Did Next*.

I'm quibbling, of course. If you gave any of my kids tickets for the South Bank they would trade them in for a Prince concert or Arsenal v Spurs at Highbury. You have to move with the times, and that is probably why *Going Live!* is so popular. Its quick-fire, helter-skelter, tongue-in-cheek format is what kids love.

And here's where I declare my partiality. I think Sarah Greene is just about the best female presenter on television. Anyone who can make sense of some of those spaced-out pop stars she interviews without being patronising or pretentious, while at the same time making you feel she's enjoying the joke, has to be serious Sue Lawley material. She's got everything has Sarah Greene. She's pretty and funny and wise and sympathetic – and didn't I see her making a reasonable job of tap-dancing as well? Sarah Greene in the next Cabinet reshuffle, say I.

Sorry, I'm getting carried away. An informed appraisal of *Going Live!* is what you want, and here it is. Perish the thought that I'm crowing about the series only so that I can have Saturday mornings to myself. This is only half the truth. The other half is that if children have to watch television (and let's face it, Dr Steiner, they do), then this potpourri of jokes, interviews, social issues, current affairs and quizzes is just the sort of thing that best fills the 'inform, educate, entertain' dictum broadcasting aims for.

Sue Arnold

GARDENERS' QUESTION TIME

1 November 1992 marked the 2,000th edition of *Gardeners' Question Time*. Daniela Soave reflects on the winning formula which has endured for 45 years

In the autumn of 1992, regular listeners to *Gardeners' Question Time* tuned in to their favourite programme to hear an edition with a difference. People with vast expanses of land, those with a modest pocket handkerchief of lawn, allotment owners and even flat-dwellers without a balcony to their name have harvested the seeds of knowledge that have been planted by the expert panel every week for almost half a century. Over the years, the gardening road

An unusual location was not, however, what made this particular programme so interesting. On this occasion *Gardeners' Question Time* was being broadcast from a Devon village where the questions were just as pertinent, the answers equally apt but, for the first time in the programme's 45-year history, the gardeners in question were all children.

The experiment was a resounding success, not only because it satisfied younger listeners but because it offered a fresh perspective on perennial problems for more seasoned gardeners. Moreover, it was comforting to realise that, in a world of computer games and amazing gadgets, gardening still beckoned its bewitching green fingers to the sophisticated youngsters of the late 20th century.

THE PANEL

- **Stefan Buczacki:** Orderly and organised, his garden reflects this. Expert on how to get rid of garden pests. Won prizes for his vegetables at the village show when he was seven. Equally happy growing vegetables, fruit or flowers.

- **Clay Jones:** Current chairman of the show. Welshman with deep, rich, reassuring voice. Started showing interest in gardening when he was three. Has been with the programme 16 years. Enjoys growing vegetables.

- **Fred Downham:** Injects humour with his down to earth observations. Comes from a family of gardeners and lives in the same cottage previously inhabited by his grandfather. Avid gardener with over 300 varieties of plants and shrubs in his borders.

- **Sue Phillips:** Encouraged to take up gardening by her grandfather. Enjoys growing vegetables, although her garden is full of unusual plants and flowers as well. Depending on whether she is abroad on a lecturing tour, there are sometimes plenty of weeds to be found as well.

- **Daphne Ledward:** Has a no-nonsense approach to gardening and can still recall her pleasure when the very first seeds she ever planted started to grow. She augments her small garden with a further five acres a few miles from her home. Appears on the show on alternate weeks to Sue.

The 2,000th programme of *Gardeners' Question Time*. (From left): Clay Jones, Daphne Ledward, Fred Downham, Sue Phillips and Stefan Buczacki

show has travelled far and wide across the British Isles to share the benefit of its vast experience, visiting gardening clubs, horticultural shows, even venturing abroad to Brussels or the British Embassy in Paris.

It was yet another milestone in the show's illustrious history but, though it marked another first, it was not by far the most important event last year for the million-plus listeners who tune in every Sunday at 2pm to tussle over the latest

horticultural mind-bender. That honour went to the 2,000th edition of the show on 1 November, a special programme broadcast from London's Royal Horticultural Halls.

The experts who make up the *Gardeners' Question Time* panel might have changed over the decades, but the formula is still the same: a satisfyingly simple recipe of problems and solutions. (Some questions pop up regularly like weeds; if you didn't remember the answer the first time, by the time you have heard it for the fifth, you will have learned the solution almost by rote.)

gradually, almost organically.

It is a brilliant blueprint, a dead cert strategy. Gardening clubs and horticultural societies jostle with one another in the five-year queue to be visited on air. Then the panel

peculiar queries too. What plants are best for a grave? Is there a gardening use for a microwave oven? What plants can be grown in a telephone box?

If anything has changed, apart from the panel, it has been the effects of new technology. Amazing plant hybrids, the advent of new strains of vegetable, even the array of gadgets and gimmickry have all kept the team on their green-wellied toes.

The arrival of garden centres has had a knock-on effect as well. With well-labelled instructions telling you how and where to plant your purchase and giving advice on feeding and pruning, there is less of a need to bother the *Gardeners' Question Time* experts with such trifles. And because it is possible and economical to purchase all manner of seedlings, fewer gardeners are pricking out or sowing their own seeds, and so another skill is gradually being lost to everyone but the experts.

With 2,000-plus editions behind them and the challenge of broadcasting into the 21st century, what does the future hold for *Gardeners' Question Time?* You can bet that slugs and snails will forever continue to cause problems for gardeners but as producer Diana Stenson says, there are no plans to alter radically a well-loved format. 'Perhaps we'll be out and about at the shows a bit more,' she says. 'There's a big event at Wembley during Easter (The News International Gardening Junket) and a *Gardeners' World* live at the NEC in June, but we've always been good about visiting the garden festivals anyway.

'I'd like to repeat the success we had with the children's edition, trying to draw in different age groups. If you get them before they reach the age of 12, you know that, even if they abandon gardening in their teens when exams and social life take precedence, they'll return to it in their 20s.'

When you consider that Dr Stefan Buczacki began listening to *Gardeners' Question Time* with his father when he was a child, it's a sound philosophy indeed.

Daniela Soave

BBC Photograph Library

A gardener puts his question to the panel in a 1951 edition of *Gardeners' Question Time* held in Rochdale

Originally entitled *How Does Your Garden Grow?*, the show was inspired by the need, in the years following the war when food was still scarce, to encourage the continuing good habits learned during the Dig For Victory campaign. Though the name was changed to *Gardeners' Question Time* three years later, two of the original panellists – Fred Loads and Bill Sowerbutts – were rooted to the programme for 30 years, giving it a reassuring sense, just like seasons, of continuity. When there has been change, it has happened

sit themselves down and address the problems put before them: of slugs and snails (the most-asked question); woodlice epidemics (easy – put out half a grapefruit overnight and it will attract thousands for your disposal); how to get rid of the swamp at the bottom of the garden; which plants to choose for dry slopes or damp corners; suggestions for a new gardening toy for the husband with everything (spring loaded daisy grubber or a compost shredder seem to be safe bets) and so on.

They have had their fair share of

A FLAVOUR OF SPAIN

It was undoubtedly the year of Spain and a glut of all things Spanish was on our screens or in the news. We were given an insight into the gastronomic delights of the country, as Christopher Middleton reports, in *Floyd on Spain* and *Spain on a Plate*, as well as a taste of the life style of British ex-pats in *Coast of Dreams*

For Italy, the Renaissance started happening around 1292. Seven hundred years later, millions of television viewers witnessed on their screens the rebirth of another Latin country, Spain.

Having in recent years acquired an unwelcome stale crust around its image, made up of Benidorm lager and half-built hotels, Spain needed something big if it was to break free.

That something big was 1992. What with Barcelona staging the Olympics, Seville hosting Expo and Madrid being the European city of culture – plus the fictional Costa Eldorado welcoming the soap of the same name – Spain was scarcely out of our living rooms during the entire year.

Furthermore, with the world's media shining the spotlight full on the nation's most obvious attractions, a score of other programme-makers sought to illuminate the lesser-known corners of the country and its culture.

And on the basis that you are what you eat, exploring Spanish food and wine was as good a means as any of uncovering the national soul.

Certainly the BBC thought so. To such an extent that it produced not just one but two gastronomically-based series on Spain. They were *Floyd on Spain* and *Spain on a Plate*.

'We were sailing a bit close to the wind, I suppose', reflects Alan Rogers, head of the BBC's Continuing Education and Training Department, which made *Spain on a Plate*. 'But it had all been carefully discussed with Alan Yentob, the controller of BBC2, and we felt that two series were justified. Firstly because Spain had been so little covered in the past, and secondly

because the two series were so different – one being very much educational, the other being pretty much pure entertainment.'

And no prizes for guessing which was which. The dynamic, pan-toting, wine-quaffing Keith Floyd did not so much visit different parts of the country as descend upon them, performing his cooking 'sketches' in a variety of impromptu, outdoor and often highly public locations.

Having adopted the creed: 'To make a good gazpacho you need happy tomatoes', he proceeded to prepare a sizzling, spitting and utterly delicious-looking range of indigenous dishes for the often bewildered residents of wherever he happened to be.

Keith Floyd gives viewers a taste of Spain in his own unique style

He made beef stew for grape-pickers in a La Mancha vineyard, he made hake with potatoes and garlic for Galician monks, and he made eels in spicy tomato sauce for a group of huntsmen in the saltwater marshes of Majorca. Elsewhere he cooked seafood hotpot on a Basque fishing boat, rabbit and red peppers for a San Sebastian dining club, and gazpacho in a bucket on the seafront at Torremolinos.

'*Floyd on Spain* is the one programme I wish I could smell' wrote a TV critic after watching a particularly garlic and olive oil-filled

episode. But as well as conveying most vividly the flavours of the food and drink, Floyd also invested the seven shows with his own verbal richness. Some idea of the contrast between *Floyd on Spain* and *Spain on a Plate* can be gleaned from the different ways in which the two presenters describe Barcelona.

Floyd, the outsider, the foreign observer, calls it 'the city of Gaudi, Dali, pimps, whores, drug pushers, itinerant tango dancers, fabulous restaurants, brilliant bars – in short the whole shebang of a culturally erotic city'.

Maria José Sevilla, Spanish-born, insider and professional promoter of the country's wines and foods, sees Barcelona as 'a beautiful Mediterranean city, with a flavour of merchant shipping and adventure. It thrives on political debate, but it is also profoundly bourgeois'.

Throughout the series, Maria José Sevilla's style was not so much to descend, Floyd-like, upon chance acquaintances, as to renew acquaintance with old friends, drawing on the five years she spent travelling the length and breadth of Spain in order to learn about the different regional cuisines.

Her role was to watch fellow craftsmen and women at work: celebrated chefs from Atlantic to Mediterranean coasts, as well as everyday cooks in farmhouses and fishing villages. And on top of the food she placed careful layers of digestible, historical and cultural material, explaining how different dishes and ingredients owed their origins to different invading races. The Romans, for example, introduced irrigation – and thereby fruit and vegetables – while the Carthaginians brought chick peas, the Phoenicians brought saffron and the Moors came bearing melons, rice, almonds, spinach, figs and pomegranates.

For her cooking demonstrations, Maria José Sevilla chose not Floyd's random harbour walls and hillsides, but a kitchen which, despite its authentic Iberian appearance (right down to the Spanish plastic shopping bags), was actually located inside a TV studio in Ealing.

Nevertheless, the food ingredients were as Spanish as you can get, as

BBC Photograph Library

Maria José Sevilla in her 'Iberian kitchen', complete with Spanish plastic shopping bags, in *Spain on a Plate*

was the patient expertise with which viewers were steered through the making of traditional dishes such as *tocino de cielo* (egg and sugar dessert), *empanada de bonito* (white tuna pie) and a type of paella which involved not just chicken and rabbit but also snails.

One regional dish Señora Sevilla did not cook was roast beef and Yorkshire pudding. However, as Channel 4's two-part documentary *Coast of Dreams* revealed, this is a favourite dish in Spain, at least among the expatriate British population on the Costa del Sol.

The first of these two programmes took a close look at the Britons living in the Benalmadena area of the Costa, and featured Mike and Betti Thompson, who had left Southend in search of their own Eldorado – the manifestation of which was their Benalmadena restaurant The Bees Knees. However, the programme showed how their dream had become a nightmare, with the Thompsons having

to contend not only with sharp lawyers and corrupt policemen but also with a 16-hour day spent churning out several hundred servings of meat and two veg, in the kitchens where temperatures often reached 38 degrees centigrade.

'Alcoholism, bankruptcy and broken marriages are the realities of life for many Brits in Spain', says *Coast of Dreams* producer-director Malcolm Brinkworth. 'Unfortunately, too many people go out there with hopelessly rose-tinted spectacles.'

Nor was all rosy on the other side of the language barrier, as the second programme showed. Entitled *Paradise Lost*, it presented a variety of native Spaniards whose feelings towards the tourism monster ranged from dubiousness to hostility. They told of farmland lost to golf courses, rural areas ruined by holiday apartments, and an economy which had become dangerously dependent on the whims of foreign tour operators.

'This is a universal problem wherever big-time tourism moves in', says Malcolm Brinkworth. 'It's happened in Portugal, it's happened in Greece and it's happened in Turkey.' It's also happened in France, which is where he has been commissioned to make a follow-up to *Coast of Dreams*. The BBC's Continuing Education and Training Department is also off to France, where it is making the second series of Mireille Johnston's *A Cook's Tour*, while Keith Floyd is bound for the Far East to make *Far Flung Floyd*.

But although they and their cameras have moved on, the effects of their programmes seem set to linger on. Having had a new, improved Spain brought into their homes, many thousands of British holiday-makers are now expected to return there after an absence of several years. As a result of 1992, there should be a lot more happy tomatoes in Spain.

Christopher Middleton

HAVE I GOT NEWS FOR YOU

Rupert Smith reviews the comedy panel game, *Have I Got News For You*, which started life on the radio and has become one of the year's most popular TV programmes. Producer Harry Thompson's winning formula of a topical, satirical look at the week's events and regulars Deayton, Hislop and Merton ensure the programme's success

Television has always had a fertile, if uneasy, relationship with satire. Ever since David Frost launched the first fusillades of *That Was The Week That Was* in 1963, small screen comedy has been an effective medium for deflating pomposity and lampooning public figures, and has caused endless anxiety in the papers, in the BBC and in parliament. *Spitting Image* was a thorn in the collective side throughout the 80s; in the 90s, the torch has been passed to a panel game, the immensely popular *Have I Got News For You*, which completed its fourth series at the end of 1992.

Like many currently successful series, *Have I Got News For You* has its roots in radio. Producer Harry Thompson started work on Radio 4's *The News Quiz* at the end of 1985 and was instrumental in shaping that show and bringing it to television. 'The News Quiz used to be a rather straight-faced quiz for journalists who could come on and show off their knowledge of current affairs,' says Thompson. 'I came along as producer when Barry Took took over the chair, and we decided that there should be at least one funny person on each team every week. Alan Coren and Richard Ingrams became the regular team captains, and the whole thing became much more entertaining and much more satirical, a sort of radio *Private Eye*.'

With the format and attitude thus established, there was a general enthusiasm in the BBC towards the idea of bringing *The News Quiz* on to television. 'There were about four abortive attempts to turn it into a TV show,' says Thompson. 'I saw one of the pilots and it was absolutely

disastrous, completely unbroadcastable, but it did have one thing in its favour: Jimmy Mulville was one of the panellists.' Mulville's involvement in this debacle was fortunate: with his wife, Denise O'Donoghue, he had formed an independent production company, Hat Trick Productions, which was busily turning out shows like *Whose Line Is It Anyway* and *Drop the Dead Donkey*. 'Hat Trick decided that they'd be the ones to take *The News Quiz* to television,' says Thompson, 'and that was precisely what they did.'

Hat Trick's first port of call was *Private Eye* editor Ian Hislop, a regular guest on *The News Quiz* who was recruited as a team captain; his opponent, Paul Merton, had risen through the Hat Trick ranks as a popular panellist on

(Left): Angus Deayton, Paul Merton and Ian Hislop of *Have I Got News For You*

Whose Line Is It Anyway. A pilot was made and sold to the BBC, after which Hislop suggested that Thompson be brought in as series producer. 'By this time I'd risen to the dizzy heights of script editor for radio comedy,' says Thompson, 'and I was reluctant to give up a good, steady job at the BBC to work on a ten-week series which, for anything I knew to the contrary, could flop and land me on the dole at the end of it. But I pitched in nonetheless, and the first thing I did was hold auditions for a new presenter. Angus Deayton turned up and we gave him the job; he was perfect.'

In 1990, the first series of *Have I Got News For You* attracted little media attention, but Thompson and company knew that the formula would work. 'We realised that we had good people and that we could

push the limits of what was acceptable on a topical quiz show,' he says. 'From then on it was just a question of waiting for people to get used to the idea of *The News Quiz* as a visual thing rather than a radio show. It didn't take long for the public to catch up.' Professional plaudits were slower to come, possibly because of the awkwardness that arose from Hat Trick effectively selling back to the BBC one of the Corporation's own products. 'There's a lot of frustration generated by this kind of situation,' says Thompson.

'Successful radio programmes like *After Henry, Second Thoughts* and *Up the Garden Path* have a way of slipping away to independent production companies or on to ITV, although in theory the easiest transition would be straight from BBC radio to BBC TV. It doesn't quite work that way, though. Radio comedy producers tend to be people who know about comedy first and who learn about production as they go on. Television comedy producers go through all the production training and then start working on comedy, so understandably they don't want a load of upstarts from radio muscling in on their livelihood. As a result there isn't as much co-operation as there should be, which means that radio comedy producers fly off to the independents, and the BBC controllers get frustrated. Hat Trick is a good case in point; nearly all the producers there have come from radio.'

Successive series of *Have I Got News For You* won ever greater critical approval, and celebrity guests began to beat a path to Thompson's door. By now, the formula is honed to razor sharpness; Thompson, Hislop, Merton and Deayton have established a chemistry that leaves guests gasping. Topicality is the key to their success; no sooner has a story broken in the papers, it seems, than the *Have I Got News For You* team is revelling in its absurdities on a Friday night. 'We have a well established weekly routine that basically knackers us when the show is running. On a Monday I sit down with the researchers and read all the Sunday and Monday papers and get a rough idea of what's going in that week's show. Then on Tuesday I get together with Angus to write his script, all the jokes that he can use if nobody else is being funny. On Wednesday we throw out half the stories because they're either not funny enough or they've become stale, and we prepare the bits of film that are going to be used. Thursday is for rewrites, then we record and edit on Friday. My working day starts as soon as I get out of bed and often doesn't finish until two in the morning.'

The only chance ingredient in each week's programme is the combination of guests; Thompson is the first to admit that some are funny and some are not. 'We have very little control over who we're going to get in a given week. We try to achieve a mixture of politicians, journalists and showbiz people, all of whom are extremely busy and difficult to pin down. MPs are particularly tricky; they have to cancel a lot. But we pursue them, because they seem to have a natural aptitude for the show. I love it when we get a big figure like Cecil Parkinson or Neil Kinnock to come on and they turn out to be really funny, I think it's a relief to them to be able to have a bit of a swipe at their colleagues. They relish it.'

Having a bit of a swipe can, of course, get a fellow into trouble. *Have I Got News For You* has to sail close to the legal wind if it is to retain its teeth, but neither the BBC nor Hat Trick Productions can afford regular libel suits. 'There are lawyers involved at every stage of the proceedings,' says Thompson, whose radio experience apprised him of the legal delicacy of satirical

comedy. 'Sometimes I get the impression that if I go to the toilet, a lawyer's going to pop round the S-bend and say "you can't do that!". But we can't work without them. Basically we're indemnified if the material's been cleared by a BBC lawyer. If, however, the BBC's lawyer said that we couldn't say something and we went ahead and said it and got sued, Hat Trick would be liable. Hat Trick's a small company and couldn't sustain that kind of financial problem, so we have to be careful on occasion. We've never been sued to date, touch wood, but we have regular fights with lawyers to bring them round to our point of view.'

One memorable fight concerned comments that were made about Imelda Marcos. 'We got involved in top-level discussions about whether Mrs Marcos was likely to sue us,' says Thompson. 'In the end, you have to accept that the law is not concerned with absolute right and wrong but with questions of likelihood. We were making allegations about Imelda Marcos that might have upset her, but it was highly unlikely that she was going to say "I must get hold of a tape of that well-known British comedy show *Have I Got News For You*, I hear they said such-and-such about me," then get someone to send the video over to the Philippines, file her libel suit and arrange to appear in a court in Uxbridge or wherever while she's got an election campaign to fight at home. So we went ahead and said what we were going to say, and of course we didn't hear a peep from Imelda.'

As *Have I Got News For You* looks forward to its fifth series in April 1993, it has become part of the curious British tradition that licenses satirical attacks on the figures and institutions it holds most dear. 'I don't see any reason why the show shouldn't go on and on,' says Thompson. 'I suppose one day the personnel will change, but we're all happy with the way it works at the moment and we all get immense satisfaction from getting away with it. It's exhilarating, and as long as it continues to feel that way, we'll be happy to keep knocking it out.'

Rupert Smith

BENNY HILL AND FRANKIE HOWERD

With uncanny timing, these two elder statesmen of British comedy died on consecutive days over the Easter weekend of 1992. Benny Hill died on 18 April, aged 68; Frankie Howerd followed a day later, just over a month after his 70th birthday. The obituaries were fulsome in their praise and eager to acknowledge both men as 'greats', yet neither Hill nor Howerd had enjoyed consistent support and popularity throughout their careers.

Benny Hill was one of the first stars of British television, a variety artist who had found his home on the relatively new medium in the early 50s. By 1955 he had his own show on the BBC, demonstrating in

Benny Hill

full for the first time the range of his visual and verbal inventiveness as well as his taste for sexual innuendo. Constantly straining against the strictures of the BBC, Hill eventually transferred his show to Thames Television in 1969 and embarked on the most successful phase of his career. In the spirit of the age, Hill's humour became less suggestive, more 'permissive', his shows full of half-naked women ('Hill's Angels') and risque jokes. At home he had a number one pop record in 1971 with *Ernie*, and his popularity abroad, particularly in the USA, soared when Thames sold edited versions of the show to foreign markets.

By the 80s, however, Hill's star was on the wane. Unloved by the new generation of 'alternative' comedians, who singled him out as

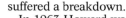

Rex Features

Double-take – Benny Hill as the bungling Fred Scuttle

suffered a breakdown.

In 1963 Howerd was tempted out of semi-retirement by Peter Cook, who put him on at the Establishment Club; regular spots on TV's *That Was The Week That Was* and a starring role in the movie *A Funny Thing Happened on the Way to the Forum* re-established him at the top of his profession. Further films followed, and in 1971 Howerd created the role he is best remembered for, the slave Lurcio in BBC TV's *Up Pompeii!*, which maintained his popularity throughout the 70s. The 80s saw Howerd, like

a representative of all that was culpably sexist in British humour, he was dropped by Thames and spent the last years of his life awaiting the comeback which occurred shortly before his death. Hill never accepted or understood the sexist tag, and to a great extent it was inappropriate; he was simply out of kilter with his times.

Frankie Howerd had gone in and out of favour many times during the course of his long career, and was

'rediscovered' on average every five years. Unlike Hill, who revelled in disguise and character acting, Howerd's stock-in-trade was his singular personality which he developed throughout many media. After the War, he became a radio star on *Variety Bandbox*, and in 1948 was topping the bill at the London Palladium. In the 50s he spread his wings in films and plays, but at the end of that decade the backlash began, and Howerd

BBC Photograph Library

Frankie Howerd in one of the most successful programmes of the 70s, BBC TV's *Up Pompeii!*

Frankie Howerd

BBC Photograph Library

Benny Hill, out of favour, but by the end of that decade he was being rediscovered again as a comic classic. His one-man show, which he had toured round the variety circuit for years, enjoyed a huge success in the West End, and at the time of his death he was about to start work on *Carry On Columbus*, which would have been his fourth *Carry On* film.

Benny Hill:
    21 January 1924 - 18 April 1992

Frankie Howerd:
    6 March 1922 - 19 April 1992

Documentary

Documentary films on such diverse subjects as fashion, natural history, science, and the arts have fascinated and informed TV audiences throughout the year.

Two 35th anniversaries took place. The BBC Natural History Unit celebrated 35 years, as did television's longest-running programme, *The Sky at Night.* And *Omnibus,* BBC1's flagship arts series, at ten years younger, celebrated 25 years.

One of the most moving documentaries of the year was *QED's Simon's Return,* showing Simon Weston back in The Falklands to meet the Argentine airman whose bombing raid was responsible for his horrific injuries.

The chapter opens with a feature by Alan Hamilton on the year's most unique documentary programme – Edward Mirzoeff's memorable *Elizabeth R,* which gave an unprecedented insight into the life of the Queen, in the year which marked the 40th anniversary of her accession to the throne.

Documentary

ELIZABETH R – A CELEBRATION OF HER MAJESTY'S 40-YEAR REIGN

The documentary *Elizabeth R*, shown for the first time in February 1992, presents a unique insight into the monarchy. Alan Hamilton, royal correspondent of *The Times*, reports on this remarkable behind the scenes look at a year in the Queen's working life

So you thought the Queen was remote and regal, unsmiling and weighed down with the twin cares of occupying the throne of the world's leading constitutional monarchy and the centre stage of the world's classiest real-life soap opera? Even a mite glum and glassy-eyed, perhaps, as she conducts her endless round of investitures and official openings, state visits and rain-soaked garden parties? Viewers of BBC1's documentary, *Elizabeth R*, will have changed their opinion for ever.

Remember the scene at the Derby, where she is watching the race on television in a room behind the Royal Box, anxiously following the progress of Generous, the horse she has drawn in the family sweepstake. The tension is electric. 'Look, it's on the wrong leg; no wonder it can't go round the corner,' she cries in alarm. 'Piggott's on the rail.'

Suddenly, the strain becomes too much. Binoculars in hand, coat tails flying in most unregal fashion, she dashes out to the balcony to watch the finish. Generous, in spite of the trouble at the corner, has done it. 'That's my horse!' exclaims the Queen, almost jumping up and down with joy. 'I've won the

sweep!' There is a look of sheer beaming delight on the face of the woman reputed to be the world's wealthiest as she collects her winnings – all £16 of them.

What *Elizabeth R* shows almost more than anything else is that its star laughs a great deal, even at the grandest of public occasions. Another time, in Washington, she is

preparing to become the first British monarch to address both houses of the United States Congress. She is disconcerted by the disaster of the previous day when, at a mere 5ft 4in, she had to make a speech from a podium designed for tall Texan George Bush; her face entirely obscured by microphones, she appeared to the worldwide televi-

On tour in Australia, 1992

Rex Features

The Royal Family and Television

Since *Royal Family* shown in 1969, various members of the Windsor clan have been sharpening their skills as television presenters, performers and interviewees, never mind being the subject of documentaries.

Princess Anne, for instance, has been interviewed by Brian Walden, has appeared on Wogan twice and even taken part in the BBC television quiz *A Question of Sport*.

The Prince and Princess of Wales were subjects of a fly-on-the-wall documentary, *In Private, In Public* in 1986, while Prince Charles, since the televising of his Investiture as the Prince of Wales, has lent his weight to many causes, including *One World*, *The Royal Collection* and *Royal Gardens*. He has even been interviewed by Selina Scott.

The Duke of Edinburgh has been interviewed in his capacity as president of the WWF and in 1987 made an introduction to an edition of *Songs of Praise*.

The younger members of the Royal Family – including the Duke and Duchess of York and Prince Edward – appeared on *It's A Royal Knockout*, an event which some feel is best forgotten.

Daniela Soave

---

sion audience as a talking purple hat.

Sir Robert Fellowes, her urbane private secretary, assures her that this time the podium has been custom-built for her. They enter the chamber to a standing ovation; she mounts the podium, glances round and announces, very deadpan: 'I do hope you can see me today from where you are'. Collapse of Congress; not even Tommy Cooper could have so adeptly won over an audience with his opening line.

Elizabeth R is the most ambitious documentary to have been made on the Queen's life for 23 years. In 1969 a BBC-ITV consortium made *Royal Family*, directed by the late Richard Cawston. It attracted a worldwide audience of 200 million, and is chiefly remembered for the scene of the Duke of Edinburgh cooking sausages on a barbecue at Balmoral.

There was, in the 60s, a perceived Royal Image problem. Monarchy was felt to be in danger of becoming remote from, and irrelevant to, that swinging era of Vietnam and student riots in Europe. To survive, monarchy must be seen.

If the Royal Family has an image problem today, it is an entirely different one. For the last ten years media coverage has concentrated on the Prince and Princess of Wales and the Duke and Duchess of York, and much of that has been concerned with their private lives. In this cascade of media attention it would be easy for the principal character to be relegated to a supporting role, and the reason for her being there at all forgotten. Which is where *Elizabeth R* comes in.

This is very much a film of the Queen's working life. It addresses the question: what does a constitutional monarch in the late 20th century actually do? It is not a film about the Queen's family, or her horses or dogs – although inevitably all make their occasional appearances.

A proposal from Will Wyatt, managing director of BBC Television, to examine a year of the Queen at her job, was accepted by

The Queen at the State Opening of Parliament

Rex Features

the Palace as a fitting way to mark the 40th anniversary of her accession. Discreet discussions were held. Directors were interviewed. The Queen herself gave her approval and signalled her full co-operation. But both sides stress that the Palace has exercised no control whatsoever over the final production. The film belongs entirely to its producer and director, Edward Mirzoeff.

Mirzoeff is a veteran BBC documentary film-maker, a master of the fly-on-the-wall technique whose office wall is not big enough to hang his collection of BAFTAs and other awards. He is probably best known for *Metro-land*, with the late Sir John Betjeman. But he has no idea why he was chosen for what was his biggest challenge.

'It may be because I have some experience in making films about institutions,' he says. 'I have done Westminster School, Scotland Yard, the Ritz and the Royal Green Jackets. It's all about access, and trust, to get inside what is essentially a closed community.'

He was granted unprecedented access, and, to help build trust, he was fortunate to have in his crew two veterans of *Royal Family*, cameraman Philip Bonham-Carter and sound recordist Peter Edwards – both experts at detecting that almost imperceptible glance from their subject indicating that it was time to stop filming.

Mirzoeff is discreetly non-committal on whether there were any areas from which his camera was barred, but says he was able to do almost everything he set out to do. His greatest triumph was to film part of John Major's audience with the Queen. We see Major, hotfoot to Balmoral from Moscow and Peking, reporting on the imminent collapse of the Soviet Union.

While proud of his exclusive footage, Mirzoeff recognises a dilemma: 'Mystique is what matters most to the Royal Family. If they don't have it, what have they got? The hardest part about making this film was pushing the frontiers back slightly, which is acceptable, without destroying the mystique, which is unacceptable.'

For a year, the crew followed the Queen about her business, beginning in October 1990 with the state visit to Britain of the president of Italy. We open with the exchange of official gifts. She gives him two pieces of porcelain, two books and a carriage clock for his wife. He gives her a piece of modern Italian sculpture.

The camera moves below stairs. We see some of the 345 permanent staff employed at Buckingham Palace going about their daily business, whether it be preparing a state banquet or running a vacuum cleaner down the seemingly endless red-carpeted corridors before an investiture.

Later, we are upstairs amid the glamour again to witness the Queen throwing a party for John Major and the other world leaders attending last year's G7 economic summit. What we don't see is Mirzoeff's most embarrassing moment of the entire shooting schedule. 'I was walking backwards with the crew, tracking away from the Queen, when I accidentally stood on someone's toe. I turned round to discover, to my horror, that it was President Bush's toe. He said "How are you doing?" I think I just smiled wanly and moved away as fast as possible.'

One of the most intriguing moments was when the crew were told to be on standby to fly with the Queen to a mysterious and unusual destination. They laid bets among themselves as to where it might be. An oil rig perhaps, or a family picnic? But what it turned out to be was the Queen's first visit to Northern Ireland since her Silver Jubilee in 1977. Security considerations dictated that they did not learn of their destination until ten minutes before take-off.

Filming ended last October with a trip to Zimbabwe where the Queen, assuming her alternative role as Head of the Commonwealth, visited the Commonwealth Heads of Government meeting in Harare. We see her talking to Nelson Mandela (only an observer at the conference, as South Africa left the Commonwealth in 1961). And what are they talking about? Why, *cricket*.

he was after all Leader of Her Majesty's *Loyal* Opposition. And is this not George Carey, Archbishop of Canterbury, come to do homage to the supreme Governor of the Church of England? It is, but we see only a snatch; the audience is even more private than that with the Prime Minister.

Watching her sitting at her desk, ploughing through her red boxes of government papers, and her mail, we learn one encouraging fact. Not all the hundreds of letters are dealt with by secretaries; a good many are read by the person to whom they

On a 1992 tour of France with the Duke of Edinburgh

Rex Features

But the royal round is not all exotic travel and pow-wows with other big chiefs. In fact, most of the film is set within these shores, whether she is visiting her subjects, poring over papers and answering letters at her Buckingham Palace desk, or entertaining at Balmoral.

Indeed, there are another two familiar faces laughing merrily with her during an after-dinner tour of the royal library – and why not? There is no reason why Neil and Glenys Kinnock shouldn't be there;

were addressed. They are acted upon if there is any chance of the sovereign unsticking a blocked bureaucratic channel. The monarch must not only be seen; the monarch must be accessible.

What we see is a woman with four distinct jobs. She is Head of State, requiring her to open Parliament, give Royal Assent to the bills it passes, visit and receive other heads of state, be seen as the figurehead of her armed services, and bestow honours. She is Head of the established Church of England. At the same time she is the figurehead of the nation. That means a heavy programme of meeting her subjects, formally and informally. And she is Head of the Commonwealth, a position she more or less invented and which she passionately believes in.

But we can read her job description in books. What Elizabeth R conveys is rather more; it is a feeling of the person herself. Having been at her shoulder for nearly 13 months, Mirzoeff is in a good position to judge his subject. 'My overall impression was that here was a great deal more relaxation and humour than the public has been led to believe. In the news coverage of public events like Trooping the Colour, we tend to see the solemn moments, because public ceremonial requires solemnity. But there is another side to her. She has a huge sense of humour; you would need one to do the job she is doing. She has a dry, sharp wit and a great talent for putting people at their ease. She is an immensely likeable woman.'

So, if this is a film about the Queen's working life, what are we doing at the Derby? 'In a sense she is working there,' says Mirzoeff. 'After all, she is a professional race-horse breeder, and besides it is all part of being seen by her subjects. But in truth, a film that was all work and no play would be a dull film indeed.' There are other personal moments, as when the whole family is posing for a photograph at Sandringham after the christening of Princess Eugenie, and a recalcitrant Prince Harry has to be collared by his regal grandmother and held firmly in place.

The Queen saw the finished version, edited from over 36 hours of film, only two days before transmission. The final result is an enlightening and appealing portrait of a woman who, at the age of 65 and 40 years into the job, is still at the height of her powers. The pictures tell the story. Observant viewers will have detected the interesting change in the Queen's hair colour over the year. It looks so much better now.

Alan Hamilton

SIMON'S LAST BATTLE

Ten years after the invasion of the Falklands, Simon Weston meets the Argentine airman responsible for bombing the *Sir Galahad*. By Brian James

Simon Weston remembers very little about the moment when he confronted the man responsible for setting fire to his face. But he advised the millions who witnessed the scene on Wednesday, 1 April on BBC1's *QED* to 'watch closely. You will see a ghost being laid'.

Weston is, of course, the young Welsh Guardsman who was appallingly damaged and yet whose

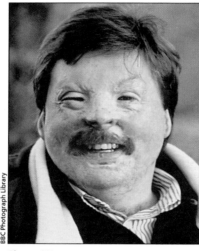

Simon Weston

courage was totally undiminished when the ship he was on was bombed in the Falklands War. He and others were set alight, and 51 of his comrades died on the *Sir Galahad*. No one could have been more visibly marked. It took 39 operations, ten years of at first unimaginable pain, and the unquenchable fortitude to make him a face, remodel his hands and rewrite his mind. Through three *QED* films on BBC1 a nation has ached for his ordeal – and become more proud of his triumph in peace than of its own in war.

On the eve of the tenth anniversary of the Argentine invasion, *QED* followed Weston back to the Falklands, to Argentina and to that meeting with ex-Lieutenant Carlos

Cachon, the Argentine pilot who bombed the *Sir Galahad*. How could he bear to go back? After all, his description of a 'personal Hiroshima...men were shadows, silhouettes with brilliant whole-body haloes of the most beautiful colours I had ever seen', of hearing burning comrades shoot themselves, of seeing one man reach with his bayonet to try to prise his own back off the bulkhead to which the blast had sealed him, remains as horrific a portrait of war as any ever written.

Yet he agreed to return with two other Falkland warriors, Sergeant John Meredith of 2 Para and Colour-Sergeant Gary Tytler of the Scots Guards, to re-visit their battlegrounds. 'I couldn't bear not to go back. Meeting this guy was something that had been waiting to happen since a few seconds after his bomb burst. The idea didn't come out of the air – I had given it an immense amount of thought. I hadn't always known his name – but for ten years Carlos Cachon was the one man in all the world I had most wanted to face.'

To get your hands on, you mean? 'No. No, no. I wasn't angry, bitter, vengeful. Had he done to my family what he had done to me, then yes. But I felt no personal animosity. He had been a professional, doing his job. My face, the bodies of 51 mates on the sea bottom, were testimony to how damn well he had done that job. Not many people get to see their would-be executioner. I wanted to look into his eyes, see if there was a human inside.

'For ten years something deep had been bothering me. Nagging at my mind. In a split second my life was changed. A flash, literally, and I was a different man. How? Why? What, exactly? Hard to explain, but something about the suddenness bugged me...I needed to know more about that moment.

'I didn't know what haunted me. My family, those closest, knew that some bogey was there. Perhaps it was this chap, the man who did it. Perhaps I needed to find him to find myself. There would be no peace. Whatever the doctors had done, my family could do, I was never going to be 100 per cent right until – well,

I didn't know what.

'I used to think about those guys in America, ex-Vietnam vets who got up one day, took a gun down to the local McDonald's and slaughtered a dozen strangers: was this something that they had suffered? Don't suggest I was going that way – I was never in a state to take an axe and slash the heads off the neighbours' goldfish, let alone the neighbours.

'But this insecurity, uncertainty, not knowing and needing to find out, haunted me. In that mood lots turn to religion, to solitude, lose themselves in music. I was luckier – I had this chance of a journey of self-discovery.'

The moment of meeting must have been unbearable. 'Waiting for it was. I was terrified. I did not know how I would react, what I was going to say. Or do.' You weren't going to hit him? Weston is not so sure. He actually tells the film crew, 'Stop filming if I lamp him upside the head with a bottle...' To me he adds, 'If he had said the wrong thing, about my mates he'd killed, or been arrogant...who knows? But then this man who had been haunting me came in. Small. Polite. Inoffensive. I can't tell you what I said. What he said. Even how long we were together. It

seemed like no more than a flash. Oh yes, one thing comes back: he said, "How could anyone as nice as you have been aboard that ship?" Odd.'

Perhaps he thought all British troops were baby-chewing barbarians? 'Don't think so. I think he was just realising that his professional, impersonal war inflicted death and injury on real, breathing people. Not an easy thing for any serviceman to confront. I think he was shaken by my looks. He knew who he was going to meet, seen pictures perhaps, but then...there I was.'

How did you feel? 'At the meeting? Don't know. But I know on the film the emotion gets across. But afterwards, next day, I felt better than for many years. Describe it? I can't. Relief, I suppose. Anyone who has ever dreaded an interview will have a clue – multiply that a million times. I felt like I had been standing outside the headmaster's study for ten years – now it was over, and no whacking.

'I know that meeting laid a ghost. I now know that Carlos Cachon was not the answer. Because the problem was me. Accepting that is the start of the cure.'

There will be controversy over

what happened next. The two men embrace. 'I didn't relish that. Up in these valleys men don't cuddle each other. You and I are talking well, but I would be horrified at a cuddle. So would you. Outside our culture. I did not resent him doing it. I resent other people criticising the moment.

'I don't think I was letting down my dead mates when that happened. They were all man enough to know wars are fought hard, but one day have to be forgotten. Old enemies from the First and Second World Wars meet and shake hands. So what's the time limit for forgiving, for men to make peace for themselves? Maybe it's hard for governments to be reconciled – but not for men, especially fighting men.

'It felt right for me at that minute to take his hand. It felt right for him to embrace. Fine. I am not about to apologise to anyone for doing so.'

Simon Weston and Carlos Cachon met twice more on this trip; the former with some reluctance. 'He seemed to want to keep this going. Wanted me to go home, meet his wife. No. Our film people were keen to keep their cameras turning. I am not criticising any of them for this. It was just we were all get-

Simon Weston meets the Argentine airman whose bombing raid on the *Sir Galahad* resulted in Weston's horrific injuries

ting something different from the meeting.

'For me, I was happy to meet him once. It was enough: I do not need him as a friend – the purpose was achieved. I came home more at peace with myself – with as much peace as I shall ever know. I came home to face the worries we all have, about work, family, mortgage. But for me to have those worries, and only those, is luxury.'

The life that Simon Weston lives now with only 'normal' headaches is centred on a sparkling house, all blue and cream and filled with the chuckles of his wife Lucy and their eight-month-old son James Andrew (named after two of the comrades who helped pull him from the *Sir Galahad's* flames), high above one of Wales's re-greening valleys.

He is back only a mile or so from where he was born, after three years in Liverpool working for Weston Spirit, the charitable venture he helped set up to 'get youngsters from areas where apathy is a killing disease up off their backsides to discover what they are made of'. He had to leave Wales to find out what he himself was made of: 'I was cocooned here, kept safe by the love of my family, the concern of my neighbours. Smothered in love. But it was a life without risk, without a gamble. And that is not a real life.'

Weston Spirit was successful (more than 1,000 youngsters have been helped by leadership and self-reliance courses, and there are now branches in Cardiff, Newcastle and, after Heysel, Turin), but Weston decided to return to Wales. 'I loved Liverpool folk. People go on about their sense of humour, as though all the city has is a bunch of comics. What about caring, their way of looking out for each other? People are as close as they are in pit villages.'

The attraction was another challenge for the man who, despite crippled hands, learned to fly a light aircraft and drive racing cars: Simon Weston was offered a Saturday programme on Radio Wales. 'I drivel on about what takes my fancy. But I also meet and interview my own heroes, people I most admire.'

Like? 'Terry Wogan. Because he is so true to his craft. And Gary Lineker. He was already up there for me, doing his job like a genius, never whining, a real ambassador for his club, his country, his game. Then this thing with his baby – you have to admire a man who sets out to make something positive from a tragedy like that, don't you?' How true.

His show, giving talks and fund-raising for the Star and Garter ex-servicemen's charity fill his days. 'Yes, I said I'd be happy to fade away and run a corner shop. But the public, who have given me so much, haven't tired of having me try to tell others that getting broken up doesn't mean gloom and doom. So while I can still wring a bit of good out of what happened to me...'

There are still moments of pain, as when girls in a passing car look across and pull 'ugh' faces at him. 'Still happens. And I feel it. But the hurt is worse for my family. Kids are cruel. We already know what young James is going to face – "Oi, your dad's ugly" – in school. My job will be to help him understand and teach him to help those who can't take how I look.'

Simon Weston is a product of war's alchemy. An elemental youngster ('face it, at 20 I was bare average – more than a bit of a waster'), he was heated in fire, brutally hammered and transformed into an articulate and assured man, possessor of properties that glint, and inspire.

Brian James

DOCUMENTARY FILMS

Anne-Marie Sapsted reviews a selection of some of the most memorable documentaries shown in 1992

Reports of the demise of the British documentary have been seriously exaggerated. So says Paul Hamann, BBC's head of documentaries, whose view is that documentary-making right across the television spectrum has never been better.

'We are fantastically well-served at the moment in this country,' he says. 'There is a terrific richness about Channel 4 and most of the ITV companies as well as the BBC, and the people who benefit are the public. Every time I go out of this country, people tell me that British documentaries are the best. And you only have to watch American, Australian or other films to know that it is true. But there is still a considerable amount of rubbish in the broadcasting press about documentary-making in this country being in crisis. It's nonsense.'

One of his favourite films, and one which broke all records for viewing figures, was the two-hour long *Elizabeth R*. First shown at the beginning of the year, shown again on ITV in the summer – all such royal films are shared in this way – the documentary attracted almost 18 million viewers, the highest ever for a documentary since statistics were first collected.

'It took several years to pull that off,' says Hamann. 'And what we all discovered when we got there was this highly intelligent, witty, charismatic woman. And the Queen herself said that it was one of the few nice things to happen to her last year.'

One series which attracted a lot of attention was *Town Hall* an eight-part, fly-on-the-wall look at local government. Made by respected film-makers Charles Stewart and Malcolm Hirst, about the workings of Labour-controlled Lewisham Council in London, the series proved to be compulsive viewing for politicians of all political shades.

'This was documentary-making at its best,' says Hamann. 'MPs from all parties said that this was real politics which affected everyone. The films were an examination of a British institution in the same tradition as *No 10*, *Strangeways* and *Ark Royal*.

Documentaries he particularly admires on the other channels include the *First Tuesday* film on the Siamese twins. 'It was an obvious one to make, but they did it brilliantly,' says Hamann. 'Any film-maker would have been proud to have done that.' He also liked Channel 4's *Cutting Edge* series.

BBC1's award-winning *Inside Story* series returned with six fascinating stories. *In Cold Blood*

Inside Story: In Cold Blood

journeyed back to the Malayan Jungle, where in 1948 Scots Guards shot dead 24 people described as terrorists in what was said at the time to be one of the most successful British operations of the Malayan campaign. The programme makers had obtained new evidence which suggested that the operation had, in fact, been a massacre of innocent civilians, concealed for more than 40 years. The film took three of the Guardsmen back and produced a harrowing but moving film.

Another in the series was *The Women Trade* where the team went undercover to expose an international gang at the centre of a cruel sex-trade involving women from the Third World and Eastern Europe being recruited and promised jobs as dancers in affluent Europe. The film broke the silence kept by so many women in fear of shame, debt and reprisals, who told how they had been tricked and trapped into work as strippers and prostitutes.

Why people are driven to a life of homelessness on the streets was examined through the eyes of 'Bag Lady' Maggie, a 42-year-old alcoholic. The team had tracked down her family and former work colleagues and found that her past held several surprises, including a job as a social worker.

Other fascinating stories including *The Assassin,* the story of a small-town American boy who joined Pinochet's secret police in Chile, one of the world's most feared organisations whose tools were torture and murder. In the words of the FBI, he was 'the perfect assassin – a man who is so blindly terrifyingly obedient he would kill anyone, anywhere, without hesitation'. Under conditions of tight security he agreed to tell his story for the first time to producer Christopher Olgiati.

Mules travelled to Nigeria to find out what compels women to embark on the dangerous mission of smuggling drugs into the UK. This was the story behind the sad statistics that one in every five women in prison in Britain today is a Nigerian drug smuggler. Closer to home, *Undertakers* entered another forbidden zone to examine the English way of death. This was another collaboration between Charles Stewart and Malcolm Hirst who went behind the scenes to find out exactly what happens in the morgue and the crematorium.

One of the most popular series this year was *Pole to Pole* with Michael Palin putting on his travelling shoes again and following the line of longitude of 30 degrees east from north to south, overland wherever humanly possible. The team crossed 17 countries, including parts of Scandinavia, Russia, the Middle East, the whole of Africa, and half of Antarctica. They also witnessed history in the making, squeezing out of the Soviet Union two days before the momentous coup against Gorbachev, crossing Ethiopia just weeks after the end of the 30-year civil war and entering Zambia on the day Kenneth Kaunda was toppled.

The journey lasted more than five months, covered 23,000 miles and transport included snowmobile, icebreaker, train, river-barge, desert-bus, bicycle, dug-out canoe, balloon, the oldest lake-steamer still afloat and the world's most luxurious train, along with a vast assortment of trucks. There were also extreme temperatures, ranging from 50 degrees below freezing in Antarctica to the searing heat of Africa.

Present Imperfect returned to BBC2 for a nine-part series chronicling the ups and downs of a year in the life of some fascinating individuals. From a fading 60s star trying to rekindle her past triumphs to a group of school leavers looking for success, to two recruiting evangelists and a dedicated foster couple, the nine programmes offered a snapshot of the changes in society affecting us all.

With perfect timing, the master of showbiz public relations, Max Clifford,

Michael Palin aboard the Nile Valley express from Wadi Halfa to Khartoum in *Pole to Pole*

Present Imperfect: Can I Call You Mum

allowed the cameras in to watch him at work. The man who successfully handled the controversy surrounding figures like Pamella Bordes and Derek Hatton was filmed guiding Sheri Stewart as she told the world of her affair with Hollywood star Kevin Costner.

In sharp contrast, another film looked at the demise of that British institution The Transport Cafe, an acknowledged favourite of Prime Minister John Major. Another film followed the fortunes of Ealing Hospital in west London as it embarked on the process of applying for Trust status.

Another BBC2 series which provided fascinating viewing and achieved respectable viewing figures was *Pandora's Box* written and produced by Adam Curtis, who set out to show how the age of science failed to live up to post-war expectations. The series told six stories from America, Britain and Russia, tracing what happened to the dream of building a better world through the power of science. It was a cultural history making use of archive footage, old cartoons and even home movies.

Though we live in a world full of the benefits of science and technology there is widespread distrust of it. *Pandora's Box* showed that it was not science which had failed the people, rather the people and politicians who had expected too much of science.

A major biography of Winston Churchill was shown on BBC1 early in the year to much critical acclaim. This, the first complete television biography of Churchill, covered in detail the major events and turning points in his amazing career and provided new material about Churchill the man, with rare insights into his character and private life. Many of his personal staff who had never before been interviewed agreed to take part, including his secretary, Phyllis Moir Forbes, now in her 90s. 'He was the most inconsiderate man I ever met,' she said. 'I soon realised I was no more to him than a fountain pen that required no time to eat or rest.'

With other secretaries she revealed how close he and his wife Clementine were and how much he valued her opinion and yet they never shared a bedroom. Churchill went to her by written invitation only. Barbara Castle and Lord Hailsham explained how Churchill became the only leader Britain could turn to in 1940 and his daughter-in-law, Pamela Harriman, revealed the depth of his personal anguish and suffering during the war at what Britain and its people had to undergo.

The research team even managed to discover Churchill's so-called 'Naughty Document'– thought to have been destroyed – on which he had written the countries of Central and Southern Europe and divided them into spheres of influence. According to Stalin's interpreter, Churchill pushed the paper across the table to Stalin during a meeting in Moscow in 1944 and said: 'Maybe we should destroy this paper because people will afterwards think how easily we decided – and cynically decided – the fate of millions of people.'

Two other BBC documentary series which proved popular during the year looked at different aspects of sport. In the year of the Barcelona Olympics, *More than a Game* looked at the pressures on top sports people. BBC1's eight part series covered issues such as the losing battle against amateur status, drug abuse, how big business has increasingly taken control of sport, the lack of sportsmanship at all levels and the lack of resources for 'sport for all'.

The world of both rugby league and rugby union was revealed in the series *Up and Under*

More than a Game – the documentary series which looked at different aspects of sport

Contributors included athletes Sebastian Coe and Carl Lewis, golfers Tony Jacklin and Jack Nicklaus, football heroes Gary Lineker and Franz Beckenbauer and legendary rugby player JPR Williams.

Rugby in all its forms was the focus of *Up and Under* for which a BBC2 team went behind the scenes to follow the 1991/2 season for two of rugby's most successful clubs.

Only four miles separate Lancashire clubs Wigan and Orrell, but they are divided by the gulf between professional rugby league and rugby union. Mixed with on-the-field action, the series also looked at boardroom dilemmas, the drive for fitness by the players and the home lives of the men who dedicate themselves to the game.

There is no animosity between the two teams who regularly see each other socially, though they are banned from playing against each other under rules formulated in 1895 when the split in rugby occurred. There was a sharp contrast between Wigan's fifth successive victory in the Challenge Cup final, accompanied by substantial bonuses for the players and Orrell's first ever bid for the Rugby Union League Championship. Their prize could only ever be the glory and the chance to contribute to the beer pot.

Anne-Marie Sapsted

35 YEARS OF THE BBC'S NATURAL HISTORY UNIT

The BBC's Natural History Unit has produced some of the most remarkable wildlife programmes ever made and has developed into the most authoritative and dedicated organisation of its kind anywhere in the world. Gareth Huw Davies looks back at the unit from its modest origins in the 50s to the present day and its innovative plans for the future

Doors lining a labyrinth of corridors and staircases in a terrace of Victorian houses in Bristol open onto astonishing vistas. In this room a producer, just returned from steamiest Africa, is examining rare film of lowland gorillas. In that room a cameraman reports on a dive among the Weddell seal beneath the ice in Antarctica. In a third a screen is alive with a swarming frenzy, discerned by a miniature camera on a hair-thin cable probed into a bivouac of army ants in Panama.

11-19 Tyndalls Park Road, Bristol, is base camp to the illustrious peaks of the natural history filmmaker's achievement. For the past 35 years the Natural History Unit has sent forth its cameramen, and women, from here to record the wild world in all its infinite complexity and magnificence.

Assignments have tested the limits of human endurance. One team spent three years in the Arctic to make *Kingdom of the Ice Bear*. Another filmed on the strand in Patagonia – with one cameraman swimming in the sea – one of the most terrifying acts of predation ever shown on TV, a huge killer whale beaching itself to snatch sea lion pups. Cameramen have been despatched inside volcanoes and deep under sea. And where the human operator finally admits defeat, the cameras are sent on alone, carried by remote-controlled aircraft. The more bizarre the idea, the more enterprising the solution: small radio-controlled cameras have been hidden in furry roller skates, disguised as prey, to show us what it's like to be pounced on and eaten by a lion.

Some of the barriers the unit has had to cross are political rather than physical. To make *Realms of the Russian Bear*, producer John Sparks cracked the most formidable bureaucracy on earth, the former USSR, negotiating his camera team's way around the vast old Soviet empire just before it disintegrated.

The location of the world's biggest factory of wildlife film making, appropriately, has never been just another annex of the BBC's sprawling London premises. Down in Bristol, as part of the corporation's South of England headquarters, the unit is close to the country. There are nest boxes nailed

Hans and Lotte Hass in May 1954

Armand and Michaela Denis in January 1962

up on trees by a senior executive to be visible from producers' offices. Until a new extension was grafted on to the old terrace, night workers would occasionally feed the foxes on the lawns at dead of night.

In the immediate post-war years the BBC wanted to disperse its specialist programme-making around the country. So agriculture was given to the Midlands and light entertainment to Manchester. Where else to site the Natural History Unit but at Bristol? It was close to Slimbridge on the banks of the Severn where Sir Peter Scott was based. Tony Soper, another of the unit's stalwarts, still lives nearby in Devon.

The unit has its roots in a series of radio nature programmes, *The Naturalist*, launched in Bristol in 1946. Radio was, and still is, a key component of the unit – Radio 4 puts out roughly as many hours of regular wildlife programmes as television – and the two media still work closely alongside one another in the same building, providing a cross-fertilisation of ideas.

Over the next ten years Bristol evolved as the natural place to report nature, as the opening eye of the TV camera began to reveal the wonders of the natural world to a wider audience. Peter Scott's *Look* series, launched in 1955, soon established an avid following for wildlife films. Two years later the Natural History Unit was formally founded, with Desmond Hawkins as its first head.

The early stars of the unit's output projected the jaunty enthusiasm of explorers – Hans and Lotte Hass under sea, and Armand and Michaela Denis in Africa. One of the early *Look* subjects was the renowned oceanographer Jacques Cousteau in the film *Silent World*. Among the pioneer presenters were Gerald Durrell, Desmond Morris and David Bellamy. But one man above all is associated with the Natural History Unit's very beginnings (although he later went to Anglia TV to help launch its *Survival* series, then the only serious competitor to the Natural History Unit). For such a renowned globe-trotter, Peter Scott's early *Look* programmes were remarkably static: he would sit in a studio with a naturalist like Heinz Sielmann, and discuss film of woodpeckers on a screen before them. Landmark films of these early days were *Private Life of a Kingfisher*, the first to be transmitted in colour and *The Major*, about the felling of a village oak tree to make way for a new road.

The great traveller, then as now, was David Attenborough, although much of his early output, such as *Zoo Quest*, was from London. Attenborough gave British viewers, and television audiences throughout the world, the 'mega series'. The *Life on Earth* trilogy attracted some of the biggest audiences for any documentary the BBC has made. It has been screened in 100 countries and seen by over 500 million people world-wide.

The concept of authoritative yet popular series on the natural history of a particular great location was pioneered by Bristol – indeed it is unlikely that any other television station in the world could assemble the talent, resources and above all the commitment to make them. *Land of the Eagle* on the USA, *Flight of the Condor* on South America, *Kingdom of the Ice Bear*, *The Birth of Europe* and others gathered in awards, a motley collec-

Sir Peter Scott

tion of Hugos, Tuskers, Apples, Antlers and Pandas, by the cabinet-full.

The unit is the biggest commissioner in the world of blue-chip, hour-long wildlife documentaries, shown in the long-running *Natural World* series on Sunday evenings. It has made important films with a serious conservation theme, such as *Ivory Wars*.

It perfected, too, the art of the crisp 30-minute film essay for prime-time BBC1, and has reaped some massive audiences: 15 million people watched *Wildlife on One*'s *Meerkats United*, close to the level of audience achieved by the most popular soap operas.

But the unit does not have to comb the earth for its subjects. In *Daylight Robbery* it challenged a genuinely wild animal to test its ingenuity in an ordinary village garden. By way of a TV advert, the sequence of a squirrel successfully negotiating an obstacle course to reach its prize has entered popular culture.

Another innovation was to report live from the animals' territory, pioneering the use of infra-red cameras developed by the military. In *Badgerwatch*, against the low drone of man's world continuing in the distance, badgers were filmed as they went about their nightly business. The unit later airlifted their outside broadcast technology

David Attenborough in *Worlds Apart*, a programme from *The Living Planet* series

BBC Photograph Library

around the world to report live from the Florida Everglades, from 50 feet under the surface of the Red Sea and from the banks of the Mara river in Kenya as the wildebeest swarmed across in one of the most dramatic mass migrations on earth.

Technical standards have improved enormously since the 60s, when a typical film might be shot by an amateur naturalist/cameraman from a hide in his back garden, with not much more competence than today's home movie makers. Since then the technological revolution, coupled with ever rising standards of photographic excellence, have

utterly transformed the unit's film making.

Electronic image intensifiers allow cameramen to work in light so dim it is beyond the sensitivity of any photographic emulsion. Tiny cameras, applied from use in medicine, can send an image down a piece of wire from inside the stem of a plant. A lens in a periscope can give a participant's eye view of the mass mating of garter snakes. Underwater teams use Acquacams, cameras for high quality marine sequences, and presenters speak live and bubble-free to the camera wearing a Bubble Helmet, developed by the unit.

The *Supersense* and *Lifesense* series pioneered new filming techniques which explored the different sensory perceptions animals and birds have of the world, using miniature, often automatic, cameras to give the creature's point of view.

Remote-controlled cameras can report from anywhere in the skies. Back in the studio, special lenses of high magnification and wide angle can close in on the tiniest subject, or mounted on finely-tuned jibs, track a moving creature from a few millimetres distance.

Time-lapse photography can provide images of the world beyond human experience. The unit's next big series, after the films on Antarctica to be shown in late 1993, is Attenborough's six-part odyssey through the plant world. It

Pandas Aren't Always Cuddly – one of the fascinating programmes from the *Wildlife on One* series

BBC / Wolfshead Production

examines plants' strategies, their fight for survival, how they compete with and prey on each other and defend themselves; it explores the fantastic ways plants evolve to cope with heat and height. But it will do it in the plants' own time-scale, using sophisticated computer-controlled equipment specially designed by the BBC.

In the past time-lapse photography has shown us no more than flowers opening and leaves unfurling. The new equipment, which is portable enough to be taken by plane to Australia, can be left on location where it will lift and move the camera automatically in tandem with the growing plant. Another computerised arm will allow cameras to track and weave through a stand of flowers like a slow motion bee. Microscopic cameras will plunge underground to see what is happening in the roots, and even probe inside the stems of plants.

John Sparks, former head of the Natural History Unit, and now one of its most senior producers, believes that, in terms of the lenses and equipment used in film-making, the unit is now up against the optical limit: 'With fibre optics and periscopes and the other technology available to us, we can't *get* any closer to the subject.'

But the unit has many more tricks to deploy, and new, young producers to bring fresh ideas. 'To some extent the greater the reality in terms of photographic excellence, the more artifice we have to employ to convey it,' says Sparks. The miracles of electronic television allow images to be overlaid one on another on the screen. By this process, the viewer can now be 'taken' into the sky to fly with a flock of starlings over London's Trafalgar Square.

Beyond the technology is a pool of some of the most outstanding cameramen available. Some series – the recent *Realms of the Russian Bear* is a good example – make little or no use of the new equipment, and instead rely on the perseverance, field-craft and brilliance of the man, or woman, behind the lens. Many famous moments are the product of an individual's dedica-

tion, rather than an inventor's genius: one of the most memorable is the sequence of the polar bears sliding down a snow slope in the Arctic, shot by cameraman Hugh Miles, who received an Emmy for his achievement.

And what now? After Antarctica and *Plants*, there will be a six-part series on insects, using the latest close-in technology. A series on China's natural history has yet to be made; South America, last filmed ten years ago for a series of only three programmes, merits another visit. It could soon be time for a big series on the world's oceans. There is talk of *The Last Eden*, a look at that third of the world that is still technically wilderness. And the end of the millennium could be the occasion for the biggest subject of all, the state of the planet.

John Sparks foresees no danger of the unit running out of ideas. 'There is an unlimited range of subjects yet to approach. There is a huge number of insects, 8,000 birds and 4,000 mammals. There are so many different ways we can tell stories about them. There will always be a fresh aspect of the natural world to report, in programmes where our aim is to create a glow of satisfaction in the viewer.'

Gareth Huw Davies

THE TRIALS OF ATTENBOROUGH

David Attenborough has changed the way in which we see wildlife since his days on *Zoo Quest* in the 50s. With the 37-week reshowing of his *Life on Earth* trilogy in May, Gareth Huw Davies tracks him to his native habitat

It's hard to imagine now, but Sir David Attenborough – friend of gorillas, target for dive-bombing skuas, master of the split sentence begun in Africa and completed in Brazil; yes, the same breathless, globe-hopping correspondent at nature's front-line – used to be in administration. He sat behind a big polished desk, attended meetings, reviewed budgets and haggled with the unions.

Of course, that was always meant

to be a short-term switch of habitat. He came from the series *Zoo Quest*, which ended in 1961, to become controller of BBC2, then director of TV programmes, knowing that the enormous whale of BBC bureaucracy was programmed to spit him out, unharmed, after eight years to resume his far-flung career. But before his demob he was troubled by a secret fear that the desk job might deprive him of a greater opportunity.

David Attenborough in Lifesize, a programme from *Wildlife on One*

It was that one day a producer would come to him from the BBC's Natural History Unit and say, 'Dave, I've got this marvellous idea. Why don't you let me make a 13-part nature special to be called something like *Life on Earth*?' Now this was the very project he had been quietly saving up for his return to programme-making: but if someone else had asked him when he was head of TV he knows he could not have refused. So we might have seen the famous gorilla in programme 12 lolling on quite another bemused presenter.

Ironically, it was Attenborough himself who had turned the request he dreaded into such a distinct possibility. As the man responsible for introducing colour TV in 1967, he recognised the need for some 'great, glorious programmes' to

On location with *The Living Planet*

show off the new medium's high fidelity. First came art – Kenneth Clark's *Civilisation*, conducting us around the West's cultural show-pieces. That was followed by science – Dr Bronowski's *Ascent of Man*. Anyone could see the next blockbuster just had to be nature.

To Attenborough's relief, no one had asked the question by the time he left administration in 1973. So he went for it himself: a series tracing the development of animal life from its beginnings three million years ago until today. Even then there were doubters. The standard nature film had been a staid biography of an animal, or the story of a habitat through a year. The frenetic world tour he proposed was revolutionary. A sceptical colleague put it thus: 'Dave, you'll make yourself the laughing stock of the scientific world. You'll be hopping around Australia and Africa and no one

will know where you are. It goes against all we know of wildlife film-making.'

Undaunted, he went ahead. *Life on Earth* took three years to make. First shown in 1979, it delighted the critics and routed the doubters. Far from confusing the viewer, the sight of Attenborough popping up in country after country to make a point held millions in thrall. Apart from some notably spontaneous encounters, such as the gorilla scene in Rwanda, it happened just as he had carefully scripted it in advance. 'I remember writing the sequence where I jump into the Mediterranean and I come up on the Great Barrier Reef, and thinking, 'This will make somebody smile'.

'So when it worked out so well, I told myself, "This is fun. Slap in for another one". So we made *The Living Planet*, another three years

exploring the earth's environments and the way plants and animals adapt to their surroundings. I thought that had pretty well done it, so I had a rest and did something on the Mediterranean (*The First Eden*). Then it dawned on us that we hadn't covered the strand of nature that TV is designed for – action and drama. So we did *The Trials of Life*, looking at how creatures use their bodies, the way they behave.'

What does he expect viewers who have watched the entire 37-week, 1,915-minute trilogy from beginning to end, from the dawn of nature to the moment a creature passes on its genes to the next life cycle, to take away from the experience? 'In a word, wonder – at the multiplicity, diversity, splendour and beauty of the natural world.

'We have now covered the three big aspects of natural science that you can do just by looking at animals. The trilogy summarises what naturalists have found out over the past 200 years.' Is it definitive? 'By no means. There are millions more things to be said. You could start the whole thing all over again. But it could be that these programmes will stand for some time, not because they are so wonderful or complete, but because no other broadcasting company in the world could have allocated the time, talent and money.'

BBC Photograph Library

The Trials of Life, in the path of a million migrating land crabs on Christmas Island

From the fruits of such a massive image-gathering, he selects one unexpected favourite offcut: frogs, a passion of his. He asked the 20-strong camera crew involved in the first series to look out for interesting frogs on their travels and commit them to film. 'After two years, the director called me in and said, "Dave, what are we going to do about all these frogs?" I sat for 90 minutes looking at them and suddenly realised that no one in the history of the world had ever seen so many different kinds of living frogs. It ended up as a two-minute montage.'

It is a matter of 'huge pride' to

him that, although it was made for general interest, *Life on Earth* is used in university courses. This has a special significance for Attenborough, whose father was principal of Leicester University. He was no naturalist, but he was a fine teacher who trained his son's enquiring mind by sending him off to the library to look things up. 'And I suppose that's what I am, a teacher.'

What now? At home in Richmond, Surrey, he is busy writing the script of a six-part series on plants. Its subject is plants world-wide – what it is to be a plant, how they solve their problems, how they get around, co-operate and fight. Just right for TV, which can adapt to the slow timescale of plants. The opening sequence lasts 12 seconds; it will take a year to film. Before that project is completed, he will travel to Antarctica as a narrator in another wildlife series. And then? 'I'll be nearly 70 when I finish *Plants*. I'll see how I feel.

'My work has been a great privilege. Can you imagine? To go wherever you want, see whatever you want.' What hasn't he seen? 'Millions of places. Particularly central Asia. But I try not to go back. A great mistake. Places always change, and not for the better.' And improvements? 'Oh yes, people's attitudes to nature have altered enormously worldwide. Thirty years ago people in Australia couldn't understand why we should go all that way to look at cockatoos. It's different now.'

David Attenborough is a national institution. But he remains totally without affectation. He is disarmingly modest, obliging, affable and matey. Even an interviewer's misfortune is cue for a funny story at his own expense. Towards the end of our chat, my tape recorder fails. He finds me a replacement, then offers a cautionary tale on the perils of technology. He was once given the first-ever interview with the Queen of Tonga. Entry to the royal presence was on hands and knees – he demonstrates on the carpet. 'And what did we discover when we arrived with this great exclusive?' He gives a hearty laugh. 'The tapes were blank.'

Gareth Huw Davies

35 YEARS OF THE SKY AT NIGHT

Colin Dunne meets Patrick Moore, presenter of television's longest running programme

It was the year when Prince Charles started prep school, Elvis Presley joined the US Army, parking meters were introduced in London, *6.5 Special* and the Flowerpot Men were television hits, petrol rationing ended, Tom Finney was the footballer of the year, Lew Hoad won Wimbledon, Ernie produced its first Premium Bond winner, and the British Prime Minister, one Harold Macmillan, assured everyone they'd never had it so good.

It was also the year that the Russians put the first Sputnik satellite into orbit and, in order to satisfy the clamour for information about what was going on above our heads, the BBC decided to screen a programme to be called *Starmap*. They had second thoughts about the title, changed it to *The Sky at Night* and asked Patrick Moore, an expert who, it was thought, could talk a bit, to introduce it. Thirty-five years later – the year was 1957 – it is television's longest-running programme and Patrick Moore is still talking.

He's the only man to become a

Patrick Moore, presenter of *The Sky at Night*

BBC Photograph Library

star by talking about them. With his tufty hair, squeaky voice, clothes like an unmade bed and torrential enthusiasm, he looks more like an inflated schoolboy than a television star, but, improbable as it seems, he's outlasted all of them. It's his passion for the subject that rivets us all to our seats, but there's another factor too: Patrick Moore is a classic in that line of much-loved British eccentrics which ranges from Gerard Hoffnung to Lucinda Lambton.

Turning in the swivel-chair in his study, he lifts his eyes to the heavens. 'There's probably someone out there exactly like me,' he says. What? Another man with flyaway eyebrows who can play the xylophone, bowl leg-breaks, and compose music? Impossible.

He lives in a rambling 17th century thatched cottage in Selsey, West Sussex, amid a jumble which reflects his extraordinary gifts. The cricket pads? Although he insists he has no talent for cricket, he plays for the Lord's Taverners, bowling medium-paced leg-breaks off a kangaroo run, and once bowled an Australian captain. 'Beat him twice, got him third ball,' he says, with the glee of a teenager.

Wooden-framed tennis rackets? He still plays regularly, claiming a tricky spin serve with very little to follow. Of all his sporting achievements, he is probably most proud of his appalling 293 on the local golf-course – 'including a masterly 32 on the 13th'.

Of the collection of pipes, one is invariably clenched between his teeth, and the faded rug is one he made with his mother when he was a little boy.

The piano he uses when he's composing his operas, waltzes and brass band march tunes, and he has played the xylophone at a Royal Command Performance.

The typewriter, which looks like a prototype Sopwith Camel, is a Woodstock which was made in 1908 and which he still uses daily, at an astonishing, two-fingered 90 words a minute. It produced the dozens of books which line his shelves, and if you happen to see another 1908 Woodstock, he'd be very glad to have it for spares.

Each year, in the village pantomime, he plays the demon, and he has worn a monocle since he was 16.

He is, as you may see, not quite as other men. It's a thought which delights him. 'I suppose I am a bit of a throwback.' To what? A shriek of laughter fills the room. 'God knows,' he says.

From the age of 6 to 16, he spent most of his time in bed with a 'wonky' heart. All he could do was read, and it was at the age of 6 that he picked up GF Chambers 1898 volume *The Story of the Solar System*, and he was hooked. With a companion volume to the moon, he became a 'moon mapper', using a telescope he bought for £7.10s. By the time he was 11, he was elected to the British Astronomical Association. He is that increasingly rare specimen, the amateur expert, and never received any proper scientific training. Yet his ability to explain science in simple terms, and to persuade people to share his

a Squadron Leader. That was his chance to go to university, but he refused because it would have meant taking a grant, and Moore doesn't believe in grants.

He turned to writing and insists that he has never done a day's work in his life, because his work is his hobby.

When the first programme went out, it shared the *Radio Times* schedules with Burns and Allen, Peter Dimmock and the *Tonight* programme. All he can remember of it was the sudden and alarming conviction that this could affect the rest of his life. A modest man, he claims it was all nothing to do with him. 'I was simply in the right place at the right time. Six months later up went the first space satellite and that's why you're talking to me now. Could've been anybody. Anyone could do it. At that time everyone was interested in what was going on up there. Television sort of fell into my lap.'

At the time the programme began,

The multi-talented Patrick Moore at his piano

BBC Photograph Library

exuberant passion, has made him one of the most influential scientists of his time.

He is a man who has very much shaped his own life. Ill-health or not, in 1940 he added a year to his age of 17 and got into the RAF, where he became a navigator and bomb-aimer on the hazardous Pathfinder flights, ending the war as

the Space Age hadn't started. 'Astronomy was still regarded as an eccentric study practised by old men with long white beards. Sending a man to the moon was little more than a music-hall joke.'

It's his personality and enormous good humour which brings the programme to life. One night, a figure in a spacesuit and fishbowl helmet walked on-screen, and announced that he was a Martian visiting earth to prove that this planet was devoid of intelligent life because of its thick atmosphere and excessive water. Beneath the helmet, Patrick Moore, of course. When he went to the Mormon state of Utah, he was welcomed by a man who said he would find no swearing, drinking or wild women. 'Then it's hardly worth coming is it?' he replied.

It's been a learning curve for Moore as much as for the viewers. In the 50s, he was convinced that man would not walk on the moon until the late 70s or 80s, rather than 1969. Nor did he expect rockets to reach the outer planets as soon as they did. For the future, he envisages more unmanned probes of the planets, an automatic landing on Mars to return with samples, a major space station and a base on the moon, possibly all before the end of the century.

He is particularly proud that he helped to inspire some of the men who have become Britain's most distinguished astronomers. 'Just before you came, had a chap here who's quite famous these days, and his first attempt was looking through my telescope. I had to hold him up to do it. He was all of 9 then.' His generosity to young enthusiasts is legendary. The son of a friend of mine, at the age of 14, wrote to him to ask his advice on a career in astronomy and Moore replied to him with a detailed and encouraging letter which, the boy, now an Oxford student, still treasures.

He never married because the girl he loved died in the war. 'It's no secret,' he says openly. 'There was never anyone else for me. I'm not the sort of chap who'd settle for second-best. I would very much have liked to have a family, but it was not to be. No good feeling sorry for yourself, got to make the best of a bad job, so there you have it. But yes, I would've enjoyed a family.'

Instead, he lived with his mother until she died ten years ago. He says he can't work without the sound of the cuckoo clock which she gave him for his seventh birthday, although when it cuckoos eight times at seven o'clock he says: 'That bird is a pathological liar.'

He reacts quite differently to the common perceptions of the stars – as a means of fortune-telling for some, and the prospect of silver-suited strangers for others. 'Astrology proves the well-known scientific fact that there's one born every minute. I did once look at my stars, and they predicted an outstanding athletic achievement for me that day. I took no wickets for 62 on a bowler's wicket, so my guardian angel must've blown a fuse that day.'

He is less sceptical about the possibility of life out there somewhere. 'I am sure there is intelligent life out there, but it's so far away that we cannot contact it at the moment.' What sort of life? 'Well, if you have a planet like the earth going round a planet like the sun, and there are plenty of them, then I would expect to find our kind of life. I can't prove it, of course. But then, if you'd told Alfred the Great that one day you could sit in Winchester and watch a man walk on the moon, he would've replied with the Anglo-Saxon equivalent of "you're nuts".'

Colin Dunne

Patrick Moore (left) and Michael Bentine demonstrate the problems of manned space flight in *The Sky at Night* in April 1968

A craftsman works on building the reproductions of the famous sailing ships in Barcelona in *Columbus and the Age of Discovery*

REDISCOVERING COLUMBUS

To mark the 500th anniversary of Christopher Columbus's discovery of America, a major new series was launched in July to find out the truth about the great navigator. Author Hunter Davies has done his own research and has some surprising revelations...

You must be aware by now that last year we celebrated Christopher Columbus. Five hundred years ago, he discovered America. If you are really aware, you will on no account use the words 'celebrate' or 'discovery'. Tut-tut. Wash your mouth out.

In 1892, when the world was remembering the 400th anniversary,

he was lauded as a hero, embodying all the known virtues. There was even a move to sanctify him, though that collapsed when it was pointed out he had produced an illegitimate son. No one at the time was worried that he had been horrible to the Indians.

All year, a flood of books and articles have poured out about Columbus, and film versions too, ranging from a Gerard Depardieu spectacular to a *Carry On*. In July, the biggest project of them all was launched, a seven-part series, *Columbus and the Age of Discovery*. It was a joint production, on a monster scale, between the BBC and television companies in the USA, Spain, Portugal, ˙Italy, Germany and Japan. They've filmed in dozens of countries and even

gone to the bother of building reproductions of those famous three ships, the *Santa Maria*, the *Niña* and the *Pinta*.

Over the past four years, I have done my own, more modest search for Columbus. As in the BBC2 series, there are two basic questions to be answered. Who was he? Should we honour him?

He was born in Genoa in 1451, the first child of a Genoese weaver called Dominico and his wife, Susanna. At times, Dominico did well, and owned a couple of houses, then he fell into debt and was put in prison. There's no evidence of Columbus's education, although when his father was in funds, he may have attended a guild school. He later boasted that he had attended the University of Pavia in

Italy. No record of C Columbus has been found, and it's now thought to be a fib.

He went to sea while young, at either 10 or 14 (he gave different ages at different times). But he did not start as a sailor, more as an errand boy for his father, then later in his own right as a commercial traveller, going up and down the Mediterranean coast, doing bits of business, buying and selling, ducking and weaving, getting himself into debts and legal arguments. Which was fortunate for us. Those documents have placed him at certain times and certain places.

While on his voyages as a maritime merchant, perhaps occasionally working his passage, he picked up navigation, found he had a gift for it, and was soon telling captains how to steer, what to look for next, sometimes hoodwinking the crew about their true position, even leading raids on foreign ships, according to the stirring tales he later told.

We have to rely on him for the details of the first big drama in his life. Sometime around 1476, he was on a fleet of Genoese cargo boats, heading for England, when they were attacked by French corsairs off the Algarve coast, near Cape St Vincent. A sea battle ensued, 500 men lost their lives, but Columbus managed to swim and paddle his way to land, arriving safely in Lagos.

He was just another shipwrecked sailor from a foreign land, with no money, no possessions, aged 25, though probably looking older, if his hair was already going grey. According to his son Ferdinand, who wrote his biography, his hair was 'blond, but when he reached the age of 30, it all turned grey'.

There are about 70 portraits which are traditionally identified as being Columbus, not counting modern versions, in which for some reason, whether it's a Spanish mural on the walls of the monastery in Palos, or a picture postcard on sale in San Salvador, he comes out looking like Robert Redford.

Columbus took up residence in Lisbon. He went to sea on several voyages, including a trip to Bristol, married a Portuguese woman and had a son, Diego (Ferdinand was a later, illegitimate son). They went to live in Porto Santo, a little island off Madeira, which even now feels cut off from the rest of the world. It was while living in Porto Santo that he first thought of his idea of sailing west, to reach the East.

In the 15th century, many of the riches of the known world came from the East, such as gold, silver and spices, but the normal trade routes had been cut off by the rise of Islam. Hence the need for another way to the East. How and why Columbus came up with his proposed route is not clear. Did he pinch it from a dead mariner, shipwrecked in Porto Santo, who had crossed the Atlantic, but never lived long enough to tell the tale? Was he given a secret map by persons unknown? Did he work it all out for himself? Columbus, naturally, maintained it was the last.

They all laughed at Christopher Columbus, but not because he said the world was round. All educated people in the 15th century accepted that, ever since the Greeks had worked it out. They laughed at him because they didn't think it was possible to sail right round. They laughed at his figures, his so-called scientific and geographical evidence. He put up his idea to the King of Portugal, who turned it down. He then moved to Spain, hung around the court of Isabella and Ferdinand for more than six years, being rejected and humiliated, till eventually in January 1492 his plan was accepted. Not because they had suddenly come round to it, but because at long last, after 800 years, the Moors had been beaten at Granada and Spain was united as a Christian country. In the euphoria and excitement of victory, they thought, why not give this Columbus chap some modest backing?

And so he set off on 3 August 1492, in his three ships, from Palos in Spain. Quite an easy voyage really. The trade winds swept them across. On 12 October 1492, he landed on San Salvador on the Bahamas, and took his first steps on what we now call the Americas.

He returned from his first voyage in April 1493 as a hero, cheered in the streets of Seville, given a triumphal procession through Barcelona. Ah, if only he had retired gracefully, as a man of his advanced years should have done. He was then 41, old by 15th-century standards.

CHRONOLOGY

- **1451**   Born in Genoa
- **1461-5**   Goes to sea, firstly as a messenger boy, then merchant trader
- **1476**   Shipwrecked off Portugal, settles in Lisbon and travels to Bristol
- **1479**   Marries Felipa Perestrello
- **1480-2**   Moves to Porto Santo, Madeira. Birth of son Diego
- **1484**   Dreams up his grand design to sail west to reach the East
- **1485**   Refused by Portuguese King
- **1486**   Settles in Spain. Puts his design to Queen Isabella and King Ferdinand. Turned down
- **1492**   Monarchs agree to back Columbus's voyage. August: *Santa Maria*, *Niña* and *Pinta* leave Palos. 12 October: Arrive San Salvador, Bahamas
- **1493**   April: returns in triumph to Spain. September: second voyage – 17 ships
- **1498**   Third voyage to the Indies: brought back in chains
- **1502**   Fourth voyage: stranded in Jamaica
- **1506**   Dies in Valladolid, Spain

Reproductions of the famous sailing ships take to the ocean in the seven-part series *Columbus and the Age of Discovery*

BBC Photograph Library

He made three further voyages, eventually reaching the mainland of the Americas (in Venezuela), but it all ended in tears, mutinies, disasters. In 1500 he was brought home in chains. Columbus died in Valladolid in 1506, aged 54, bitter and twisted, in poverty, so he said, protesting he had been cheated out of his honours and rewards. Even America was named after someone else.

As a navigator he was outstanding, always curious, always adventurous, always looking for new lands. As a governor he proved incompetent, which was why he was brought back in chains. As a personality, he was obsessive, self-willed and, with age and ill health, became paranoid and rather unstable.

The achievement of Columbus was to reach the Americas, to get back, tell his story and begin permanent European settlement of what to Europe was a brand new land. Technically, it should not be called 'discovery', as how can you discover a land with about 20 million people living there?

As for celebrating, many people who are environmentally, ethnically, and ecologically minded will disagree. When Columbus arrived on the island of Hispaniola, for example, there were three million Indians living there. Fifty years later, long after Columbus was dead, only 200 remained. It is a terrible indictment of white colonialisation.

However, there are a few points to bear in mind. The vast majority of Indians were killed by disease, such as smallpox (in return, the Spaniards brought back syphilis to Europe). It is easy to over-idealise the native way of life – the Aztecs had a ruling class and kept slaves – and dangerous to use 20th-century values when judging 15th-century behaviour.

It seems to me that if villains must be found, 500 years later, the real baddy is humanity. The Spaniards were occupied by the Moors for 800 years, then went on to dominate others for 400 years. We had the Romans for 400 years, then in turn we ruled our own empire. It appears to be human nature that the exploited turn exploiters, given half a chance. In 1992 it is time to remember the past, but to move on, vowing to do better in future.

Hunter Davies

• Hunter Davies is author of *In Search of Columbus*, published by Sinclair-Stevenson, price £16.95

FASHION ON TV

First there was *The Clothes Show*, the highly successful consumer-orientated programme, which looks at fashion trends from the international design studio to the high street. Then came *The Look*, which goes behind the scenes of the fashion industry and reveals a world of big business, glamour and intrigue. By Daniela Soave

If you were asked to devise a recipe for a fail-safe television series, what could be better than a heady cocktail of sex, celebrity, money, beautiful clothes, devastatingly beautiful women, glamour and jealousy, all set in a cutthroat world? For six weeks last autumn, that is exactly what was served up to viewers tuned into *The Look*, and it worked. From the very first episode, they were hooked.

Was this the long-awaited succes-

Red or Dead at London Fashion Week

sor to *Dallas* or *Dynasty*? No. For all these ingredients, *The Look* was not a sizzling soap. Instead, it was a compelling, tightly-constructed documentary series, made by husband and wife team Jeremy and Gina Newson, that took the lid off the fashion industry as never before. Like the successful runway fashion shows it depicted, *The Look* too was a runaway success, drawing

praise from critics, (many of whom had previously dismissed fashion as a frivolous television subject) and viewers alike.

When one considers that the fashion business is Britain's fifth biggest industry – we spend £16.8 billion a year on clothes – it is a subject that merits further investigation. Via exclusive interviews with top designers – such as Karl Lagerfeld, Ralph Lauren, Giorgio Armani and Christian Lacroix – through to unprecedented access to the catwalk shows, *The Look* was the most analytical series ever made about the topic.

Deliciously irreverent yet satisfyingly informative, it struck a chord both in disciples and detractors. By the end of its run, it had explored the political map of fashion, looked at the evolution of the superstar model, analysed the power of the fashion press, examined the lure of lucrative licensing deals, demonstrated the impact of fabric on three designers and profiled one of the most influential figures in fashion, Yves Saint Laurent.

But what was the secret of *The Look*'s success? Was it the spy value of spotting celebrities like Elton John and Eric Clapton at the catwalk shows? Was it the sheer shock of seeing the evolution of a jacket from the designer's pad to the finished article with a staggering price-tag of £30,000? Was it the voyeurism of watching world famous supermodel Linda Evangelista lose her patience with the television cameras and shout 'Go away!'? Or the revelation that Yves Saint Laurent was such a nervous wreck? Or Lowri Turner, fashion editor of the *London Evening Standard*, describe the bitchiness and back scratching between fashion houses and journalists?

'I think it was because the fashion industry is close to everyone,' explains Jeremy Newson. 'We all wear clothes; everyone is conscious of how they look and how their appearance affects the way other people see them. So viewers were interested to learn more about the people who control the way we look. Everyone knows about fashion designers but not so much about the complexity of the indus-

***Haute couture* from Yves Saint Laurent**

try. For example, I don't think people realised how successful the more successful designers are. They earn billions of dollars a year.

'It's very difficult to make good television programmes and we were lucky that the fashion industry is a very rich topic, one which bore fruit. It's a charismatic world with built-in drama and the tension of getting the collections together in time. It is the perfect soap subject.'

The Look's compulsive quality had much to do with the fact that it was neither a history of fashion nor a consumer guide but an independent, sassy view of a flamboyant macrocosm, its rituals and foibles. The Newsons had no previous inside knowledge of the fashion industry and their introduction to the highly-strung, secretive and often paranoid world of designers was truly a baptism of fire: they would be told that one designer superstar would not be interviewed unless a certain other also said yes; they would be on tenterhooks waiting for confirmation that they could film the backstage events of a fashion show only seconds before the event was about to commence; they would spend a year corresponding with a designer in the hope that he would agree to be filmed. To those working in the fashion industry, such idiosyncrasies would be accepted without question but for outsiders like the Newsons, these rituals were evidence of the workings of a world apart, and ripe for the plucking.

That fashion has become a subject suitable for serious television debate is largely due to the influence of *The Clothes Show*, which, although completely different in format, broke new ground by looking at trends in design, colour and the transition from *haute couture* to high street. Its success can be measured by *The Clothes Show Live*, now a popular annual event, which draws viewers in their thousands to experience for themselves all that is best in British fashion and *The Clothes Show Magazine*.

Without *The Clothes Show* it is debatable whether the British Fashion Awards, which could be described as the fashion Oscars, and draws as much interest and anticipation as its celluloid counterpart, would have ever reached the television screen. And would Janet Street-Porter and Alan Yentob have commissioned the Newsons to make six programmes about fashion had the interest not already been proven?

Clothes Show presenters Caryn Franklin and Jeff Banks

BBC Photograph Library

'The Look and The Clothes Show are two completely different programmes,' says Jeremy Newson. '*The Clothes Show* is more consumer-orientated. I think it is very good, but it is more within fashion. Our series looked at fashion from the outside. We didn't know about fashion and we weren't part of the machine. It was as much an eye-opener for us as it was for the viewer.'

Where else is there to go in the television world of style? That *The Look* figured so highly in viewers' esteem and in the ratings, shows it is a subject not yet exhausted – 'although we were exhausted by the end of it,' Jeremy Newson admits. 'You could go deeper and wider. In about five years' time it would be interesting to see what has happened, because all the current top designers will be getting to a certain age and there will have to be a new wave. That's when the fun will begin.'

Daniela Soave

THE ARTS

1992 produced a wealth of documentary films relating to the arts, with established programmes *Omnibus*, *Arena* and *The South Bank Show* continuing to show innovative films covering a huge spectrum of cultural subjects. Anne-Marie Sapsted reviews a selection of the year's most notable programmes

On BBC television alone, output from the Music and Arts department accounted for more than 375 hours of programmes each year, covering an enormous range of arts and cultural topics in both documentary-style and performance-based programmes.

The most watched arts documentary series on television in this country is *Omnibus*, BBC1's flagship arts series which celebrated its 25th anniversary in 1992. The birthday season opened with a film which, because of her death shortly after the completion of filming, became a moving tribute to English novelist Angela Carter. The programme explored her clever, witty

BBC Photograph Library

A scene from the *Omnibus* programme: *Angela Carter's Curious Room*

and inventive style which has inspired films such as *The Company of Wolves* and *The Magic Toyshop* and included the last interview she gave before her death.

A film on Leonora Carrington, the Surrealist artist, who now lives in Mexico, also included sequences of film shot in her English childhood home, which contrasted vividly with her surroundings in her country of adoption. This was the

The artist Leonora Carrington, who was featured in an edition of *Omnibus*

BBC Photograph Library

woman who inspired Max Ernst, Andre Breton and Paul Eluard, and whose own writing and painting is highly original, but who proved difficult to draw out on the subject of her own inspiration. She preferred instead to let her work speak for itself, though by agreeing to be filmed going about her daily routine, she provided some illumination into her very individual attitude to life.

One of the UK's most successful film directors, Ridley Scott, was filmed working on his multi-million dollar version of the Christopher Columbus story starring Gerard Depardieu and Sigourney Weaver which was released in October. *Omnibus* traced his career. Another subject was Irish-American film director John Ford, who died in 1992 after making 112 feature films, starting in 1917 with silent westerns, eventually turning out classics such as *The Grapes of Wrath, How Green was my Valley* and *The Quiet Man.*

There were also programmes about Piero della Francesca, the accomplished Quattrocento painter, whose mathematical precision and stark simplicity continue to influence painters today; about the multi-talented actor-director Canadian Robert Lepage whose production of *A Midsummer Night's Dream* opened at the National last summer; about the Paris-based Israeli painter Avigdor Arikha; about the Disney approach to fairy tales with unseen footage from their archives; and about Sebastiao Salgado, one of the world's leading photo-journalists whose photographs of famine-stricken Africa and of his native Latin-America have captured the imagination of people the world over.

The first *Omnibus* programme appeared in 1967 called *Everybody's Expo* and since then has profiled such artistic giants as Graham Greene, Sir John Gielgud, David Hockney, Dmitri Shostokovich, Charlie Chaplin, Alfred Hitchcock and Joan Sutherland. There have also been explorations of subjects as diverse as Madonna, stand-up comics, the cleaning of the Sistine Chapel ceiling, the Royal Shakespeare Company, art in the Third

Reich and poems by schoolchildren. One outstanding success was the recording in New York, by leading opera singers, of *West Side Story* conducted by its composer Leonard Bernstein. And the Prince of Wales was offered the chance to air his views on architecture in a programme called *A Vision of Britain*.

Bookmark, BBC2's lively look at the literary scene, returned with a new series which included PD James's first in-depth interview about her life and work, to coincide with the publication of her latest novel *The Children of Men.*

In another programme, Yasher Kemal, a Kurd who is regarded as Turkey's leading novelist, spoke about a key moment in his life in a film which was interwoven with scenes from his finest story. Under Turkish law, it is the duty of the family to avenge the murder of one of its members and Kemal's own involvement in a blood feud forms the basis for *Childhood* which was shot in the writer's native village with an entirely Turkish cast.

Enid Blyton's Famous Five celebrated their 50th birthday in 1992. Ken Howard profiled this classic children's author in a film which included an insight into her life provided by characters from her books, which proved to be far from the sunny carefree stories she served up to her young readers.

Oliver Reed in a scene from *Dante's Inferno*, which was televised in the first series of *Omnibus* in December 1967

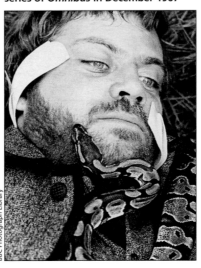

BBC Photograph Library

BBC2 also produced *The Royal Gardens*, in which Sir Roy Strong, a practised gardener in his own right who helped Prince Charles in the design of Highgrove, explored this glorious but often forgotten part of British Heritage. Since Tudor times, the Royal Family has created some of the world's greatest gardens and this series showed the gardens of successive monarchs through the eyes of their creators and in the context of history.

The six programmes were filmed in changing seasons over the course of a year with the participation of the Queen and the Prince of Wales, and locations included private gardens at Frogmore, Windsor and Highgrove which are not open to the public. Sir Roy, the former director of the National Portrait Gallery and the Victoria and Albert Museum wrote and presented the series.

A new and highly unlikely television star was born with the transmission of *Sister Wendy's Odyssey* a series of six short programmes on BBC2. Sister Wendy travelled the country in search of some of the art treasures which she had never seen but which have inspired her life. The hermit nun living in a caravan in a Norfolk wood, whose life of prayer had not prevented her from becoming an art connoisseur captured the public imagination with her knowledge and fervent enthusiasm gleaned from art postcards and reproductions in books.

Her frank and often graphic descriptions of some particularly erotic old masters and her personal re-evaluation of some 20th century artists delivered as she visited galleries all over the country, made the series very popular and a somewhat unexpected success. 'So many people are frightened of art,' she confided, 'but they shouldn't be. Art is a window into something greater than yourself, a way of enriching your life through someone else's experience.' Even Wogan and his guests listened to her with undisguised interest.

Arena is BBC2's major arts documentary series and its 1992 season included some fascinating subjects. *Masters of the Canvas* followed

Ulster poet Paul Yates and Pop Art supremo Peter Blake's quest to portray champion masked wrestler Kendo Nagasaki in words and paint and to explore the enigmatic man behind the mask. A triple bill on Argentinian culture was directed by the renowned ethnographic film-maker Jana Bokova and featured the gauchos and their music, the dance music of the Andes foothills and the culture of the Indians of the High Andes.

In sharp contrast *Chi Chi the Panda* examined both the role of this high-profile animal as diplomatic currency, and the social issues raised as she became a TV superstar. Another film looked at Dean Reed, the greatest rock star the Communist world has ever known who was found mysteriously drowned in East Berlin in 1986. Reed was an American who converted to Communism in South America and sold more records than anyone else behind the iron curtain.

Arena also explored the controversy surrounding everyday objects purporting to be art and art purporting to be everyday currency in a film which looked at Duchamp's *Fountain* and Boggs's paintings of money and how they contravene the normal definitions of art. In this series, Robert Frank, one of the top US photographers and a member of the Beat generation was invited by *Arena* to make a film reflecting life in downtown New York and some of his own interests and concerns.

A three-part documentary series *City of Strangers* on BBC2 looked at Los Angeles in the first half of the century, growing up with a new art form – the cinema – at a time when many European artists and performers were gathering there. These émigrés came from Berlin, Paris and Vienna, cities with rich cultural traditions, to a brash new city which was striving to create a blueprint for the future.

America's topical film show *Siskel and Ebert* was brought to BBC2 this summer for a short series. Gene Siskel, film columnist for the *Chicago Tribune* and Roger Ebert, film critic for the *Chicago Sun-Times* are two of America's most powerful and famous film critics known for their verbal volleys,

often disagreeing about the latest movie releases. Syndicated all over America and watched by an estimated 15 million viewers each week, the programme has received four national Emmy award nominations.

Composers, artists, choreographers, film-makers and poets from all over the UK were commissioned to create new works especially for television as part of a BBC2 season of programmes called *Commissions and Collaborations*. According to Alan Yentob, controller of BBC2, the series 'highlights the vital role of BBC2 in developing and encouraging creativity and originality from a

Arena devoted a programme to the late Dean Reed, the greatest rock star in the Communist world

wide variety of artists,' and it will 'not only confirm the BBC's position at the cutting edge of cultural activity in the UK, but will also bring poetry, dance, music, film and fine art into the homes of millions of viewers in an accessible, entertaining and stimulating way.'

The BBC Billboard Art Project was an exciting idea taking art onto the streets in May when more than 15 artists, including Richard Hamilton, Helen Chadwick, Howard Hodgkin, Sarah Raphael, Bill Woodrow and Damien Hirst created works for around 200 billboard sites throughout the country. The project was mounted in association with *Radio Times* and several of the artworks were displayed on a

billboard in the foyer of London's Tate Gallery.

Ken Russell returned to BBC television for the first time in 25 years with an hour-long film *The Mystery of Dr Martinu* examining the work of Czech composer Bohuslav Martinu. Dramatising his inner life and dreams as well as telling his life story, the film took the form of a psychological detective story.

Six writers combined poetry and film to create six personal documentaries in verse in *Words on Film* and six distinguished contemporary artists returned to the inspirational source of a chosen artist from the past in *Artists' Journeys*. One of the country's most talented young composers, Mark-Anthony Turnage was commissioned to create a new musical work based on poems written by long-serving prisoners, and *Killing Time* directed by Rob Walker was the striking result.

Cross Channel was a 30-minute dance film created especially for television by choreographer Lea Anderson and director Margaret Williams. And *Dance House* was a series of 12 short films designed to show the diversity of British dance today.

Major concerts are regularly screened and this year ten Proms were shown. Viewers were also treated to *Tosca* starring Placido Domingo, staged in Rome in the exact locations and times intended by Puccini. This was a unique BBC/Channel 4 collaboration, with viewers able to see the entire opera on Channel 4. More than 45 countries on five continents received the live transmission, involving 27 cameras, four crews in four locations, a helicopter crew, 1,000 kilowatt lighting and five satellites.

There was also a gala concert from Glyndebourne, the last public performance in the theatre there and a fund-raising event for its new opera house; a Royal performance of *Don Giovanni* from the Royal Opera House to celebrate the 40th anniversary of the Queen's accession to the throne; and on Good Friday, the screening of Harrison Birtwistle's new opera *Gawain*, based on the medieval poem *Sir Gawain and the Green Knight*.

BBC Photograph Library

Rhythms of the World: Bombay and all that Jazz

The autumn music documentary season included profiles of Rachmaninov, the Labeque sisters, a history of operetta, and conductor Simon Rattle's journey into Stravinsky's musical landmark *The Rite of Spring*. Music of a different kind was the subject of *Rhythms of the World* with lots of performance-based programmes, including New Orleans jazz and the Finnish tango.

The Late Show was launched in 1989 to provide a live arts and media magazine programme four nights a week and continued to explore a wide range of subjects. An archive unit was set up in *The Late Show* and *TV Hell* in the autumn which provided an entertaining look through television history. There was also a major tribute to Granada Television.

London Weekend Television's *South Bank Show* continued to entertain and inform and lean towards more popular subjects with programmes about Sir Richard Attenborough, Lenny Henry, Pet Shop Boys, and Terry Gilliam but also Seamus Heaney, Alice Walker and Cecilia Bartoli. Ken Russell

also made a film about composer Arnold Bax.

Channel 4's major series *Without Walls* continued to take programmes from a range of different production companies. This year saw subjects ranging from Harold Pinter directing his own play *Party Time*, to an examination of three artists and writers (Michelangelo, DH Lawrence and Shakespeare); Sir Jimmy Savile and Norman Wisdom composing their own obituaries; a celebration of the tenor, and histories of the E-type Jaguar and the Volkswagen Beetle.

Anne-Marie Sapsted

CRIMEWATCH UK

With an invaluable source of vital information from viewers, *Crimewatch UK* has helped the police solve some of the country's most serious crimes. Julie Allan meets the *Crimewatch* team

The Stephanie Slater kidnapping case may be among the most notorious of the crimes solved as a result

of *Crimewatch UK*, but editor Liz Mills has a personal favourite.

'Back in 1990 some workmen renovating flats in Cardiff found bits of a skeleton wrapped in a carpet,' she says. 'It turned out that the body was of a young woman named Karen Price and had been in the ground for nine years. The police were desperate for us to do an item because they had practically nothing to go on.'

Crimewatch nearly turned the case down. 'I was working as a director making the reconstructions at the time,' says Liz Mills, 'and we wondered if there were too few clues to make it worthwhile. In the end we thought we'd try simply because the police were so keen.'

Despite the nine-year gap and apparent lack of witnesses or even much knowledge of the woman's movements, there turned out to be one thing the team hadn't anticipated. 'The forensic people came up with enough information for us to build a model of Karen's head,' remembers Mills, 'and we also made a film using an actress as Karen Price and visiting some of the places that she used to frequent.'

It was still quite a long shot, but *Crimewatch* was in for a stroke of luck. 'It turned out that an accomplice to the murder was watching with some friends,' she says. 'When the model was shown, he said he recognised her. I don't know why, but he even rang the programme. Perhaps he couldn't back down in front of his friends.'

The police investigation that followed revealed flaws in this man's story and he was eventually convicted. 'It made me realise that it really is possible to solve a crime that at first sight seems impossible,' says Mills.

In fact, *Crimewatch* generally only tackles crimes with which the police are stuck; cases in which it seems that every lead has been followed. 'It seems that *Crimewatch* viewers remember the most amazing things,' she says. 'Things they didn't give a second thought to at the time but that turn out to be important.'

The programme, which has been running for eight years, goes out once a month and is watched by at least 12 million people each time. Police and BBC researchers staff 28 studio telephone lines, ready to take calls from viewers with information. And they have to work extremely hard: an average programme will attract an incredible 2,000 calls.

So who actually calls in? 'All sorts of people,' says Nick Ross, co-presenter with Sue Cook. 'It's not a question of goodies against baddies. Did you know, for example, that one-third of all British men have a criminal record by the age of 30? Everybody has their own code of honour: there are people who may be involved in gang warfare, for example, who won't put up with sex crimes; burglars who will help catch a murderer; murderers who disagree with armed robbery and so on. And people will call in even if it's painful – maybe they're a relative of the criminal. People have even called in about themselves.'

By last December *Crimewatch* had featured 934 cases, leading to 326 arrests. In general, one in five of the crimes it shows are solved – crimes that the police might otherwise have had to leave the book open on.

Detective Constable Jacqui Hames, a police presenter of the programme, along with her colleague Superintendent David Hatcher is not surprised by *Crimewatch*'s success. 'It reaches a bigger audience than the police by themselves could hope to do,' she says. 'And I'm impressed by the attention to detail put in by the production team – the high standard and the genuine interest in the job the programme does.' She is sometimes surprised, however, by *which* crimes get solved. 'On the face of it some seem almost too tough to stand a chance,' she says. 'Yet sometimes it's the most obscure case that's sorted by the end of the evening and the one you thought would be no problem is still sitting there a month later.'

Crimewatch uses as many ways as possible to jog the memories of viewers who might unknowingly be able to solve a crime. The most elaborate are the three reconstructions featured on each programme. 'We start with whatever information the police have and then do our

own research,' says Mills. 'We make sure we've talked to any witnesses, and the victim if possible. Sometimes people are prepared to be interviewed for the reconstruction film itself and it's up to them if they want to be seen in silhouette or just have their voice used. When it comes to casting actors as villains, the victims and witnesses often help us to find somebody with a good physical resemblance.'

Do some crimes make better reconstructions than others? 'The type of crime doesn't matter in itself,' says Mills, 'but usually it needs a national implication; perhaps looking for somebody who

programme interesting but without glamorising the crimes and without making people feel too frightened to leave their homes,' she says. 'We always take care to point out that the crimes we feature are actually rare. What's important to me is the knowledge that somebody dangerous has been taken out of harm's way or that other people are being protected from falling victim to the same criminal. I'm pleased to say that we get a lot of letters and I even get stopped in the street by people saying the same.'

'The thing is,' adds Nick Ross, 'that we're actually showing that something can be done. Yes, sometimes we

Crimewatch UK **presenters Sue Cook and Nick Ross (seated) with Superintendent David Hatcher and DC Jacqui Hames**

could be anywhere in the country or somebody regarded as particularly dangerous. And we have to be sure there are enough clues or else there's no point. An artist's impression, a car or number plate, dropped jewellery or a pen found at the scene. Perhaps even an unusual make of gun left behind. Anything that people might have information about.'

Presenter Sue Cook, is, like the rest of the team, very aware of the tightrope they walk between providing the information needed to get a response and turning crime into some kind of voyeuristic entertainment. 'We have to make the

portray a disturbing event, but we're also offering people the opportunity to do something about it. To ring in and help stop it happening again.'

And that's just what people do. 'It may be 200 calls, like a case last year when a prostitute was murdered,' says Cook, 'or it might be just a vital one or two. It only needs a couple of calls, if they're the right ones.'

DC Hames agrees. 'Sometimes it seems like pure luck,' she says. 'The right person just happens to be watching. So you cross your fingers, thank your lucky stars and hope that even more people watch next time. I'd definitely recommend it.'

Julie Allan

BBC Photograph Library

Sport

In the year of the Olympics, British sportsmen and women returned from Barcelona with five gold medals, Lennox Lewis emerged as the great British heavyweight boxing hope, and Nick Faldo won the Open.

Nigel Mansell became Formula One World Champion and was voted BBC Sports Personality of the Year, and World Cup Cricket was the first big sporting event to be broadcast on satellite TV.

All the major sporting events – from the European Championships to Wimbledon – are included, as well as behind the scenes features and profiles of the top sports personalities.

1992 was a remarkable year for sport and the chapter concludes with Clement Freud's unique and entertaining Sports Review of the Year.

5

Sport

WINTER OLYMPICS

Hugh Costello reflects on what might have been for British competitors at the Albertville Winter Olympics

It is a tradition of the Winter Olympics that the British media rarely has anything to get excited about outside the ice rink, where the like of John Curry, Robin Cousins and Torvill and Dean have excelled. In the absence of such prodigious talents, British teams go into competition with the spirit of the Games – it's not the winning that counts, but the taking part – very much in their minds.

But in the build-up to the 1992 Games, contested in an area of over 2,500 square miles around Albertville in the French Alps, it was a skater of a different type on whom all the hype was focused. Wilf O'Reilly, a 27-year-old from Birmingham, had won gold in the spectacular and precarious sport of short-track speed skating when it was a demonstration event in Calgary in 1988, and was the reigning world champion in the event. The Albertville Games, it was confidently predicted, provided the stage on which O'Reilly would claim his place in the Olympic Hall of Fame.

Alas, that most experienced and astute of commentators, David Coleman, hit the nail on the head when he pointed out in the *Radio Times* preview of the Games: 'It's a dangerous sport and all kinds of things can go wrong.' O'Reilly duly proved the point by taking a tumble during the semi-final, when he was ideally placed to make it through to the showdown.

O'Reilly's exit was somewhat controversial. His coach, Archie Marshall, alleged that the world champion had been interfered with by New Zealand's Mike McMillen. But the affable O'Reilly refused to be drawn into a slanging match and took his disappointment philosophically: 'A real champion is not the person who wins but one who can lose occasionally and come back and win again.' When the four-man relay team led by O'Reilly was eliminated in the semi-final a few days later, Britain's golden boy returned to Birmingham with nothing to show for his efforts but a few cuts and bruises and a promise to set the record straight next time round.

Meanwhile, medal hopes were rising to the east in La Plagne,

where Britain's bobsleighers were aiming to take advantage of the fall of the Berlin Wall. For the first time, they had access to the bobsleigh technology that had made East Germany virtually unbeatable for years and 31-year-old Mark Tout was determined to lead his crew to Britain's first victory in the event since Tony Nash and Robin Dixon won two-man gold in 1964.

It can't have helped Tout's chances that O'Reilly's fall had made him the new focal point for a British press corps desperate for something positive to report from an otherwise glum Games. Despite being given an exceptionally quick start by his colleagues in the four-man bob, Tout, who had already finished a creditable sixth in the

Britain's medal hope, speed skater Wilf O'Reilly in action at Albertville

Action-Plus

two-man event, made a series of uncharacteristic driving mistakes on the lower part of the run, demonstrating that the pressure of carrying the hopes of the entire British team was too great.

'I just couldn't relax,' Tout admitted. 'I was steering far too hard and cutting a lot of ice, which shaves off time. This is a tough competition and it's all about doing it on the day. Unfortunately, I didn't.'

As the Britons struggled, the nations that traditionally dominate the Winter Games were racking up their medals. In Alpine skiing, Petra Kronberger and Patrick Ortlieb were warming the cockles of the Austrian hearts, and flamboyant Italian Alberto Tomba was making history by retaining his giant slalom title. America's Kristi Yamaguchi and the Unified Team's Viktor Petrenko were the stars of the figure skating events, in which Joanne Conway made a valiant but ultimately fruitless bid to restore British pride.

For many television viewers, the Games came alive late at night, when coverage of the ice hockey tournament threatened to achieve cult status. Speed, strength and stick control were the watchwords as a succession of thrilling matches enthralled the crowds at the Meribel ice-rink. Sweden, Czechoslovakia and the United Sates were fiercely competitive but it was the Unified Team and Canada who made it through to the final on 23 February. The Canadians, in their national sport, were seeking their first gold medal in nearly 40 years, but the Unified Team proved worthy guardians of the Soviet Union's pre-eminence in recent Games and ran out 3–1 winners.

Just as the pundits were beginning to complain that the Albertville Games lacked a real star, a worthy inheritor of the mantle of Franz Klammer or Torvill and Dean, 16-year-old Toni Niemenen from Finland launched himself off the ski-jump ramp in his bright pink suit and stunned the world by winning two gold medals.

Niemenen went into the scenic and spectacular event with an unenviable burden of expectation on his young shoulders, and could manage only bronze in the 90m category. But he picked himself up for the team competition and won the gold for Finland with a breathtaking leap of 122m. Using the recently-invented V technique, in which the jumper uses his skis as wings rather than keeping them close together, Niemenen, at 5ft 6in and less than eight stone, proved himself to be an unlikely boy wonder and left us with perhaps the most memorable images of the Games.

The Winter Olympics will, henceforth, follow a different four-year cycle to its high-profile Summer counterpart, starting at Lillehammer in Norway in 1994. The switch has prompted some sponsors and television companies, especially in the USA, to question whether the Games attract sufficient public interest to justify the expense of mounting them (the British team invested almost half a million pounds in its ill-fated journey to Albertville). There is talk of boosting the Winter Games by moving some of the more popular indoor events such as boxing and basketball into the Winter cycle, replacing them with advertiser-friendly sports like golf or American football.

The British, too, had a suggestion to make. Sports Minister Robert Atkins could be seen wandering the slopes of Albertville lobbying for the inclusion of curling, a Scottish invention, as a competitive Olympic sport. It may not do much to boost American television ratings, but at least curling would give the beleaguered Brits something to cheer about.

Hugh Costello

Austria's Patrick Ortlieb – Men's Downhill Gold Medallist

Action-Plus

THE OLYMPIC GAMES

The Barcelona Olympics was arguably the most memorable sporting event of the year. But how did the city cope with the staging of the Games? And how did the BBC cope with such extensive sporting coverage? Hugh Costello reports on the greatest show on earth

The Best of British

It is an unwritten rule of the Olympic Games that for every triumph there is a tragedy, and for every joyful celebration a disconsolate trudge back to the changing room. That rule has never held so fast for the British team than at Barcelona 92. Take the men's sprints, for example. While team captain Linford Christie was crowning a glorious career with a gold medal, young Jason Livingston was destroying a promising one with a positive dope test. And we witnessed hurdling heaven and hell: heaven for Sally Gunnell from Essex as she ran the race of her life to win gold, hell for Welshman Colin Jackson as he wrote off a fantastic season with disaster in the Olympic final.

In all, Britain won five gold medals at the 1992 Olympics. Here's how.

Linford Christie

At 32, the grand old man of British sprinting had a cabinet full of medals and a list of records as long as your arm. He was British, European and Commonwealth champion, and had a silver to his name from the 1988 Games in Seoul (upgraded from a bronze after the disqualification of Ben Johnson).

There were those who believed that he was too old to handle the intensity of another Olympic final, but Christie wasn't among them: he was on a high after being one of four men to break the world record at the Tokyo world championships in 1991, and knew himself to be stronger and fitter than ever before.

The failure of Carl Lewis to qualify for the American 100m team a few weeks before the Games caused a ripple of excitement. In the absence of the greatest modern

Linford Christie wins the 100m gold medal

Olympian, Christie was the senior statesman of the blue riband event. But he still faced a stiff challenge from Americans Leroy Burrell and Dennis Mitchell and the Namibian Frankie Fredericks.

The final took place in the Montjuic Stadium on 1 August. Christie had romped through his heats and semi-final, and was now using all his vast experience to concentrate on the task ahead. While others fidgeted and false-started, Christie kept his eye on the tape. They got away third time, and 9.96 seconds later Christie was breasting the tape to strike a blow for the thirty-somethings.

Sally Gunnell

At the world championships in Tokyo in 1991, Sally Gunnell was heartbroken to be pipped for gold on the last stride of the 400m hurdles by Tatyana Ledovskaya of the Unified Team. But rather than accepting that she was second best, the 26-year-old from Chigwell in Essex set to work on her technique, and she reaped the rewards in the Montjuic Stadium on 3 August.

Gunnell, the reigning Commonwealth champion and ladies' captain of the British team, was lifted by the victory of her male counterpart Linford Christie two nights earlier: 'I wanted to follow in his footsteps,' said Gunnell. Between her and a gold medal were her old rival Ledovskaya and the formida-

Sally Gunnell goes for gold in the Olympic 400m hurdles final

ble Americans Sandra Patrick-Fermor and Janeene Vickers.

Gunnell ran a faultless race and found herself in front going over the penultimate hurdle. Patrick-Fermor was close behind but Gunnell found an extra gear and rather than hanging on she extended her lead to take gold. 'I gave it everything I could,' she said later. 'I have to say there is not much of the race I remember. It is just beginning to sink in. I am so pleased, so delighted.'

Chris Boardman

Going into the Barcelona Games, individual pursuit cyclist Chris Boardman had a sneaking feeling that the astonishing bike designed for him by British company Lotus would take him to a gold medal, but he wisely played down any potential hype: 'We all knew this bike was something extremely special but you are always nervous. Anything can go wrong at the last minute. But I think having it was probably the difference between gold and bronze.'

Chris Boardman on his Lotus superbike wins Britain's first individual Olympic gold for cycling for 84 years

The 23-year-old from the Wirral, whose past record included bronze medals at two Commonwealth Games, took full advantage of his bike's revolutionary design. Boardman annihilated Denmark's Jan Petersen to reach the semi-final, where he easily outpaced Australia's Mark Kingsland around the circular wooden track.

In the final on 29 July, Boardman was up against the world champion, Jens Lehmann of Germany. A last-minute technical hitch threatened to justify Boardman's earlier caution, but the behind the scenes team solved the problem and Boardman was away. The Briton took the name of the event to heart: not content to simply record a better time than his opponent, he set out in hot pursuit of Lehmann. With one lap to spare he overhauled his rival to win Britain's first cycling

gold since the tandem team of Harry Ryan and Thomas Lance won at Antwerp in 1920.

Steve Redgrave and Matthew Pinsent

Thirty-year-old Steve Redgrave, a farmer's son from Marlow, is one of the greatest British Olympians of all time. His 6ft 5in, 15 stone frame first contributed to a rowing gold in the coxed fours in Los Angeles in 1984. Four years later, he switched to coxless pairs and again took the gold, with partner Tony Holmes. Barcelona 92 gave him a shot at a unique hat-trick, and he took his

opportunity with both hands.

For four months leading up to the Games, Redgrave was afflicted with a severe dose of colitis that drained his reserves and threatened to disable him from competing in this most intense of sports. But Redgrave drew on his vast wealth of experience and determination to take his place alongside new partner Matthew Pinsent on the rowing lake at Banyoles.

Pinsent, a 21-year-old Oxford undergraduate who will compete in his third Varsity Boat Race this spring, was the perfect partner. Young, super-fit and dedicated, he provided the power at stroke while Redgrave controlled things from the bow. From the outset, it was obvious that their closest rivals, from Germany and Slovenia, were outclassed. The gold was theirs, and no sooner were they back on dry land than Redgrave was hinting at his plans for Atlanta in 1996: 'I felt extremely relaxed and I want to do it again. It seems to be getting better the more it goes on.'

The Searle Brothers

Of all Britain's gold medal-winning performances in Barcelona, the Searle brothers' effort on the lake at Banyoles was perhaps the most unexpected. No-one doubted that Jonny, 23 and Greg, 20 had the talent, but they were up against Italy's Abbagnale brothers, rowing legends in their own lifetime. Even to suggest that the two giants from Surrey could outpace the masters from Pompeii was tantamount to heresy, but the Searles went into the

Steve Redgrave and Matthew Pinsent

coxed pairs final on 2 August with heresy on their minds.

Egged on by cox Garry Herbert, they overturned a seemingly hopeless deficit with just 250m of the 2,000m course to go. As the line loomed, the British brothers made a superhuman effort to keep their rhythm going. 'We had no idea what was going on in the last few metres,' said Greg. 'Everything had gone black. We switched to autopilot and, because we are brothers, we were both doing the same.'

Associated Press

The Searle brothers with emotional cox Garry Herbert during the medal ceremony after their victory in the coxed pairs

In one of the most dramatic finishes in the entire Games, the Searles beat their Italian rivals by a matter of inches to take gold. As the Abbagnales slumped despondently over their oars, Greg and Jonny punched the air in jubilation, while Garry Herbert climbed from his cockpit to join in the celebrations. The tiny cox had been out of sight throughout the race, but when it came to the medals ceremony his tears of joy provided some of the most moving and memorable images of the Games.

The Games in your Living Room
The 1992 Olympic Games in Barcelona were memorable for British viewers and listeners for one very simple reason: not since the Moscow Games of 1980 had they been able to watch or listen to the major events at a sensible time of the day. Los Angeles (1984) was eight hours behind, while Seoul (1988) was ten hours ahead, and most of the big events seemed to be on at an ungodly hour of the morning. Last summer, though, Europe got its revenge, and British fans were able to tune-in to top athletics

BRITAIN'S MEDAL WINNERS

GOLD

Athletics:
100 metres	Linford Christie
400 metres hurdles	Sally Gunnell

Cycling:
4,000 metres individual pursuit	Chris Boardman

Rowing:
Coxless pairs	Steven Redgrave, Matthew Pinsent
Coxed pairs	Jonathan Searle, Greg Searle, Garry Herbert

SILVER

Canoeing:
C1 slalom	Gareth Marriott

Judo:
Light-heavyweight	Raymond Stevens
Light-heavyweight	Nicola Fairbrother

BRONZE

Archery:
Individual	Simon Terry
Team	Richard Priestman, Steven Hallard, Simon Terry

Athletics:
400 metres hurdles	Kriss Akabusi
Javelin	Steve Backley
Women's 4 x 400 metres relay	Phylis Smith, Stephanie Douglas, Jennifer Stoute, Sally Gunnell
Men's 4 x 400 metres relay	Roger Black, David Grindley, Kriss Akabusi, John Regis

Boxing:
Light-middleweight	Robin Reid

Hockey:
	Women's team

Judo:
Middleweight	Kate Howey
Half-lightweight	Sharon Rendle

Swimming:
200 metres breaststroke	Nick Gillingham

Yachting:
Soling class	Lawrie Smith, Robert Cruikshank, Ossie Stewart

as they tucked in to their tea.

The Barcelona Games were the biggest ever, and to ensure that the armchair spectator could share in the occasion, the BBC mounted the most extensive sporting coverage in its history. To cope with the densely packed schedule, BBC TV showed more than 250 hours of action; an average of 16 hours each day.

The preparations began on the day in October 1986 when International Olympic Committee president Juan Antonio Samaranch announced that Barcelona had been awarded the Games. Within half an hour, the London office of British Telecom International had received a telex booking satellite links between Spain and London six years in advance. The accessibility of Barcelona, along with the technological advances in broadcasting in recent years, meant that BBC TV could, for the first time, present the entire Games *in situ*, without having a London studio to link events.

Needless to say, the bureaucracy and paperwork involved in mounting the coverage were breathtaking in their scale. Fees and facilities had to be arranged, equipment and personnel had to be got hold of and security clearance had to be obtained. By the time the Games began, BBC TV's executive producer Martin Hopkins was moved to admit: 'When form-filling becomes an Olympic Sport, I'm a

real medal prospect.'

The years of preparation paid off once the events were underway. It took the images of the world's greatest sporting event just a quarter of a second to make the trip from Barcelona to Television Centre, via a Eutelsat satellite hovering 23,000 miles above Europe.

A flaming arrow leaves the bow of Antonia Rebollo to light the Olympic Torch at the opening ceremony of the Barcelona Olympics

With Desmond Lynam presenting the evening events, it fell to Steve Rider to keep the millions watching at home up-to-date with the daytime action. Rider is in no doubt about which of those daytime events will live longest in his memory.

'From a professional point of

view, the Searle brothers' victory was the most exciting. Not only was it quite unexpected, but the manner in which they won had us all jumping up and down in the studio.

'In the evenings, I was in the fortunate position of being able to wander up the hill to the Montjuic Stadium to watch the big athletics finals. Being in the stadium for Linford Christie's win was tremendous, and I thought Sally Gunnell's gold medal run was an immaculate performance. For atmosphere, though, the last night of athletics, when Spain's Firmin Cacho won the 1,500m gold, was the best.'

How Barcelona Coped

For Barcelona, the staging of the Olympic Games brought to an end a 70-year wait. The city first bid for the Games in the early 20s, but Paris was preferred. The next target was the 1936 Games, and the Catalans were so confident of getting them that they went ahead and built a stadium on top of the Montjuic hill. Alas, the Spanish Civil War was brewing and Barcelona lost out to Hitler and Berlin. Hopes were rekindled for 1972, but by that time the stadium had fallen into disrepair and another German city, Munich, was chosen instead. Not until one of the city's leading figures, Juan Antonio Samaranch, became the president of the International Olympic Committee in the 80s did a

The Montjuic Stadium, Barcelona

real bandwagon of support build up behind Barcelona's bid.

Once chosen, the city fathers resolved not just to rebuild the original Montjuic stadium but to embark on a modernisation programme for the whole city. Construction began on a new airport terminal, a motorway, telecommunications tower, marina and apartments to house competitors and officials (the apartments are now helping to solve the city's housing shortage). The railway line that once ran across the beach was moved, opening the centre of the city up to the Mediterranean. In all, more than £4 billion was invested in making the city an appropriate venue.

Coping with the influx of 18,000 competitors and officials and a similar number of media representatives was never going to be easy for a city of just 1.7 million people, but Barcelona rose to the occasion. Says BBC TV presenter Steve Rider: 'I've been to four Games now and I always approach them with some trepidation because there are so many things that can go wrong. For quality of organisation and style of presentation Barcelona was the best. It was very efficient but never allowed the need for efficiency to strangle the atmosphere, as sometimes happens at major sporting spectacles. It was bright, colourful and relaxed.'

Barcelona had a strong incentive to prove itself worthy of the Olympic honour. Elsewhere in Spain, 1992 was a vintage year. Seville hosted Expo 92 and Madrid was the European City of Culture. For Barcelona, fiercely proud of its Catalan identity and weary of being seen by the rest of Spain as a troublesome relation, the Olympics were an opportunity both to reaffirm its cultural separateness and demonstrate that separateness does not have to be accompanied by chaos, violence or disorder. With a style and heritage all its own, Barcelona is a mature city with a clear idea of where it stands within Spain and Europe as a whole. The trouble-free success of the 1992 Olympic Games provided a lesson that other regions of Europe would do well to learn.

Obscure Sports at the Barcelona Olympics

With 25 sports in official competition, there were more medals on offer in Barcelona than ever before. But while the athletics, swimming and gymnastics events captured the world's imagination, others were barely noticed outside those countries hotly contesting for medals.

Take baseball, for example. The professional variety is almost a religion in the United States, but the amateur form that made its official Olympic debut in Barcelona was contested by an unlikely hotchpotch of nations: Japan, Taiwan, Puerto Rico, the Dominican Republic, Spain, Italy, the United States (college boys all) and Cuba. The latter nation made it clear that the baseball gold was not so much desirable as imperative.

Fidel Castro, who once tried to ban the Yankee game but found it too engrained within his country's culture, saw the Olympics as perhaps the last throw of the Cold War dice. The Cubans duly obliged, sweeping aside Taiwan 11-1 in the final. The Americans failed to win a medal, yielding third place to Japan.

Then there was badminton. Its arrival on the Olympic scene completed a remarkable resurgence for racket sports. In 1984, there were none in the Games: four years later tennis and table tennis were given official Olympic blessing, and to the joy of the Asian nations who dominate the sport, badminton joined them at Barcelona.

The Indonesians and South Koreans dominated the four badminton events, finishing with two golds each, China and Malaysia failed to live up to their own expectations. Only Denmark, with one bronze medal, managed to prevent an Asian clean-sweep.

The three demonstration sports on show in Barcelona had one thing in common – aggression. First there was taekwondo, a Korean martial art in which hands and feet are used to such deadly effect that competitors have to wear helmets and body pads to avoid serious injury. Then there was the fast and furious sport of roller hockey, of which IOC president Juan Antonio Samaranch was himself a practitioner in his youth.

Finally there was pelota, a game as beloved in the north of Spain as rugby league is in the north of England. This spectacular sport, in which a four and a half ounce ball

The fast-moving sport of pelota

Action-Plus

is flung against a huge wall at 150mph by a wicker basket which is strapped to the hand, was the most popular of the demonstration sports. Combining speed, strength and danger, the Basque national sport made a big impression at Barcelona 92, but it may not yet have sufficiently international credentials to justify full inclusion in future Games.

merka of Algeria defying the fundamentalists at home to win the women's 1500m; and Jackie Joyner-Kersee of the United States retaining her heptathlon title in magnificent style.

America's basketball dream team joined professional tennis stars to mark the beginning of the end of a truly amateur approach to the Games. The Cubans returned from

wonders against the backdrop of the city spread out below them. And in the swimming baths, Kristina Egerszegi of Hungary won three golds to add to the one she achieved in Seoul.

As ever, the gymnastics provided a graceful counterpoint to the more boisterous exertions of track and field. Tatiana Gutsu and Vitali Chtcherbo of the Unified teams were the stars. Another indoor sport, weightlifting, was a late-night favourite on television. Turkey's Naim Suleymanoglu confirmed his status as the greatest lifter of his generation by retaining the featherweight gold.

Spare a thought too, for the celebrated losers at Barcelona 92. In the 200m, Michael Johnson was deemed to have the gold sewn up but failed to make the final. Sergie Bubka, the greatest pole-vaulter of all time, suffered a similar fate. Jamaican sprinter Merlene Ottey went into the Games knowing it was her last chance for glory but came away with nothing to show but a bronze at 200m.

The real winners at the 1992 Olympics, though, were the thousands of competitors in events as obscure as modern pentathlon and handball who were content simply to be there, taking part in the world's greatest sporting spectacle.

As the countdown begins to Atlanta 1996, it is these most traditional of Olympians who will continue to give the Games its special flavour.

Hugh Costello

The USA men's 4 x 100m relay team celebrate their world record of 37.40. From left: Carl Lewis, Mike Marsh, Leroy Burrell and Dennis Mitchell

Summary

It is the beauty of Baron Pierre de Coubertin's brainchild that although each modern Olympiad may be very different from the others, none is ever disappointing. Even the Boycott Games of 1976, 1980 and 1984, when first the Africans, then the Americans and Germans (and some Britons) and finally the Eastern-bloc chose to make the Games the focus of a political statement, managed to be utterly memorable. It seems the good Baron knew what he was doing when he revived the Olympic concept back in 1896.

The 1992 Games will be remembered for Carl Lewis, the greatest Olympian of all time, adding two more golds, in long jump and 4 x 100m relay, to his collection, despite failing to qualify for the 100m; for South Korea's Hwang Young-Cho leading the marathon field up Montjuic hill, the toughest finish to the 26-mile race in Olympic history; for Hassiba Boul-

self-imposed Olympic exile to win seven gold medals in the boxing ring. It might have been eight but for Michael Carruth of Ireland, who won his country's first gold since 1954 amid some of the most joyous scenes of the Games. The Chinese diving team thrilled spectators and viewers alike as they performed

Romania's Lavinia Corina Milosovici scored a perfect ten and won the gold medal in the floor exercises in the women's gymnastics competition

THE EUROPEAN CHAMPIONSHIPS

In a competition both England and Scotland would rather forget, the underdogs, Denmark, triumphed to win an astonishing final against the might of World Cup winners Germany. By Chris Peters

It isn't often that the dustcart upstages the Lord Mayor's Show but Denmark's European Championship triumph in Sweden was as popular as it was unexpected.

The Danes, who had failed to qualify for the final stages of the tournament, were called in at the 11th hour when United Nations sanctions against war-torn Yugoslavia forced the withdrawal of their national team. Denmark, we thought, were just there to make up the numbers. They would battle gamely throughout the group stages before bowing out to let the big boys get down to business.

The Danes had other ideas. They not only won – causing one of the biggest upsets in recent soccer history – but played with an open, attacking style in a competition which often threatened to die of fright.

Faced with just three group games and little margin for error, too many countries employed a 'safety first' tactic in the hope that their rivals would make the mistakes. Denmark had nothing to lose. They had already been eliminated from the competition once and regarded anything else as a bonus. Their 2-0 victory over world champions Germany in the final brought a fairy-tale ending to a tournament barely deserving of it.

The Danes were refreshingly simple in their approach. Throughout the tournament, manager Richard Moller Nielsen put his side's strength down to a diet of Swedish boiled salmon and compared their strategy to the structure of his mother's old corsets.

It was his straightforward style which so nearly upset England's plans in the opening group game in Malmö. Moller Nielsen's side – assembled in just ten days following Yugoslavia's withdrawal – drew 0-0 but would have launched their campaign with a win had the post not denied John Jensen's goalbound effort. That miss looked to have cost Denmark dear when they were defeated 1-0 by the host nation but they refused to be written off and goals from Henrik Larsen and Lars Elstrup earned them victory over pre-tournament favourites France and a place in the semi-finals.

It was a sad reflection on the negative nature of the competition that France and England, strongly tipped to qualify from Group One, should go home early having amassed a meagre four points and three goals between them.

While everybody applauded Denmark's achievement, few expected them to progress beyond the semi-finals where they met Holland, the reigning champions. Holland's AC Milan triumvirate of Gullit, Rijkaard, and Van Basten are revered throughout the world; many of Denmark's players were unknown outside their own country.

However, that counted for little in Gothenburg's Ullevi Stadium as the

Peter Schmeichel – Manchester United and Denmark goalkeeper

Action-Plus

Dutch twice fell behind to Henrik Larsen goals before forcing a penalty shoot-out. Manchester United goalkeeper Peter Schmeichel was the Danish hero, saving Van Basten's spot-kick to clinch their place in the final.

Holland, it was revealed later, had taunted their opponents with offers of tickets to watch the final, and Schmeichel said: 'After Holland scored the first equaliser they had the appearance of a team who thought they had won the match – they were wrong weren't they.'

Modesty was never the Germans' greatest attribute either. Berti Vogts's team had booked their reservations at a Gothenburg hotel in anticipation of a final appearance and they didn't disappoint.

Victory over Sweden meant they were just one game from becoming the only World Cup-winning side to conquer Europe at the first attempt. 'We want the title, Denmark are going to experience the real world champions,' declared Vogts. Even the most ardent Dane found it hard to disagree.

However, on the most memorable night in the history of the European Championships, a team regarded by many as the whipping boys of the competition humbled Germany 2-0 to complete an astonishing achievement. John Jensen gave Denmark an early lead but it was the scorer of the second goal, Kim Vilfort, who best personified his team's battling spirit.

Vilfort had spent most of the championships travelling between Stockholm and Copenhagen where his daughter was being treated for leukaemia. It was fitting that his goal 12 minutes from time should seal victory, not only for Denmark but for all the romantics and 'neutrals' who supported their cause.

If Denmark's triumph was wholly unexpected, England's shortcomings had been all too evident in the months leading up to the tournament.

Manager Graham Taylor's preparations were also disrupted by the loss through injury of defenders Rob Jones, Lee Dixon, Mark Wright and Gary Stevens, and winger John Barnes.

Despite using an incredible total of 73 players during his two years in charge and adopting numerous different strategies, Taylor arrived at his first major championships in a state of disarray. There was no Paul Gascoigne and no Barnes; Taylor had lost both his right backs and was without a recognised sweeper. 'There is no-one capable of making you think "Hey, look at that". We may lack that little bit of flair,' he admitted.

How right he was. England survived that rocky opening game against Denmark to earn a draw which, the optimists in the camp were quick to point out, was more than they had done in the whole of the disastrous 1988 championships. But there was no glossing over the weaknesses and Taylor once again shuffled his pack for the disappointing 0-0 draw with France in Malmö.

In a game more reminiscent of rugby union encounters between the two countries, France lacked the desire, and England the ability,

Gary Lineker

Action-Plus

to win. A match which had received top billing will be remembered more for an unsavoury encounter between Basile 'Boom Boom' Boli and Stuart 'Psycho' Pearce than any piece of soccer artistry the two sides had to offer.

Pearce suffered a nasty cut to his head in an off-the-ball incident but so nearly snatched victory for England when his fierce free kick hit the bar and bounced off the goal line to safety. 'I was looking across for the Russian linesman from 1966 and wondering where he'd gone to,' joked Taylor in reference to Geoff Hurst's controversial goal in the 1966 World Cup final.

Unfortunately England's predicament was no laughing matter and neither were the scenes in Malmö's main square that weekend as rival fans ran amok, shattering the image of the 'friendly finals'.

England had reached their final group game needing to win to stay in the competition, just as they had in Mexico in 1986 and Italy in 1990. Taylor's side knew they had to shrug off the stifling fear of failure against the host nation in Stockholm's Rasunda Stadium and they were off to the perfect start when David Platt scored after only four minutes.

However, England's hopes were dashed by a Swedish side who employed a typically British approach of direct, attacking football. Eriksson and Brolin scored the second half goals which sent Sweden through to the semi-finals and consigned England to an early exit.

Perhaps the saddest sight of all was that of captain Gary Lineker leaving the field on his last appearance in an England shirt. Lineker, who had already decided to quit international football and join Japanese side Grampus Eight in Nagoya, was hoping to end his glittering England career on a high note. It was not to be and the 31-year-old could barely hide his disappointment when he was substituted in the second half.

Taylor came under fire but defended his decision by claiming that 'it was not Gary's type of game'. Yet Lineker was renowned for rising to the big occasion.

Action-Plus

The England squad at the European Championships

It was his goal against Poland in Poznan which had booked Taylor's ticket to Sweden in the first place. It was his hat-trick, also against Poland, which saved England from elimination in the 1986 World Cup finals (not to mention earning Lineker the coveted Golden Boot award and a lucrative transfer to Barcelona). And four years later in Italy, it was his two penalties which averted a humiliating defeat at the hands of Cameroon.

The ability of a player who scored 322 goals in 631 games during his career cannot be questioned. The former Leicester City, Everton, and Spurs star was feared for his clinical finishing the world over. But in the months leading up to Sweden he had been burdened by talk of surpassing Bobby Charlton's record of 49 goals for England. When Lineker scored his 48th goal it seemed unthinkable that he would not add to that tally in the time available before his retirement.

There was to be neither a record nor a happy ending. The harsh truth was that, in three European Championship games, he failed to have one genuine scoring chance. 'Bobby was a better player anyway,' declared Lineker, who will be remembered as much for his mild manners and modesty as any of the many goals he scored (he never received so much as a yellow card throughout his career).

Asked if there was a rift between himself and Taylor, he added: 'Well, I would never hit him'. Maybe not, but there was a distinct unease in the relationship between player and manager which was to re-surface when Lineker's autobiography was published later in the year.

It was an unsatisfactory finale to a career which was rewarded with only two major honours – winner's medals in the European Cup Winners Cup with Barcelona and in the FA Cup with Spurs.

The failure of Lineker and England to make their mark in Sweden somewhat overshadowed another brave display by the ever unreliable Scots. Scotland have built up a reputation down the years for capitulating to minor nations in major championships as Zaire, Iran, Peru and Costa Rica will testify. But they are also famous for glorious defeats and the European Championships were no exception.

Faced with the might of Germany, Holland and the CIS in Group Two, Andy Roxburgh's side, like Denmark, had little to lose. Their raw endeavour so nearly earned a draw in the opening game against the Dutch but they were beaten by a late goal.

Scotland's next challenge, against Germany in Norkopping, proved to be one of the most exciting encounters of the tournament. Germany eventually won 2-0 but the Scots were highly praised for their open, attacking approach.

Their enterprise was rewarded in the final game against the CIS as Paul McStay, Brian McClair and Gary McAllister scored to complete a 3-0 win – the biggest victory by any side in the competition.

Scotland were going home early once again but they had managed to outstay England and proved once more that they are capable of rubbing shoulders with the best in the world.

Chris Peters

PAUL GASCOIGNE

After the saga of 'the knee', 1992 saw Gascoigne back in action with Italian club Lazio. Chris Peters reports on Gazza's long-awaited comeback

Terry Venables admitted to having mixed feelings the day he waved goodbye to Paul Gascoigne. 'I'm pleased for him, but it's like watching your mother-in-law drive off the cliff in your new car,' quipped the Spurs chief.

Venables was responsible for nursing Gascoigne through the most traumatic period of his life. From the tears of disappointment which captured the hearts of a nation during Italia 90, through the tears of despair which signalled his exit from the FA Cup final 11 months later, to the smiles which greeted his transfer to Lazio, Gascoigne's fortunes had come full circle.

He had left Italy on a tide of emotion after the World Cup and returned there bigger and more boisterous than ever. En route he made a detour through soccer's wilderness and at times threatened to disappear for good. But if Italia 90 – and the multi-million pound move to Lazio that followed – confirmed Gazza as a truly world class performer, the interim period did as much again to underline the irrepressible character of Britain's favourite footballing export.

Bold, brash, and blissfully irreverent (he insisted on hugging Margaret Thatcher when the two posed for pictures outside No10), Gascoigne embodies everything that is great about the bulldog spirit. As ex-pros and pundits queued up to write him off, the colourful Geordie buckled down to battle his way back from a crippling injury.

It occurred in one fateful moment at Wembley in May 1991 when, with his £8 million move to Italy agreed, he was attempting to end his Tottenham career with an FA Cup winners' medal. A dreadfully mistimed tackle on Nottingham Forest's Gary Charles left Gazza with a ruptured cruciate ligament in his right knee and so began a 12-month fight to save his career.

The transfer fee dropped to £5.5 million, although many doubted the deal would ever go through at all as Gascoigne underwent a series of complex operations, including one to repair damage inflicted on the knee in a nightclub fracas.

However, each month brought new progress and by April he was ready for action for the first time since Wembley. The press turned out in force for a training match at Spurs' Mill Hill training ground and Gazza didn't disappoint. Never one to shy away from the cameras, he treated them to a goal and celebrated by diving headlong into a big puddle. 'I'm feeling fine,' he declared. Lazio believed him.

He was flown to Rome and, a year to the day after being carried off at Wembley, Gascoigne began rigorous tests to decide whether or not his recuperation was complete. While England boss Graham Taylor selected his European Championship squad around one notable absentee, Gazza was paraded through Rome as an all-conquering hero. The Lazio fans had waited a long time to savour the moment.

Lazio are traditionally Rome's second club, destined to suffer in the shadow of their more illustrious neighbours Roma. Both clubs play in the city's Stadio Olimpico but that is about all they share. As in most cases where two big clubs are competing for local supremacy, there is no love lost.

Lazio have been starved of success. Besides winning the league title in 1974 and the Italian Cup way back in 1958, there has been little else for the fans to celebrate. They looked upon Gascoigne as their saviour, for the time being at least, and the club took every precaution to ensure he was up to the challenge.

He came through the preliminary tests on his heart, lungs and brain with flying colours ('You won't find my brain in there, it's in my feet,' he told professor Aldo Maiotti). Finally, despite a last-minute scare over a scan on the right knee, Lazio club doctor Claudio Bartolini declared himself satisfied and the deal went through. From first bid to completion, the transfer had taken 427 days.

Gascoigne's contract, signed two days before his 25th birthday, guaranteed him in excess of £500,000 a year, not to mention a house, car, armed bodyguards, and all the other trappings that accompany star status in Italian soccer. 'Not once did I think that I wouldn't come through it all,' he said. 'I'm not scared one bit – I'm out to prove that I'm still one of the best in the world.'

Lionello Celon, Lazio's managing director could hardly contain his excitement. 'I thought he was a bargain at £8 million but he's even more of a bargain now,' he enthused. 'We will build our team around him and I think he will fill the hole left in Italian soccer when Maradona went.'

Celon's flagrant devotion to the sport is typical of a nation who live, eat and breathe soccer. It comes second only to pasta in their staple diet. Italy's top clubs splash out staggering sums to attract the best players, making their Serie A the most skilful league in the world.

Italian soccer is also notorious for its cut-throat approach, a breeding ground for hatchet men and con artists. Whichever way he looked at it, Gascoigne knew he was submitting himself to the toughest test of all. Genoa's Mario Bartolazzi provided a timely reminder 44 minutes into Gazza's senior debut with a tackle which left the England man clutching his right knee. His pained expression was matched only by that of Celon and his financial advisors as they watched Lazio's prize asset and squirmed in their seats. When Gascoigne eventually rose to his feet, Rome breathed again.

Lazio weren't the only ones expressing relief. England manager Graham Taylor had been made acutely aware of his side's lack of finesse during a disastrous European Championship campaign in Sweden and knew Gascoigne could provide that missing spark.

Like Lazio boss Dino Zoff several weeks earlier, Taylor was coming under increasing pressure from the media to play his trump card sooner than he would have wished.

Gazza was recalled in October for the crucial World Cup qualifier against Norway at Wembley – four

Action-Plus

Gascoigne plays for England in a 1-1 draw against Norway on 14 October 1992

months earlier than Taylor had expected. Rarely have the England fans demanded so much of one man and even the usually fearless Gazza felt it necessary to urge caution. 'If I have a bad game it's not the end of the world,' he said, guardedly. 'We still have to go home, we still have to eat, we still have to live on and that's exactly what I will do.'

Gascoigne's reservations proved unfounded. Not only did he surprise everyone by lasting the full 90 minutes for the first time since his injury, but he produced a man of the match performance to inspire renewed confidence in the England side.

Norway scraped a 1-1 draw but Turkey did not get off so lightly when they arrived at Wembley a month later. Gascoigne was in match-winning mood. He scored two goals – doubling his tally from 21 previous caps – and created another for Alan Shearer as England triumphed 4-0 to hand Taylor the biggest victory of his international reign.

It was no fluke that Gascoigne's reappearance had coincided with an England revival. Taylor, like predecessor Bobby Robson, had seen his future become inextricably linked with Gazza's.

Gascoigne was born to be in the spotlight, and when Robson called him 'daft as a brush' it was as much an admission of defeat in his battle to resist the irresistible as a fond salute to England's clown prince.

Robson and Gascoigne marched on to Italia 90 hand-in-hand and came within a whisker of a place in the final. A similar pattern is unfolding now.

As Graham Taylor watches the path to the 1994 World Cup in the USA unfold before him, the dark clouds hanging over the past year are beginning to break.

And Gascoigne's star burns brighter than ever.

Chris Peters

CRICKET AND BROADCASTING IN 92

With the ever increasing potential of the broadcasting media, and the growth of satellite television, sports coverage has undergone dramatic changes. John Collis examines the impact of the media on televised sport and reviews the year's cricket highlights

Cricket in 1992 was dogged – or enlivened, perhaps – by a relentless series of controversies, and the role of broadcasting was one factor in the continuing story.

The neatest symbol of the growing influence of the media in sport, however, came late in the year, and in the boxing ring rather than on the cricket field. Lennox Lewis has the potential to become the first British-born heavyweight champion this century, and fought an eliminator against Donovan 'Razor' Ruddock in London on 1 November.

However, the bout took place in the middle of the night, to suit North American television, and British fight fans needed to subscribe to BSkyB in order to see it. Most people in this country had neither the stamina nor the technology to see their man's stunning victory.

Now that television broadcasting in the UK has almost infinitely widened in potential, with the advent of satellite and the spread of cable and pay-as-you-view, sport has become *the* battleground for viewers. It is the signing of exclusive rights to a major sporting event by BSkyB, even more than their first-run screening of the latest Hollywood movies, that sends an increasing number of us to the television dealers. Compared to the unrepeatable immediacy of live sport, Tom Cruise is just an image on dead celluloid, and he'll still be there tomorrow.

The first skirmish of 1992 involved cricket's major international competition, the World Cup, which was staged in Australia and New Zealand in February and March. This was packaged and promoted with a commercial awareness unparalleled in cricket. The old-school-tie brigade who still administrate the game are slowly coming to terms with the fact that they must now negotiate with slick marketing men, and that their fiefdom is increasingly being invaded by the demands of business.

This influence had taken its first giant step forward in 1975 when the Australian media magnate Kerry Packer, frustrated at being unable to buy the rights to televise Test cricket, simply bought the players instead and set up his own international competitions, staged specifically for commercial television.

Once peace had been restored, we could see that many of the changes were beneficial – more imaginative camera-work from a greater number of angles (including, eventually, from within the stumps and the batsmen's helmets) being the main one. Personally, I shall never get used to the main camera switching every over so that it is always behind the bowler's arm: the batsmen constantly seem to have

sneaked singles that you didn't notice, and one's mental picture of the ground is destroyed. By and large, however, a more upbeat approach to camera-work has enriched the television view of the game.

But the dangers are also apparent. A rain-affected World Cup match between England and South Africa ended in bewildering farce, largely because the match had to fit into pre-determined television schedules. And in autumn 1992 a Test match between Zimbabwe and New Zealand was interrupted not by the traditional 'rest day', but by a limited-over contest between the same two sides! Many feel it is unsatisfactory to interrupt a county match for the Sunday knockabout; at international level it is a nonsense.

The brash approach of the commercial entrepreneurs helped to make the World Cup an exciting event to a broad and youthful international television audience, many of whom bought 'replica' shirts

declaring their national identity, but the golden eggs of marketable 'instant' cricket will no longer be laid if the goose of the traditional, bedrock, epic game is killed by greed, or by lack of understanding of its essential character.

Most of us, of course, could not watch the World Cup at home. In one of their most successful coups in the overall battle plan of hurling money at major sport, BSkyB secured exclusive UK rights, and refused the BBC even the consolation of 'highlights' packages until the very last dish had been sold by the exercise.

In February, after saturation advertising, 78,000 new dishes were installed. In March, as the World Cup approached its climax, the monthly figure rose to 94,000. At this point 2.4 million households could receive satellite transmissions, a million more than a year previously. Allowing for those who had signed up earlier in anticipation of the World Cup, cricket had played a significant part in this growth.

Imran Khan in action in the final of the World Cup

Action-Plus

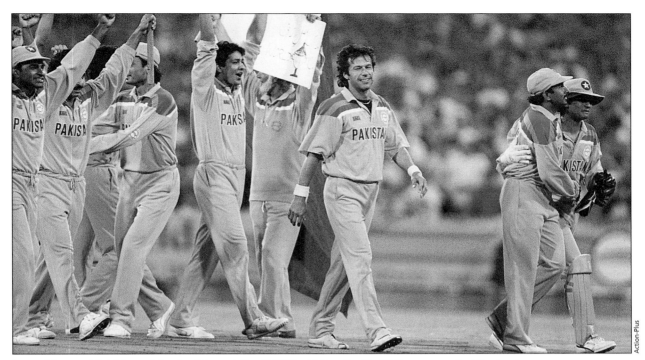

Action-Plus

Imran Khan and Pakistan celebrate victory at the 1992 World Cup final in Melbourne against England

BSkyB continued this momentum by buying the rights to live coverage of football's new Premier League (with the BBC showing highlights), though when you add to this ITV's Sunday-afternoon matches, Channel 4's coverage of Italy's *Serie A*, regular internationals and proliferating cup competitions, there are already fears that the appetite for constant televised football will become jaded, as it has for the much cheaper schedule-filling sport of snooker.

Eighteen months before the World Cup, the first major cricket event to be screened exclusively on satellite was the Benson and Hedges Cup Final – BSB, soon to be swallowed up by Sky, briefly owned the television rights to the competition. But there's a huge difference between the lesser of the two domestic cup competitions and the World Cup – in February 1992 cricket irreversibly entered the satellite era. What next? The Boat Race wouldn't sell too many dishes, but the Grand National? Wimbledon? Home Test matches? The FA Cup Final? Those hitherto sacrosanct events will surely come under fire from the skies, and from Sky.

South Africa, with the blessing of the African National Congress and after much multi-racial groundwork by their cricket supremo Ali Bacher, had already returned to international cricket with a brief visit to India – the most hard-line nation in opposing sporting links with South Africa under apartheid, India had broken off relations with Pretoria in 1948.

The World Cup was the next stage in the rehabilitation, followed by a historic visit to the Caribbean, which was also screened here live on satellite. In Barbados, South Africa and the West Indies contested their first-ever official Test match.

It was a classic. The hosts made two modest totals and South Africa had a comfortable first-innings lead. But even by this stage the visitors had shown their inexperience, allowing the West Indian batsmen to recover from almost certain defeat. When South Africa lost eight wickets for 25 in 20 overs on the final day, the natural order – a West Indian win – had been restored.

With South Africa accepted back into international cricket the authorities were faced with a prob-

lem over Zimbabwe. The standard of their cricket did not demand Test status – isolated one-day victories had been their only successes at top level, but the same can be said of Ireland and Holland. Without encouragement, though, their best players would presumably move over the border in search of Test cricket, as they had done in earlier years before South Africa was ostracised.

This would perhaps fatally reduce the game in Zimbabwe to a nostalgic, whites-only ritual. Under cover of the more headline-worthy decision to 'forgive' those English players who had been banned for touring South Africa, the International Cricket Conference quietly gave Zimbabwe Test status.

The domestic authorities also decreed a number of changes to the county game for 1993. Predictably, the Championship will consist of four-day games, with each of the 18 first-class counties playing each other once. In recent years three-day cricket has too often followed an artificial pattern – the sides jockey for advantage over two days and then the captains agree on a contrived last-day formula involving a declaration and a run chase. Four-day cricket may make this less likely, but professional sportsmen have always shown a talent for thwarting the best intentions of administrators.

The Benson & Hedges Cup will become a straight knock-out: until now it has been contested in four leagues with the top teams proceeding to a knock-out stage. From 1993 it will resemble its senior partner, the NatWest Trophy, and many cricketers are of the opinion that the old system maintained interest and revenue for longer, in that one bad game didn't immediately eliminate your club.

The main change is an attempt to revive spectator interest, both at the grounds and as television spectacle, in the Sunday League. Now on Sky, with consequently a smaller audience, it was without a sponsor in 1992.

All players are bemused and most are annoyed at the decision to start earlier and play for longer (50 overs per side rather than 40). It's more work, it makes the Sunday knock-about more like the other competitions, and for spectators it destroys the pattern of Sunday lunch followed by an afternoon's cricket.

Few players, however, will object to the garish clothing, with each county sporting its own colours. As the World Cup proved, there's a brisk market among younger supporters for 'replica' shirts, and if this increases both county support and revenue, all to the good. As for the white ball – I'm convinced that if cricket was invented tomorrow, the ball *would* be white. Sighting a dull red ball against trees or spectators, particularly as the light fades, is a hair-raising (and sometimes face-denting) handicap.

In 1992 Pakistan came to England as World Cup champions, and with the West Indies in a 'restructuring' phase they pressed their claim, simmering for some time, to be the best in the world at all forms of the game. In fact England beat them in the one-day matches, but Pakistan prevailed in the Tests.

Great fast bowlers have often hunted in pairs, and Pakistan have two of the greatest in the right-left punch of Waqar Younis and Wasim Akram. The television cameras now zoomed in on the biggest cricketing row since Mike Gatting exchanged pleasantries with Pakistan umpire Shakoor Rana. Surely bowlers this good, capable of swinging an old ball into the batsman's toes at murderous pace, must be cheating?

Bowlers have always worked on the ball to their advantage, but never under such scrutiny from TV replays and zoom lenses. In the old days, when the slow bowlers took over from the pacemen, they would openly scuff the ball in the dirt to give them more grip. A bowler can legally use sweat to smooth and polish, use spittle to weight one half of the ball, use a thumbnail to clean mud from the seam. But as soon as the thumbnail raises strands of the seam, in an attempt to achieve movement off the pitch, or scars the leather to increase the wind resistance, the bowler is cheating.

The dividing line is impossible to judge with precision, and most professionals would probably prefer 'all or nothing' to be the rule. Either they should not work on the ball, handing it to the umpire for cleaning, or they should gouge on regardless.

Accusations of cheating spread from the pitch to the television screen and the front pages of the press, and ultimately to the law courts. And as a welcoming prelude to Pakistan's winter visit to New Zealand, a television executive allegedly offered his cameramen a bonus for on-screen evidence of foul play. Once more, the broadcasters had overstepped the mark, ensuring that the contest was launched in an atmosphere of suspicion and acrimony.

As the English season ended and a winter of unprecedented international activity commenced, cricket made yet another invasion of the television news and the front pages. The selectors announced their squad for the visit to India. It did not include David Gower, an in-form and truly great player with a Test average in the mid-40s. It did not include Jack Russell, widely regarded as the world's most accomplished wicket keeper. It did include fast bowler Paul Jarvis, who had recently toured apartheid South Africa, whose season was dogged by injuries and could only manage a modest haul of wickets.

With press campaigns, mentions in the House and a threatened revolt in the MCC. Whoever said that cricket was dull?

John Collis

Allan Lamb (England) lbw Mushtaq Ahmed (Pakistan) in the 2nd Test at Lord's

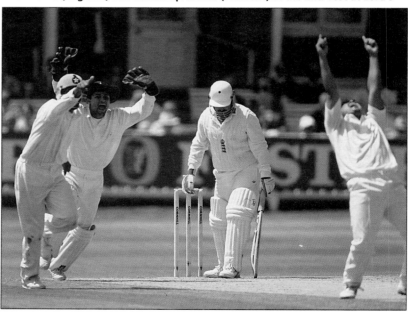

Action-Plus

WIMBLEDON 92

The All-England Lawn Tennis Championships gave the home crowd cause for celebration when Jeremy Bates won through to the final 16. Hugh Costello reviews the highlights of Wimbledon 92, goes behind the scenes with the Radio 5 team and pays tribute to Dan Maskell, one of the most respected names in the tennis world

They said it couldn't be done. Steffi Graf, plagued by injury, bad form and troubles in her personal life, to beat Monica Seles, the undisputed empress of women's tennis? Nonsense. Andre Agassi to prevail over the power of Becker, the stealth of Edberg and the serving of Stich? No chance.

If Wimbledon 92 proved anything, it proved that rules are made to be broken, dreams to be shattered and fairy tales to come true. Twelve months earlier, Andre Agassi, the golden boy from Las Vegas, had wowed the Centre Court crowd with his ironic whiter-than-white kit, his gracious charm and his fierce hitting. But he had been forced to admit that when it came to grass-court tennis he had a lot of catching up to do on the boom-boom brigade, the big men whose serves sent the ball hurtling over the net at the speed of a Formula One racing car.

Last July, though, Agassi found the elusive solution to one of the great dilemmas in world tennis: how does a baseliner with a comparatively pedestrian serve manage to outplay a big server at Wimbledon? The answer lay in the power and accuracy of his returns, the relentlessness of his double-handed passing shots, the sheer demoralisation his opponents felt when they saw yet another searing winner send up a tell-tale cloud of chalk as it landed plumb on the line.

At the start of Wimbledon fortnight, Agassi was fast earning a reputation as the sport's nearly-man. He had contested three grand slam finals and lost them all. What's more, his form in the months leading up to Wimbledon suggested that he'd be spending more time in the commentary box than on court. But like so many before him, Agassi came under the spell of the Wimbledon phenomenon. Exuberant victories over Boris Becker, many pundits' favourite for the title, and the rejuvenated John McEnroe (who had the consolation of a doubles win with Michael Stich) established that he was in the mood.

When he threw away a two-sets-to-one lead against the Croatian ace-machine Goran Ivanisevic in the final, it looked like the baseliners' revenge would have to go on hold for another year. But Agassi conjured up a brilliant fifth-set recovery that left his exasperated opponent flustered and frustrated. 'This tournament has offered me and my life so much,' said the victorious American afterwards. 'This is the greatest title in the world. It is the greatest achievement I have ever made.'

Agassi was one of the most popular men's singles winners in years. Perhaps only a British victor could have earned more popular acclaim. And, for once, a Briton raised his game in front of the home crowd to blaze a brilliant, if unlikely trail through the earlier rounds.

Jeremy Bates will probably remember Wimbledon 92 as the occasion on which his front lawn was colonised by reporters and paparazzi eager to find out where this unheralded saviour of British tennis had come from, ('I don't know if I'm more famous than Gazza but it certainly feels like it,' remarked Bates wryly).

A seasoned pro with years of disappointment and unfulfilled potential behind him, 30-year-old Bates suddenly found an extra gear, and despatched several highly-rated opponents to the tennis equivalent of an early bath. The quality of Bates's serve-and-volley technique was never in doubt. His ability to sustain it for a whole match, never mind an entire tournament, was. But it all came good against seventh seed Michael Chang, Spaniard Jaime Sanchez and France's Thierry

Andre Agassi hugs his trophy after defeating Goran Ivanisevic to win the men's singles final

Associated Press

Action-Plus

Jeremy Bates

Champion before Bates went out in five sets to number nine seed Guy Forget in the last 16.

In the women's final, it took Steffi Graf only 58 minutes of playing time to ruin Monica Seles's chances of a grand slam, though vintage Wimbledon weather meant that more than five hours elapsed between first point and last. The other feature of the final was the conspicuous absence of Seles's trademark grunt. Some experts attributed the world number one's capitulation to her efforts to stifle her natural noise-making, but it is doubtful whether Seles could have found any answer to Graf's impeccable grass-court tennis. The reigning champion won her fourth Wimbledon title in five years with consummate ease, using her unrivalled athleticism to run her less mobile opponent into the ground. Nonetheless, the German expressed surprise at the way she had won: 'Seles is not the type of player you beat 6-2 6-1. It's difficult to play your best against her. I never expected it.'

Graf is still only 23, and her 1992 victory gave notice that she has now set her sights on emulating, or even surpassing, Martina Navratilova's record of nine Wimbledon singles titles. There are those who would argue that it is only a matter of time before Seles, who has just turned 19, stamps her authority on the

world's most prestigious championship, but Graf, like her compatriot Boris Becker, has an almost spiritual affiliation with Wimbledon and it will take something special to remove her from the throne.

Associated Press

Steffi Graf with the ladies singles trophy, after defeating Monica Seles to take the championship

Wimbledon on Radio 5

The commentary team who work on Radio 5's coverage of the Championships certainly can't be accused of seeing tennis as just another sport. 'Some of them spend the morning playing on Wimbledon's indoor courts,' explains producer

Joanne Watson. 'John Inverdale in particular is very keen.'

Inverdale hosts the all-day coverage from a small 'presentation box' adjacent to the main commentary box overlooking Centre Court. The radio team have several commentary positions scattered around the All-England Club, as well as Perry's Perch, a vantage point high above the courts from which the various matches can be surveyed. The perch is so named because it is near a bronze statue of the great Fred Perry, three times Wimbledon champion in the 30s, who, at 83, celebrated his 46th year behind the microphone at the last Championships.

In common with their television counterparts, the Radio 5 team face the eternal dilemma posed by the weather. During the 1992 women's final, rain interrupted proceedings no fewer than four times. So how do they fill in the blank spaces? 'We have a certain amount of feature material prepared,' says Joanne Watson. 'And we look around for special guests who we can drag in to the presentation box and witter away to.'

At the end of what Watson describes as 'a shattering fortnight' the team take a well-deserved rest. For commentators David Mercer and Tony Adamson, it's a chance to go easy on their vocal chords. 'Tennis commentary on radio is an art form,' explains Watson. 'It's remarkable how well they do it, considering that they don't get much practise.'

Dan Maskell

The All-England Championships, and the whole tennis world, lost one of its greatest names late in 1992, when Dan Maskell, the undisputed voice of Wimbledon, died at the age of 84.

Ironically, his death came just months after the doyen of tennis commentators had decided to hang up his microphone after more than 40 years.

Maskell was the seventh of eight children in a working-class family, and his first involvement with the game was as a ball boy at Queen's Club in London in 1923. As a player, Maskell was the world professional champion in 1927, and won the British Professional Championship no fewer than 16 times. He became Wimbledon's first professional coach in 1929, and had never missed a single day's play since then.

By the time he retired Maskell had become an institution almost as venerable as the event itself. Like all great commentators, he knew instinctively when to speak and when to stay silent. When viewers

Dan Maskell at Eastbourne 1991

heard Maskell describe a cross-court volley as 'glorious', they knew he meant it. Likewise, his most famous catch phrase, 'Oh, I say', was reserved for moments of true inspiration. Maskell was never partial, showing a heartfelt respect for all the men and women who played the game, but he did deign, after his retirement, to name his all-time greatest men and women champions. He chose Rod Laver and Martina Navratilova.

Perhaps the most fitting epitaph for Dan Maskell was provided by 1975 Wimbledon champion Arthur Ashe, who once said: 'If you had been in a long sleep and suddenly woke up and heard Dan Maskell broadcasting from Wimbledon, you'd know all was well with the world.'

Dan Maskell:

11 April 1908 – 10 December 1992
Hugh Costello

FALDO'S OPEN VICTORY

In a year of British sporting successes, Nick Faldo conquered the world's top golfers to win the Open. Hugh Costello reviews Faldo's victory and rounds up the highlights of 1992's golf

In 1987, a 30-year-old budding superstar called Nick Faldo won his first Open Championship at Muirfield with an astonishing display of consistency and, apparently, nervelessness. Faldo shot 18 consecutive pars in the fourth and final round to consolidate the lead he had built up on the first three days and lift the title. In July 1992, history repeated itself as Faldo, now established as the world's pre-eminent golfer, kept his head to pip John Cook, one of the less well-known of the American contingent, over the final few holes of the same historic course in one of the most dramatic showdowns in Open history.

After the first two rounds, the 121st Open Championship seemed to be developing into a contest for second place. Faldo had scored a record-breaking 66, 64 to open up a three-shot lead. On the third day, his 35th birthday, he extended his lead to four shots with a solid 69. The fourth day opened with golf writers already penning their post-tournament eulogies, leaving blank spaces into which they would later insert the contemptuously large margin of Faldo's victory.

As the main contenders teed off on the Sunday afternoon, a swirling wind and heavy rain showers blew across the Firth of Forth suggesting that low scores would be few and far between. Leading the chase were the Americans Steve Pate and John Cook, neither of whom were recognised major championship specialists. After nine holes, little had changed. Faldo had dropped a shot at the first but regained his composure with a string of pars. Pate was playing erratically, gaining and dropping shots with equal regularity, while Cook had shown signs of mounting a challenge until a double bogey seven at the ninth hole undid all his good work.

What happened next was one of the most astonishing turnarounds in

Faldo in action at the British Open at Muirfield

Open history. Faldo dropped three shots between the 11th and 14th holes, and Cook, spotting the chink in the great man's armour, took full advantage. Out of the blue, the American found himself with a two-shot lead. Faldo later recalled: 'Boy, I was making it tough for myself. I said: "You'd just better play the best four holes of your life right now".'

It is a mark of sporting greatness that a competitor can summon up the resources to respond to such inner exhortations. Faldo gritted his teeth and put together a birdie-par-birdie-par finish to claw back the lost ground. The unfortunate Cook waited until the last hole to shoot his only bogey of the back nine, and it was that one slip that denied the American a play-off place. Faldo played a textbook approach shot to the 18th green and rolled his first putt to within a foot. He made the last short putt look easy but reflected afterwards: 'I couldn't have handled it if it was from three feet. My legs were gone. I was shaking.'

The importance of the victory to Faldo was clear to the millions tuning in to BBC coverage of golf's greatest event. His customary reserve was dropped as he shared with presenter Steve Rider the agony and ecstasy of the final few holes. Any suspicions that Nick Faldo's appetite for victory had diminished were well and truly laid

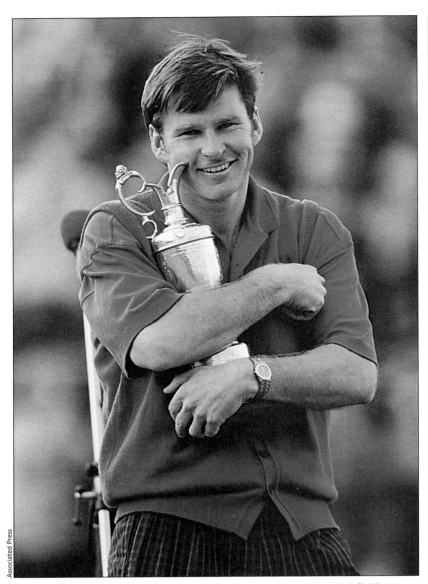

Britain' Nick Faldo hugs the British Open golf trophy he won at Muirfield

one sure-fire way to reach the top and stay there. He now has a total of five major championships to his credit, having won the US Masters in 1989 and 1990, and has set his sights on adding the US Open and US PGA titles to his list. As Europe's golfers prepare for another Ryder Cup showdown with their American rivals, the presence of the name Nicholas Alexander Faldo MBE on their team-sheet will be hugely reassuring.

Elsewhere in 1992

Three of golf's most notorious 'nearly men' broke their major championship ducks in 1992. Between them, Fred Couples, Tom Kite and Nick Price had an impressive, if somewhat depressing, collection of second places and near misses to their names.

Couples, the popular American whose good-natured and even-tempered personality had prompted cynics to question whether he had the gumption to lift a major title, came good on the tricky greens of Augusta, Georgia. Four consecutive British victories in the US Masters had left the fanatical American golfing public panting for a home victor. Couples obliged with a performance of skill and consistency, proving that his outstanding displays in the 1991 Ryder Cup were more than a flash in the pan.

Tom Kite was the king of the

Fred Couples at the Johnnie Walker Golf Championship in Jamaica in December 1992

to rest, as was the myth that his clinical approach to the game had made him incapable of an emotional response. 'At the end it becomes a battle of the mind, a battle for control,' said the first Briton since Henry Cotton in 1948 to win a third Open title. 'You try so hard to do the right things, to relax, but pressure takes over. It wears you to a frazzle.'

To British fans, of both the armchair and 36-handicap variety, Faldo's third Open victory (he also won at St Andrews in 1990) was a shot in the arm. British golf has prospered in recent years, as four consecutive victories in the US Masters between 1988 and 1991 proved, but apart from a single Open victory for Sandy Lyle in 1985, it has been left to Faldo, of the new generation, to reclaim the ancient silver claret jug from the clutches of the Americans, the Australians and Seve Ballesteros.

The boy from Welwyn Garden City, who never wanted to do anything but play golf and be the best, has shown critics of his obsessively meticulous approach to the game that single-mindedness is the

Nick Price at the Toyota World Matchplay at Wentworth in October 1992

NIGEL MANSELL – FORMULA ONE WORLD CHAMPION

BBC Sports Personality of the Year, Nigel Mansell, made 1992 a year to remember with his Formula One world title victory. Hugh Costello reviews Mansell's remarkable achievements

It is commonplace in the world of sport to hear tales of courage triumphing over adversity, of tenacity and dogged determination keeping a competitor going through thick and thin until the ultimate goal is reached, often against the odds and at an age when most sportsmen and women would happily rest on their laurels. Linford Christie is one such exemplar, Martina Navratilova another. But for a sheer, stubborn refusal to bow to disappointment and shuffle unfulfilled off the sporting coil, few achievements can rank with Nigel Mansell's victory in the 1992 World Drivers' Championship.

Ever since he started racing karts in the 60s, the 39-year-old from Upton-on-Severn had set his sights on winning fame and fortune in that most intense and life-threatening of sporting arenas, the Formula One championship. By the time he started what was to be his dream season in South Africa last March, Mansell, one of the highest paid sportsmen in the world, had already taken care of the fortune side of things. But the crown he had come so close to wearing on several occasions in the past remained elusive.

There was, in retrospect, an inevitability about Mansell's victory in 1992. His Williams-Renault team had at last put together a machine worthy of his ambition and it was obvious from the very first race that only a technological miracle or a tragic accident would stop him. But, Mansell being Mansell, there was also an undercurrent of misgiving, a lingering sense that the bad luck and recklessness that characterised his career would undo him yet again and hand the title to a less flamboyant but more predictable rival.

Even as Mansell was stringing together a record-breaking run of

nearly men. In his long and hugely successful career, he had come agonisingly close to a major victory on many occasions. Going into the US Open at Pebble Beach in California in June, he was widely regarded to be the best player never to have won a major. He passed that undesirable label on (to Spain's Jose Maria Olazabal) with a courageous display in blustery conditions to overhaul clubhouse leader Colin Montgomerie.

In 1991, Nick Price had pulled out of the US PGA championship at the last minute when his wife went into labour. His replacement, a rookie called John Daly, went on to win the title. It must have crossed Price's mind that fate had denied him a richly-deserved first major, because he went to the Bellerive Country Club in St Louis in August with only one aim: victory. The popular Zimbabwean, who came close to winning the Open Championship more than once in the 80s, duly laid claim to the prestigious title.

Hugh Costello

Tom Kite at the British Open at Muirfield

Associated Press

Nigel Mansell celebrates on the podium after winning the British Grand Prix Formula One race at Silverstone in July

five successive victories at the start of the season, saloon-bar cynics could be heard muttering darkly into their pints: 'It's too good to be true. He'll blow it again.' Mansell had made a habit of losing out, and even among his many fanatical supporters there remained doubts that their man could keep his head for long enough to seal one of the most richly-deserved title wins in Formula One history.

Their doubts were unfounded. With the previously dominant McLaren-Honda outfit lagging behind technologically, the man most likely to thwart Mansell's ambition, reigning champion Ayrton Senna, was out of the reckoning. The great Alain Prost, Mansell's mortal enemy of old, was rumoured to be eyeing up a challenge with the French team Ligier, but it failed to materialise. The young German Michael Schumacher, surely a world champion of the future, showed flashes of inspiration but his Benetton-Ford was no match for the Williams dream machine. Only the Italian Riccardo

Patrese, Mansell's team-mate, could mount a serious challenge. However, despite constant reminders from the Williams camp that the two drivers carried equal status within the team, it was apparent early on that Patrese lacked the burning ambition to overhaul the Briton.

It was those five straight wins that laid the foundations of Mansell's triumph. With maximum points under his belt after South Africa, Mexico, Brazil, Spain and San Marino, Mansell was virtually unassailable. It came almost as a relief when a loose wheel caused him to falter at Monte Carlo, never the happiest of hunting grounds. Somehow it seemed right that a talent as mercurial as Mansell's should be given the opportunity to wax and wane, to go off the boil before re-expressing itself in a special and significant way. And where better than at Silverstone, the long-disused wartime airfield that had shrugged off the challenges of Brands Hatch and Donington Park to establish itself as the home of British Formula One racing.

The events of 12 July provoked a fierce debate about the extent to which British motor racing fans should be allowed to demonstrate their passion for their sport and the man who embodies it. Mansell's magnificent victory – his fifth in the home race – prompted a track invasion more redolent of Millwall Football Club in the 70s than of a sport in which the lethal prowess of the machinery traditionally prohibits the public from encroaching on the battleground. In the event, no lasting damage was done and Mansell managed to escape the clutches of his adoring faithful to reach the safety of the winner's rostrum, but not before his car was subjected to a buffeting that threatened to cause problems at the post-race technical check-up.

Mansell's victory at Silverstone all but sealed his title bid, but he had to wait another month before putting himself out of reach of his rivals once and for all. Ironically, he clinched the title not with a victory but with a rather fortuitous second place at Hungaroring in Budapest on 16 August (his daughter Chole's tenth birthday). More ironically still, the man who led him home by over 40 seconds was none other than Ayrton Senna, who 12 months earlier had tightened his grip on the championship with a victory at the same track after Mansell had threatened to overhaul him.

For Mansell and his travelling entourage of fans it mattered not a jot that the title had been won with a second place finish at one of Formula One's less glamorous circuits. Their mutual joy was unbounded. As the new world champion stood side by side with his predecessor on the rostrum, the look on his face told the whole story.

Mansell admitted in a post-race interview that he felt he had been 'carrying a 100-ton weight' around with him, and the lifting of that burden showed. The heartache of 1986, when a blow-out in the last race at Adelaide handed the title to Prost, and the anguish of 1987, when a crash during practise in Japan gave Nelson Piquet a surprise third title, were soothed at last. The frustrations of the 1991 season, when Mansell did everything in his power to close the gap on Senna's vastly superior McLaren, no longer mattered. The first British cham-

pion since James Hunt in 1976, and the seventh in all, had righted a wrong and proved himself worthy of the ultimate accolade.

When Mansell's boss Frank Williams, head of the team that was now streets ahead in the constructors' championship, congratulated Mansell and Renault on their successful partnership and vowed that 'it has only just begun', it seemed certain that the new champion would be shaping up for a defence of his title in 1993. But even as Mansell was going on to notch-up records for most wins (nine) and most pole positions (14) in a season, and to extend his record number of wins for a British driver to 30, the wheel of fortune, oiled by the motor racing industry's money men, was taking an astonishing turn.

The events leading up to Mansell's decision to sign a contract with the American Indy Car team Newman-Haas are shrouded in confusion and an element of farce. First Williams made it plain that they wanted Mansell in their 1993 team, then they apparently changed their minds, and finally they restaked their claim on the world champion, by which time Mansell's mind was made up. Speculation

about Mansell's departure centred on the fact that his new Williams team-mate would have been Alain Prost, with whom he has had a notoriously difficult relationship in the past. Then there were allegations that money was the real reason. But those in the know are inclined to put Mansell's absence down to his pride rather than his pocket.

'Mansell was not sensibly handled,' says BBC TV commentator Murray Walker. 'He is a very thin-skinned, sensitive man, while those who run the sport are businessmen and politicians. He got fed up with the whole thing.'

To complete a disheartening end to a great season, Mansell's final race at Adelaide in November was marred by yet another controversial incident involving his old rival Senna. Mansell was leading and seemed to be on course for a victorious farewell, when Senna, in second place, crashed into the back of his car and put both of them out of the race. A disgusted Mansell looked to the stewards for confirmation that Senna had deliberately shunted him off the track, but their verdict was that the crash was an accident and no action was taken.

Mansell's title-winning year ended

Nigel Mansell at the South African Grand Prix

Action-Plus

in a manner that reflected the drama and tension that have dogged his entire career, but the scale of his achievement was in no way reduced. Even the knockers who put his success down to the pre-eminence of the Williams-Renault car were left clutching at straws by the magnitude of his triumph. 'The superiority of his car in no way detracted from his victory,' says Murray Walker. 'The fact is that the bloody good drivers get the bloody good cars. Mansell handled his car better than his team-mate Patrese and that's why he won. His achievement ranks with that of all the previous British world champions. He is one of the greats of all time.'

And what of the rumours that Mansell may well make a surprise reappearance next season, when Britain hosts two grands prix? 'It could be true,' says Walker. 'He's a totally unpredictable chap. I'd love to see it.'

Hugh Costello

MARTIN OFFIAH

Martin Offiah has broken every record in the book and now rates as one of the top rugby league players in the world. However, there is more to Offiah than sporting brilliance, as Chris Peters discovers

Rugby League has never lacked endeavour. Firmly rooted in the working class heartlands of northern England, the sport has always reflected the true grit and honest toil of its origins: a game played by 26 strapping young lads doing their utmost to tear each other limb from limb in the name of local pride.

A game proud of its flat-cap, alehouse image; brash, brawling men of principle with deep northern burrs.

What rugby league has lacked, however, is the ability to mould itself into a marketable product, to thrust itself into the public eye as a sport for all.

That has changed in recent years and it is no accident that the change has coincided with the arrival of a certain Martin Offiah.

Offiah wasn't the first player to switch codes from rugby union, nor will he be the last. But he has made a greater impression on the game than anybody before or since.

In the five years after turning professional, the live wire winger has broken almost every record imaginable and now rates as the most prolific try scorer in the world.

But there is more to Offiah than sheer sporting excellence. To many, he is the public face of rugby league, a dream ticket for all the ad-men and promoters attempting to capture a wider audience.

Why? Because he is different, both on and off the field. An educated black southerner (he learned independence from an early age after being sent to Woolverstone Hall boarding school in Suffolk), Offiah was brought up in Stoke Newington and dreamed of playing soccer for Arsenal. He couldn't be more different to the stereotype rugby league player.

No-one is more aware of that than Offiah himself. 'Kid from London, no background in rugby league, signs up at 21 and makes a success of it – bit of a fairy tale really,' he says. Offiah, now 27, is happy to take his share of the credit for the game's new faster, fitter image.

'The game is changing, the way it is marketed is changing and the stereotype of the players is changing,' he adds. 'It has become more of a spectacle. The player earns more and dedicates more of his time to playing so at the end of the day you get a far superior product.

'I would like to feel that I did contribute in some small way.' A personal revolution? 'On a small scale, perhaps, but I feel it would have changed anyway. It's been good for both rugby league and for myself – it's helped project me.

'A lot of people who are not directly associated with the game have had a go because they relate to me.' (Both boxer Gary Mason and sprinter Ade Mafe have tried their hand at rugby league in the last 12 months.)

On the pitch, besides his blistering pace and unrivalled strike rate, Offiah sets himself aside from the rest by his extravagant behaviour.

He delights the crowd with an exaggerated high-kicking stride as he glides imperiously towards the try-line before launching into lavish celebrations with the supporters.

'I was doing the same in rugby union although it didn't go down too well,' he says. 'But that's me. People say I'm playing up to it all but I'm performing to a crowd, not just cultivating an image.'

Maybe so, but Offiah is not about to fall victim to his own publicity and takes fame and fortune in the same confident stride that has become his trademark down the years. 'You need hype to survive but you can never let it go to your head. Rugby league is pretty down to earth. It has changed but it's still got a pretty macho image and I find it hard to correlate "star" and "rugby league player".'

Unlike many of his fellow union converts, Offiah heralded from the relatively humble surroundings of Rosslyn Park. Selected for the Barbarians, he was spotted by then Widnes coach Doug Laughton during the annual Middlesex Sevens and abandoned the opportunity of a sports scholarship at Bath University to turn professional.

Widnes's gamble in offering the inexperienced and largely unproven youngster a lucrative 10-year contract had sensational results. Offiah scored 181 tries in 145 games for the Naughton Park side, topping the national scoring charts for four consecutive seasons. He soon broke into the international squad and set a new record for Great Britain by scoring five tries in one game against France.

His marriage to Widnes turned sour, however, and in May 1991 Offiah demanded a transfer. The split was a complicated bitter affair and Offiah's lengthy contract became a millstone around his neck. Widnes used it to quote outrageous transfer fees and the player was put up for sale at £700,000.

The asking price was enough to scare off all but a couple of clubs. The local hero was left in limbo and became a target of abuse from the Widnes fans, not least because of his desire to join arch rivals Wigan.

'Things were so bad that I just wanted to get out,' admitted Offiah, who played only 30 minutes of a reserve team game between September 1991 and January 1992.

'It affected me to be out of the game for five months and there were lots of times when I thought I wouldn't play again,' he concedes. 'But I detached myself from the game and used it as a rest.'

Wigan eventually splashed out a world record fee of £440,000 to get their man on 3 January 1992, forging a partnership which was to bring both club and player an enormous amount of success.

Within a month Offiah had helped Wigan to the World Sevens title in Sydney, scoring ten tries – including all four in the final against Brisbane – and earning the Player of the Tournament award.

He ran in five tries against Bradford Northern in the Challenge Cup semifinal and ten against Leeds at the same stage of the Premiership (a new club record and one off the world best) as Wigan scaled new heights.

They duly clinched their third successive league title and a fortnight later retained the Challenge Cup at Wembley. Offiah scored two tries and only missed out on becoming the first player to claim a Cup final hat-trick because a linesman adjudged his foot was in touch. Not surprisingly, he was awarded the Lance Todd Trophy for man of the match.

Wigan went on to beat St Helens 48-16 in the Premiership final – another record – with Offiah scoring twice to make it 30 tries in 16 games since his transfer.

The only blemish on an otherwise impeccable season came in the World Clubs' Championship, which Offiah had previously won with Widnes, as Wigan surrendered their crown to Brisbane Broncos.

Offiah admits that success with the Wigan 'Dream Team' does have its drawbacks, however. 'If you're at the top then there is only one way to go and that's down,' he says. 'You fight to be the best and I suppose the fear of failure is pretty big. You've done it all before but you have to blank it out and start all over again.

'I always go out and try to better myself. Each season I do something

Martin Offiah of Wigan in action

Action-Plus

I haven't done before. There have been a lot of high pressure games in the past and maybe I shouldn't have played in a lot of them. But Linford Christie and Carl Lewis are over 30 years old and they're the fastest men in the world so maybe I've got a few years left.'

On the international front, Offiah was one of 13 Wigan players in the Great Britain squad to tour Papua New Guinea, Australia and New Zealand.

It proved to be the most successful tour since 1970, although Britain once again failed to prise the Ashes from Australia's grasp, losing the deciding Test 16-10 in Brisbane.

While having to swallow a third successive Ashes defeat at the hands of Australia, Offiah had underlined his standing as the deadliest finisher in the world.

He was to get his chance for revenge in November when the two sides locked horns again, this time in the World Cup final at Wembley.

With only a handful of countries playing the sport, rugby league's World Cup is perhaps not quite the challenge of its soccer counterpart.

Teams qualify on the strength of their Test match results and Britain had to rely on superior points difference to book their place in the final ahead of New Zealand.

The big match failed to live up to expectations, however, and there was little in a tight, tactical battle to excite the 73,000 Wembley crowd.

Offiah and fellow winger Alan Hunte rarely touched the ball while Britain snuffed out the danger of Aussie playmaker Allan Langer.

Britain scored all their points in the first half, Deryck Fox kicking three penalties to give them a 6-4 interval lead, but the game always seemed destined to be decided by a single try and Australia looked the more likely to break through.

The crucial score came 13 minutes from time when Steve Renouf sprinted through a gap in the Lions' defence to touch down and Aussie skipper Mal Meninga – the architect of so many British defeats down the years – added the conversion to put his side 10-6 ahead.

Mal Meninga celebrates Australia's 6-10 victory against Great Britain in the World Cup final

Britain failed to claw their way back and at the end were left to reflect on what might have been had they shown a little more enterprise.

It was particularly frustrating for Offiah, of whom so much had been expected, and he was booed off the pitch after refusing to collect his loser's medal. 'Nobody likes losing, I don't think anybody can say they are a good loser,' he says. 'I don't begrudge people their success, I didn't feel cheated, and they were the better side.

'But the Cup final was the lowest point for me, even more so than losing the third Test in Australia. I feel that I didn't contribute and that I wasn't able to contribute. After all the hype surrounding myself and the team, it was a bit of a damp squib on the day.

'Sometimes you feel people expect too much of you but the only time it relates to pressure is when things aren't going too well and I certainly felt it after the World Cup.'

Offiah's eye for an opportunity and his appreciation of public image made the defeat all the more disappointing. Britain had not only lost a game of rugby but the chance to promote the sport nationwide.

'We had the chance to really boost rugby league in this country and the general opinion was that we'd blown it. The big step now is not only to conquer the Aussies but also to conquer Britain. As the Australians have shown, it's very important to make the game bigger in your own back yard.'

Ironically, Offiah will spend this summer 'guesting' with Eastern Suburbs in Sydney for a reputed £3,000 a match (his third, and he claims final, stint Down Under).

'You've got to make hay while the sun shines because you never know what tomorrow may bring,' he adds.

'I would just like to be remembered as an exciting, entertaining player who people wanted to watch.'

Chris Peters

LENNOX LEWIS

Britain's brightest boxing hope, Lennox Lewis, emerged as one of the world's top heavyweights during 1992. Hugh Costello looks back at the career of the rising star of British boxing

On 17 March 1897, world heavyweight champion 'Gentleman' Jim Corbett lost his title in Carson City, Nevada, to a balding Cornishman called Bob Fitzsimmons. The first Briton to hold the title managed to retain it for two whole years, but only because he wasn't called upon to defend it. When his first defence came, in June 1899, he succumbed to an eleventh round knockout by the alliterative James J Jefferies, who duly restored the honour of the United States.

British boxers have fought for the title on 13 occasions since then, but none has managed to win it. The most gallant effort was by Welshman Tommy Farr, who took the great Joe Louis to 15 rounds in New York in 1937. The most recent was by Frank Bruno, who briefly alarmed Mike Tyson in Las Vegas four years ago before being stopped in the fifth round.

Now, however, there is a new British contender in the challenger's corner. Introducing Lennox Lewis, an East End lad with Jamaican parents, a Canadian passport and a graceful fighting style that has prompted cautious comparisons with Muhammad Ali. Lewis is already recognised by the WBC, one of the sport's two main governing bodies, as world champion, but he achieved that honour by default and no-one, least of all Lewis himself, will start celebrating until he has gone one stage further.

Ever since he won Olympic gold for Canada in the super-heavyweight division at the 1988 Olympics, Lewis's hat has been in the ring. He has had his detractors, who argued that he lacked the bulk and the punching power necessary to be world champion, and his defenders, who pointed to the speed at which he moves on his size-15 feet and his impressive reach (at 6ft 6in he is one of the tallest heavyweights around). All

Action-Plus

that remained to be said was Lewis's own word on the subject, which he articulated very forcefully indeed at Earls Court on 31 October, when he took America's Donovan 'Razor' Ruddock for the right to be called the main contender. Lewis let his 14in fists do the talking, and his unfortunate opponent got the message after just 226 seconds.

Ruddock, who once survived eight rounds against Mike Tyson with a broken jaw without yielding, was served notice of Lewis's intentions when he was felled with a majestic right at the end of the first round. Suddenly the fanatical Earls Court crowd sensed that their man was going to put on a show. Lewis, too, had no doubt that the finest hour of his professional career had come: 'As he got up his feet were wobbling and his eyes had widened, so I knew he was still feeling the pain. But I knew I must stay cool and not waste the situation.' Less than a minute later, the job was done and the British boxing public were hailing the coming of a saviour.

The clarity of thought revealed by Lewis's post-fight comments is one of the trademarks of a man whose peripatetic childhood gave him a maturity and sense of his own worth uncommon in British heavyweight hopefuls. After leaving London at the age of 11, Lewis, now 27, grew up in Kitchener, Ontario, where he was the only black boy in his school. When it became apparent that young Lennox would use his natural aggression to stand up for himself, his headmaster coaxed him into joining the boxing club. Lewis's adopted country reaped the rewards of the headmaster's foresight when Lewis returned from Seoul with the coveted gold medal.

Many column inches have been devoted to the debate about Lewis's national identity. Some pundits ask how the British boxing establishment can be so brazen as to claim Lewis for itself when it played no part in the development and encouragement of his talent. Others argue that Lewis, having spent his first 11 years in the East End, has simply reclaimed his British identity, not reinvented it. Lewis himself concurs with the latter view. He is fond of citing his support for West Ham United as the ultimate proof of his Britishness.

Lewis's victory over Ruddock in a fight he was not obliged to contest put paid to any doubts about his ability, but it also catapulted him into the maelstrom of heavyweight politics. No sooner had he been lined up as the next opponent for reigning champion Evander Holyfield than Holyfield lost to Riddick Bowe, the man Lewis beat in the 1988 Olympic final. The new champion immediately signalled his intention to avoid an immediate champion of the world late in 1993 or early in 1994.

The financial wranglings in the Machiavellian world of the ringside supremos has tarnished what would otherwise have been a magnificent year for Lewis. But it may have played into the hands of the indefatigable Frank Bruno, who still has hopes of going out with a bang. The man who carried the banner for Britain almost single-handedly through the 80s is known to fancy a crack at Lewis, and given the state of flux world heavyweight boxing finds itself in at present it is not inconceivable that the WBC might give him that chance.

Lennox Lewis after his victory over Derek Williams in April's Triple Heavyweight contest

Action-Plus

defence against Lewis, and thus forfeited the title in the eyes of the WBC. Lewis became the WBC world champion without so much as throwing a punch. Bowe remains the WBO champion, however, and is likely to mount his first defence against Ray Mercer in March.

Lewis, meanwhile bolstered his reputation further as a man of principle when he declined a lucrative $11 million offer to be Bowe's second challenger. Instead, he will probably fight 42-year-old former champion George Foreman in April, in the first defence of his WBC title, and meet Bowe in a contest to decide the undisputed

With Lewis installed as the crown prince of British heavyweight boxing, Bruno is in danger of becoming the court jester, but he confirmed his reputation as the hardest-hitting pantomime dame around with his comprehensive demolition of South Africa's Pierre Coetzer in October. Lewis, though, remains the great hope, and as the centenary of Bob Fitzsimmons's victory over Corbett draws ever nearer, it is heartening to think that by this time next year, Britain may be heralding the arrival of its second undisputed heavyweight champion of the world.

Hugh Costello

CLEMENT FREUD'S SPORTS REVIEW

In a year of outstanding British sporting achievements, Nigel Mansell was voted BBC Sports Personality of the Year. Clement Freud selects his own 'Sports Personality' and considers the successes of the many contenders for the title

Linford Christie waves to the crowd after receiving his gold medal

In an Olympic year I began by looking at the medallists: Linford Christie's memorable ten seconds was accorded my most careful consideration; had it not been for the 4 x 100m relay and the 200m, I would have looked no further.

Sally Gunnell was different. Sally Gunnell looked tense and hollow-eyed, also lantern-jawed as she carried our colours, and our hopes, into the 400m hurdles final. When she won – brilliantly, courageously, to our rapturous delight – her face was suffused with beauty. It was not just a duckling becoming a swan, a before-and-after picture on a beautician's pamphlet. We witnessed the fulfilment of years of work and hope, the elimination of self-doubt. It was a moment to be cherished and I want to remember her like that.

At Wimbledon, there was Jeremy Bates: for the first week we had a man for whom to cheer, who gave us much to cheer about. Had he played three more successful matches you would have remembered the name yourself.

If 1992 was more than a run-of-the-mill year for darts, I must have been watching *Eldorado* at the time. The two programmes have in common the fact that if you have an urgent desire to watch, you could tape any half-an-hour of either and gaze contentedly.

I am sorry about bowls; for years I saw David Bryant and his pipe, and marvelled both at his skill with the woods and his ability to focus through the tobacco fumes. He seems to have stopped smoking and others have usurped his position, but until outdoor bowls affords TV cameras clear access to the play and does something about all those bums who get between the lens and the head, major sports personalities will not come from the bowling green.

There is a case for Nigel Mansell: Formula One world champion after all those years and all those near misses. Two factors persuade me to withhold recommendation: the huge financial rewards that are already his, and the decision to leave the discipline and move to Indy racing.

Football and cricket are the natural sources for major awards: Gary Lineker deserves high praise for keeping the game in repute, though 1992 was not his best.

Bruce Grobbelaar must be on the list for introducing a whole new perspective to goalkeeping, but it is success rather than innovative approaches to the game that qualifies. Sadly – after the FA Cup win – this has become one of Liverpool's fallow years.

David Mellor, reputed to have achieved the rare feat of scoring in a Chelsea shirt, is not a serious contender, but Newcastle manager Kevin Keegan deserves attention: a man who has brought back life, self-respect and joy to St James's Park, where they turn away great multi-

Sally Gunnell wins gold in the 400m hurdles final

Kevin Keegan, manager of Newcastle United

tudes of Geordies who hang around outside basking vicariously in the pleasure of the full house within.

It was just an average year for cricket, with bad tempers and suspect umpiring getting a narrow verdict over good play. We lost the World Cup final and the Test series, but my choice for honours would be David Gower, whose elegance and unpredictability endear him to

lovers of the game he adorns, even if purists and disciplinarians go apoplectic at his name. Gower is a star; he had a good season with the bat and performed stylishly both at his stag night and the wedding.

British boxing is regaining respectability; we shall have to wait and see whether the comebacks of yesterday's men are genuine. Frank Bruno and Nigel Benn would both look good on the victory podium; I am less sure of Chris Eubank's ability to create the blend of happiness and humility which we expect of the winner; if things go to plan, Lennox Lewis must be odds-on for 1993.

Both codes of rugby deserve a mention for the huge enjoyment they have given, but contenders for my 'Sports Personality of the Year': Will Carling, Jeremy Guscott, Martin Offiah? Now if David Campese played for a British team...

There have been genuine heroes in racing. Old Lester Piggott; young Peter Chapple-Hyam, who trained the Derby winner and was loyal to his unfashionable jockey; Clive Britain, for whom George Duffield won two classics. Michael Roberts would grace the victory platform: cheerful, modest likeable. His success was achieved by hard work, brilliant judgement and intelligent engineering by his agent. Pat

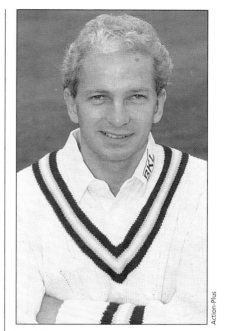

David Gower

Eddery, whose championship he took, has retainers that demand his presence in France and Ireland when there are winners to be ridden at Redcar. Roberts's agent banked on that and backed his man to win at odds of 100-1.

Had Britain's women won the Olympic hockey crown, there would have been a case for Jane Sixsmith (nicknamed Jasper for her carrot-coloured hair), who scores goals from penalty corners; her joy is contagious, she would have become everyone's first choice to perform supermarket openings; perhaps another year.

A Briton did win the Open. Nick Faldo bestrode the fairways and greens of the world like a giant and only twice in a season of unrelenting graft did he behave like ordinary mortals and crack. And all the while, at his side when he drove, crouched behind him when he lined up a putt, stilling the photographers, never moaning about the weight of the bag or the lengths of the delays, was his caddy, Fanny Sunnerson.

I would vote for her as my 'Sports Personality of the Year', but I shall not blame her if she mentions the fact that she owes it to the lad.

Clement Freud

Jane Sixsmith at the Barcelona Olympics

News and Current Affairs

Television news was dominated by the harrowing scenes from war-torn Bosnia, and the chapter opens with BBC Overseas Correspondent Martin Bell reporting on this devastating human tragedy.

It was the year of the General Election and the American Presidential Election, and as well as reviews of both events – from Robin Oakley and Charles Wheeler respectively – Peter Snow takes us behind the scenes to discover the secrets of the Swingometer.

The Maastricht treaty, the threat of pit closures, and the Earth Summit all hit the headlines, and with conservation issues to the fore in the aftermath of the Rio Summit, a special feature on the fate of the whale is included.

There is also a unique insight into a day in the life of BBC2's *Newsnight*, revealing the fast-moving world of a TV news programme.

Doom and gloom dominated the news with reports of famine, war, disasters and recession from around the world. Polly Toynbee's News Review of the Year reminds us of some of the events which hit the headlines in 1992.

News and Current Affairs

CIVIL WAR IN BOSNIA

Stories of the devastating situation in the republics of the former Yugoslavia have hit the headlines throughout the year. BBC Overseas Correspondent Martin Bell, who has spent much of 1992 in Bosnia, reports on this overwhelming tragedy

It was a sharp introduction to the hazards of the Bosnian war. Drunk and aggressive, the Serbian militiaman stood squarely across our road five miles from Zvornik – a town which the Serbs had just captured. No, he assured us, we could not pass. We had no business to be there. We were *Ustashe* (Croatian) spies. If we did not turn back at once we would be shot. He unslung his rifle and fingered the safety catch speculatively.

Every road block has its own Napoleon and ours was no exception. We beat a prudent retreat. At the local Serb headquarters my resourceful interpreter had better luck with Napoleon's commander. Our mission was explained, our credentials examined, and much was made of our personal relationship with the leading Serbian warlord in the area. At the second attempt, we were through.

And soon enough we came upon the reason why the Serbs had been so reluctant to let us pass. We caught up with the rearguard of a great and forced migration. Here it was in its early stages. It later came to be known as 'ethnic cleansing'.

Two thousand people were camped pitifully in the next village. They were Moslems and Croats driven out of Zvornik and the settlements around it by the ever-advancing Serbs. They had no possessions but what they could carry: no transport, no shelter, no hope. Along mountain paths and cart tracks some 20,000 of them were on the move that day, heading for safer territory on a trail of tears. The ethnic map of a doomed republic was being redrawn before our eyes.

Beset by such misery, we were embarrassed and humbled to be treated as saviours, which sadly we were not. The refugees applauded us as we passed among them, for we were the first indication they had received that the outside world knew of their plight, or cared.

'Terrible things are happening', said one, a schoolmaster, 'and have been happening for two days. It is a terror which has been made by the Serbs and is being made right now. You can hear even now some shells.' We could, and so could the straggling column of refugees which had come to a halt around us, as the crump of artillery stirred the morning air. They appealed for our help. I felt, though I could hardly say so, as helpless as they did. But I made them the speech that they wanted to hear, and promised to tell the world.

That, tragically, was the pattern of the year: ethnic cleansings, expulsions, concentration camps, documented and evident atrocities, funerals and fire-fights, the explosion of mortars among innocent and unarmed people. I have, in my sometime trade of war correspondent, reported 11 conflicts around the world, but never one so brutal as this – in our continent and in our time – in which civilians were not

Bosnia-Herzegovina – A sniper takes aim

Rex Features

only not spared, but targeted with particular ferocity.

When it came to the blame-laying – a delicate task, for the BBC World Service News was rebroadcast nightly on Belgrade television with simultaneous translation – the Serbs were rightly held responsible for most of the aggression. But there were also Serbian refugees by the tens of thousands; Serbian villages torched and abandoned; Serbian civilians massacred. Nothing was as simple as it seemed. And the more you knew, the more you knew that you didn't know.

It was, to a reporter coming fresh to it, a Balkan tragedy in many acts but with no final curtain in sight. Also, a story of quite unique horror and complexity. After all, this was supposed to be the new world order made possible by the Cold War's end. Yet there was no peace dividend here. Bosnia was shaken by ancient hatreds, distilled and inherited from the blood feuds of the past. It was hard to explain, hard to understand, harder still to frame in an acceptable way on the nightly TV news.

It was as if there were an iron law of the place: the worst that *could* happen *did* happen. And yet it was a year of such chances missed, such paths of peace not taken.

It began, indeed, with a moment of rare hope: the signing of the 15th cease-fire agreement in Croatia, the first one that actually worked. It was, inevitably, breached from time to time, and the Croats especially grew impatient with it, for it froze the front lines in place at the very time when the Zagreb government was starting to regain lost territory (which was precisely the reason why the Serbs accepted it). But for the most part the guns fell silent; the Federal Army withdrew peacefully from its remaining barracks in Croatian-held areas; and the blue helmets of the United Nations were deployed for the first time on the continent of Europe.

They came from at least two dozen countries, in an alphabet soup of initials. First there was UNMO, a small group of intrepid military observers who were much in the line of fire, with casualties to match. Then there was UNPRO-

Martin Bell and General Lew Mackenzie, UN Commander, in Sarajevo in June 1992

FOR, mandated to keep the peace in Croatia, from the ruins of Vukovar to the bleakest of mountain passes around Knin. But its headquarters were set, with unjustified optimism, in the Bosnian capital, Sarajevo. And when that blew apart, and the mixed UN force of French Ukranians and Egyptians was simply unequal to the task before it, it was supplemented by UNPROFOR II: more men and more armies – including this time a substantial British force spearheaded by the Cheshire Regiment – but now with a more limited mission of escorting convoys and trying to save lives. Peace-keeping was no longer part of the mandate, for there was no peace to keep.

Surely in Bosnia, we told ourselves, it didn't have to be so. Bosnia, with its mosques and churches nestling companionably across the fault line of two old empires, was a patchwork quilt of a

A typical scene in war-torn Sarajevo

republic, and in better times a model of ethnic and religious harmony. Of all the territories of ex-Yugoslavia, it was the one where the communities lived closest to each other, where there were most mixed marriages, the greatest fears of war and incentives to peace.

It was said against the Serbian leaders that, before the war, they had gone out into the Bosnian uplands and urged their people to sell a cow and buy a gun. In short, they knew what was coming and were ready for it. The Moslems did not and were not. They proclaimed an independence they could not defend. (A Moslem friend said, months later and with the benefit of hindsight, 'While they were arming, we were singing folk songs.')

But there was a strong peace movement, in which some Serbs were also involved, and peace marches which grew larger, and their placards more urgent ('No Vukovars Here') as the first fatal shots were fired. That was in April, after a false start in March, and from then on Bosnia slid instantly into the most lethal and ferocious of the wars of ex-Yugoslavia.

Its principal feature, as with most civil wars, was its mercilessness. It was fought without the benefit of the Geneva Convention, or any rule of war except 'kill or be killed'. And if a cease-fire were signed, as happened from time to time, it was a signal to head for the deepest bunker available. 'What are they doing?' I asked a friend during a particularly heavy bombardment. 'Oh, that's the Serbs. They are celebrating the cease-fire.'

To the viewer at home it was most often seen as the siege of Sarajevo, in which the Serbs in the hills bombarded the Moslems below.

But it was actually more complex than that. For the besieged population of some 350,000 included many thousand Serbs (some of them were rounded up and accused of collaboration; others were victims of the random shelling just as much as the Moslems and Croats, and buried alongside them in the overflowing Lion Cemetery). The government of President Alia Izetbegovic, fighting the Serbs, included not only Croat but

Moslem members who served the Bosnian cause. The Moslem commander of the garrison at Dobrinja, holding out for months against the Serbian onslaught, had a Serb as his personal bodyguard.

If it was a hard situation to understand, it was harder still to survive. From a strictly professional point of view, I found that the most difficult part of reporting it was, quite simply, staying alive.

It has to be said, that our plight was as nothing to that of the people of Sarajevo. We had flak jackets, which they did not. We could escape, which they could not. We could bring food in with us and subsist (albeit with a twinge of guilt) on a diet of something other than

hotel in the suburb of Illidza in May, but suffered no more than a damaged editing machine, which subsequently turned up repaired and functioning in the hands of the new TV service of Serbian Bosnia. (They called it the spoils of war.) We then brought in new equipment and set it up in the basement annexe of the main UN base, protected by 3ft of concrete overhead and welded steel plates at the windows. This time, the machines came through unscathed.

The people, however, did not. Rob Celliers, a redoubtable cameraman from our allies at Visnews, the TV news agency, was wounded in the arm on his third day in the country; his only comment after-

Martin Bell with Colonel Doyle (formerly Lord Carrington's special representative), during a break in negotiations with the Serbs at Lukavica Barracks outside Sarajevo

rice and nettles. In a spirit of solidarity I did one day sample dandelion soup...but I do not recommend it.

Sarajevo, by our subjective reckoning, was and is the most dangerous place on earth: like Beirut without the civilities. By its grim standards, we have led a relatively charmed life there. We were bombed out of our headquarters

wards was that it ruined his golf swing, but he was always given to understatement. Just a month later, the CNN camerawoman Margaret Moth, on whose unflinching work we had also come to depend, was badly wounded by sniper fire on the airport road, which is Sarajevo's Death Alley. Less seriously, I myself had an argument with some mortar fragments in August, which characteristically I lost.

Then, in November, one of our true local heroes, Tihomir Tunukovic, was killed by Serbian machine-gun fire on the road to Travnik. Tihomir, a Croat whom we knew as Tuna, was one of the best and bravest of them all. In both the Bosnian and Croatian wars he covered the front lines where others feared to tread, and brought back images of extraordinary impact and power.

With some 40 journalists killed so far, the wars of ex-Yugoslavia were the most dangerous in the experience of any of us. So we took what action we could to limit the risks. An early step was to cut back on the habitual competitiveness of the business, by pooling our combat footage with our rivals'. In so doing, we surrendered some unilateral advantages, for we maintained a more constant presence than they did. But it made evident sense to have only one camera team, instead of a number, at the scene of the daily gun battles.

Next, we borrowed from the experience of the military, in travelling under armour. This was also an innovation, and it followed an incident on the airport runway, the only route across no man's land to the Serbian side, when our rented car was hit by a burst of sniper fire. From an inspection of the bullet holes – one at head level, the other in the driver's door – I concluded that this was not the way I wished

Martin Bell donning body armour in the BBC's bunker in August 1992 – three days later he was wounded

to carry on. So I asked the BBC for an armoured vehicle, and within two weeks they had one on the way to us: a reinforced Land Rover acquired on the second-hand market in Belfast.

The BBC, to its credit, really did care about safety – and armed us, further, with a whole sheaf of memos urging us not to take unnecessary risks. My favourite was a ringing declaration that 'Macho journalism will not be countenanced'.

But it is an uncertain world out there. You often don't know what is a necessary risk until after you've

taken it. And you cannot report a war from the inside of a bunker or armoured vehicle. From time to time, you have to get out into the open to do the business. That in fact is exactly how I had my own mishap. It was simply a failure of fieldcraft – I stayed out of cover for too long. The only courses open are to take some risks, or to leave the field completely.

By the same token, we chose most of the time to forego the benefits of staying with the rest of the press at the Holiday Inn. It was surely the ultimate war hotel, with its upper floors completely destroyed, and every remaining window holed by sniper fire.

But it was also a target. And what we needed was not a hotel room at ground zero, but a vantage point. We found one in a friend's flat high above the old town and the Presidency. From there, at the end of the day's work, and often coinciding with a gunner's change of shift, we would view the evening and overnight bombardments of the city. (The 5am barrage I tended to ignore, but would pull up the covers, like a child, till it was over. In Sarajevo, you got your wake up call from the barrel of a gun.)

It was also a home, an unusual comfort to find in a war zone, and soon enough our neighbours became our friends. There Nigel

Martin Bell at Sarajevo Airport, 28 June 1992 – President Mitterand's helicopter, damaged by sniper fire, in the background

Bateson, my larger-than-life South African colleague, was able to combine the roles of cook and cameraman. One evening, as tank shells hit the Parliament office building, he had left his balcony-based camera switched on. And he obtained his most vivid images while cooking spaghetti.

It is, I know, a charge often made against television news that we dwell too much on the darker side of things (though, aside from the heroism of so many of its people, there was hardly a brighter side to be seen in Sarajevo), and that by our presence we somehow exacerbate the conflicts that we witness.

In Bosnia, this was certainly not so. Its people pleaded with us to stay and tell the world their story. They had a touching if misplaced faith that the extremity of their plight would lead to military intervention. All they got was food and sympathy, and not enough of either. ('Fattening us,' said the defence minister, 'so they can kill us'.)

The presence of the cameras even had a calming effect. Both sides felt so, for they would require our attendance at such events as an exchange of prisoners – each in the belief that, under the eye of the camera, the other side would be less likely to break its undertakings.

Nor were the Serbs invariably hostile. Routinely, we were threatened at their road blocks. But just as often, a local commander would have us sit down with him, as the price for passing through his territory, and deliver a lecture on his people's ancient grievances. The tone was friendly: history laced with slivovitz.

And besides, as we soon became aware, so much that had happened was done outside the camera's range, in remote parts of Bosnia where whole communities were overrun, and the only witnesses were the victims, who did not survive.

What we did see tested us beyond our ability to communicate. We were surrounded by suffering which was in a real sense both unspeakable and unshowable. When a mortar exploded in a crowded market place, it was a story that had to be told. Yet the images of carnage were so horrific it was hard to know what to do with them: like the mortars themselves they would land with a fierce numbing pain.

It was often the gentler moments that carried more impact – as when Bodran Smilovic, a cellist who had played the concert halls of Europe, appeared one day in full white tie and tails on the streets of Sarajevo. Both suit and streets had seen much better days. He set down his cello on the spot where 16 people in a bread queue had been killed in an earlier mortar attack. All other attempts to save the city having failed, his aim was to mobilise the world's musicians, at midday the following Friday. 'Let everyone', he said, 'take his instrument in every place, maybe the metro, maybe an aeroplane, open your instrument and play Albinoni.'

I don't know what effect it had on the world, but for a moment it transformed the city. For at the appointed hour the musicians did appear – a trumpeter at one corner, a violinist at another, a cellist at yet a third – and they played Albinoni's Adagio. Douglas Hurd was visiting at the time, and the strains of the Adagio followed him like the anthem of this doomed and desolate city – still intact at the start of the year, but a ruin at the end.

For me, after so much else, it was time to question a lifelong habit of distanced, 'objective' reporting. Somehow the old rules seemed inadequate. We were standing at the edge – sometimes it seemed the end – of the civilised world.

And it was time to take sides – not with one community against another, but with the unarmed against the armed, the weak against the strong.

It is already past the eleventh hour. These people need our help. And they need it now.

Martin Bell

A musician plays Albinoni's Adagio in the doomed city of Sarajevo

Rex Features

POLITICS

The General Election, the Maastricht treaty and the proposed closure of the coal-mines were three of the most significant national news stories of 1992. Robin Oakley, the BBC's Political Editor, reports on these important issues

The BBC's Political Editor Robin Oakley

GENERAL ELECTION 1992

The Conservative victory in the General Election of 1992 confounded the opinion polls, and the winning party leader, John Major, overturned conventional theory about campaigning techniques. Labour, opening with an average opinion poll lead of 1.6 percentage points and ending with an average lead of 2.3 per cent, was held, as in 1987, to have run the better, more professional campaign. No government had ever been as unpopular as the Tories in mid-term and won the subsequent election. The 9 April contest was not called at a moment of Conservative choice but at very nearly the last resort, the government having been unable to wrest the political and economic cycles back into synchronisation.

Neil Kinnock, a fine orator, had spent years disciplining Labour into an organisation capable of competing once more for the centrist vote. After three Tory victories in a row for Margaret Thatcher, the Labour cry of 'Time for a change' has rarely

had greater resonance. And yet John Major managed against the background of the longest post-war recession to win a marginally higher share of the vote for his party than Margaret Thatcher had done in a comparative boom and to come home with a working majority of 21.

The Tory campaign was criticised throughout as jerky, negative and uninspired. Following a 'Budget for recovery' which had concentrated limited tax cuts on the lower paid, it argued that a Tory victory would bring an end to recession. Virtually all Conservative energies were spent on attacking Labour as the party of high taxation. It was a traditional 'Don't let Labour ruin it' campaign weakened by the fact that many voters, notably those 'natural Conservatives' who had bought homes or set up businesses encouraged by the enterprise culture of the Thatcher years only to find themselves crippled with high interest rates, clearly felt that things could scarcely get much worse.

The Tory campaign, relentlessly insisting 'You can't trust Labour' and harking on the potential

'double whammy' of higher taxation and higher national insurance contributions for many under Labour, was notable only for some spectacular gambles by the Prime Minister.

Against, Mr Major risked accusations of defeatism in emphasising the perils of a hung parliament. It proved to be a tactic which helped to push wavering would-be Liberal Democrats back into the Tory fold in the last few days. He ignored appeals to soften on a Scottish Parliament and played the unionist card, reckoning there was no benefit for the Tories in being the fourth best devolutionist party. His reward was seeing the Tories gain a net two seats in Scotland against the predictions of a near wipeout north of the border. And Mr Major, making little impact with his 'meet the people' sessions sitting on a stool amid an elaborate set, ignored advice that it would be electoral death in a television age and took to a soap box in the streets to sell his message.

Labour played a safety first game, leaving the government to lose the election. Well-drilled press conferences were devoted to the caring

John Major campaigning in the run-up to the General Election

Rex Features

themes of education, health and pensions on which opinion polls demonstrated its pulling power.

Neil Kinnock, as punchy a platform orator as ever, contrasted Labour's readiness to take action to halt unemployment and boost public services with what he called a government supine in the face of recession. And Labour played on the solidity, respectability and credibility of shadow chancellor John Smith. He tackled the Tory tax arguments head on by introducing a formal 'Shadow Budget', complete with posed photographs outside the Treasury. Mr Smith insisted that eight out of ten voters would gain from Labour's tax and spending plans, which included a new 50 per cent tax band and the removal of the £21,000 a year ceiling on national insurance contributions as well as a boost to pensions and child benefit.

The Tories shifted their attack to the overall burden of Labour's spending plans, arguing that these would require an average tax increase of £1,250 a head. Mr Smith's problem was underlined with opinion polls showing, in response to the Tory barrage, that more than 50 per cent of electors reckoned they would be worse off under Labour.

Promising a Japanese-style partnership with British industry, Labour looked fresher, recycling the policy ideas developed through the opposition years. Its campaign gave prominence to its leading women like Margaret Beckett, Mo Mowlam and Harriet Harman, a deliberate contrast with John Major's then all-male cabinet, and shut out less telegenic figures like the able Gerald Kaufman.

The Liberal Democrat leader Paddy Ashdown demonstrated formidable energy criss-crossing the country while his party's manifesto insisted that proportional representation was the minimum price for Liberal Democrat participation in any coalition government. They promised a £6 billion package to kick-start employment and jobs, a merger of the tax and national insurance systems and an extra penny on taxation to pay for increased provision for education. That went down well. The Liberal Democrats won their highest-ever policy ratings on education.

There were few new 'big ideas' however in any of the party manifestos. Labour's 'It's time to get Britain working again' marked the contrast with the past by emphasising strong commitment to the

European Community and pledging to retain a nuclear deterrent for Britain until the world's stock of such weapons had been eliminated. The nearest to a nationalisation pledge was the promise to take the national grid and the water utilities into 'public control'.

The Conservatives' 'The best future for Britain' promised a new ministry, soon nicknamed the Ministry of Fun, to take over responsibility for sport, arts and the national heritage, special help for the inner cities, a new openness in Whitehall and the franchising out of British Rail services.

The Liberal Democrat document reflected Paddy Ashdown's quest for greater definition. Their sharpest election document ever, it committed the party to significant increases in petrol prices in a shift to environmental taxation of finite resources.

Practice in phoney war skirmishing ensured there were few notable gaffes. Biggest excitement of the campaign was the affair of Jennifer's Ear. A Labour election broadcast about NHS waiting lists and 'queue jumping' highlighted the cases of two little girls needing the same operation, one of them rich enough to afford it privately. Details leaked of the real family on which the case was based. Tories complained of the exploitation of children, Labour was caught out in some inaccurate research and Health Secretary William Waldegrave admitted putting the *Daily Express* in touch with the consultant in the case.

After a few days of claim and counter-claim both parties limped away. But meanwhile a British Medical Association vote of no confidence in the government's health reforms attracted relatively little notice, and Labour never made quite the headway on health expected.

The government, dogged by poor economic statistics, grew edgy as the Labour poll lead continued while the youthful 'brat pack' under party chairman Chris Patten at Conservative Central Office was criticised by Thatcherites involved in previous campaigns for the lack of 'oomph and fizz', as the lady herself was said to have put it.

Paddy Ashdown drums up support for the Liberal Democrats

Rex Features

Rex Features

Labour defeated – Neil Kinnock speaks to the media

A Mori poll in *The Times* on 1 April gave Labour its biggest lead yet at 7 per cent. As City markets took fright at the prospect, Labour politicians allowed a huge rally in Sheffield that night to take on a triumphant tone amid much show business style razzmatazz. Some later believed that to have been a crucial mistake. As Neil Kinnock closed his campaign by calling the Tories a 'spent force' John Major warned voters not to let Mr Ashdown become 'the doorkeeper to a Labour Britain'. Mr Kinnock may have helped him persuade voters that Liberal Democrats and Labour would combine by beginning in the later stages of the campaign to flirt with PR in an attempt to win over Lib Dem floaters.

Labour needed an eight point swing to win power in its own right and it had never looked like a sea change election. But the relentless message of the polls through the election, led commentators to expect that the best the Tories could hope for was to be the largest party in a hung parliament, a result which most expected to lead to a Labour victory in a second election soon after.

The final round of pre-election polls put party support at Labour 42 per cent, Conservative 39 per cent (NOP); Labour 39 per cent, Conservative 38 per cent (Mori); Labour 38 per cent, Conservative 38 per cent (ICM); and Conservative 38.5 per cent, Labour 38 per cent (Gallup). Presentation of exit polls on election night for both BBC and ITN encouraged hung Parliament expectation. Although the NOP/BBC exit poll put support at Conservatives 40 per cent, Labour 36 per cent, and the Harris/ITN poll made it 41:36 in Conservative favour, the predictions for seats were realigned to take account of other factors. The BBC opening forecast of seats was Conservative 301, Labour 298, while ITN put it at Conservative 305 seats, Labour 294.

In the event the UK result was Conservative 41.9 per cent, Labour 34.4 per cent, Liberal Democrats 17.8 per cent, Nationalists 2.3 per cent, others 3.5 per cent. The new House of Commons contained 336 Conservatives, 271 Labour, 20 Liberal Democrats, and 4 Welsh and 3 Scottish Nationalist MPs, as well as the 17 from Northern Ireland (9 Ulster Unionists, 3 Democratic Unionists, 1 Ulster Popular Unionist, 4 Social Democratic and Labour party).

Opinion polls are temperature gauges, not barometers, but the pollsters, impressively close in previous elections but 8.5 per cent out on average in their final verdicts this time, admitted they had never got it so wrong. Anguished debate has been going on since to decide how much of the error to attribute to late swing, differential turnout, the 'shame factor' of people voting Tory with a grumble, or faulty polling methodology.

The Conservatives' historic fourth election victory was marred for John Major by the loss of his party chairman Chris Patten, who was defeated by a Liberal Democrat in Bath and who soon after accepted the offer of becoming the last governor of Hong Kong.

Other prominent casualties were the overseas aid minister Lynda Chalker, who was rapidly sent to the Lords to carry on with the same job from there, and two able Treasury ministers Francis Maude and John Maples, both of whom might have expected cabinet status in the current Parliament had they survived.

In forming his new cabinet John Major dropped the former Home Secretary Kenneth Baker and former Defence Secretary Tom King retired. Peter Brooke, former Northern Ireland Secretary, dropped out to seek the Speakership but, having failed in that ambition, was invited back as National Heritage Secretary when David Mellor resigned a few months later. Two women, Virginia Bottomley (Health) and Gillian Shephard (Employment) came into the cabinet.

On the Labour side, Neil Kinnock and veteran deputy leader Roy Hattersley both resigned. After a contest with Bryan Gould, John Smith was elected Labour's new leader in July by an overwhelming margin with his former shadow Treasury colleague Margaret Beckett gaining the deputy's job in a contest with John Prescott and Mr Gould again.

Robin Oakley

THE MAASTRICHT TREATY

Deep-seated Tory divisions on Europe helped to cost Margaret Thatcher her crown as Conservative leader. In one way or another Europe saw the departure from her cabinet of Nicholas Ridley, Nigel Lawson and Sir Geoffrey Howe. But Tory tensions have not lessened under a new leader who combines his determination to put Britain 'at the heart of Europe' with describing himself as 'the biggest Euro-sceptic in the party'. They have merely shifted focus.

In the second of two Parliamentary divisions on the night on 4 November 1992 over the Maastricht treaty, John Major's government squeaked through by a margin of only three votes. Six Tories abstained and 26 voted against, despite the most intensive whipping

operation seen in years. Had the government been defeated, a number of cabinet ministers believed the Prime Minister would have resigned. And the concession Mr Major was forced to make that night, promising back-bench doubters that the bill would not come up for the third reading until after a second Danish referendum in May 1993, earned him the obloquy of his European Community counterparts.

Ratification of the Maastricht treaty, an issue almost totally neglected in the 1992 election, was the major political preoccupation of the year. It divided all parties but damaged the Tories the most.

Mr Major was proud of the hand he played at Maastricht in December 1991. In intensive negotiation he refused to sign up to the 'social chapter' of the treaty, covering industrial relations and welfare policies, so this was omitted from the

The Prime Minister underlines the British Government's total commitment to the Maastricht treaty at the UK Presidency Conference in London

Associated Press

treaty proper and became a separate protocol agreed between the other 11 countries. He also secured the concession that Britain would have the right at a later stage, subject to Parliament's will, to opt in or out of the proposed single currency, the eventual goal of the treaty on economic and monetary union. British negotiators argued that the treaty, for the first time in EC history, put centralising tendencies into reverse by reserving areas such as foreign and defence policy for co-operation between sovereign national governments, outside the framework of community institutions. The treaty also introduced the concept of 'subsidiarity', or 'minimum interference', saying that the EC institutions should only tackle matters which were best performed at Community level.

Tory critics continued to insist that the treaty marked another step towards federalism and an unacceptable sacrifice of national sovereignty. They disliked the concept that Britons were to become citizens of the 'European union' and they argued that a single currency and a single central bank would lead inevitably to a single European government. Nevertheless the Commons endorsed the Prime Minister's deal on 19 December 1991 by a massive majority, although 15 Tories, including Margaret Thatcher, abstained and seven voted against.

The Major government, after one brief wobble, rejected calls for a referendum on the treaty, insisting that the decision was for Parliament. But with the general election fought between three major parties all committed to ratification of Maastricht, Euro-sceptics argued that opponents of the treaty were denied the chance to express their views.

After the election the bill ratifying the Maastricht treaty (the European Communities (Amendment) Bill) was given a second reading in the Commons on 21 May 1992 by 336 votes to 92. The majority of 244 looked handsome. But it was an indication of troubles to come for a government with an overall majority of only 21 that 22 Tories voted against the second reading, with another four abstaining. Labour proved even more divided. Its MPs were instructed to abstain, on the grounds that the party's policy was to have the Social Chapter included in the treaty. But 59 Labour MPs voted against the bill and two voted in favour.

A series of events then piled up trouble for the government. The new intake of 63 Tory MPs, mostly selected during the Thatcher years, proved to be a self-confident group containing many Euro-sceptics in the lady's own image. And scepticism on Europe ran deeper in the Tory ranks than had been revealed in votes. Both government and Tory party had tended to glory in the Maastricht deal for the British exceptions rather than for the substance of the treaty. As other EC nations began, after the negotiation, to conduct the debate which had taken place in Britain before December 1991 it became apparent too that there were more Continental doubts about economic and political union than their politicians had reflected at Maastricht.

While John Major continued to defend the treaty on the grounds that Britain could not afford to scowl on the sidelines while others made decisions in Europe with a vital influence on our future, the Euro-sceptics in his party mobilised effectively. Events then played into their hands as concern over the continuing British recession became inextricably linked with the Maastricht debate.

On 2 June, by just 23,000 votes, the Danish people voted 50.7 per cent against ratification. None of the Danish parties which had all backed the deal were quite sure why, but there appeared to be a growing mood across Europe questioning the judgment of political leaders. John Major's strategy of rebuilding a Tory coalition around a platform of pragmatic pro-Europeanism was dealt a hefty blow. Loyal Tories who had previously swallowed their reservations in acknowledgment that the Prime Minister had secured more than they had hoped at Maastricht now felt that it was open season on the treaty once again. They believed that the growing doubts across Europe about rapid integration had opened up a real prospect of renegotiation. More than 90 Tories signed a Euro-sceptical Commons motion greeting the Danish decision as a chance for a 'fresh start' in building a less centralised Europe.

To the little disguised fury of John Major, President Mitterrand, believing it would help him divide the anti-Socialist opposition in France, decided that he too would hold a referendum. With France one of the two great architects of the EC, the result was considered a foregone conclusion. An Irish referendum on 18 June backed Maastricht by 69 per cent to 31. But in July and August a series of opinion polls indicated real doubts about the outcome in France, where the government was deeply unpopular. The political uncertainty helped to create turbulence in foreign exchange markets, which had been held together only by the glue of the expected moves towards economic and monetary union in the Maastricht treaty.

The pound was vulnerable because many dealers believed that the 2.95 Deutschmark to the pound rate at which Britain had entered the ERM was unrealistic and because the election result had failed to produce the lift-off for the British economy predicted by the Tory government. On Black Wednesday, 16 September, Britain was forced to leave the Exchange Rate Mechanism and devalue. Acrimonious exchanges followed between Britain and Germany. Other EC nations refused to recast the ERM, which Britain argued was faulty. British opponents of Maastricht, constant critics of the Deutschmark-dominated ERM which had forced Britain to maintain high interest rates, were able to crow that they had been right all along. A further fillip was given to the anti-Maastricht cause.

The position was further complicated for Mr Major by the fact that from 1 July Britain had been in the chair as custodian of the six-month presidency of the EC, responsible for undoing any Maastricht tangles and getting the Danes back on board.

By mid September some British

ministers were admitting privately that a *'non'* in the French referendum might be the easiest way out. Instead there came what was politically the most difficult result of all, a French *'oui'* by the narrow margin of 51.05 per cent to 48.95 which pushed the onus back on Britain while boosting the case of the doubters.

After John Smith had secured the backing of the Labour party conference for a pro-European party John Major and the cabinet faced one of the most difficult Tory conferences in years in the aftermath of devaluation. A raucous, emotional debate on Europe, including an anti-Maastricht onslaught from former party chairman Lord Tebbit, concluded with a cool restatement of the government's case from Douglas Hurd which helped the government win the day. The Prime Minister then devoted the bulk of his leader's speech to insisting how robustly he would fight for British interests within Europe. As the conference concluded, Tory Euro-sceptics conceded it was likely the government would succeed in pushing through the Maastricht legislation, however long and bloody the battle.

The government, unwisely in the view of many Tories, then decided, in macho mood, to take on their internal party critics, staging a 'paving' debate to herald the return well before Christmas of the Maastricht bill, suspended during the summer's uncertainties, for its committee stage. It was a tactical miscalculation, which maximised the potential opposition.

Following devaluation and the pit closures debacle, Labour saw the opportunity of fatally wounding a floundering government. Arguing that it was not a vote on Maastricht but in effect a vote of confidence in Mr Major, Labour decided to oppose and with a cohesive and well-organised group of around 36 anti-Maastricht Tories preparing to vote against the motion, the government faced the serious prospect of defeat. Their only ray of hope was that the 20 Liberal Democrats, save their one anti-EC MP, said that they would stick with their pro-European principles and back the Maastricht bill, so long as the

government did not claim it was a vote of confidence in Mr Major.

A special one-day EC summit in Birmingham, designed to spell out the practical implementation of the principle of subsidiarity (and convince fractious Tories that it really meant a blow against the bureaucrats of Brussels) proved a damp squib, totally overshadowed by the pit closures row. And in the run-up to the crucial vote there was a dramatic interlude when Downing Street failed to deny a spate of stories that the Prime Minister might call an election if he failed to win endorsement for the treaty which, he maintained, was a question of Britain's good faith with her European partners.

Mr Major and his senior ministers called in squads of backbenchers to persuade them of the case for Maastricht and there were squeals of protest about the allegedly tough tactics used by the Tory whips. The result remained in doubt until the end. But in the first vote, on a Labour amendment, the government survived by six votes at 319 to 313. And, after the concession on the later timetable of the bill, Mr Major won through on the government motion by just three votes at 319 to 316.

Although Labour and the Tory rebels are unlikely to end up in the same division lobby again, except perhaps over the question of an independent central bank, the opposition will not co-operate in timetabling operations. So the committee stage through to May will be long and bruising.

Robin Oakley

PIT CLOSURES – CRISIS IN THE COAL INDUSTRY

The announcement by British Coal on 13 October that it was to close 31 of Britain's remaining 50 pits, with devastating effects on mining communities and the direct loss of 30,000 miners' jobs, set off a spontaneous outburst of national protest which all but engulfed the Conservative government. The Tories were only saved from Parliamentary defeat by a series of dramatic U-turns, involving a comprehensive,

open-minded review of their entire energy policy and a 90-day suspension of the closure programme.

A series of factors combined to produce the political crisis: the government was still floundering in search of a new economic policy following its forced withdrawal from the ERM, the promised economic lift-off following the General Election had failed to materialise, and as unemployment rose inexorably there was alarm that recession was turning to slump. Amid concern at the de-industrialisation of Britain the sheer scale of the redundancies announced by British Coal and the speed with which they were to be implemented proved a lightning conductor for public discontent.

Michael Heseltine, the President of the Board of Trade, and his fellow ministers had badly miscalculated. They seemed to have assumed that the winning from the Treasury of a £1 billion package of redundancy benefits for the sacked miners and past public distaste for the militancy of Arthur Scargill, the NUM president, would see them through what they said was a painful but inevitable decision to run down the coal industry.

Instead they found themselves faced by a wave of public protest from all quarters as Opposition, churchmen and Tory MPs combined to denounce the planned redundancies and to demand a rethink. The admission by Neil Clarke, British Coal's chairman, that productivity had more than doubled in the past six years increased public sympathy for the miners and amplified Mr Scargill's complaint that the closure programme was 'a deliberate political act of industrial vandalism perpetrated against an already decimated industrial landscape'. Even those who accepted the economic case for closures argued that they had to be phased over a longer period in a more humane way.

Coal had been in decline throughout the century. Previous blows to the pits had included Winston Churchill's conversion of the Royal Navy from coal to oil in 1911, British Railways' phasing out of steam locomotives in the 60s and

Rex Features

One man speaks for millions with his simple message

environmental regulation in the late 80s requiring the gradual reduction of sulphur dioxide emissions. Then British Steel, one of the few non-power coal customers, began importing cheaper coal from abroad. Pit workers who had numbered 718,000 on nationalisation in 1947 were already down to 53,000. But the crucial factor was the privatisation of the electricity industry.

Even the old nationalised Central Electricity Generating Board, oper-ating alongside the National Coal Board had attempted to reduce its dependence on coal with some nuclear and oil-fired power plants. The electricity privatisation pushed through first by Cecil (now Lord) Parkinson and then by John (now Lord) Wakeham split up the CEGB into National Power and Powergen and pushed the regional distribution companies too into the private sector.

The new wave managers were bound to seek the cheapest fuel. This led to the purchase of foreign coal, which the NUM claimed was subsidised, and then the 'dash for gas' as the generators sought environmentally clean power stations and the regional distribution companies looked for independent supplies. More power was being bought too from Nuclear Electric. Margaret Thatcher, a nuclear enthusiast, had been keen to ensure alternative power supplies after the pit strikes of the early 80s. After the vast costs of running down old nuclear stations were revealed there was a European Community deal under which Britain was allowed to subsidise its nuclear industry (withdrawn from privatisation) while Germany subsidised its coal mines.

Coal contracts had been agreed for three years ahead with the electricity generators but in autumn 1991 when negotiations began on a new round, British Coal was in a weak position. The Rothschild study on privatisation of the coal industry had argued for a reduction to just 12 pits, foreign coal was available much cheaper and British Coal stocks were mounting at a million tons a month. No deal was achieved by the time of the election and after that the Department of Energy was no more, its functions absorbed into the new Heseltine-led DTI. The government went on approving licences for gas-fired stations.

That was the background as Mr Heseltine backed the British Coal announcement that six pits would stop work in a week, a further 13 by Christmas and 27 by March 1993, with just four mothballed for possible future reactivation, saying: 'This is a dreadful thing to have to do, but it is the right thing to do.' Output, it was argued, had to be run down by 25 million tonnes a year. Keeping all the existing pits open, said Mr Heseltine, would cost £100 million a month in subsidies. The economic case was 'unanswerable'. Energy minister Tim Eggar insisted: 'There can be no going back on the pit closures programme. It is a completely unavoidable decision.'

But then, with Labour arguing that 70,000 more jobs would be lost in mining-related industries, came

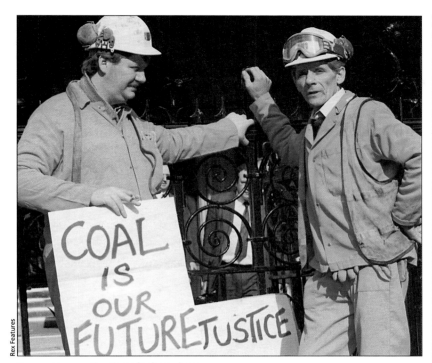

Two miners make their feelings known

becoming irresistible. Sir Marcus Fox, chairman of the influential 1992 Committee of Tory backbenchers, said that the government's approach to pit closures was 'unacceptable'. John Smith, the Labour leader, said that a 'foolish government' would be called to account 'in the name of a very angry people'. Tory MPs Winston Churchill and Elizabeth Peacock visited pits to proclaim their support for the miners, arguing that a strategic mistake was being made that would enable others to hold Britain to ransom for fuel supplies in future. Amid bitter accusations that the government was out of touch, opinion polls revealed Mr Major as the most unpopular Tory leader ever. The Tory press joined the onslaught, comparing the British people to the 'lions led by donkeys' of the First World War and complaining that the 'scale of the government's incompetence is breathtaking'.

Ministers sought to hold the line over the weekend by arguing the economic case. But with an overall Commons majority of only 21 and with at least a dozen Tory MPs threatening to vote against the government in the debate to be staged by Labour the next Wednesday it was clear that concessions would have to be made. The government's difficulties were patent as rebels on the Maastricht

the storm. The manufacturing core of the country, said Norman Willis, the TUC chairman, was 'starting to melt'. The NUM and the non-TUC Union of Democratic Mineworkers, to whom Tory MPs felt especially committed for their past role in combating Mr Scargill's militancy, both applied for court injunctions to halt the closure programme. Churchmen led by the Archbishop of York wrote to *The Times* complaining of a 'self-inflicted disaster'. Roy Lynk, UDM chairman, began a sit-in 1,000ft underground at the threatened Silverhill Colliery, Nottingham.

Public and political reaction intensified when it was revealed that the closures had not been discussed by the full cabinet and some of the ministers affected, notably employment secretary Gillian Shephard, were said to have been furious at the lack of consultation. As the storm grew, Norman Lamont, the Chancellor of the Exchequer, sought to divert pressure with the announcement of a one per cent cut in interest rates. The Prime Minister, in Birmingham for an EC summit, was dogged by the domestic crisis and was forced

to give a separate press conference at its conclusion, revealing that he had been worried enough by the closure plan to insist on a last minute review of all options. It was, he said, 'wrong to go on producing coal for which there is no demand and for which, alas, there is going to be no market'.

But the political pressures were

Arthur Scargill joins the protest march

Rex Features

Miners and their families from all over Britain take part in peaceful demonstrations in the capital

treaty sought to exploit its weakness and right wingers who blamed Mr Heseltine for Mrs Thatcher's downfall saw the hope of forcing his resignation in revenge.

On Monday, 19 October, Mr Heseltine was given one of the most uncomfortable grillings a minister has ever survived in the Commons and the backdown began. Saying that the government recognised public concern at the speed of the rundown, he said that British Coal would be allowed to go ahead with the closure on only ten of the 31 pits. There would be a moratorium for the others while interested parties were consulted. He announced too a further £165 million package of help for the affected areas. But it remained doubtful whether he had really promised the review of the closure programme sought by many MPs.

By the next day Lord Wakeham, in the Lords, did seem to be promising such a review, with the implication that at least some of the 21 pits could be saved. He agreed too that the government would 'look again' at the switch to gas. The Prime Minister, refusing John Smith at question time the formal inquiry he sought, did promise full government co-operation with a review by the all-party Trade and Industry Select Committee and conceded that Mr Heseltine's new study would be in the context of the government's energy policy.

But Tory MPs were still grumbling and with the outcome of the vote remaining in doubt it took a further string of assurances from Mr Heseltine and from David Hunt, the Welsh Secretary, in the debate on Wednesday, 21 October to ensure the government's survival.

With tens of thousands of miners and their families marching peacefully through London in protest, this time Mr Heseltine conceded that his inquiry could actually halt rather than merely postpone some closures. Provoking rowdiness on the Labour benches allowed Mr Heseltine to enlist Tory support for his skills in assaulting the Opposition. He was able to win the day in Parliamentary terms. But the price of ensuring Conservative support in the voting lobbies was considerable.

The President of the Board of Trade promised that his review of the closures would be genuine. International consultants would review the viability of every pit. Care and maintenance would continue even for the ten pits not in the moratorium and development work at the 21.

He promised to amend electricity privatisation if his review found it prejudicial to the coal industry, to look into the 'dash for gas' and whether it provided cheaper energy, to re-examine nuclear energy subsidies and to report on the economic implications of coal imports. There would be no pre-ordained outcome.

If it was not quite the full-scale energy review demanded by Labour's spokesman Robin Cook, who said the government had created a nation 'united in anger' and promised to harry them at every turn, it was certainly a massive series of U-turns compared with just a week before. The government was, in effect, committed to a full-scale energy review in just 90 days.

The government won the vote 320-307. Six Tories voted with Labour on the Opposition motion and five abstained. But ministers had postponed rather than ended the pit closures crisis. As the government wrestled with its energy review the courts found that British Coal had acted illegally. A report by the Commons Employment Select Committee sharply criticised the government's handling of the affair. And although technical reports by mining consultants offered support for the closure programme in a declining market they suggested that changed working practices could keep up to 13 earmarked pits open. As the Trade and Industry Select Committee inquiry took shape in January ministers became resigned to subsidy to keep open a number of the threatened pits. But they were divided over how much help should be provided, and for how long.

Robin Oakley

BBC Photograph Library

Rio de Janeiro – harbour

THE EARTH SUMMIT

Gareth Huw Davies reports on the impact of the Earth Summit, held in June at Rio de Janeiro, Brazil

Ask any Briton, or for that matter European, to name the most important diplomatic measure of 1992 and they would almost without exception answer 'Maastricht'. Few would nominate Agenda 21, which in its scope and vision has the potential to relegate the Maastricht treaty to a mere footnote in the history books, even when the conference which brought agreement on this visionary article was the most publicised peacetime gathering in history.

So, Agenda 21? This hefty 40 chapter action plan, agreed at the Earth Summit at Rio last June, does nothing less than list the priorities and targets for a sustainable world. And living sustainedly, in rich North as well as poor South, is now accepted to be the key to launching the planet into the next century, and millennium, with any hope of it coming out more or less intact at the other end.

Agenda 21 warns us in the developed countries that our present life style and patterns of consumption are not sustainable. We have a quarter of the world's population, yet we consume 70 per cent of its energy, 75 per cent of its metals, 85 per cent of its wood and 60 per cent of its food. These global economic imbalances are responsible for most of the environmental threats we face. Agenda 21 addresses how we must tread more lightly on the planet, and use its resources more sparingly, and fairly.

There is, however, little applause for Agenda 21 among environmentalists. They agree it would go a long way to redressing the imbalance between North and South, by providing the resources so that the countries in the South could meet the demands of their own populations and manage their environments in a sustainable way. They note its impeccable aspirations on Third World economic management; they endorse its 115 clean-up proposals, its specific commitments to piped water for all, land reform, combating poverty and managing fragile ecosystems. But then they point to the figures.

Implementing the whole of Agenda 21 would cost $625 billion in increased resources, of which $125 billion would have to come in extra money from industrialised nations. But it contains escape clauses, with phrases like 'where appropriate' or 'cost effective action', which allow too much scope for business as usual. Are governments prepared to make the policy shifts to draw us in the rich North away from our extravagant life style to a level of consumption which does not jeopardise future generations? By the end of recession-hit 1992, there was no sign that the industrialised world was in any mood to do so.

The rich North's unwillingness to fund the non-binding Agenda 21 – at least not yet – is at the heart of the widely perceived failure of last summer's UN Conference on the Environment and Development (UNCED) at Rio. But other commentators take considerable comfort from the fact that the 12-day-summit happened at all. It was the largest ever gathering of world leaders, with 178 governments represented, 114 of them by heads of state, supported by armies of civil servants and 15,000 representatives from environmental bodies and other lobbyists. It was also by far the biggest media event on the environment. The woes of the planet were reviewed on television, radio and in print as never before. A constituency of billions is now infinitely better informed.

Rio, the culmination of two years of preparatory meetings and negotiations, *did* conclude with agreements, signed by many countries. And, the optimists would proclaim, those treaties come as the *stage* of a process, not the end. The world can go forth to tighten progressively the provisions that those treaties contain, and make them more effective.

Certainly, after Rio, environment and development issues can never again be seen as peripheral matters. They are centre stage in local, national and international politics. The imbalance between North and South is firmly on the international agenda. The enormous publicity of Rio can only benefit the cause of the poorest people and degraded environments, by increasing the pressure on politicians and businesses to tackle the problems they cause.

Environment groups like Greenpeace do not share that view. They argue that Rio was actually the end of a process that began 20 years ago with the 1972 Stockholm Conference on the Human Environment. This produced a raft of real achievements, such as a convention on transboundary air pollution, the Convention on Trade in Endangered Species (CITES), and the United Nations Environment Programme (UNEP). It beefed up the International Whaling Commission, which went on to agree a ban on commercial whaling. It also led to the establishment of environment ministries in many countries.

Stockholm was followed by the Montreal Protocol on Ozone Depletion, the Brandt Report, the World Conservation Strategy, and the Brundtland Commission. So to say Rio was a tremendous leap forward, the conservationists argue, is nonsense.

The disappointment of Rio stems from the lack of political commitment to go beyond statements of concern to a specific, timetabled programme of action. 'We looked in vain for a change in political will, that governments will take the sustainable development path,' said Chris Rose of Greenpeace. 'In order to make future progress we have to point out that Rio was an empty vessel, because otherwise politicians will get away with doing nothing, convincing people that something really happened when it didn't.'

One of the most negative factors at the summit was the attitude of the USA, where vested interests lobbied hard against change that might compromise business. President Bush came to Rio proclaiming his government's environmental credentials, but was widely criticised for his cautious approach as he struggled to defend his electoral position. He would support no initiative that might cost American jobs or jeopardise the profligate US life style. Most significantly of all, he refused to sign the biodiversity treaty. Other countries found the US attitude a convenient cloak for

World leaders assemble for the Earth Summit

Rex Features

Rex Features

Crowds demonstrate against (former) President Bush's failure to sign the biodiversity treaty at the Earth Summit

their own lack of commitment. The atmosphere of the entire summit was soured.

But already a more positive view can be taken about the attitude of the USA. Mr Bush is replaced by President Clinton, whose Vice President Al Gore was widely agreed to be the greenest of senators, a lucid advocate of environmental protection. Environmentalists, correctly sceptical of all politicians until they see their works, remain to be convinced that the new administration will be any better disposed, but it is hard to believe that the Clinton-Gore administration will not signal a softening of its predecessor's attitude on the environment, perhaps

by signing the biodiversity treaty.

What were the lobbyists' hopes before Rio, and what precisely did Rio achieve? They were looking for clear signals that the international community was willing to relieve the debt burden on the poorest nations, to create a fairer balance in trading relations with the rich world and to make commitments of increased aid to underdeveloped countries. They wanted firm measures which would slow the destruction of tropical rain forests. They wanted movement on measures to limit the pollution that leads to climate change and to protect biodiversity – the plant and species richness of countries,

particularly in the tropics.

And what did Rio actually deliver? The summit did produce two new legally binding agreements – treaties on climate change and on biodiversity. They respectively recognise the threat posed by global warming and the extinction of species caused by man, but, significantly, they do not oblige nations to tackle the problems.

Climate Change

Slowing the accumulation of CO_2 in the atmosphere – chiefly the product of the North's over-consumption of energy resources – and reducing global warming, is the biggest challenge facing the planet. Work on a climate convention had been under way for two years, independently of UNCED. It was then decided to make climate a pivotal issue at Rio. In the event, the climate treaty did not oblige any government to go further than it was already committed in setting CO_2 emission targets.

Again recession was partly to blame, causing, for instance, the Germans to water down earlier commitments. But so was political caution. The USA would not commit itself to specific targets, or timetables, (an attitude in which it was supported by the UK). So the treaty sets only the 'aim' of stabilising emissions at 1990 levels by 2000. Most countries were already committed to this. (The Intergovernmental Panel on Climate Change stresses the need to *reduce* significantly rather than stabilise emissions.)

Biodiversity

This treaty, under discussion for ten years, encourages governments to conserve the plants and animals within their borders, but does not compel them to protect them. It was the summit's one official failure. A measure originally designed to protect natural life turned into something addressing how living organisms, mainly in the bio-rich tropical countries, should be commercially exploited by chemical, pharmaceutical and pesticide industries, and who should have the patent rights. It was weakened by the USA, which refused to sign on the grounds that it might threaten its biotechnology industry by interfering with patent rights. US support might have changed the entire mood of the conference.

Forest Principles
Environmentalists wanted Rio to address and tackle the root causes of deforestation in the tropics, such as the West's overconsumption of raw materials, Third World debt and poverty, and the actions of multinationals. Instead the forest discussions became a vehicle for a wider argument about the resources the South expected from the North, and the commitments to conservation the North expected from the South.

Friends of the Earth believe the best way forward on forests now is for national governments to take action, using domestic legislation to promote the market in timber from sustainable sources (where only as many trees are taken as are naturally replaced). The UK, for example, imports tropical timber worth £500 million a year from non-sustainable sources, the largest importer in the EC. The money it collects on VAT on timber alone dwarfs what it spends on tropical timber conservation.

Earth Charter
The set of 'ten commandments' that environmentalists sought was replaced by this bland declaration,

able Development, a success, at least on (the conference's non-recycled) paper. Its purpose is to monitor the way governments implement the Rio agreements, and particularly Agenda 21, reviewing action reports from over 170 countries. It will have 50 members, representing all continents, and a permanent secretariat. The commission's terms of reference will be set by the UN General Assembly by early 1993. It could play an important role if it succeeds in providing a genuine forum to assess governments' environmental behaviour.

Environmentalists want the commission to address the way the economics of the developed world act as a brake on sustainable development in debt-distressed nations, particularly in Africa. They feel it will be vital for the commission to influence the working of international financial institutions, which have an impact on Third World economies and dictate how things are done in these poor countries, such as whether they invest beneficially in public transport and infrastructure and health schemes, or in dams and defence.

Aid and Debt
Rio saw no commitment by the rich nations to reduce Third World debt. In 1991 developing countries transferred $31 billion more to the North in debt repayments than they received in new loans. The loss of revenue from the trade imbalance between North and South, according to the UN Development Programme, is running at $500 million a year. Yet all the resources needed to implement Rio could be met by a more liberal trade regime.

Even then, poor countries often trade in items which are wrong for their economies. One way they raise money to pay off their debts is by concentrating on cash crops, such as coffee, taking good land from sustainable peasant farming, and forcing people off the land into cities.

The UNCED secretariat estimated it would cost developing countries £350 billion in new resources by the year 2000 to implement Agenda 21 and meet environmental obligations called for at Rio. It suggested a

One of the many banners displayed in Rio de Janeiro during the Earth Summit drawing attention to environmental issues

In the end the summit agreed on a statement of principles for the sustainable management and conservation of tropical forests. But this went no further than existing agreements, some said not even as *far* as existing agreements. There are still no binding measures at all to preserve tropical forests. Third World countries refused to give up their right to cut down their natural resource; they were unimpressed by the West's threat to withhold aid.

which includes 27 principles for protecting the environment and promoting greener economic growth.

Agenda 21
This is the programme of action designed to implement the principles of the Earth Charter, covering everything from pollution to poverty and biodiversity.

This in turn is to be supported by a new UN Commission on Sustain-

Rex Features

The *Rainbow Warrior* arrives at Rio

donation of £70 billion by the developed countries, including the £30 billion already given. The figure the developing countries pledged, around $2.5 billion a year, fell below even the most pessimistic forecasts of between $5 and $10 billion a year made before the summit.

The aspirations of Agenda 21 could be met if OECD countries donated the established UN recommended target of 0.7% of GDP as aid to the poor South. Rio reasserted this target, but no date was set for meeting it. Some countries, such as Denmark, have already met it; others are committed to do so by the year 2000. The USA, UK and Germany gave no indication when they might meet the target. UK aid budget is at its lowest ever: it currently gives 0.32%, just under $2 billion, compared with 0.51% in 1979.

The Global Environment Facility, jointly administered by the World Bank and the UN, is a separate fund to assist poor countries to carry out conservation work which could be of international benefit. At Rio it was agreed that this will be more than doubled, to £800 million. The UK pledged an additional £100 million to this fund.

The Darwin Initiative
In addition, the UK government made its own specific commitments at the summit. It announced the Darwin Initiative, a research programme by which the enormous expertise of certain UK scientific institutions would be harnessed to help poorer countries to assess their natural resources and species and draw up biodiversity strategies. However by the end of 1992 the likely participating institutions, including the Botanic Gardens at Kew and the Natural History Museum in South Kensington, still did not know when or by how much the programme would be funded, and when the programme would begin.

The UK also announced it would launch a global technology partnership to share environmentally-sound processes with developing countries, leading to a conference in the UK in 1993. And it said it would call another world conference, for non-governmental organisations concerned with the environment and development.

The Cost of Progress
One factor behind the reluctance of First World governments to make a radical shift in the way they run their economies, and meet the challenge of Rio, is the apparent conflict between profit and conservation.

Clearly there will be a cost to the rich North in replacing existing, inherently-polluting, technologies. But there are unassessed costs from pollution itself – and these environmental costs are not included in our national accounts. However this concept of environmental economics, or 'green' cost accounting, did creep onto the agenda at Rio in the discussion of Agenda 21.

There are enormous potential markets for the clean processes and technologies that tackle over-consumption of resources and the excessive generation of waste. The switch to cleaner technologies will require government intervention; it cannot be left to market forces which, for example, would not have brought about the coming ban on ozone-destroying chemicals.

Environmentalists argue that the transition from the most polluting aspects of our present life style to cleaner production can be planned without major dislocations of society or mass unemployment. There are already signs of a more interventionist thinking in the West, with a shift away from the Reagan-Thatcherite formula of market individualism, and particularly in the new US administration, that might facilitate the change.

Those searching for a model are looking with interest to see how Japan, which was reckoned to have had a good conference, responds to the challenge, by moving into the technology of energy efficiency and renewable energies as an alternative to fossil fuels. Japan's intervention here could give the same sort of boost to the market as it did as a car manufacturer.

An example of an area where developed countries could intervene and begin to meet their obligations (moral if not actual) under Rio, is transport. Many urban areas are now seriously disrupted and polluted by traffic, particularly the private car. Yet countries like Britain are committed to enormous further capital expenditure on new roads, which is almost bound to lead to a growth in traffic and further pollution. Promoting more fuel efficient vehicles and speed limits, coupled with investment in attractive public transport could make a big difference in resource consumption. At the same time it need not involve any sacrifice to the quality of urban life.

Summary

So, at the start of 1993, is there real hope that the world will become a better place than it would if so many influential people had not assembled at Rio?

Richard Sandbrook, director of the International Institute for Environment and Development, believes there are two ways of looking at Rio. 'In the short term the outcome is all very negative. But looking over the hill, one thing that Rio did establish is that the old East-West axis is finished. A new North-South axis is beginning. The triumph of the summit was in assembling Agenda 21, which gives a very sound basis to the North-South agenda for the next decade.

'When we look at what is implied in Agenda 21, the short term problem of financial resources – at the end of the day the cost of financing it is the price of one swing-wing bomber – becomes unimportant. Ten years on we will be looking only at its strategic importance.

'The public in the rich North saw Rio as an environmental conference; in the poor South they saw a development conference. And we can't expect quick results in development. Rio was part of a continuing process. It is just another step. Yes, in the short term I am pessimistic, but in the long term I am rather more optimistic.'

Gareth Huw Davies

A boat with a message sails past Sugar Loaf Mountain, Rio de Janeiro

Rex Features

THE FATE OF THE WHALE – SURVIVAL OR EXTINCTION?

Gareth Huw Davies examines the conservation issues concerning the most magnificent creature in our oceans

Can we save the whale? In 1993, as in every year, the members of the International Whaling Commission (IWC) will sit down to debate the future of a huge, mysterious and highly intelligent sea mammal, which, over two centuries, the world has ruthlessly pursued almost to extinction.

There is a particular significance to the 1993 meeting. It will be held during May in Japan, which is the most determined of the three remaining whaling nations – the other two are Iceland and Norway. In the face of enormous world public opinion, which sees the cause of the whale as symbolic in the battle to save the planet, Japan resolutely refuses to give up whaling, which it maintains is part of its culture. Western nations, for their part, see the salvation of the whale as one of the few attainable goals in a world beset with environmental problems.

The fate of the whale is delicately balanced. The 1993 meeting could either considerably improve, or seri-

ously undermine, its cause. Two proposals are coming close to a vote. On the one hand the scientific committee of the IWC is in the final stages of drawing up a revised management procedure (RMP), which could allow some resumption of commercial whaling, suspended since 1986 when an indefinite moratorium imposed by the IWC took effect.

On the other hand the proposal by France to set up a no-whaling zone in Antarctica, which would have the effect of protecting one of the last relatively unexploited whale populations on the planet, is gaining support. It was not ready to come to the vote at the 1992 meeting. It could do so this year.

Mankind has the utmost regard for the whale. The song of the humpback whale, the longest and most complex in the animal kingdom, is aboard the Voyager spacecraft, now on the way out of the solar system as part of the planet Earth's 'message in a bottle'. On the face of it, then, saving such a creature ought to be one of the least complicated of international conservation challenges, compared, for instance, with ending the destruction of the rain forest. Many people may wonder why whaling cannot now be banned outright.

The whale is the only creature to

have an entire international body dedicated to its management, although, unfortunately for the whale, not to its protection. The IWC, as Japan insists on pointing out, is a body to *regulate* whaling, not an anti-whaling organisation. It was founded in 1949, with 12 members – when many nations were still whaling and the enormous reductions they had made to whale populations were still not realised – to address the mismanagement of one of the planet's largest animal stocks.

Commercial whaling began in earnest in the last century. By 1850 there were 700 whalers afloat, pursuing the creature across every ocean on earth. By the turn of the century ignorant and greedy hunters had rendered the whale populations of the northern hemisphere virtually extinct. They turned their attention to the southern hemisphere and, following the introduction of factory ships in the 20s, systematically destroyed them there too.

In the past 50 years at least 1.5 million whales have been killed in southern seas. A report based on six years of sightings carried out in the 80s in Antarctic waters estimated that populations of the blue and fin whale have been reduced by between 98 and 99 per cent. The blue whale, the largest creature that ever lived on earth, bigger than the biggest dinosaur, is down from 250,000 to between 500 and 1,000. In the 30s, 30,000 were taken in a single season. But the slaughter was actually greater *after* the IWC was set up.

The IWC, whose terms of reference were 'to provide for the proper conservation of whale stocks', was powerless to do what was intended of it. It presided over an unprecedented slaughter, with the crash of stock after stock. Between 50-60,000 whales were taken a year and by the mid-60s the figure reached an all-time high of 70,000. As they depleted the bigger, more profitable, whales (and many of these species show little or no sign of recovery, despite years of protection), hunters turned to the smaller whales. The minke, smallest of the great whales and previously considered too insignificant to pursue, was

A magnificent whale dives beneath the ocean

Rex Features

Rex Features

Inquisitive whales swim near a sailing boat

not hunted until the 70s. Now all three whaling nations have their eyes on it, the only whale surviving in sufficient numbers to be worth hunting.

The IWC underwent a belated sea change following a call by the 1970 UN Conference on the Environment for its strengthening. New management of the catch was tried and failed. Only a moratorium could save the whale. The idea was first voted on in 1972. It failed. By the early 80s the ranks of the whalers were reduced to the then Soviet Union, the Republic of Korea and a number of smaller pirate whaling fleets, as well as Japan, Norway and Iceland. In 1982 the IWC, by then with 37 members, finally voted for a moratorium on commercial whaling, to take effect from 1986.

Japan, Norway and Iceland now present the only real obstacle to a permanent end to commercial whaling. Under IWC rules they were able to continue whaling after lodging an objection. Later, Japan and Iceland introduced 'scientific' programmes, catching whales in order to research their populations. As many as 14,000 whales may

have been killed since the moratorium came into effect, over and above small numbers caught by indigenous peoples.

The whaling debate at the IWC is now dominated by scientific argument over the size of stocks. But, say the conservationists, there *is* no effective way of counting whales. Any count is subject to a margin of error of plus or minus 50 per cent. So, they claim, scientists have to proceed on 'guesstimates' of how many survive to sexual maturity and add to the stock. The IWC scientific committee is moving towards a very conservative formula which could allow a limited commercial catch of certain key populations, such as the Antarctic minke whales, which Japan has been hunting for the past few years for scientific research.

The 1992 IWC meeting in Glasgow saw two big developments. First Iceland left the Commission altogether. But, paradoxically, it is worse off outside than in the IWC. As one observer put it: 'Iceland may have harpooned itself in the foot.' During the first few years of the moratorium, Iceland caught whales for scientific purposes, apparently sending all the meat to Japan. It has

not whaled since 1989. If Iceland wants to resume hunting now, it will have to do so illegally, outside the only international framework for whaling, and could become the target of international sanctions.

Norway, when the moratorium came in, carried on whaling under an objection, and killed 800 whales. Then, bowing to international pressure, it switched to a research programme and killed, respectively, 30 whales in 1989, 20 in 1990 and none in 1991. Norway has announced that it intends to restart whaling in 1993, for further 'research', probably in May or June. It is hard to define Norway's motives, particularly when Prime Minister Mrs Brundtland has otherwise some of the most impressive conservationist credentials of any world leader. Anti-whaling activists point to the votes available in the northern coastal region where most whaling takes place.

Norway argues that minkes eat too many fish in the North East Atlantic and need to be controlled. And it claims, together with Japan and Iceland, that, anyway, the North Atlantic fin and minke and Antarctic minke populations are large enough to withstand commercial exploitation. Conservationists counter that it is not safe to take even the 382 minkes Norway proposes. The IWC scientific committee recently stated that minke in the North East Atlantic had been depleted by between 50 and 70 per cent of its pre-exploitation level. Once a whale population falls by over 54 per cent, under IWC rules it becomes protected.

Now a debate has broken out in the Norwegian press over hunting methods. A recent report by a Norwegian inspector suggested atrocities in recent hunts. There have been reports of exploding harpoons that failed to go off, of whales being inflated alive and of whales shot to pieces. These are unconfirmed, but then it is extremely difficult to monitor the conduct of whalers at sea. Norway's fisheries minister hinted that the promised hunt might not go ahead if problems with the exploding harpoon could not be resolved.

Japan, the world's leading whaler – only Norway has killed more whales than Japan this century – remains as intractable as ever. Since the moratorium began, it has taken 7,000 whales in Antarctica. Last summer in Antarctica, Japan killed 288 minkes for so-called research, in defiance of the IWC which has never validated Japan's programme. There is now a ban on whaling in Japanese coastal waters, but, claims Greenpeace, minkes are still being killed there illegally.

Whale meat is in demand only by the epicure in Japan. (There are no essential commercial uses for which there is no substitute to whale meat, and it has long since ceased to be an essential part of the Japanese nutritional requirement.) In early 1992 Greenpeace found it selling in a Tokyo supermarket at 6,500 yen for 100 grammes, or £138 per pound.

Such prices certainly support the anti-whalers' contention that the short term profit motive dominates whaling to the exclusion of long term conservation. Whales may reproduce at only between 1-4 per cent of their total population a year, while the income from a dead whale, selling at £25,000 on the

quayside in Japan, might reap 10 per cent annual interest in the bank. It would make more sense to kill now and invest the money than wait for whales to recover. Japan appears to live in hope that the IWC will agree to a resumption of whaling, allowing it to take up to 5,000 minkes a year.

The USA is effectively the only nation with either the domestic legislation or the economic muscle able to take action against the countries which go against the spirit of the IWC's decisions, and is probably the cause of Japan withdrawing its objection to the moratorium. Norway never has withdrawn its objection, so technically there is no reason why it should not legally continue whaling.

Otherwise the IWC is the best, and the only effective, forum for protecting the whale. (Three to one majorities are required for any change.) This is why the next few IWC meetings could be so crucial, with the certainty that the revised management procedure (RMP), which could trigger the re-start of commercial whaling, will be put to the vote.

France's proposal to set up a no-whaling zone in Antarctica is supported by strong scientific evidence, and could potentially be carried in by IWC members at a single meeting on a wave of popular support, as the moratorium was in 1982. The most recent convert to this cause was the powerful voice of Russia, until recently, as most of the USSR, one of the most determined whaling nations. Japan could ignore an Antarctic exclusion zone, but it would be one more moral impediment against a nation eager to advance itself diplomatically, and with eyes on a UN Security Council seat.

There are pressing reasons for setting up a Southern Hemisphere whale sanctuary. The ozone hole above the Antarctic is threatening the delicate balance of marine life. Depletion of ozone is leading to damaging levels of ultraviolet B radiation, which destroys phytoplankton, which in turn reduces zooplankton such as krill, the staple diet of so many species of Antarctic baleen (filter-feeding) whales. Other

wider threats in the oceans are pollution, particularly the accumulation of persistent toxins such as PCBs (polychlorinated biphenyls). Then there is over-exploitation of the whale's prey fish species. Global warming may alter ocean currents and further disrupt food availability for the whales. Other threats to the whale include entanglement in nets and human encroachment into sensitive areas.

Quite apart from the uncertain effect on whale numbers, there are strong moral arguments for ending the hunt. The notion of killing creatures with a high degree of sentience is repugnant to many people. And the way in which whales are killed is still fundamentally inhumane.

The IWC banned the cold harpoon as unacceptably cruel in 1983, but among the other instruments used, including the penthrite harpoon which kills by shock rather than by laceration, and another method that includes electrocution, there is still no humane way to kill a whale. Data from Norwegian and Japanese hunts show the average death time of minke whales to be just under ten minutes. The RSPCA in a 1991 report 'The Cruel Seas – Man's Inhumanity to Whales' described the killing of whales as 'completely unacceptable'.

The Japanese counter that we should treat whales with the same attitude as domestic livestock in the west, both being killed for food. UK agriculture minister John Gummer replied to this in 1988 by saying: 'We are very tough in this country on the way animals are killed for meat. I would not allow a farmer to throw a harpoon at a cow and allow it to run through five fields before it died.'

The RSPCA calls for a complete cessation of whaling. World public opinion wants it stopped. Greenpeace argues that, given the uncertainty over whale numbers, and the apparently long time it takes depleted populations to recover, the only way to be sure of saving what whales remain is to turn the current moratorium into a permanent ban.

Gareth Huw Davies

BEHIND THE SCENES OF TELEVISION'S ELECTION COVERAGE

The Swingometer has come a long way since its debut in the 50s, and in a year which gave us both the General Election and the American Presidential Election, BBC presenter Peter Snow describes the huge advances in high-tech computer graphics which have made television coverage of these events more exciting and innovative than ever before

At a quarter past midnight on Friday, 20 November, stifling hot inside a tear-off suit held on with Velcro, I leaped onto the stage of the BBC's *Children in Need* programme to introduce their own special Swingometer. Moments later four dancers were stripping the suit off me, and I was left standing there in a leopard skin – singing 'I'm the King of the Swingers'. Such is the price of being the BBC's election night presenter! Of all the years of dancing around in front of displays of election graphics, 1992 has been the most stimulating – but it has also presented the greatest challenge.

The two big events were the British General Election in April, and the American Presidential Election in November. For the first, David Dimbleby and I were on the air live for six hours on results night, and another seven hours the following day: in Washington we were live for nine hours all through the night. On both occasions the result was clear after the first hour and a half. So the greater part of my job on each election programme was explaining what had happened *after* the race was already over. Imagine commentating from a racecourse for several hours after the end of the last race, and you have an idea of the problem. The way we solved it was to invent a whole repertoire of graphic displays that would describe *why* people voted the way they did, and what political tasks lay ahead of the winners and the losers.

But before the story of how those two big results programmes were made, there is another one to tell –

(From left) Peter Sissons, David Dimbleby and Peter Snow – presenters of BBC TV's election night coverage

about how we monitored the British election horse-race from day to day through the campaign from early March to polling day on 9 April. On almost every night I sat with a small team of BBC computer experts in a corner of the newsroom – preparing the nightly BBC poll of polls. In nearly all past elections the polls had given a pretty accurate guide to party fortunes during the campaign and, at the end of it, a

good prediction of the outcome. We were not to know how badly wrong they were to be in 1992. Mind you, even if the polls had had a poor record in previous elections, we would still have felt bound to report them. They remain the only means – however unsatisfactory – by which we can get a feel for the ups and downs of the race as polling day approaches.

We told that story with a set of graphics that could absorb new poll figures right up to the time we went on the air. And not only could we slap on the screen charts that would show the very latest opinion poll scores for all the parties, but we could re-calculate the shape of the House of Commons and redraw it – in a three-dimensional model of the Commons chamber – within minutes. And so, each night between seven and nine o'clock, as the pollsters revealed to us the figures that would be appearing in the newspapers the following morning, we fed them into our computer to calculate the BBC's poll of polls, and then rushed the result and the House of Commons forecast to our team of graphic artists.

We kept the night's headline poll of polls figures a closely guarded secret each night: they were not allowed out until they'd been announced on the *Nine O'Clock News*. In the event, the graphic

Peter Snow demonstrates the Swingometer

display we were most proud of – a beautiful revolving hexagon that showed the trend of the poll of polls – showed a Labour lead over the Conservatives of between one and three points from the beginning to the end of the campaign. That would have produced a hung Parliament on polling day. Only on one night, 31 March, did we have a Labour lead of four points – just enough to put Labour in power with an overall majority of one. Even then, of course, I reminded

Mackenzie scored a big hit with BBC viewers by introducing the concept of swing to explain the shift in the vote from one election to another. And he illustrated it by moving a wooden pendulum across an arc that had painted on it a different outcome for every one per cent of swing. All that the programme producers required was a cut-out pendulum and a nail on which it could pivot.

When we began to plan for the 1992 Election, we began to experi-

swing. Rather conveniently, a swing of the pendulum of four percentage points along Labour's red arrow would deprive the Conservatives of their overall majority, and an 8 per cent swing would see Labour in with an overall majority.

All we had to do was find some way of making those little blue figures turn red *precisely* as the pendulum passed over them. And the solution was to replace Bob Mackenzie's nail at the top of the pendulum with a potentiometer

Peter Snow in the studio on election night

people that the margin of error in most opinion polls could be up to 3 per cent for each of the parties, and that meant a party's *lead* could be up to six points out. But even that was not good enough to explain what happened on election day: the Conservative lead was a whole *eight* points away from the final prediction of the pollsters.

All the excitement of illustrating the campaign was just a taste of what was to come on results night. The great firework display of television graphics we showed then was the product of the best part of three years of planning. We began with the Swingometer.

Back in the 50s, Professor Robert

ment with ways of bringing the Swingometer up-to-date. The story had not changed – it was still the swing between Labour and the Tories that would decide the election. But the technology had leaped forward. We could now design a Swingometer that would be part computerised display, and part mechanical pendulum.

We had the idea of planting the Labour MPs (in red) and Conservative MPs (in blue) on the Swingometer, and making them change colour as the pendulum passed over them. We would be able to show people how many blue Conservative MPs Labour would be able to turn red for a given amount of

made of conductive plastic. Any movement of the pendulum was tracked by the computer, and a message sent to the little blue and red figures to change colour the moment the arm passed over them. So I only had to sweep the pendulum across the display and more and more of the figures would change from blue to red as the swing increased to Labour.

I had to memorise the names of the seats the little figures represented – each one in its precise place on the Swingometer. The most important one at the bottom of the display was Basildon: that would turn from Conservative blue to Labour red with a swing of just 3 per cent. Pendle – up in the north – required a swing of 3 per cent too.

It was the variability of the swing that made the first hour or so of the programme so exciting. Pendle changed colour: the Labour swing there was enough to snatch it from the Conservatives. But Basildon did not. Basildon turned out to be more typical of the country than Pendle, and the Conservatives held on to their majority. Labour achieved a swing of just 2 per cent over the whole United Kingdom – half what it needed to upset the Conservatives' overall majority.

But if the Swingometer stole the show, the Battleground also provided us with a very clear illustration of Labour's failure to capture enough of those Tory seats. This too had been one of Bob Mackenzie's favourite displays, a rather more complicated piece of carpentry than his Swingometer. It was essentially a list of seats which the challenging side had to capture if it was to throw the government out of office.

That was the idea behind our 1992 Battleground too, but instead of the list of seats being a static display, we invented another gigantic computerised graphic. The seats spilled out in a long list – over 90 of them – and, as the last one popped on in the colour of its forecast winner, it triggered open the door to Number 10 Downing Street to reveal the next Prime Minister. I remember very well – at the start of the programme – when our computer was forecasting a hung Parliament, how John Major was predicted to be hanging on in there with only a few seats more than Labour. As the results came in, and fewer and fewer of those Battleground seats were forecast to turn from blue to red, the extent of Labour's failure became clear. Of the 94 seats on the list, Labour managed to gain less than half.

The election graphics that we spent the most time designing were the ones that appeared on the small screen in the studio: these were the pictures that told the essential story of how and where the seats were won and lost, and how the parties shared the vote – nationally and by region. All of them – like the displays on the big screen – were generated by the computer and reacted in real time to the very latest changes in the vote – as the results came in. I selected, controlled and animated these graphics on a keyboard.

Each picture had a number, and by just tapping that number out on my keyboard, and then punching the 'return' key, I could call up the required graphic on the screen. I could even bunch together a set of pictures and make a sequence of them. The problem of course was remembering the numbers. I never quite knew when David Dimbleby might bowl a fast ball like: 'Peter, how are the parties doing in the Northeast?' I am glad to say that normally I was given a few moments notice of what I was expected to do!

The final excitement of 1992 – the American Presidential Election – provided us with a quite new opportunity. For the first time ever, we decided to take a whole package of computer-operated graphic displays across the Atlantic and operate them in real time from the BBC's Washington studio. And just to be really ambitious, we again had

Peter Snow presents the American election results

a go at two quite different types of display. We had a full repertoire of small screen graphics – magnificently designed in full three-dimensional animation.

We also had a dazzling map of

Technical wizardry behind the US Presidential Election map

the United States which lit up in the colours of the winner in each state, and spinning presidential heads and scores in electoral votes – like a giant fruit machine. It was designed and constructed by Andy Bowman, one of those technical wizards only the BBC employs these days. He spent every day of two whole months wiring up three bulbs for each of the states and attaching each of them to a relay and a transformer, and then finally to a computer that would tell them when to fire up and in what colour.

We had a blue bulb in each state for Bush, a red bulb for Clinton and a yellow one for Perot – just in case he won a state or two. He did not, but for one glorious moment he *appeared* to have taken most of the industrial states in the Northeast. A whole bunch of them suddenly shone yellow while I was live on the air, and I just had time to say 'If Perot really has taken Pennsylvania, I'm a Dutchman', when a little voice in my ear said: 'It's wrong: it's wrong', and the map and I were swept off the air. It was not Andy's fault. Someone had pressed the wrong button well before it reached his computer.

Technology is opening up new and even more challenging ways to exploit computer graphics. The most impressive feature of it all is the speed at which pictures can now be constructed and animation developed. By the time of the next election, goodness knows what magic we'll have to conjure with!

Peter Snow

THE AMERICAN PRESIDENTIAL ELECTION

In the wake of Bill Clinton's victory, veteran reporter Charles Wheeler recalls past election dramas

For those of us who were betting on a Democratic victory, and were incautious enough to say so in public, there was a short, sharp shock some ten days before polling day: a slight but perceptible surge in the opinion polls showed President Bush drawing level with Governor Clinton. Could it be, we wondered, that Bush was about to make fools of us by repeating the miraculous recovery that had won him the Presidency in 1988?

nounced as a liar. Bush won. I shall never forget his chief strategist, the late Lee Atwater, rushing into the press room. 'Three days ago our guy was dead,' he shouted. 'You're watching a resurrection. Been nothin' like it since you-know-who.'

A second resurrection was perhaps more than any mortal man deserves. As America went into the last days of the Presidential campaign, there was every chance that for only the third time for 60 years an incumbent President would not be elected to a second term. It happened to Herbert Hoover in 1932. In 1980 it was Jimmy Carter the voters threw out. The reason was the same in each case: a President's failure to prevent a fall in the nation's standard of

year was to fly from one military base to another: only thus could he avoid the crowds of anti-war protestors, chanting 'LBJ, LBJ, how many kids did you kill today?'

It was election year in 1968. For America's sake, I hope there'll never be another one like it. What we watched was the checks and balances of the US political system at their most violent. They came into play in snowbound New Hampshire, where an anti-war Democrat, Senator Eugene Mc-Carthy, won a startling 42 per cent of the vote. 'You know when I first thought I might have a chance?' McCarthy said later. 'When I realised you could go into any bar in the country and insult Lyndon Johnson, and nobody would punch you on the nose.'

McCarthy's successful challenge in the first of the primaries split the Democrats and brought Senator Robert Kennedy into the race. Two weeks later Johnson abdicated, appearing on TV from his White House Oval Office to announce: 'I shall not seek, and will not accept, the nomination of my party for another term as your President.' And with that he passed the electoral chalice to his loyal but privately dovish Vice President, Hubert Humphrey.

For a few months it was fun to crisscross the country with the candidates. Although TV was already a powerful political force, it was not yet all-consuming. On a whistle-stop tour through Nebraska, my camera crew and I would have Kennedy to ourselves for 20 minutes without being trodden underfoot by the heavies from the networks. Then, one Californian summer day, the campaign turned into tragedy when the winner, the likeable, and surprisingly shy Bobby Kennedy, was shot and killed by an assassin.

At the Democratic convention in Chicago the decibel level rose to a scream, as night after night anti-war demonstrators and dissident delegates fought police in full view of network television. By the time he won it, Humphrey's nomination seemed worthless, and the Republican's choice, Richard Nixon, had a 15-point lead in the polls.

Associated Press

Bill Clinton on the campaign trail through the state of New Hampshire in February 1992

As Vice-President and heir-apparent to Ronald Reagan, Bush had lost the very first of the primary contests, in Iowa, not only to Bob Dole, the Senate's Republican leader, but also to the Reverend Pat Robertson, a former faith healer. A second defeat, one week later in New Hampshire, where he was trailing, would have put him out of the race. But Bush had engaged the brightest, and least scrupulous, team of handlers in the business. They made a TV commercial accusing Dole of secretly planning to raise taxes, and in the last 60 hours before the polling booths opened voters saw Dole repeatedly de-

living. Now it was George Bush who was perceived to have let the people down.

Why is it, I wonder, that American presidents are so rarely permitted the relative dignity of a gentle, downward drift in the popularity polls? Invariably, they crash. When I moved to the United States in 1965 President Lyndon Johnson was a giant. Elected the year before in a stunning landslide, he had only to lift a telephone for the Congress to obey. Yet by 1967 his escalation of the war in Vietnam had turned the home front into a battleground. To travel around America with the President in the latter part of that

George Bush greets residents of Findlay, Ohio during an unscheduled stop in his campaign tour

But this was the year we learned that nothing is certain in politics, especially American politics. With three weeks to polling day, his campaign funds at zero and his organisation a shambles, Humphrey wrenched himself free from the war policy of the lame duck Johnson administration, called for a bombing halt and began to recover. In the event, Nixon did win. But he limped home with no more than 43 per cent of the popular vote, the lowest percentage for a victor since 1912. What was worse, he became the first president in 120 years to begin his White House tenure facing Congress controlled by the opposition.

The Watergate scandal shook the institution of the presidency to its foundations. It also had the curious effect of opening the road to the White House to the temporarily unemployed. Two years before the 1976 election it occurred to the former Democratic Governor of Georgia, now engaged in farming peanuts, that a palpably honest, born-again Christian might win

over the by now deeply disillusioned electorate and succeed to the highest office in the land.

So Jimmy Carter set off for rural Iowa, whose voters would be the

Bill Clinton (left), H Ross Perot (centre) and President George Bush (right), participate in the first presidential debate in St Louis, Missouri on 11 October 1992

first nationally to hold a primary. For month after month he trudged around the state, visiting 114 towns and countless villages and farms in between. 'I'm Jimmy Carter and I'm running for President,' he would say. By the time another ten Democratic aspirants joined the field, early-bird Carter had impressed Iowa. And although he only came second in the poll, and only one in ten eligible Democrats bothered to go to the polls, Carter's smiling face made the cover of *Time* magazine, a bonus that propelled him through the next half a dozen primaries.

Results night showed that most American elections become closer as they reach the final weeks. In 1976 Carter was challenging Gerald Ford, who assumed the presidency after Nixon resigned over Watergate. It was a long, nail-biting night for both camps, and a classic example of the complexities of the American electoral system, with its heavy premium on the political weight of the larger, more populous states. To carry one of these – California, New York or Texas – is more important than winning up to five or six of the smaller states. Moreover, the winner takes all. This means that a candidate can win Wisconsin by a margin of a million votes and score 11 points, and minutes later lose California by a single vote and watch his rival run off with 54. In 1976, while Ford carried California, Carter won Texas and New York and beat him. But it was close: an independent candidate, the former senator, Eugene McCarthy, cost Carter four lesser states. If he had been a little stronger, he might have cost Carter the election.

In 1992 the Third Man, billionaire Ross Perot, won a surprising 20 per cent of the popular vote. But he didn't win a single state and he can't be said to have thrown the election to Bill Clinton. Clinton deserved his victory: he ran a determined and very cleverly judged campaign. But what brought about the result was Bush's inept and unimaginative performance as President. He seems never to have grasped that in 1988 Americans voted for a continuation of Ronald Reagan's policies, and not for

George Bush. Neither did he understand that a leader must stand for something, must have ideas, programmes and above all clear beliefs. Bush was no Reagan. He was content with the *status quo* to the point of complacency, and to the voters his inaction in the face of recession was seen as indifference.

Associated Press

Bill Clinton takes part in the first presidential debate in St Louis, Missouri

America now has a President who has come to office on a tide of rising expectations. It will not be easy to deliver. If Clinton also fails, look to a return of the Third Man. For better or for worse, Ross Perot is waiting in the wings.

Charles Wheeler

THE DEATH PENALTY IN THE USA

In a year when 31 men were executed by the state in the USA, distinguished reporter and broadcaster Charles Wheeler investigates the case of Roger Coleman, found guilty of rape and murder and put to death in the electric chair

On the night of 20 May 1992, at Greenville Prison in Virginia, a 33-year-old miner named Roger Keith Coleman was put to death in the electric chair. He was one of 31 men executed in the United States last year.

Ten years earlier, Coleman had been convicted of raping and murdering his 19-year-old sister-in-law, Wanda McCoy, at her home in the little coal-mining town of Grundy, in the Appalachian Mountains. Coleman always insisted he was innocent, and throughout his years on death row he fought for a re-trial, taking his case all the way to the Supreme Court of the United States.

It was a brutal and extremely bloody murder. Wanda had been raped, twice. She had been stabbed and her throat cut. Her body was found indoors by her husband, Brad McCoy, on his return from night shift, at about 11.15pm. The police surgeon put the time of death at half an hour earlier. Brad told the police that the crime must have been committed by someone well known to his wife, who would never have opened her door to a stranger. That led the police to Coleman, who had been convicted as a teenager of attempted rape.

Coleman's three-day trial was held in Grundy, following a blaze of publicity. A poster opposite the courthouse read: 'Time for another hanging in Grundy'. Coleman was represented by two young, inexperienced, court-appointed lawyers. They failed to visit the scene of the crime, failed to check Coleman's alibi, and failed either to interview key prosecution witnesses or investigate the state's evidence. Coleman complained to the judge, but to no effect.

On the night of the murder Coleman had left home for work at 8.30pm. En route he heard that his shift had been laid off. Arriving at the mine to collect his belongings he met several of his mates, who testified in court that he left the mine at 10.30pm. From there he drove eight miles to a trailer camp, passing the McCoy home on the way, and collected an audio-tape he had lent to a Mr and Mrs Gary Stiltner. According to Coleman, he then drove a further five miles to a public bath-house to shower before arriving home a few minutes after 11.00pm. Coleman's wife and grandmother both testified to the time of his return. However, at the trial a year later Coleman's wife, who by then had left him, said she could no longer remember when he reached home.

There was no obvious motive. Coleman's relationship with the McCoys had been good; Brad had asked him to be a pallbearer at his wife's funeral. But at the trial the prosecutor, Thomas Scott, offered a motive, together with a vivid if unsubstantiated reconstruction of the crime. According to Scott the accused man had driven to the trailer camp with the specific intention of raping and killing Mrs Stiltner and only abandoned his plan because her husband was at home. As the prosecutor put it to the jury:

'The murder had not yet taken

Reporter and broadcaster Charles Wheeler

BBC Photograph Library

place. His plan had been foiled. Coleman could not rape and kill Sandra Stiltner, fortunate for her and unfortunate for the poor Mrs Wanda McCoy. From there, probably distressed and anguished because he was not able to carry out what I submit he planned to do at the residence of Mrs Stiltner, he proceeds down State Creek and it dawns on him that his sister-in-law lives in the Longbottom section (of Grundy) and he knows she will let him in the house.'

When I interviewed Mr Scott a few days after Roger Coleman's execution he said: 'I made that up'. But he insisted that as prosecutor he had every right to draw inferences from the evidence and from Coleman's previous conviction for attempted rape. He added that if defence counsel had failed to challenge his case that was no concern of his.

So what other evidence may have persuaded the jury to convict? The forensic evidence presented at the trial – involving blood group and colour of pubic hair – was ambiguous in that it neither implicated nor exonerated Coleman. No witness was found who spotted Coleman or his pickup truck anywhere near the built-up area in which the victim lived. However, the prosecution did produce a witness – a fellow prisoner called Roger Matney – who claimed that Coleman had confessed to the murder while in jail awaiting trial.

After a succession of appeals had been rejected by state and federal courts in Virginia a prominent Washington law firm took up Coleman's case. Together with a clergyman turned investigator, Jim McCloskey, his new lawyers spent many months in Grundy. An advertisement in the local paper now brought several leads.

First a former Grundy policeman, Walter Hinkel, revealed that the jailhouse informant, Roger Matney, had received favours in exchange for his evidence – including an early release after serving only nine months of four concurrent four-year sentences. Matney's mother supported Hinkel's testimony.

Next, the investigators discovered that on a wooded hillside above Grundy a pair of heavily blood-stained sheets had been buried under several feet of rubbish. They were found on the morning after Wanda McCoy's murder in a pickup truck within sight of the scene of the crime. Its owner reported his discovery to the county sheriff and to Grundy's chief of police. Neither man showed any interest whatever.

Coleman's new lawyers had long suspected that a family living directly behind the McCoy house might know something about the murder. In the summer of 1990 a young woman, Teresa Horne, volunteered an affidavit implicating the older son of the family. Three years earlier – so Horne alleged – the man had tried to rape her, and during the attack had told her that if she didn't stop struggling he would kill her, as he had killed Wanda McCoy. In March 1991 her mother persuaded Teresa to tell her story on local television. Next day she was found dead. Since then others have come forward to say that the man in question, who still lives in Grundy, has been heard to boast that because the Coleman case is 'closed' he will never be charged with the murder.

For purely technical reasons none of this new evidence was ever tested in court. In 1986 Coleman's lawyers misinterpreted a procedural rule peculiar to the State of Virginia and filed a petition one day after a deadline. Accordingly it was rejected by a district judge. His decision was upheld by a series of higher courts, including the Supreme Court of the United States.

Another obstacle was a Virginia law that requires an appellant to submit *any* new evidence within 30 days of his conviction, even if it has lain undiscovered for years. As Roger Coleman pointed out when I spoke to him shortly before his execution, the attempted rape of Teresa Horne did not occur until 1987, five years after he was convicted. Again the US Supreme Court refused to intervene.

But even without the new evidence it is hard to see how Roger Coleman *could* have murdered Wanda McCoy. The work clothes he was wearing that night, and handed to the police next day, were thick with coal dust. But not a speck was found in the house or on the victim's body. According to the prosecution he reached the house, and avoided being seen, by wading through a fast-running stream. No trace of water or mud was found in the house or in Coleman's truck. And although the lower 12 inches of his trousers were damp (from the bath-house floor, said Coleman) his boots and socks and long johns were dry. Finally there is the description given to me by Grundy's police chief, Randall Jackson, who was the first law officer at the scene of the crime. According to Jackson the victim's blood was spattered not only over two walls and much of the furniture but had reached the ceiling. Yet there was not a trace of blood in Coleman's truck, or the wash-house, or on Coleman's towel or wash-cloth. True, forensic investigators found two minute specks of blood on Coleman's jeans. But it took a microscope to find them.

Coleman's conviction in 1982 had been widely welcomed in Grundy. Ten years later many members of this tight and isolated little community had changed their minds.

'Nobody could have got a fair trial in Grundy', one woman told me. 'We wanted somebody caught and tried, and after Roger was convicted we felt safer. Then just before the execution people were talking about all the new evidence that never got to be presented, and all kinds of people came up to me and said they no longer believed Roger was guilty, and that even if he was he deserved a fair trial. I think if a man's going to be executed it should be beyond reasonable doubt. But we went ahead and killed him. I have nightmares about it now that they've killed this boy. It's unbelievable that anything like that should happen in this country.'

It is impossible to prove that Roger Coleman was innocent of the crime for which he was sent to the electric chair. All one can say with certainty is that his defence at the trial was grossly inadequate, while the refusal of higher courts to consider new evidence was a shocking miscarriage of justice.

Charles Wheeler

NEWSNIGHT

BBC2's *Newsnight* with up-to-the-minute live news reports of the day's events and cool, calm, professional broadcasting gives no hint of the hectic world which exists behind the scenes. However, a day in the life of the *Newsnight* team could never be described as uneventful as Julie Allan discovers...

Imagine spinning four plates on sticks while conversing with passers-by and wondering where you're going to get a fire-eater at short notice. What's more, should one of the plates fall, not only will you need to keep the other three going while finding another but you may even have to make the new plate. Meanwhile, several likely stilt-walkers have had to cancel and the trapeze artist is trying to tame the lions because the lion-tamer has been sent to tame lions elsewhere. But the show must go on.

One thing is for certain, you need nerve and humour to work for *Newsnight*. Every weekday the curtain rises on a cast busy looking through the first editions of the newspapers over breakfast, and falls around midnight with sandwiches and a chat about how it could be done differently next time. In between, six producers, correspondents, the daily editor and his assistant, presenters, researchers, film crews and a host of others sail calmly by. They know it will be all right in the end – it has to be and it always has been before – but like ducks heading upstream, the calm surface belies the frantic fancy footwork below.

It's 11.30am on Monday, 23 November and Richard Clemmow, the editor of the day, is frowning. He's not the only one. He discusses with his assistant, Andrew Thompson, the lack of a lighthearted story in that night's programme and is concerned that the whole thing is looking dull. At the moment, various teams are working on a European economic growth story, a possible story about the house of Windsor, an Iraq item (James Cox is following the debate in the House) and a piece involving the Turkish Prime Minister who will be inter-

viewed live in the studio by Jeremy Paxman, that day's presenter.

'It'll be OK if the Windsor thing turns out to be interesting,' comments Clemmow in the tone of voice that says he thinks it probably won't. Like everyone else, he knows the story has been on the news all weekend following the fire at Windsor Castle and he's not sure there's any new way of tackling the debate about who should pay for it. A researcher is despatched to ring every local radio station and find out what their opinion polls on royal tax-paying have to say.

Shortly after midday Richard Clemmow rings the producer of the Turkey story, who is down in the graphics department, to voice his concern about the choice of 19th century *Punch* cartoons being used to accompany the report. The producer comes up. So does reporter Olenka Frankiel. They don't want the studio debate to get off on the wrong foot either, but they do think there's a genuine human rights story that shouldn't be fudged just because the Turkish Prime Minister and associates will be in the studio at the time. They want to set the scene so that Jeremy Paxman can then ask Turkey's Prime Minister if he really thinks he can integrate his country more closely with Europe – which is what Demirel is proposing. Clemmow sees the point but remains unconvinced. Two of the cartoons can stay, but the one headed 'The Unspeakable Turk' is out, even if the words are removed.

Meanwhile, in Brussels, Mr Lamont declares he's only willing to do a face-to-face interview for the European story and what's more, he won't be back in Britain that night. Richard Clemmow thinks Jeremy Paxman or Graham Ingham the economics correspondent, should interview him but Ingham is currently scheduled to do a piece in a factory in Hertfordshire and Paxman has to be back to present the programme. Decision postponed while the Brussels debate is monitored to see how interesting it becomes.

As lunchtime approaches, Her Majesty's majesty is debated again for the struggling Windsor story.

The polls show a bit of a swing against the monarchy. 'Doesn't make your hair stand on end,' is Clemmow's uncheery response. He's starting to look for a replacement item. Paxman, while not questioning the import of the stories already in progress, agrees that the programme could do with something a bit more, er, accessible. 'Don't go to bed yet, mother,' he quips, 'the Turkish Prime Minister's on in ten minutes.'

At 1pm all eyes are on the *One O'Clock News*. Headsets on every desk allow users to listen in to all major TV and radio channels and throughout the day news bulletins are monitored to make sure that no relevant information is missed. A very close eye is kept on the 'wires' from Reuters and other news agencies, and the BBC's own computers allow the *Newsnight* team to read storylines and synopses of all material for the other news programmes. Also on computer are the producers' and reporters' scripts in progress for that evening's *Newsnight* and Andrew Thompson is creating and updating running orders for that evening: which stories will go out at what point in the programme and what they involve – filmed or live interviews, animated graphics, links from Paxman – including how long each part will be, to the last second.

The news over, reporter Graham Ingham and the European story team discuss their approach with Richard Clemmow. They explore the ins and outs of how the long-awaited European unity seems still far off, with various countries leaving the ERM and Germany not cutting interest rates. A German banker needs to be tracked down for comment and Ingham will go off to report on the implications for British business. The serious and even-handed conversation serves to highlight the irreverent, albeit informed, approach that *Newsnight* in general, and Paxman in particular, delights in: 'Blame it on the Germans?' Paxman will ask later, before he interviews a Bonn banker. 'Absolutely,' will be the reply.

The Windsor producer has conjured up new enthusiasm. He passes by on his way to lunch, talking about the Sex Pistols and wondering if he could get an off-the-wall studio discussion going about the classless society. Richard Clemmow raises an eyebrow. The conversation continues at 2.15pm. Perhaps Johnny Rotten and the editor of *Hello!* magazine as studio guests? It is not until around 6.30pm, just four hours before the programme goes out, that the Windsor item finally bites the dust. Since no exciting news has broken during the day, Clemmow decides to substitute a film already made by the team about Wales apparently having suffered fewer job losses than other parts of Britain.

The office is quiet in the afternoon. The teams are writing and polishing scripts, out with camera crews, or down in the graphics unit discussing the electronic production of coloured maps, charts and graphs. Paxman has shut himself in an office, 'probably contemplating Turkey,' comments Clemmow. 'Later he'll have his scripts to write or introductions to other items to record.'

At 3pm, Graham Ingham, on his way to a British factory in Hertford, is called on a car phone, told to go home and get his passport and be ready for further information. Clemmow makes a mental note to memo everybody about carrying their passports at all times. A 1655 from Heathrow to Brussels is located (he won't be in time to catch the 1600 from the City) and a seat booked while Andrew Thompson gets on the phone to Brussels to make sure that Lamont will still be around when Ingham arrives. It will be tight, but they're going to try.

At 3.45pm, Clemmow is briefing Ingham by telephone while Andrew Thompson is on the telephone to the researcher who will also be going, telling her where to pick up the Belgian currency that will be organised from the office. The studios are put on standby too – this interview might not arrive until 7pm or later and will then need editing and fitting into the rest of the story.

At 4pm, the Iraq story is under discussion – there are thoughts about comparing the resources Britain puts into investigations with what the Americans did for Iran-gate and Watergate. Generally,

volume and speed of movement is starting to pick up. The once-deafening telephone buzzers now seem to be a more reasonable volume. Faxes fly between Britain and the Bonn banker to finalise interview time, location and content. Clemmow reads draft scripts, as does Paxman.

It's difficult to say what seems more unreal, the office madness or the picture on the television at the end of the desk – assorted children are covering their white boiler suits in chocolate and then licking it off.

At 5pm, Scotland Yard calls in to say they're in transit with Demirel the Turkish Prime Minister, and entourage. BBC hospitality has been arranged, extra staff provided to act as hosts and arrangements made for the Turks to be present in the control gallery above the studio while Demirel is interviewed. The World Service calls to ask if they can have him after *Newsnight*. Meanwhile, the Windsor story, shortly to get the boot, has progressed as far as failing to get author Sue Townsend (*The Queen and I*) confirmed as a guest. By 6pm they will also have failed to get Ludovic Kennedy.

The 5.30pm meeting – every day there's a gathering of whoever is around to discuss progress and to iron out problems before the final push begins. Today it's an opportunity to check who is around to oversee the editing of which bits – the Hertfordshire factory, Lamont from Brussels, the Bonn banker – and to make sure that there's studio space for everyone who needs it.

By 6.30pm producer Fiona Anderson is working on the script for part of the Europe package. She writes it to length, while monitoring the Channel 4 news and Reuters for up-to-date information. Words are listed down the right of the page, pictures down the left. It's at this point in the day that walking seems to be abandoned in favour of a barely-disguised trot. When the script is written, she and Jeremy Paxman will trot to a sound studio and record it. Later, they'll trot back there and change some of it. Half an hour later than she thinks is a good idea, Anderson will trot the sound tape, graphics, location film from

the British factory and footage pinched from the *Six O'Clock News* down to the video editor, who will use the script as a guideline to fit the pieces together. If he didn't have to sit still, he'd be trotting. Graham Ingham is running late in Brussels so his contribution will have to be added later.

With just half an hour to go, Paxman is still working on his own scripts. Some of the stories are ready to go – but not all. Clemmow is making last-minute adjustments to the script for the 'menu' at the start of the programme. The studio is ready and in the control gallery the tension mounts.

At 10.20pm Paxman, scripts in hand, heads for the studio. Last-minute adjustments are made to the lighting. On BBC1, Barry Norman is listing the top ten films in America, while here, the Turkish Prime Minister settles in to his seat. At 10.25pm, a piece about the Commons is still being edited. At 10.27pm, Olenka Frankiel reports that the last pictures are being added to her Turkish report. A close call, but it's there.

With ten seconds to go, the countdown begins and the bank of monitors in the gallery show what the nation is seeing – the spinning *Newsnight* graphic and theme tune. Three seconds to go before Mr Paxman makes his appearance – the three seconds are counted down, he stops shuffling papers – the show is on the road.

The plates are handed, still spinning, to the director, the studio crew and Jeremy Paxman.

Paxman blames the Germans, he blames the Turks. The Germans and the Turks argue back in good part. Ingham blames Lamont, whose fault it doesn't seem to be either.

Last-minute bits of script arrive throughout the programme, Paxman is kept informed throughout. But he's a pro. While the pre-recorded reports go out, he checks scripts, looks at the papers, chats briefly to guests and never for one moment looks as if he's doing anything other than watch *Come Dancing* on the other side.

By 11.15pm it's all over – until tomorrow, at least. Those who want to, meet in a room housing two large trays of welcome sandwiches. They discuss life, the programme and everything. They'd do it differently next time. They remember stories from the past that they really thought would never be ready in time, days when everything went wrong and still the programme made it on air. Today has been altogether sedate. 'Come again,' urges Olenka Frankiel, in the taxi taking us home. 'You should see it on a really busy day.'

The plates have stopped spinning. My head has not. And yes, I'll return. As the taxi driver said, 'they do a good programme, those *Newsnight* people, and they are all so nice.'

Julie Allan

Rex Features

Jeremy Paxman
Born in Yorkshire in 1950 and brought up in Worcestershire. Took an English degree at Cambridge University. Worked in local radio before going to Belfast in 1974 and spending three years as the first full-time television current affairs reporter there, specialising in investigative work. Moved to London in 1977. Was a reporter on *Tonight* and *The Bear Next Door* about countries bordering Russia. In 1979 joined *Panorama*, where he stayed until 1985. Joined the *Six O'Clock News* as a presenter, then went to *London Plus* before joining the *Breakfast News* team in 1986. Has written books on chemical warfare and Central America. Likes to ski, walk in the mountains and fish. Has been known to cycle to work,

weather permitting. Joined *Newsnight* on 1 October 1989.

Peter Snow
Born in Dublin in 1938. Took a BA in Classics, Ancient History and Philosophy at Oxford University. National Service (1956-8) with the Somerset Light Infantry. In 1962 joined ITN news and worked as a newscaster, diplomatic and defence correspondent until 1979. Has written two books: *Leila's Hijack War* (1970) and *Hussein* (a biography, 1972). Known for being the man with the maps and swingometer during election times. Likes sailing in his spare time. Joined *Newsnight* in 1979, ready for its launch in January 1980.

BBC

Sue Cameron
Born in Lewes, Sussex in 1946. Read History at University College, London then spent a year with

Voluntary Service Overseas, teaching English at a girls' school in the western Sudan. Started a journalistic career in 1967 on various local newspapers and then specialised in labour relations for the *Times Educational Supplement*. Joined *The Times* in 1976 and in 1985 became political editor of *Today* before moving to television as a presenter/reporter on Channel 4's *A Week in Politics*. In 1988 she wrote and presented *A Model Mandarin* about cabinet secretary Sir Robin Butler and a three-part series *On Trial*, about the English legal system. Joined Channel 4's *The Parliament Programme* in 1989 as presenter. Became a member of the *Newsnight* presenting and reporting team in October 1991.

BBC

Francine Stock
Born in Devonport in 1958. Went to Oxford University to read French and Italian. Began her career in 1979 on the magazine *Petroleum Economist* and then worked as a newspaper journalist specialising in energy, economics and the Middle East. Joined the BBC in 1983 as a radio producer. Produced *World at One*, *PM* and *World This Weekend*. In 1985 became a reporter for BBC radio's *The Financial World Tonight* and *Moneybox* before moving to television in 1986. Joined BBC2's *Money Programme* as a reporter before moving to *Newsnight* in July 1988.

EL ALAMEIN – THE 50TH ANNIVERSARY

October 1992 marked the 50th anniversary of the battle of El Alamein. Christopher Middleton looks back at this historic battle and the events which commemorated what was seen as the turning point in the Second World War

In October 1942 Field Marshals Erwin Rommel and Bernard Montgomery faced each other across the desert sands, at a small Egyptian railway halt called El Alamein.

Fifty years later, their two sons stood side by side in Westminster Abbey, at a service commemorating the epic, 13-day battle their fathers' armies went on to fight.

The turning point of World War II is how Alamein has always been seen. Had Rommel's Axis forces triumphed, they would have reached the Suez Canal and severed the Allies' supply lines. As it turned out, though, the 'Desert Fox' and his Afrika Corps were driven westwards by Montgomery's victorious Eighth Army, and forced to surrender three months later.

Some 65,000 men are thought to have been killed, wounded or captured at Alamein – four times as many on the Axis side as on the Allied. It was the collective sacrifice of all the troops – Germans and Italians under Rommel and British and Commonwealth under Montgomery – that lay at the heart of the Westminster Abbey service on 14 October, marking the beginning of the Alamein anniversary commemorations.

The service was attended by the Queen, the Prince and Princess of Wales, the Duke and Duchess of Gloucester, along with some 2,000 fellow guests, many of them veterans of the North Africa campaign. The BBC's television coverage of the service incorporated footage of the battle that gave some idea of the chaos and destruction that prevailed at Alamein: the heat, the tank tracks, the minefields, the flames and the sheer confusion and terror of battle. Nevertheless, the overall theme of the occasion was peace, rather than war.

'The service celebrated reconcilia-

tion between nations rather than the victory of one army over another,' said the BBC's head of events Philip Gilbert, who was in charge of television coverage from the Abbey. As well as being broadcast throughout the UK, pictures were also being recorded in London by German TV station ZDF, for use in a documentary on the Queen's visit to Germany.

Viewers heard prayers in English, German and Italian, as well as bible readings from the two opposing commanders' sons. Viscount David Montgomery read a passage from Micah, containing the verses 'They shall beat their swords into ploughshares and their spears into pruning hooks', as well as 'Nation shall not lift a sword against nation'. Manfred Rommel chose a section from Romans 12, which concluded with the words: 'If possible, so far as it depends on you, live peaceably with all'.

As service commentator Tom Fleming pointed out, the date bore special significance for Herr Rommel; it was on 14 October 1944, as a teenage boy, that he watched the Gestapo arrest his father on suspicion of involvement in the failed Stauffenburg plot to assassinate Hitler. He was never to see him again. Given the choice of committing suicide or risking reprisals against his family, the former hero of the desert chose poison.

For Montgomery, a happier fate

awaited. He went on to spearhead the successful Normandy landings in 1944, was made a viscount in 1946 and served as deputy supreme commander of NATO's forces in Europe from 1951 to 1958. He died in 1976, some 32 years after the man he had defeated at Alamein. Montgomery's life was chronicled in Jeremy Bennett's documentary *Monty – In Love and War*, which was broadcast by the BBC on 23 October – the day Alamein began.

Mixed in with the glowing tributes from the soldiers he had inspired were less charitable assessments from people with whom he had crossed swords. Someone who could take an objective view of Montgomery was Godfrey Talbot, the BBC Radio war correspondent who reported on Alamein from the battlefront. As well as reading out his wartime despatches at the Westminster Abbey service – 'Tonight this once desert wilderness is just one khaki cauldron, boiling with men' – Talbot also appeared on ITV's *Highway* on Remembrance Day.

Standing in front of Montgomery's own sand-coloured tank, the veteran reporter described Monty's arrival in North Africa, in August 1942, as a 'tonic' to the Eighth Army.

'Monty came as a firecracker,' he recalled. 'Before, the men hadn't known their commanders, but Monty made a point of making

British Premier, John Major (left), and his French counterpart Pierre Bérégovoy lay wreaths at the Commonwealth cemetery in El Alamein to mark the 50th anniversary of the battle which was fought there

Associated Press

himself known to everyone, particularly those in forward positions. They all knew this cocky, little sharp-nosed man who kept telling them they were going to win.'

Although this interview was filmed at the Imperial War Museum, the rest of *Highway* was recorded at the memorial ceremony held on 25 October at the Alamein War Cemetery, on the site of the battle itself. Here, amid immaculately pruned bougainvillaea bushes and graceful Mediterranean pines, viewers saw wreaths laid by scores of Eighth Army veterans and their relatives, as well as by serving members of the armed forces and by visiting political dignitaries, including the British Prime Minister John Major. 'As significant a victory as Agincourt' was how Mr Major described Alamein to reporters at the ceremony.

Meanwhile, men who 50 years ago had bombed and bayoneted each other shook hands and stood side by side, as they paid silent tribute to fallen comrades. Some walked on sticks, others were pushed in wheelchairs. The feelings of the returning warriors were summed up by Eighth Army veteran Les Witts. 'I came here to see some good old pals I left behind,' he told *Highway* presenter Sir Harry Secombe.

Throughout the run-up to Remembrance Sunday, BBC2 ran a season of films, dramas and documentaries under the title 'War and Peace'. Two specially commissioned series led the way.

Battlecries was the story of Britain's fighting men, told in their own words; interviewees ranged from RAF Tornado pilot Robbie Stewart, shot down during the Desert Storm conflict, to Colonel Robert Daniell, the first British soldier to witness the horrors of Belsen.

Splendid Hearts sought to make flesh and blood the names inscribed on war memorials, tracing the stories of men and women who lost their lives in places as far apart as Enniskillen and the Falklands. The season also saw a repeat dramatisation of Vera Brittain's powerful World War I autobiography *Testament of Youth*, starring Cheryl

Campbell. And reinforcing the same message – though in a more light-hearted way – was a rerun of the comedy series *Blackadder Goes Forth*, starring Rowan Atkinson and culminating in the chilling, freeze-frame scene where the heroes go over the top to their deaths. Poet Tony Harrison's *Gaze of the Gorgon* explored the paralysing moral effects of war, while other programmes examined the experiences of conscientious objectors, war cameramen and black servicemen in the British Army.

The aim of the War and Peace season was to give extra meaning and poignancy to the Remembrance period, which this year culminated as usual in the Festival of Remembrance, at the Royal Albert Hall, and in the Cenotaph ceremony in Whitehall – both broadcast on BBC TV and Radio.

Again, Alamein featured prominently. In what was one of the most moving moments from the Festival, two widows of the Eighth Army servicemen led a small group of six women who had all lost their husbands while on active service. And at the Cenotaph march-past the next day, it was a group of some 300 Eighth Army veterans who were at the head of the first column. Many wore the distinctive red, black and sand-yellow medal of the North Africa desert campaign. All wore the proud exteriors of men who knew they had helped turn the tide of the war. Commentator David Dimbleby recalled the words of Winston Churchill, who said that in years to come it would be enough simply to say 'I fought with the Eighth Army'.

Of course, as the years go on, there are fewer and fewer men who can claim that distinction. 'We are by nature a finite organisation,' says Colonel Michael Jeffrey, chairman of the Eighth Army Veterans' Association, as he surveyed the ranks of graves at Alamein. 'However, we all feel very strongly that with all the events and television programmes recording the 50th anniversary of the battle, El Alamein has been properly recognised once and for all. Not in the spirit of victory, but in the spirit of remembrance.'

Christopher Middleton

NEWS REVIEW OF THE YEAR

BBC Social Affairs Editor Polly Toynbee considers the events which hit the headlines in 1992

If the Queen thought it was her *Annus Horribilis*, she was not alone. Around the world 1992 was a year of exceptional horrors, the death of many hopes, and very little sign of new dawns. Amid war, famine, recession and strife, very few countries escaped a sense of world-wide malaise.

The question that stayed unanswered at the end of 1992 was this. Is there now a new world order, following the death of the Soviet bloc and communism? Is there a new sense that peace can now be policed by the United Nations, fronted often by the United States, to push forward the onward march of freedom, democracy, and protection of minorities against the tyrannies of dictators and despots?

Proxy wars disgracefully supported and armed by both superpowers during the Cold War would surely end, we thought, as the Berlin Wall crashed and petty tyrants found themselves without big backers. Yet everywhere small and terrible wars have multiplied since then. The new world order struggled all year to assert itself in former Yugoslavia, in Iraq and in Somalia but the jury remains out. Doubts abound.

All year the world watched helpless and hopeless as the worst famine in 30 years gripped Somalia, a country already stricken. The spectacle of a rudderless country, without government, out of control, assailed by pillaging war lords reckless of human life, bombarded the television screens of the world. Children lay dying of starvation, 1,000 a week in Mogadishu alone, while food stockpiled in abundance, gifts from the richer world, was guarded and purloined by gunmen. Eventually the USA intervened, with troops to guard the shipments of food and to help distribute food around the country.

Despite the best of intentions, despite the clear fact that the USA had absolutely no political or financial stake in Somalia, some sections of the world looked on with unease, uncertain that they wanted a new world order that looked so American. The test of this expedition, and to some extent of the idea of the new world order, will rest on whether the Americans can withdraw within a reasonable time, leaving behind some kind of stable government and a people who will not be plunged again into war and famine.

The torment in Yugoslavia worsened. Bosnia drawn into the fighting, Sarajevo besieged, as Moslem, Croat and Serb fought three ways against each other. The intervention of UN forces was strongly criticised by many who thought that nothing could be done, no settlement found in a country where ethnic hatred was so fierce, yet different ethnic groups lived so intermingled amongst each other.

But others, less defeatist, thought the world, and especially Europe, could not stand by and watch 'ethnic cleansing' as savage and deliberate as the Nazi holocaust, concentration camps, mass rape, enforced pregnancy and systematic torture, and do nothing. Fears abound that we shall be drawn into a situation far worse than Vietnam, with no clear objectives or solutions, with potential huge loss of life among peace-keeping soldiers. The unclear line between keeping the peace, and

The tragic consequences of war in Bosnia

fighting off aggressors, vies with shame at doing nothing at all. That dilemma remained unresolved at the end of the year, as the world awaited a new American President.

The year started well in South Africa, full of hope for a bright and peaceful new beginning, as the white minority voted two to one to support constitutional reform, and to move towards black majority rule. But mighty change needs to keep up a rapid momentum if it is not to falter, and somewhere in the protracted negotiations that impetus was lost. In June, 44 deaths in a

massacre in Boipatong lead to bitterness that inflamed ANC supporters against both Inkatha and the government. Troops moved in, three more were shot dead and Nelson Mandela, to contain and express the fury of his people, announced the end of negotiations, and the start of mass actions. A march on the Siskei border followed, the Siskei soldiers opened fire and 29 died. Relations between the ANC, and white government and Inkatha were left in tatters, with still no date for elections, nor a transitional timetable.

The tragedy of famine in Somalia

Boipatong, South Africa, where 44 were killed in June

The Soviet Union was officially declared dead on 1 January, Boris Yeltsin taking power but not control of Russia. Overnight, prices rose in the shops by 400 per cent, with price deregulation and a chaotic attempt at reaching out for capitalism. Suddenly a week's pension money would no longer buy a cigarette or a potato. Soup kitchens were set up to feed the hungry, and the grim return of some of the disgraced old communists

Neo-Nazi riots took place in Rostock, where young Germans from the former Eastern bloc inflicted horrific violence on the immigrant population

brought demonstrations onto the streets, and the setting up of a communist National Salvation Front, which was promptly banned. Yeltsin never had control of the communist dominated parliament, and they inflicted a humiliation by voting out his young, dynamic, modernising Prime Minister, forcing him to appoint one of the old guard instead. The long march towards capitalism has turned into a miserable and uncertain stumble, with too many hopes dashed, too much disillusion to bear.

Out in space a Russian astronaut, a solitary Major Tom figure, floated neglected month after month in a decaying space station, while the bickering nations of the old Soviet Union niggled about who should pay for the expedition to bring him back to earth. This was tragic symbolism, as state after state turned itself to small, largely unnoticed, but vicious internecine wars: Tajikistan, Moldova, Armenia, Georgia all took to the gun and self-destruction, instead of freedom and hope for the future. Meanwhile, more elegantly, but just as tragically, Czechoslovakia voted to split into two countries to the probable harm of each, but at least with no fighting.

Europe shuddered at the spectacle of growing unrest in the newly united Germany. Race riots in Rostock by young neo-Nazis were watched with the approval of multitudes in the ruins of derelict East German industry, unemployment soaring, and a West German government that seemed indifferent or incompetent to deal with the sufferings of the old East. Foreign guest workers, and Romanian refugees were the target of the violence that shocked the world.

their feet as equals to the West. The further they fell behind and the more violent they became, the more the Westerners despised their cousins, accusing them of idleness, their spirit of enterprise and work ethic sapped by years of communism. The greater the need of the East, the less sympathy they gained from the West in a downward spiral of mutual dislike and resentment. So the biggest and richest power at the heart of Europe turned inwards on its own troubles just when Europe needed it most to turn outwards and offer help, through lower interest rates to the recession-struck continent.

At times last year civilisation seemed to be a perilously thin veneer. Riots broke out in Los Angeles in May, killing 58 people, some murdered in front of the television cameras. The riots were sparked by an all-white jury acquitting four white police officers seen on coast-to-coast television kicking Rodney King, a black motorist

The aftermath of the race riots in Los Angeles

Chancellor Kohl had said the country could be united without raising extra taxes, without sacrifices for the wealthy West.

The East saw their industry demolished, West German predators taking the best parts of it, and little new investment to set them on

almost to death. Other American cities and other countries including Britain who had experienced riots in the past, waited nervously to see if they would spread. Youths with AK 47 rifles roamed the streets in a frenzy of looting and arson, often directed at other ethnic minorities

Chancellor Norman Lamont speaks to the press amidst the sterling crisis in September

the pound was hurtled through the floor of the European Exchange Rate Mechanism by the money markets. The government's critics said the pound had been brought into the ERM at too high a level, and refusal to devalue gracefully had forced this humiliation upon Britain, plunging the government's economic policy into chaos. 'On Skid Row' read the headline of one tabloid next day, and knives were out for the Chancellor for the rest of the year, but John Major stood by him, through this and several other controversies.

Norman Tebbit's full frontal assault upon the government at the Conservative Party Conference in October started a terrible autumn and winter for John Major, through the long drawn out Maastricht process, and deep unease on his own back benches, rumbling through every policy. Meanwhile Labour, with John Smith as their new leader, was judged not to have found their feet as an effective opposition, even in these dark days for the government.

Violence, always ebbing and flowing in waves, continued in Northern Ireland, with the tragic 3,000th death since the troubles began. Particular acts of savagery among the regular shootings stirred the by now battle-hardened British. The IRA blew up a group of Protestant

in South Central Los Angeles, a tinder box of racial tension. By the time the riots abated a large area of the poorest part of LA was laid waste. By the end of the year there was little sign of any attempt at rebuilding or repairing that shattered community who were themselves, as usual, the main sufferers.

Even Nature seemed to conspire to make this a truly horrible year. Disasters, man-made and natural, were worse than for many years. Even the natural disasters had an unnatural tinge, as people queried whether global warming might be partly responsible for ferocious storms, floods, hurricanes and tornados. Fifty died in Californian storms, many swept away by floods. In Italy and southern France, which saw the worst storms in decades, 44 died.

Two thousand died in Pakistan's floods and three major earthquakes left at least 500 dead in Turkey. In clearly man-made catastrophes 70 died when a 747 cargo plane crashed into a block of flats in Amsterdam and 200 died in Mexico when the state-owned oil company allowed explosive gas to leak into the sewers, causing an appalling explosion. This dismal litany of tragedy sets much of the tone for a year many parts of the world must be glad to see the back of.

At home, there was little cause for rejoicing either. The brief belief that recession would be over, green

shoots sprouting, the flurry of optimism surrounding the election, was dashed as Britain plunged further into the worst and deepest recession since the 30s. At the end of the year unemployment was galloping towards the three million mark. Twice as many families were projected onto social security as ten years ago.

A fantasy that the pound could replace the Deutschmark as the benchmark currency was mocked into ridicule on 16 September when

The Amsterdam air crash – 70 were killed when a 747 cargo plane plunged into a block of flats

workmen returning from an army base. The Ulster Volunteer Force retaliated with a shocking massacre in a betting shop where five died, including a 16-year-old boy, and ten were injured. As the politicians again began an attempt at talks, under the then Northern Ireland Secretary Peter Brooke, hopes in so far as they were ever raised, were dashed yet again.

1992's new tactic by the IRA was revealed in the biggest bomb on the mainland since the War. A 1,000lb bomb all but destroyed the Baltic Exchange in the City of London, killing three, one of them a 15-year-old girl, and injuring 91 others. The IRA gave notice that many other such bombs were planned.

It marked a new concerted effort to destroy property, a tactic the IRA has used for years in Northern Ireland, devastating business and industry. The estimated cost of repairing the Baltic Exchange was £800 million and it succeeded in causing a crisis in the insurance world. Following this colossal loss, insurance companies refused to continue to cover major buildings for bomb damage, unless the government offered the same kind of compensation for IRA damage on the mainland as it did for business loss in Northern Ireland. This threatened to become a major propaganda coup for the IRA demonstrating their ability to disrupt London's business community, until the government finally came to an arrangement with the insurance industry to pay a part of bomb damage costs in future.

It has always been a danger that bombs on the mainland, and especially in London, tend to get more publicity than outrages in the Province. This is a danger both in encouraging further London bombings, and it rightly deeply offends those suffering similar horrors in Ireland.

However, the London authorities had good reason to feel they had a good year against the IRA. Several large and potentially catastrophic bombs were detected and defused before they could explode, saving the huge Canary Wharf complex. The Christmas period was scarred by a succession of small devices in the Oxford Street area, designed to frighten shoppers away. Many commentators, however, noted that the British have become inured to these, and they had remarkably little impact on people's determination to come and go as they pleased. After so many years the hazard is seen in perspective as a very small risk for any one individual, among all the other far greater hazards of urban life. However, it does still seem to alarm foreigners, especially Americans, and impacts badly on tourism.

Good news? The Church of England voted to allow the ordination of women though there may be a bitter price to pay in schism. London Zoo has been reprieved, though in what form is yet to be decided.

Women rejoice at the news that the Church of England is to allow the ordination of women priests

Rex Features

David Mellor, who resigned his Cabinet post after revelations about his private life

Curious events, if unfortunate for the participants: David Mellor was eventually drummed out of office after gruesome details were published of his affair with an actress, and he was shown to have accepted lavish free holidays for his family from the daughter of a prominent PLO leader. His fall was brought about by the press he had been charged with investigating, and bringing to heel in a possible new privacy act. Was his downfall delivered as a warning to any politician foolhardy enough to cross the terrible power of a largely Tory tabloid press grown arrogant on its power, as it nestled so close to government for the last decade?

Kevin and Ian Maxwell, sons of disgraced publisher Robert Maxwell, were arrested and charged with fraud offences totalling at least £128 million. Despite claims of penury, they were observed frequently by the tabloids enjoying their usual life style in grand houses, with children in the most expensive schools.

On a lighter note, at Marne-la-Vallée on the outskirts of Paris there was razzmatazz, oompah's and have-a-nice-day's, when Euro Disney opened its gates in April. There was carping from the French, with their native disdain for American culture, and they failed to pour in, in the expected numbers. The

Rex Features

Euro Disney

British, Germans, Spanish and Italians showed more enthusiasm, but it wasn't enough to prevent a first year loss of £30 million. However, few doubt that the profits will flow, eventually.

The weather was one problem, though the sale of yellow Mickey Mouse macs at £2.60 each flourished. Then the French lorry drivers blockaded the place in fury over the GATT negotiations with the Americans. Train strikes and the French air traffic controllers took their toll, and then the French transport ministry kept issuing warnings to drivers to avoid the area because of likely congestion. But the underlying reasons for the less than brilliant first year were economic. When the

pound and lira plummeted, it added 20 per cent to the cost of a trip for the British and 10 per cent more for the Italians. The world-wide recession meant many people had less to spend on holidays. Those who have already experienced two hour queues for the main attractions puzzled over how on earth they planned to push yet more visitors through.

1993 can only be better. At least it starts with lower expectations. Hopes are already dashed, new dawns already become tired dusks. Disillusion reigns in a recession-torn world, from Japan, who thought it could never happen to them, to Britain where Stop-Go has been a way of life since the War.

Polly Toynbee

Film

Film 92, the perennially-popular guide to the movies celebrated its 21st birthday, and to commemorate 21 years of this entertaining and informative guide to what's new at the cinema, we take a look at 1992's most memorable films.

Also included is a profile of Michelle Pfeiffer, one of Hollywood's biggest stars, who turned in a show-stopping performance as Catwoman in *Batman Returns.*

On the small screen many films had their TV premieres, and viewers could indulge in their favourite recent movies. An abundance of TV film seasons which catered for all tastes – from Hitchcock to Disney, from horror to romance – were shown during the year and we review the highlights.

Sadly, the film world lost some of its brightest stars during the year. We pay tribute to Marlene Dietrich, Denholm Elliott, Robert Morley and Anthony Perkins.

Film

A REVIEW OF THE YEAR

Angela Thomas looks back at the box-office winners of 1992

It was the year in which Oliver Stone made a movie that woke up Congress and put forward the conspiracy theory to end all conspiracy theories. It was the year in which Sharon Stone forgot her underwear and became the hottest blonde since Madonna put *her* underwear on display. The world learnt to hurl with the help of two overgrown teenagers with a taste for bad jokes and heavy metal. And we all discovered that our homes were under threat from single, white, females, killer cops and nannies from hell. The most romantic movie of the year featured a cartoon beauty and a beast, and an English-

man played the ultimate red-blooded American. We saw the last of superwoman Ripley and discovered a new, sexy side to cool, quiet Michelle Pfeiffer, while the world suddenly recognised the cover girl beauty of 'queen of kook' Geena Davis.

The year began with a bang as Oliver Stone unleashed his mind-blowing investigation of the assassination which rocked the world, *JFK*. With Stone in control, Kevin Costner proved he really could act and held his own at the head of a stellar cast which included Oscar nominee Tommy Lee Jones, veteran Jack Nicholson and Britain's Gary Oldman who gave a brilliant performance as Lee Harvey Oswald. Nick Nolte continued to prove he's one of America's most talented actors by giving dramatically different perfor-

Rebecca De Mornay in *The Hand that Rocks the Cradle*

mances in two contrasting films. In Barbra Streisand's lushly romantic *Prince of Tides* he was a man unable to come to terms with his past. In *Cape Fear* his past came violently back to haunt him, in the shape of a wildly over the top Robert De Niro.

The stars came out in the spring for Spielberg's *Hook*. It looked great but was curiously lacking in the usual Spielberg magic. As one of the few major family movies of the season, however, it still cleaned up at the box-office. Family matters were also at the heart of the chiller *The Hand that Rocks the Cradle* in which angelic Rebecca de Mornay turned a family's dream life into a nightmare.

Michael Douglas found himself

Spielberg's *Hook*

caught up with another dangerous blonde in the controversial sex thriller *Basic Instinct*. Douglas was a bad cop fatally attracted to bad but beautiful Sharon Stone in the film which generated as much publicity as it did mega bucks at the box-office.

Guild Film Distribution

Michael Douglas and Sharon Stone in ***Basic Instinct***

The summer brought an outbreak of 'sequelitis' as three blockbuster movies dominated the UK box-office. First came Tim Burton's inventive *Batman Returns* in which Michael Keaton returned as the Dark Knight pitted against the petrifying Penguin (Danny DeVito) and the show-stopping sexiness of Michelle Pfeiffer. While Pfeiffer turned on the sex appeal, Sigourney Weaver shaved her head to make one last appearance as the unluckiest woman in the galaxy, Ripley, in the dark and depressing *Alien 3*.

There was nothing dark and depressing about the third instalment in the Lethal Weapon series. *Lethal Weapon 3* was jam-packed with explosive action and cracking one-liners, and featured old hands Mel Gibson and Danny Glover along with Joe Pesci and *Lethal* newcomer Rene Russo.

Movie man of the year was golden boy Tim Robbins who aimed straight at the heart of Hollywood with the star-crammed *The Player* followed by his own darkly humorous and very timely political satire *Bob Roberts*.

Statuesque Geena Davis stepped into the leading role in the baseball comedy *A League of Their Own* and found herself on the cover of *Vogue* and countless other magazines on both sides of the Atlantic.

Columbia Tri-Star Films (UK)

Geena Davis in *A League of Their Own*

Following hot on the heels of her Oscar nomination for *Thelma & Louise*, the lightweight comedy finally proved that Davis is a leading lady to be reckoned with.

The romantic leading lady of the year was cute and colourful – and a cartoon! Disney animation enchanted a whole new audience with the release of *Beauty and the Beast*. The title song hit the charts, the film became the first animated feature to

Disney's enchanting *Beauty and the Beast*

The Walt Disney Co

receive a Best Picture Oscar nomination, and the critics and the public simply fell in love.

In contrast, misplaced affection brought out the beast in blue-eyed cop Ray Liotta when he spotted Madeleine Stowe in the next loony-on-the-loose-in-suburbia film, *Unlawful Entry*.

A month later the home again provided the battleground for the room-mate from hell – Jennifer Jason Leigh in *Single White Female*. Leigh continued to live up to her reputation as the most gifted actress of her generation while Bridget Fonda finally lived up to her famous surname by giving a quietly impressive performance as a woman who lets a stranger into her home, and her life, with deadly results.

We had to wait until the autumn to see the best of the three films dealing with Christopher Columbus. Ridley Scott's magnificent *1492: Conquest of Paradise* sailed into cinemas looking stunning and featuring a mesmerising performance from Gerard Depardieu.

Also stunning to behold was Michael Mann's sweeping, romantic epic *The Last of the Mohicans*. Britain's Daniel Day-Lewis made a highly successful bid for mainstream leading man status with his performance as Hawkeye. Impressive battle scenes and emotion-packed performances enthralled audiences on both sides of the Atlantic.

Christmas marked the return of the million-dollar kid, Macaulay

Depardieu in *1492: Conquest of Paradise*

Culkin, in the sequel to the most successful box-office comedy of all time, *Home Alone*. Obviously deciding not to mess with a good thing, director Chris Columbus turned *Home Alone 2: Lost in New York* into a basic re-run of the first film. Instead of causing havoc on his own doorstep however, the tiny terror took a bite out of the Big Apple, turning increasingly violent in his bid to stop the notorious wet bandits from robbing a toy shop.

Angela Thomas

Macaulay Culkin is 'Lost in New York' in *Home Alone 2*

TWO FROM 92

During the year, BBC1's *Film 92* kept film fans up-to-date with all the latest releases at the cinema. Two of the box-office hits of 1992 were *Batman Returns* and *The Last of the Mohicans*

Batman Returns

Director Tim Burton's magical imagination is given full rein to create this visual masterpiece which combines the darkness of his first *Batman* with the beauty of *Edward Scissorhands*. This time, Batman (Michael Keaton again) is pitted against three foes even more bizarre than Jack Nicholson's Joker. Leading the pack is the grotesque Penguin, played with diabolical relish by Danny DeVito. Then there's the slinky, acrobatic Catwoman, played with show-stopping sexiness and some caustic one-liners, by Michelle Pfeiffer. Completing the trio of twisted adversaries is Christopher Walken, as wild-haired, evil businessman, Max Schreck.

As in the first film the real weakness in this visually breathtaking film lies in the fact that Burton once again spends so much time creating his villains, there's little opportunity for us to get to know Batman himself. This flaw is all the more noticeable because in Keaton, Burton has a gifted and intelligent actor who can make Batman much more than just another two-dimensional super-hero.

Keaton's best moments come as Batman's alter-ego Bruce Wayne, the mysterious millionaire who this time romances enigmatic secretary Selina Kyle (Catwoman's other self). But Batman's screen time is so short it's no wonder Pfeiffer's feline creation dominates the action. Whether she's kick-boxing her way through any opposition or whipping up attention on the streets of Gotham, she's the main attraction.

The plot, such as it is, centres on the creation of the Penguin and Catwoman. The film opens with the baby Penguin being abandoned by his horrified parents. The baby with the beak is adopted by some real penguins and grows up in the sewers of the city plotting his

Michelle Pfeiffer as Catwoman in *Batman Returns*

revenge against the big-wigs.

As the Penguin plots, businessman Max Schreck makes his own plans for a city takeover. When his mousey secretary Selina stumbles on his evil plot he throws her out of his office window. But Selina doesn't die, she's brought back to life by a bunch of stray cats. The reborn Selina however, has a whole new tougher personality, a whole new wardrobe, and a new, separate identity – Catwoman. Determined not to let anyone push her around again she sets her sights on tackling Batman and destroying Schreck.

While Pfeiffer looks sensational, DeVito's Penguin is just too gruesome and malevolent to gain too many admirers, and it's left to his penguin army to raise some much needed laughs. With two such bizarre bad guys it's no wonder poor old Walken's evil businessman is somewhat neglected.

What's not neglected is the production design, which comes courtesy of Burton's *Beetlejuice* and *Edward Scissorhands* partner Bo Welch. Welch's dark, grandly Gothic sets remain in the memory long after the final credits.

The Last of the Mohicans
Beautifully filmed and powerfully acted, *The Last of the Mohicans* is movie-making on a grand scale. Director Michael Mann takes James Fenimore Cooper's classic story of Hawkeye, the white boy raised by the Indians and turns it into a romantic adventure story packed with scenes which simply take your breath away.

Britain's Daniel Day-Lewis is almost unrecognisable as the same actor who won the Oscar for his performance in *My Left Foot*. For his big budget US debut he looks every inch the lean, intense romantic hero. American Madeleine Stowe (*Unlawful Entry*) is also perfectly cast as the beautiful British woman he falls in love with. There's so much chemistry between the screen lovers that a few smouldering looks say more than any explicit love scene ever could.

The passionate romance is matched by the sweeping cinematography and the brutally realistic battle scenes. Mann (*Manhunter*, TV's *Miami Vice*) employs his usual attention to detail to ensure the action is powerful to watch while never allowing it to overshadow the central, passionate romance between Hawkeye and Cora.

As well as introducing a much more defined love affair between the two central characters, Mann has paid closer attention to the historical setting of the story and the characterisations of the Native Americans than Fenimore Cooper's novel. Apart from the inspired casting of Day-Lewis and Stowe, Mann has also assembled an excellent supporting cast. Most noticeable are charismatic Indian activist Russell Means as Hawkeye's adopted father Chingachgook, newcomer Eric Schweig as his sensitive Indian brother Uncas, Stephen Waddington as his rival for Cora's affections and Wes Studi as the bloodthirsty but powerfully human, Magua.

The intense performances and visual splendour of the cinematography are enhanced by the haunting soundtrack from Trevor Jones and Randy Edelman. The result is a true piece of movie magic which should finally get Mann the kind of credit and respect he should have received when his masterful *Manhunter* was released.

Angela Thomas

Daniel Day-Lewis in *The Last of the Mohicans*

MICHELLE PFEIFFER

The past decade has seen Michelle Pfeiffer soar to superstar status, becoming one of Hollywood's most sought after actresses. In the summer of 1992, Pfeiffer gave a show-stopping performance as Catwoman in *Batman Returns* demonstrating, once again, her versatility and box-office appeal

Michelle Pfeiffer is Hollywood's reluctant superstar. Although the fragile, blonde beauty may look every inch the movie queen on screen, away from the camera she dresses down and guards her privacy jealously. But the usually shy and retiring actress surprised almost everyone when she went all out for one of the flashiest roles in the movies, Catwoman.

Pfeiffer's eagerness to play the rubber-clad villainess may have taken her fans by surprise, but she insists it's a role she wanted to play ever since childhood. 'Catwoman was certainly a childhood heroine of mine. I used to watch the TV series and just wait for her to come on, and she was never on enough as far as I was concerned,' she says. 'I guess she just broke all the stereotypes of what it meant to be a woman. I found that shocking and forbidden. Also, I was probably at the age where I was really just coming into my own sexuality, and I just found Catwoman thrilling to watch.'

Pfeiffer was desperate to play Catwoman and when the first Batman was being made she asked friends who were working on the film to let director Tim Burton know, 'that I wanted to play Catwoman. I said, "please, I'll do it for free! One scene, a cameo, anything".' To get in shape to play Catwoman, Pfeiffer studied kick-boxing and martial arts and she even had whip training!

Did You Know...?
Before being cast in the comedy *A League of Their Own* each actress had to pass try-outs to prove she had the ability to look like she really could play baseball. A veteran baseball coach was enlisted to help director Penny Marshall choose her team.

Pfeiffer's turn as the whip-wielding Catwoman was just the latest change of direction for the actress who could quite easily have become just another forgotten Hollywood blonde. A beauty queen at 19, she signed on with an agent and made her acting debut in the television

Michelle Pfeiffer

Rex Features

Rank Films

Pfeiffer in *Married to the Mob*

series *Fantasy Island*, in which she uttered just one line, 'who is she, Naomi?'

Forgettable film roles followed in *Falling In Love Again* in which she played a younger version of a char-

Pfeiffer with John Malkovich in *Dangerous Liaisons*

found time to play a 30s movie queen who falls in love in the well-received TV film *Natica Jackson*.

Pfeiffer suddenly found herself on Hollywood's A list when she joined Cher, Susan Sarandon, and Jack Nicholson in *The Witches of Eastwick*. She followed that high profile performance by playing the cool blonde at the centre of a love triangle with Mel Gibson and Kurt Russell in the disappointing thriller *Tequila Sunrise*.

Next, she became a gum-chewing brunette in the Jonathan Demme comedy *Married to the Mob*. She was back to being blonde as the virtuous object of John Malkovich's amorous attentions in *Dangerous Liaisons*. Her performance earned Pfeiffer her first Oscar nomination.

Did You Know...?
Over 1,000 extras were employed to pack the set for the fake Academy Awards ceremony in the Kevin Costner/Whitney Houston film *The Bodyguard*. But strict regulations surrounding the use of the Oscar statuette prevented the Oscar itself actually making an appearance.

She demonstrated her versatility once again with her hot-blooded performance as a sultry lounge singer in *The Fabulous Baker Boys*. Her knockout performance

acter played by Susannah York, the equally missable comedy *Hollywood Knights* and the rather silly *Charlie Chan And The Curse Of The Dragon Queen*. In between she had a recurring 'bimbo' role in *Delta House*, the television spin-off of *National Lampoon's Animal House*.

Her first major feature film role was very nearly her last – she was cast as the leading lady in the disastrous *Grease 2*. Few actresses could have survived such an inauspicious beginning. But Pfeiffer just picked herself up and started again from scratch. Her first step on the road to success was as a coke-sniffing moll in Brian De Palma's violent *Scarface*.

Did You Know...?
A complex series of sets were built on seven soundstages at Pinewood Studios for *Alien 3*. The biggest set was the lead works and blast furnace built on the 007 stage, the world's biggest soundstage.

She turned to comedy for John Landis's offbeat *Into The Night*, and her ethereal beauty was put to

good use as the enchanted heroine of the romantic *Ladyhawke*. Good reviews followed for her performance as an actress playing the leading lady in a chaotic movie on the American War of Independence in *Sweet Liberty*, and she even

Pfeiffer with Al Pacino in *Frankie and Johnny*

BBC Photograph Library

Barry Norman with Michelle Pfeiffer in a *Film 92 Special*

21 YEARS OF FILM 92

Barry Norman and *Film 92* celebrated 21 years of film watching in October 1992

The longest-running TV programme about the movies, *Film 92*, celebrated its 21st birthday in 1992 with a look back over two decades of movie watching and Barry Norman on the cover of *Radio Times*. In 21 years the format of the show has stayed very much the same.

Long-time presenter Barry Norman holds court interspersing his reviews of the latest cinema releases with interviews and occasional on-set reports. The son of film director Leslie Norman, he's established himself as the leading British authority on the movies. Apart from the 'Film' programmes he's also presented related specials including *The Hollywood Greats*, and *The British Greats*.

BBC Photograph Library

Barry Norman on the set of *Film 92*

Norman briefly left the programme in 1982 to present the arts documentary series *Omnibus*. In his absence producer Ian Johnstone took over the hot-seat. But Norman was soon back in the stalls after he left *Omnibus* and has remained there ever since.

In the past decade the only major changes to the hit formula have come in the opening titles and in the increased video coverage. And in 1992, as in other years, the big stars turned up to talk about their latest movies, from Michelle Pfeiffer in January to Meryl Streep in December.

Angela Thomas

won her another Oscar nomination. She went deliberately downbeat to play a Russian woman who falls in love with book publisher Sean Connery in *The Russia House*, and then tried rather unsuccessfully to look even more dull and ordinary in *Frankie and Johnny* opposite Al Pacino.

Did You Know...?
Christopher Walken's *Batman Returns* character was named Max Schreck in a sly tribute to the German actor who played Nosferatu the vampire in the 1922 classic movie.

She went from frump to vamp to play Catwoman and in so doing confirmed her position as one of the handful of superstar actresses at the top of the Hollywood tree. Pfeiffer's latest film, the inter-racial romance *Love Field*, has just been released in the USA, after being caught up in the financial problems of its distribution company Orion.

The actress who once said she acted for love and accepted the high salaries for the inconvenience of being regarded as public property, has already completed Martin Scorsese's period drama *Age Of Innocence* with Daniel Day-Lewis. And with talk of Pfeiffer donning her skintight rubber suit to play Catwoman once again in the next *Batman*, it's clear that her low-key versatility will keep her on the Hollywood fast track just as long as she's willing to live her life in the spotlight.

Angela Thomas

TV FILM SEASONS

With subjects as diverse as French classics, mobsters and Arnold Schwarzenegger, the year's TV film seasons had something for everyone. *Radio Times* film editor Derek Winnert reviews the highlights

Film buffs – and that means almost everybody – will remember 1992 as the year some of their favourite recent movies had their premieres on TV. At Christmas *Indiana Jones and the Last Crusade* (the one with Sean Connery as Indy's dad) and *Shirley Valentine*, with frustrated housewife Pauline Collins romancing Tom Conti on a Greek island, rightly attracted the biggest audiences. ITV put all their biggies on just before Christmas to attract the shoppers' advertising, like Tom Hanks in *Turner and Hooch* and Bob Hoskins in the mixed cartoon and live action film *Who Framed Roger Rabbit*.

Casablanca

But if 1992 was about the big new blockbuster, the surprise of the year was the return of the good old-fashioned film season. In the spring, *Radio Times* launched its new series of movie magazines called simply *Films*, and in our autumn edition I asked readers if they remembered the days when there used to be wonderful, almost complete seasons of Alfred Hitchcock,

Francis Ford Coppola, Jack Lemmon or Meryl Streep. From September, the BBC decided to revive the idea with seasons on three nights a week – Tuesdays at 11.15pm, Fridays at 11pm and Saturdays at 9pm. The Tuesday season was all-time classics, ranging from *Casablanca* (of course) to *Cabaret*, from *The Elephant Man* to *King Kong* (the original, naturally), from Wayne's swansong in *The Shootist* to Anthony Perkins (who died in September 1992) in his finest hour in *Psycho*. This great season was still running well into 1993.

Did You Know...?

Danny DeVito's penguin army consisted of real penguins, puppet penguins, short people in penguin costumes and 3D computer generated images.

Friday's season was of human dramas, and included a mini-season of underrated Sissy Spacek movies: *Crimes of the Heart*, with Jessica Lange and Diane Keaton, a penetrating tale of three southern sisters; *The River* with Mel Gibson about a troubled farming couple; and *Marie*, with Spacek as a divorcee who exposes Tennessee corruption. Saturdays brought 'first run' premiere showings of new films, many of them scarcely three years old. These included Kevin Costner and Susan Sarandon in the sexy baseball drama *Bull Durham*; Michael Keaton in *The Dream Team*, a comedy about psychiatric patients at large in New York; Peter O'Toole in *High Spirits*, the engagingly silly comedy set in an Irish haunted house; yuppies on the run from mobsters in a funny black comedy *Weekend at Bernie's*; and last but not least *Tremors*, a spoof

---

Did You Know...?

Pretty Woman Julia Roberts' Tinkerbell in Spielberg's *Hook* was originally planned as a floaty, feminine fairy. But the costume designer soon realised that pretty dresses weren't going to hide the bulky harness she had to wear for all the flying sequences. So he gave her a female Robin Hood look instead.

Bagdad Café

monster movie that in America notched up the highest audience for a film in 1991.

But it was a year of seasons. The BBC started it off with *Moving Pictures Presents* – films like *Jagged Edge*, *Pat Garrett and Billy the Kid*, *Brazil* and *Bagdad Café*, all connected to reports in BBC2's film magazine, then at the end of January a season from director Billy Wilder included *Ace in the Hole*, *The Lost Weekend*, *Stalag 17* and *Sabrina Fair* with the late Audrey Hepburn.

February brought a short run of mobster movies, including Jack Nicholson in *Prizzi's Honor* and Danny DeVito in *Wise Guys*. The end of May put Alex Cox back in

Tremors

Jean de Florette

the spotlight introducing another *Moviedrome* season and there were four films in tribute to Marlene Dietrich, who died in May 1992.

Did You Know...?
British Olympic gold medallist Robin Cousins was the choreographer and technical adviser for the ice-skating romance *Cutting Edge*..

July brought four memorable Woody Allan movies and *Classic Chillers*, a season of vintage scares with the likes of *Son of Franken-*

Conan the Barbarian

stein and *I Walked with a Zombie*. In October there were four Italian classics from Roberto Rossellini, and around a score of films were screened in celebration of John ('I make westerns') Ford in November which also saw the start of the BBC's French classics season running till the Christmas showing of *Jean de Florette* and *Manon des Sources*.

Did You Know...?
The producers of *Bugsy* ran into all kinds of trouble trying to recreate the gangster's casino in the desert for the multi-million dollar film.

'I don't know whose folly was grander, Bugsy's or ours. We built this hotel in the middle of nowhere and we were up against the same conditions as he was. The single most destructive element was the wind. We had signs blown away. We had grass blown away,' says producer Mark Johnson.

In the autumn ITV retaliated with a season devoted to the biggest star in the movies today, Arnold Schwarzenegger, who rose from being a 70s bodybuilder fighting a losing battle with his Austrian accent to the number one superstar who gets paid in percentages and aeroplanes. The films were *Conan the Barbarian* (1981), a beguiling mix of fantasy tale and violent action that rescued him from the small time and set

the pattern for the career to come; *Commando* (1985), a gung ho actioner as Arnie rushes around South America zapping baddies while looking for his daughter; *Predator* (1987), an exciting Rambo-style film about a mission into the jungle that turns into a terrific monster movie; and *Red Heat* (1988), for which Arnie got $10 million as a Russian cop teaming with James Belushi to rid Chicago of drug dealers. Stallone's still better at the straight action, but *Conan* and *Predator* show Arnie's the king of the myths.

Did You Know...?
The production team behind the Christmas hit *Home Alone 2: Lost in New York* had to create the perfect toy shop for one of the key sets in the sequel to the smash hit *Home Alone*. 'Duncan's Toy Chest is the kind of toy store you would always want to have been in as a kid. The visual style of Duncan's is based on Gepetto's workshop in Pinocchio, only on a grander scale,' says director Chris Columbus.

Over on Channel 4, the big season was a well-deserved celebration of a decade of *Film on Four*, the saviour of the British cinema throughout the 80s. The picture that toasted the anniversary was a TV movie, *Bye Bye Baby*, a sweet exercise in nostalgia by Jack Rosenthal, writer of the fondly remembered *P'tang Yang Kipperbang*, transmitted on Channel 4's second evening in the *First Love* series.

Others in the season had all played successfully in the cinema,

The Lady Vanishes

Nightbreed

including Sting and Melanie Griffith in the moody Newcastle film noir *Stormy Monday*; the late, much lamented Ray McAnally as a young boy's fisherman grandpa in *Venus Peter*; a hilarious black comedy with *Making Out*'s Margi Clarke, *I Hired a Contract Killer;* and Charlotte Rampling as a ruthless Tory politician in *Paris by Night*, one of the most pertinent political dramas of the 80s.

Other Channel 4 seasons during the year were devoted to Dirk Bogarde – *By Myself* in January; Peter Sellers's British features – *Early Sellers* in February; a horror season – *Chilling Out* in April; *Cinema Canada* devoted to one of the most accomplished but least noticed filmmaking countries; *Mondo Cinema* in June, a pick of new foreign movies; *Cinema Cinema* – a wonderful selection of French films; *Hindi Nights*, a wide range of Indian films, starting in August and still running in 1993; *All in the Mind* – a selection of Hollywood films about mental illness and psychiatry; and a valuable series of about a dozen Gerard Depardieu films kicked off in November as it should with the terrific *Cyrano de Bergerac*, a nose ahead of the rest of the season which ran up to Christmas and included controversial films like *Danton*, *Police*, *Tenue de Soirée* and *Les Valseuses*. It was certainly a good year on TV for the growing minority warming to French films.

Channel 4 also gave us daytime seasons devoted to American favourites like Joan Crawford (including the delirious *A Woman's Face*), Edward G Robinson and Alice Faye. They livened (or should that be deadened?) late night Fridays with *The Killer Bs*, compromising some dreadful old horror tosh, in which jolly spirit they were also showing a Godzilla monster season over the new year, films as pathetic as they come but arguably amusing in the shortest of doses. At Christmas they singled out Sidney Poitier, in a surprise but deserved tribute, with films like *The Blackboard Jungle, The Bedford Incident, A Raisin in the Sun* and *The Slender Thread*.

The Christmas seasons on BBC were a huddle of Hitchcocks (*The Lady Vanishes, The 39 Steps, Suspicion, Notorious, Marnie, The Birds*) and all nine Astaire and Rogers films. Who cares that these films are shown so often? Well, film buffs care. These cinematic gems should be displayed like the crown jewels at least once a year.

ITV's only Christmas season was devoted to its Disney back catalogue, and though they were all second or third-rate Disney that's still entertainment enough, certainly for volume as there were two on almost every morning of the holiday

Cyrano de Bergerac

fortnight. There were premieres of *Baby Secret of the Lost Legend*, *The Legend of the Sleepy Hollow* and *The Sword in the Stone*. And there were re-runs including *Herbie Goes Bananas*, *Candleshoe*, the cartoon *Robin Hood*, *Pollyanna* and *Blackbeard's Ghost*.

Although we don't all have the magic dish, we mustn't forget satellite. Sky had a busy year with seasons too. The main ones were: *Family Affairs*, for two months beginning in February, including *Ghostbusters 2*, *Field of Dreams* and *Witches*; in March a *Tough Girls* season, with *Blue Steel* (Jamie Lee Curtis), *Blood Money*, *Arizona Hide* and *Assault of the Killer Bimbos*; in May, *Masters of Horror*, with films representing all the big scare names like Stephen King (*Firestarter*), Clive Barker (*Nightbreed*), George A Romero (*Dawn of the Dead*), Sam Raimi (*The Evil Dead*), Tobe Hooper (*Spontaneous Combustion*) and Wes Craven (*A Nightmare on Elm Street*); in June came a gangster movies season with *The Krays*, *Scarface*, *Married to the Mob*, *The Freshman*, *Goodfellas* and *Once Upon a Time in America*; and

Stormy Monday

Misery

finally in December, king of horror Stephen King got his own season, with *Misery*, *Graveyard Shift*, *Silver Bullet*, *Carrie*, and *The Shining*. There were also seasons devoted to superheroes, sci-fi, martial arts and current movie darling Julia Roberts.

Those were the seasons that actually happened. But *Radio Times* came up with ones that haven't – yet. I asked readers to write in with suggestions for the TV bosses. Here's what they asked for: a Life after Bond season starring Sean Connery; Directing Firsts on major directors' debuts; the Oscar-winners of each year; People and Places (*The Third Man* for Vienna, *Oliver Twist* for London); Composer Biopics; TV Pilots; Widescreen; and Comics and Pop Stars in the Movies. The idea for a 50s cinema night with widescreen, spectacular colour epics won the editor's prize as best suggestion. Let's hope the telly moguls are listening.

Derek Winnert

OBITUARIES

MARLENE DIETRICH

'Your name begins with a caress and ends with a whiplash,' said Jean Cocteau of Marlene Dietrich, the last survivor of the great age of Hollywood glamour, who died in May, aged 90. Dietrich, like Garbo, Davis and Crawford, established herself as a star on the strength of her screen presence rather than her material.

Marlene Dietrich

A star in her native Germany by the end of the 20s, it was Josef Von Sternberg who created her first international success in *The Blue Angel* in 1930, leading to a Hollywood contract and a series of spectacular starring roles, directed by Von Sternberg. In *Morocco*, *Dishonoured*, *Shanghai Express*, *Blonde Venus*, *The Scarlet Empress* and *The Devil is a Woman*, Dietrich and Von Sternberg refined the mixture of eroticism and hauteur that remained potent for the rest of her life.

When their professional association ended, Dietrich made a handful of great films (including *Destry Rides Again* and *Touch of Evil*) and many not-so-great; it was during the Second World War, however, that she found her second career. Having spurned Hitler, she embarked on a massive tour entertaining American troops and, after the War, she was at her best in her one-woman cabaret show, accompanied by Burt Bacharach.

Marlene Dietrich in *The Blue Angel*, the film which turned her into an overnight legend

She continued to perform until 1976, when she retired from the stage; '*je vous dire adieu*,' she announced to her final Parisian audience, '*parce que c'est fini*'. She spent the rest of her life in relative reclusion in Paris, collaborating with Maximillian Schell's 1984 film *Marlene* on condition that she would provide only her voice, not her filmed image.

Marlene Dietrich:
27 December 1901 – 6 May 1992

ROBERT MORLEY

One of the most consistent and successful actors of the century, Robert Morley had a strong line in self-deprecation. 'Not many easier ways of making a living than acting,' he said. 'I don't work; I merely inflict myself on the public.' Unlike others in his profession, he had a clear idea of where his value and his limitations lay. He turned down Sir Peter Hall's offer to play Falstaff at Stratford, and in 1970 even refused a knighthood on the grounds that it was an unsuitable honour for a light comedian.

It was in light comedy that Morley excelled. Although his career had embraced many performances of depth and complexity (he portrayed Oscar Wilde on stage and screen, and appeared to great effect as Katharine Hepburn's father in *The African Queen*), he had his greatest success in light boulevard comedies, often self-penned, which kept him busy in the West End throughout the 50s for runs of up to three years.

Robert Morley as Emile Carpeau in BBC1's *The Deadly Game* which was televised in 1982

As well as acting and writing, Morley was a successful manager and director, the author of several books, and a noted raconteur. He was always unquestionably the master of his own destiny. When he starred in Alan Ayckbourn's 1970 hit *How the Other Half Loves*, Morley insisted on changing the lines to emphasise his character: 'I've left a trail of richer but sadder authors behind me,' he explained to the disgruntled Ayckbourn. In 1940 he married Joan Buckmaster, daughter of the actress Gladys Cooper, with whom he had three children, among them the critic and writer Sheridan Morley.

Robert Morley:
26 May 1908 – 3 June 1992

DENHOLM ELLIOTT

'Never act with children, animals or Denholm Elliott,' quipped Gabriel Byrne after the two actors had co-starred in *Defence of the Realm* in 1985, testifying to Elliott's effortless ability to steal every scene in which he appeared. From the end of the Second World War until his death in October 1992 at the age of 70, Elliott had developed a unique persona, combining dignity with a seedy, sinister edge that he put to good use in countless stage and screen performances including *Alfie*, *A Private Function*, *A Room with a View* and, shortly before his death, *Noises Off*.

Denholm Elliott in *Hotel du Lac*

Elliott's acting career got off to a false start when he left RADA (where he had enrolled on his psychiatrist's recommendation) after a year; it was not until he spent three years in a PoW camp in Silesia that he concentrated on acting, and launched his post-War assault on the British stage.

Spotted by Laurence Olivier, Elliott enjoyed considerable theatrical success in premieres of work by Christopher Fry and TS Eliot; in the 60s, he concentrated increasingly on films. His returns to the British stage were few but remarkable, always in challenging material such as Ibsen, Strindberg or, most recently, David Mamet. He was married twice: to actress Virginia McKenna in the 50s and to Susan Robinson, with whom he stayed for 30 years.

Denholm Elliott:
    31 May 1922 – 6 October 1992

ANTHONY PERKINS

Psycho made Anthony Perkins world famous and in so doing, successfully obliterated anything he did on stage or screen before or since, until his Aids-related death in September 1992.

He was born in New York in 1932 and began acting when he was just 15. His first screen role was opposite Jean Simmons in *The Actress* in 1953. He followed that with a steady stream of roles on stage and on screen, often playing the shy young man and appearing alongside acting greats like Gary Cooper, Sophia Loren, and Henry Fonda.

Then came Hitchcock's classic chiller *Psycho* in 1960. Perkins's outwardly normal, inwardly troubled, tortured and extremely dangerous young man was as much a horror classic as the film itself. While *Psycho* was earning its place in movie history Perkins was in Paris starring opposite Ingrid Bergman in *Goodbye Again*. From that point onwards he divided his film and stage career between France and the USA, working with everyone from Brigitte Bardot to Orson Welles. High spots included a small but effective role in *Catch 22* (1970) and a cameo in *The Life and Times of Judge Roy Bean* (1972). He was a mad fashion photographer in *Mahogany* (1975) and a murder suspect in *Murder on the Orient Express* (1974). He was cast over and over again as sinister or psychotic characters on screen while on stage he still managed to be cast in shows like *Romantic Comedy*.

Anthony Perkins

Eventually Perkins decided to do what Hollywood had been hoping he would do for over 20 years – play Norman Bates again. *Psycho II* was quickly followed by another vintage crazy from Perkins in Ken Russell's controversial *Crimes of Passion*. Then he resurrected Norman Bates again for *Psycho III* which he also directed. By this time Perkins was obviously resigned to the fact that he would be playing variations of Norman for the rest of his career. He went over the top in the dreadful *Edge of Sanity*, and appeared in the TV films *I'm Dangerous Tonight* and *Psycho IV The Beginning*.

Anthony Perkins:
    4 April 1932 – 12 September 1992

Charity Events

The two biggest TV charity events of the year – ITV's *Telethon* and the BBC's *Children in Need* – took place to raise funds for a huge range of deserving causes. The events provided viewers with hours of entertainment and fun, as well as information on the work of the charities which would benefit from their donations.

The most unusual TV charity event was *Trading Places*, where celebrities swapped life styles for a day and took on a diverse range of tasks. Viewers also took part and were invited to become their favourite TV stars by donning wigs and costumes and taking on the appearance of their chosen celebrity. The event was organised to raise funds for Breakthrough, a charity set up to combat breast cancer.

The NSPCC Children's Royal Variety Performance changed its style and departed from its usual variety format. Many of Britain's favourite personalities took to the stage to raise funds for the NSPCC in an entertaining and innovative show.

On Easter Monday, Wembley Stadium staged one of rock's most spectacular concerts, when the stars turned out to pay tribute to the late Freddie Mercury. It was not primarily a fund-raiser, but a celebration of the man and his music, and a means of increasing global awareness of Aids, with any funds raised being made available to Aids charities.

Charity Events

TRADING PLACES

One of the most unusual televised charity events of the year raised funds for Breakthrough, a charity set up to combat breast cancer

'The mind boggles at the idea of thousands of people being me for the night,' said Cilla Black who hosted what must have been television's most unusual charity fundraising event this year. *Trading Places* was billed as the country's largest mass participation event since *Comic Relief*'s Red Nose Day, and the idea was that anyone who wanted to could be sponsored to be someone else for the day.

So all over the country people were donning auburn wigs and having 'a lorra lorra laughs' as they traded places with Cilla. Back in March that evening's television also featured some highly amusing life style swaps. Viewers followed Westminster Council's glamorous new dustbin lady, Joanna Lumley, who took the job very seriously and got very grubby clearing her share of the rubbish on the round.

One of London's top chefs, Raymond Blanc, got rather more than he bargained for when he agreed to run a transport cafe with Geoff Capes. It was certainly a good deal more down to earth than his posh restaurant kitchen, equipment was fairly basic and there were no minions to do his bidding. But the clients seemed satisfied.

Comedians Hale and Pace took their lives in their hands when they volunteered to trade places with the England rugby team for a training session. They only narrowly survived! Cilla herself tried her hand at

being an ITN reporter and discovered that without the back-up of her usual studio team, life out in the wide world was a little more hectic.

For members of the public who didn't come up with their own idea, *Trading Places* produced celebrity packs of a selection of Britain's best-loved characters which people were able to send off for, free of charge. There was a wide range of talent to choose from: Rab C Nesbitt, Michael Fish, Gary Glitter, Cher, Nora

Batty, Gazza, MC Hammer, Dame Edna Everage, Kylie Minogue and of course, Cilla. The packs included a letter signed by the celebrity, a funny booklet outlining exactly how to become that person for the day, a signed certificate declaring official change of character and a foreword by the celebrity on the official sponsor form.

But what was it all for?

At the end of the day £800,000 was raised for a new cancer charity

Cilla Black and Gary Glitter who took part in *Trading Places*

Breakthrough which was set up specifically to fight breast cancer. Breakthrough was founded in 1989 by Canadian Bill Freedman, whose actress wife, Tony Robins (she had appeared with the Royal Shakespeare Company and shortly before her death starred in the West End production of *The Aspern Papers* together with Christopher Reeve and Vanessa Redgrave), died of the disease in 1986. What had shocked Bill Freedman was that his wife had not been in any of the high risk categories associated with the disease: she didn't smoke, she didn't drink, she wasn't overweight and had had her three children before the age of 30.

After her tragic death, Bill made a commitment to find a way of reducing the chances of his daughter, Lisa, developing the disease. He talked to a number of specialists in the field about the problems of combating the disease before he met Professor Barry Gusterson, then professor of histopathology at the Institute of Cancer Research in London.

His idea – to bring together under one roof a team of the best breast cancer scientists in a co-ordinated programme focused exclusively on breast cancer – seemed to Bill to offer the best hope of finding a cure for the disease. More precisely, the new research programme would concentrate first on the 'basic science' of the disease: what is it in a previously normal, healthy breast which causes the cancer to develop?

The centre would be the first of its kind in the world and Professor Gusterson calculated that to create and equip it and to provide a core team of research scientists would cost around £15 million. Additional research within the centre would then be funded by the Cancer Research Campaign and the Institute of Cancer Research and other funding organisations such as the Wellcome Foundation.

So Breakthrough Breast Cancer was founded. After two years of lobbying companies, trusts and individuals to establish the charity, it was publicly launched in October 1991. It was felt that a big fund-raising scheme was needed and the

Freedman family had just the idea: Bill's son Peter and his wife Fiona Halton, who had directed *Comic Relief*'s Red Nose Day, came up with *Trading Places*.

By the end of this first public fund-raising year, Breakthrough had raised over £6 million. This was the sum needed to acquire and refurbish the new research centre building which is alongside the Royal Marsden Hospital and the Institute of Cancer Research in Surrey. Together the three form Europe's largest cancer complex. Two million pounds will be used to buy state-of-the-art equipment and the remaining £7 million will be spent on securing long-term funding for key scientific teams.

The Breast Cancer Story
The disease kills 15,000 women every year; that means 300 women every week. The figures have not changed over the last 30 years, despite research into treatment and the introduction of a national breast screening programme.

One in five of all female cancer deaths in Britain are due to breast cancer – it kills more women than any other cancer. Every year 25,000 new cases are diagnosed.

Dr Daphne Pearson who was treated at the Royal Marsden Hospital, has spoken honestly and openly about her breast cancer and mastectomy and is an enthusiastic supporter of Breakthrough. More than two years after the experience she is often asked to talk to other women who have been newly diagnosed with cancer. 'You need a lot of counselling,' she says. 'I found myself turning to the Macmillan nurse at the hospital, who was wonderful. She was the only one I cried with.'

Over 20 years of marriage and three children, Dr Pearson had several problems with breast lumps, but all had been non-cancerous. Another small lump five years ago did not seem anything to worry unduly about. Tests showed it, too, to be benign. But the lump did not disappear and it was suggested the tests be repeated. A letter arrived two weeks later telling her that the mammography was 'suspicious'.

'I knew that meant they'd found

malignant cells, but it was only when I got to the hospital and saw my husband waiting for me – he'd never been with me before – that I realised this was the full thing.'

She can laugh about it now, but her husband's work as professor of haematology at St Thomas's Hospital, London kept him in regular contact with cancer patients, and meant that he knew the implications of the diagnosis.

'It certainly didn't help that we were both doctors. We were at different stages at different times. At first you deny it. You tell yourself that the next test will be normal. Then, when you do accept that they're right, you think, "It's only cancer of the breast, I can cope with having that off, no problem." You're still denying the major problem, which is cancer.'

In little more than a week, Dr Pearson found herself in a hospital ward recovering from a mastectomy and breast reconstruction. 'I insisted on that. A month later I was sitting in a bikini by a pool in Portugal without feeling at all abnormal.'

The next phase of treatment, chemotherapy, proved more difficult. Her skin was a greyish, yellow colour, half her hair fell out, she suffered nausea and vomiting and because of her age – menopausal symptoms too. After five doses, she could take no more. So she was put on Tamoxifen, an experimental drug treatment which has shown promising results in clinical trials, combined with hormone replacement therapy to combat the menopausal symptoms.

'I bought a wig which I wore for three months and I felt better. Now I feel good, I've got a new short haircut which I like, and people say I look ten years younger.' Though she is now clear of the cancer, Daphne Pearson is well aware of the statistics and the risks. 'I must admit that I have to stop myself worrying about little aches and pains. But then I worry a lot less now than I used to. I'm keen that Breakthrough gets off the ground. That's why I'm prepared to talk about it, for the sake of our daughters and our younger sisters.'

Anne-Marie Sapsted

THE FREDDIE MERCURY TRIBUTE – A CONCERT FOR AIDS AWARENESS

Wembley Stadium played host to a unique event on Easter Monday, 1992 when a star-studded line-up paid tribute to the late Freddie Mercury and helped to communicate a vital message. By Rupert Smith

It was entirely suitable that the Freddie Mercury Tribute Concert for Aids Awareness was not only the biggest rock spectacle of the year, but was also fraught with contradictions, controversies and misunderstandings, much like the man it honoured. The scale of the grieving which followed Mercury's death in November 1991 surprised everyone, and when the surviving members of Queen announced in February 1992 that there would be a grand testimonial concert at Easter, top flight rock acts fell over themselves to get on the bill. It was not, as some cynics suggested, simply a good platform from which to boost flagging careers; it marked an acceptance that Aids could affect everyone, even superstars, and that anything that could get that message across was a life-saver.

The 72,000 tickets for the show sold out within three hours, long before the bill had been decided;

Elton John (left) and Axl Rose

throughout the weeks leading up to the concert, the papers reported in minute detail the complex negotiations that led to the final line-up. 'It's been hard turning down a lot of good people,' said Queen drummer Roger Taylor, 'so we chose performers who had some links with Freddie and who were very famous.' The final artists roster would have been breathtaking in any event, but the fact that such diverse acts had come together in the name of Aids awareness was unbelievable. True, George Michael and Elton John had supported Aids charities since the late 80s, but to see traditional, macho rock acts such as Metallica, Def Leppard and Roger Daltrey mustering behind the Aids banner

was astonishing. Nothing, however, could top the appearance of American band Guns N' Roses. One of the best-selling acts in the world, they had nevertheless alienated liberals everywhere by their aggressively anti-gay, xenophobic lyrics. Their decision to appear at the Freddie Mercury concert was, perhaps, an act of atonement; whatever their motives, it was proof that the rock establishment had at last acknowledged the health crisis.

Mercury is an unlikely hero for Aids awareness campaigners. Until the day before his death, he refused to make a public statement about his illness. He had been what the tabloids delight in calling 'promiscuous' with both sexes. But his death finally brought home to millions of people of all ages that somebody they knew could be affected by a disease that until then had been remote. 'Freddie's death brought Aids so close to so many people,' says Jacky Gunn, who runs the Queen fan club. 'Young kids of 12 or 13 who were in the fan club were completely devastated, but were writing us letters saying that they were now aware of Aids. From that point of view, Freddie didn't die in vain.'

The concert was a unique opportunity to spread a very basic message about Aids to the widest possible audience, and Queen Productions were quick to realise that they needed expert advice on how best to exploit the situation. The Terrence Higgins Trust, Britain's leading Aids charity, had already benefited from sales of *Bohemian Rhapsody*, re-released shortly after Mercury's death, and were keen to continue the relationship with Queen.

'We've learnt a lot about the mass media over the years,' says Daryl Upsall, head of fund-raising for the Terrence Higgins Trust. 'You have to realise the limitations of what you can get across in an event like this. You can't teach people all about HIV, about safer sex, in one fell swoop. But you can make people realise that Aids is a reality for all of us, not just for a few minorities. An event like the Freddie Mercury show is so big that the best you can hope for is an

(From left): John Deacon, Roger Taylor and Brian May

acknowledgement that Aids exists, that we all need to think about it. I think it was a great success in that respect, and we've been processing requests for further information ever since.'

Fans gather to pay tribute to Freddie Mercury at Wembley Stadium

Unlike Live Aid, the nearest comparable event, the Freddie Mercury concert was not primarily a fund-raiser. The purpose was threefold: to pay tribute to Mercury, to increase global awareness of Aids, and to ensure that the concert made an overall profit which would be available to Aids charities worldwide.

For many of the fans who arrived at Wembley Stadium on Easter Monday, 20 April 1992, the concert fulfilled the function of a memorial service. 'Queen felt that the fans needed some way of paying their last respects, because the funeral had been such a private affair,' says Jacky Gunn. 'There had been no opportunity for them to let off steam, and the best way to do that was by having a big party. Freddie loved a good party, and he would have hated the idea that people were miserable because of him. At all the parties he gave, he was the perfect host; he would always make

sure that you were really enjoying yourself. There was some trepidation about Wembley, though. A lot of the fans felt it was a great idea but that it would be sad because any minute they'd expect Freddie to

launch himself out on to the stage.'

The concert itself was a masterpiece of organisation, its three-and-a-half hours running almost without a hitch. Musically, the standard was high – particularly given that most of the artists were performing songs Queen had made famous. Technically, it was a huge achievement, not only within the stadium but also in the massive operation that provided the satellite link to 76 countries. The first half started punctually at 6pm with sets from Metallica, Extreme and Def Leppard, all bands who reflected Queen's roots in heavy metal. Bob Geldof and Guns N' Roses finished off the first half's musical offerings, but they were little more than a warm-up act for Elizabeth Taylor, whose non-musical role still managed to upstage virtually everyone else at the concert.

Miss Taylor took to the stage with an air of authority; she has, after all, single-handedly rallied Hollywood

stars to come out in support of Aids charities. Resplendent in a sequined jacket decorated with images of herself as Cleopatra, she magisterially silenced a lone heckler who yelled 'Get off!'. 'I'll get off,' she snapped, 'but I've got something to say first.' What she had to say was the evening's most unambiguous statement about the dangers of HIV; in two weeks, she announced, there would be as many new HIV infections as there were people in Wembley Stadium. She paid a characteristically florid tribute to Mercury, to the artists and the audience; sentimental it may have been, but it was undoubtedly the emotional focus of the show.

Elizabeth Taylor speaks to the crowd on Aids awareness

'I was rushing around trying to watch the show and do some media work as well,' says Daryl Upsall of the Terrence Higgins Trust, 'but Liz Taylor brought me to a standstill. I don't want to single anyone out, because all the performers were great, but she really brought a tear to my eye. When she dealt with that heckler, I felt very proud for some reason; not just proud of her, but proud of the courage and commitment of everyone who's involved with the fight against Aids.'

The second half of the show put the emphasis on fun and nostalgia as Roger Taylor, Brian May and

John Deacon, Queen's drummer, guitarist and bassist, provided musical backing for a succession of guest vocalists who interpreted Freddie's greatest hits. Friendly competition was the order of the day, not least when Annie Lennox and David Bowie duetted on *Under Pressure*, with vocal honours going to Ms Lennox, who also came a close second to Elizabeth Taylor in the sartorial stakes. Bowie, not to be outdone, elicited gasps of disbelief by dropping to his knees and reciting the Lord's Prayer on behalf of everyone with HIV or Aids. 'In an age of few surprises, the sight of David Bowie in prayer still has the power to shock,' said Ben Thompson, The *Independent's* rock critic.

George Michael, Elton John and Axl Rose raised the proceedings to fever pitch, at which point the only person left (and possibly the only person who could have handled the finale with sufficient panache) was Liza Minnelli, who led the company in a full-throttle rendition of *We Are the Champions*. After 20 acts had performed, 20,000 hamburgers had been consumed and 26,000 pints of lager quaffed, the show was over, and a worldwide audience in excess of one billion had been exposed to the Aids awareness message.

But how successful was the concert? Certainly it was a good send-off for Mercury, who had crossed all audience barriers in his life and now, in death, brought together figures from a broad musical spectrum who might never otherwise have met. But had the other ends been achieved? Before long, reports were appearing in the newspapers claiming that the concert had failed to raise as much money as the promoters had hoped, while others claimed that the subject of Aids had been too low on the agenda.

Queen Productions was swift to reply. The concert, they said, was never intended to be a fund-raiser. It had cost £1,087,000 to put on and had taken a net amount of £1,160,000 at the box office. Television sales to North America had raised considerable amounts which were distributed to Aids charities across the country. Substantial sums from the sale of merchandise were all handed over to the Mercury Phoenix Trust, a special trust set up to distribute all monies raised in Mercury's name in Britain.

Adverse reports persisted, however. 'The press started believing its own headlines,' says Daryl Upsall. 'One headline which was particularly damaging claimed that Freddie had left £25 million to Aids charities, and a lot of people felt that was far too much, and that Aids organisations were over-funded. In fact, Freddie left about £5 million in his will, all to private individuals; none of it went to Aids charities. Then there were reports that the concert had failed to reach its financial targets. There never were any financial targets, so that was nonsense. The result of all this misinformation was a massive confusion about what had been done, which is quite destructive; people are always ready to believe the worst about this kind of event.

David Bowie recites the Lord's Prayer in an unprecedented moment during the concert

'Nobody involved in the Freddie Mercury concert would claim that it was an effective piece of health education – nobody left Wembley having learnt how to put on a condom. But it wasn't meant to be that. It was a very broad, general statement about Aids, and in that respect it was very successful. It brought a lot of people into the Aids arena who would never have considered getting involved. The Terrence Higgins Trust has benefited from a number of subsequent record releases: Extreme and U2 have both donated royalties to us, Elton John continues to donate royalties from all his singles, and now there are other artists approaching us. Right Said Fred have given us a lot of money. That's exactly the kind of thing we wanted: to set a precedent for people to carry on working for Aids in Freddie's name.'

Thanks to the efforts of his many friends, fans and colleagues, Freddie Mercury has the mixed honour of becoming the most significant figure in the Aids crisis to date. When Rock Hudson died in 1985, the Hollywood community closed ranks and remained tight-lipped, terrified to join the fight against Aids lest that be interpreted as a personal statement about sexuality or HIV-status. But when Aids touched the music business, the reaction was swift and remarkably positive. Of course, not all of the stars of the Freddie Mercury Tribute Concert for Aids Awareness would have any clear statements to make on the subject; some of them, indeed, may have agreed to perform for less than charitable reasons. But, for the duration of the concert at least, individual motives were subsumed in the greater impact of the day. 'It was a new type of pop music event,' says Upsall. 'There were grandparents and grandchildren there, heavy metal fans, young professional parents, gay people, straight people, all sorts.

'Everyone connected, and everyone had a positive feeling about what we could achieve together to raise awareness about Aids. It may sound ridiculous, but the atmosphere was somewhat akin to being in church. It wasn't perfect, and there were a few things that I might have changed, but it reached a billion people all over the world and I honestly think it changed lives.'

Rupert Smith

TELETHON

Anne-Marie Sapsted finds out about *Telethon*, the non-stop television fund-raiser. How is it organised? How did it all begin? Who benefits? The 28-hour marathon of fun, entertainment and fund-raising all happened one weekend in July

It's the television marathon to beat them all, but *Telethon 92* was also a personal marathon for Michael Aspel who, while most people were planning their summer holiday, was preparing for 28 hours of non-stop fun and fund-raising. And coolly and calmly he hosted a television spectacular which was a feat of technical expertise.

For behind the scenes, British Telecom had put in 3,200 tele-

phones all over the country to cope with the deluge of giving, which at one point reached a peak of a quarter of a million simultaneous calls. Between them, BT and NatWest Bank provided 15,000 volunteers to man the telephones over that July weekend which finally raised over £15 million while on the air, with donations pouring in for weeks afterwards.

Joe Simpson, coordinator of the event explained: 'Over a million people up and down the country have been involved. The money *Telethon 92* raised is money that would not otherwise have gone to help charities all over the UK. These are difficult times and we have never set ourselves a financial target.'

Simpson and his team were particularly gratified by indepen-

dent research which showed that the whole event, which was sprinkled with short appeal films – some only ten seconds long, others lasting three minutes or longer – had a significant educational impact on viewers. There were about 60 national appeal films, carried at the rate of around three every half hour, with the 16 regional companies making their own local films.

'The research showed that viewers were the regular ITV audience and that heavy TV watchers were the most likely to see the programme. The more *Telethon* they watched, the more noticeable was their change in attitude and the more empathetic they became. I think it's what I like best about the programme. It's an amazing thing to be able to witness the impact a very powerful and personal state-

Michael Aspel, who hosted 28 hours of non-stop fun and fund-raising in *Telethon*

ment about disability can have on the audience. We can make a direct correlation between what's happening on the programme with what's happening with the phones ringing.

'The particularly interesting thing about it is that because it's live television, we can improve as we go along. We knew when we were off beam and could do something about it. The strongest responses came when we got someone to tell their own story about disability in their own words. That for us was one of the most important things about *Telethon*, that we wanted to raise awareness as well as to raise money.'

Susannah Wheeler, the national fund-raising coordinator for *Telethon*, says: 'We knew that with the recession it would be very hard to raise money. But we showed that the British public is prepared to come out in droves and support something they feel strongly about. This has never been a celebrity driven show, it's a people-based appeal.

'It shows the power of television, but we're moving away from the idea that it's a chance to get on television. We've got people into the habit of doing something for charity once a year. For first-time fund-raisers we wanted them to feel that they had enjoyed themselves and to look around for another charity they could do something for. That's always been one of our aims.'

The idea for using the telephone as a fund-raising tool came from America, where stars like Jerry Lewis have been doing Telethons for almost 30 years. There are now regular Telethons in Italy, France, Australia, New Zealand, and even Russia is planning one to raise money for the children affected by Chernobyl.

Michael Aspel's Recipe for *Telethon* Success

TV's Mr Cool, Michael Aspel is the man with the job of guiding the audience through the 28-hour *Telethon* marathon. In fact, Aspel and fellow presenters around the country hold the record for the longest stand-up stint on television. When *Telethon* was first considered

Aspel went over to America to watch Jerry Lewis in action on the American version of *Telethon* which lasted 21 hours.

'After the first *Telethon*, the prospect wasn't so daunting because we had some idea what to expect. But there was slightly less gleeful anticipation because we didn't see how we could possibly raise as much money again. But when we raised even more, I have to say it was the nearest I've ever been to being emotionally overwhelmed on television.'

For Aspel, it's quite a relief that 'most of the mayhem goes on outside the studio'. But how does he get through that gruelling 28 hours? 'I don't sleep, even during the longer breaks, because once sleep claims you, it takes a long time to claw your way back. I'm lucky in that I don't sleep very much anyway. I usually have about four hours a night, with five or six at most.

'There are several changes of clothes to keep you on your toes and I make sure I drink as much as I can – no alcohol – and there are plenty of nibbles about. But to liven myself up I do a good old bop round out of camera shot because there's a lot of good music. Even if it is alone, there's nothing better to keep you going.

'You do get more tired than you care to think and I did start to hallucinate slightly on one occasion. I was introducing Cilla Black and I suddenly realised I wasn't doing a bit of filming, this was going out live. There are low spots, too, usually about eight in the morning when it begins to catch up with you, but we shake those off quite quickly.

'And when it's over it's a wonderful feeling, as high as anything produced by alcohol. You really feel alive. Then after a couple of days you feel jet-lagged for a while.'

A New Look *Telethon 92*

Telethon 92 had a new look. There was a move away from the idea of stars dropping in to do a turn and instead viewers were treated to special editions of their favourite programmes.

Blind Date: A special junior

edition of *Blind Date* was introduced by Cilla Black where young love was much in evidence. Participants were aged between seven and nine and were the children of Safeways staff. The company were one of the show's biggest sponsors and had raised £350,000.

Coronation Street: Vera went on a summer outing, intent on re-living her courting days, while Reg Holdsworth took possession of a mysteriously shaped package!

This Morning: Husband and wife team Judy Finnigan and Richard Madeley hosted a special edition of their programme live from Liverpool which included a mass makeover for 20 couples and a spectacular parachute jump on the famous *This Morning* floating weather map.

You Bet!: Matthew Kelly threw down the gauntlet to various companies who came up with some unusual challenges. Victoria Wine staff did a live bottle wrapping challenge, and Magnet Trading built a complete kitchen and cooked a meal in it in a record-breaking time.

The Disney Club: A special edition was hosted by Andrea Boardman, John Eccleston and Paul Hendy with live music from top bands. And many stars were on hand to take telephone pledges in person.

There was also a special *Bullseye* show hosted by Jim Bowen and *The Hit Man and Her* starred Michaela Strachan and Pete Waterman.

Four of TV's favourite detectives along with a host of stars took part in a specially written treasure-hunting murder mystery spanning more than a century and running over two nights. When Sherlock Holmes (Jeremy Brett) discovered a double murder it started a chain of circumstances which then involved the Dutch detective Van Der Valk (Barry Foster), led on to Glasgow where Taggart (Mark McManus) picked up the trail before reaching Ruth Rendell's Inspector Wexford (George Baker). Not only did he find the treasure, but he also solved the mystery of the double murders.

Telethon also had a royal appearance when Prince Charles, patron of *Telethon*, appeared to introduce the very best of the Prince's Trust

Telethon included a special junior edition of ***Blind Date***

concerts which included classic clips ranging from Elton John and Phil Collins to Sting and George Michael.

The spirit of *Telethon* was reflected in a multi-denominational service of hymns, songs, dances and readings from Hope Street and conducted by Archbishop Derek Warlock with Bishop David Sheppard, the Roman Catholic and Anglican Bishops of Liverpool. Each region featured its own live contribution and choirs from the Hanna Street Black Pentecostals, the Salvation Army, and the Cross-Community Choir from Northern Ireland took part.

Everything You Wanted to Know About *Telethon*

• 36 million viewers watched *Telethon 92* over a period of 28 hours.

• It is the only nationally-run charity where every penny pledged by telephone in a region, stays in that region.

• *Telethon 92* set a new record as the longest running continuous programme in the history of British television.

• Over a million people around the country were directly involved in making money.

• The total weight of all the coins counted by NatWest staff in *Telethon 90* amounted to 16,500 kilograms.

• NatWest Streamline terminals used more than 25 miles of tally roll during *Telethon 92* – the terminals processed a credit card donation in 27 seconds.

• It took the main autofile computer less than one second to process each pledge made.

• The record for computer pledges is 23.59 per second.

• *Telethon* is the biggest single mail operation – 660,000 pledge forms were sent out free of charge by the Royal Mail in 1990.

• There were over 13,000 registered events throughout the country.

• It was the most technically complex TV programme ever mounted involving every technician employed in ITV along with many freelances, using enough wiring to go to the moon and back.

How *Telethon* Began

Telethon first began in 1980 on a very small scale on Thames Television and was an occasional feature. In 1988 came the first national *Telethon*, which along with *Telethon 90* raised over £50 million to make it the second largest grant-giving body in the country, giving 30,000 charitable grants. In 1990, more than 14,000 charities benefited, though not everyone who applied was fortunate. In total a staggering £157 million was requested.

Each ITV company has a regional Telethon Trust which distributes the funds raised locally while the Independent Broadcasting Authority Trust funds initiatives of national importance. In 1992 the aim was to help charities working with children, young people, older people and people with disabilities and their carers.

Incredible feats have included a sponsored gnome hunt, a haggis hunt, a sponsored tooth-brushing, a man walking 60 miles with a pint of milk on his head, a sponsored silence in schools, a group emptying a 110,000-gallon swimming pool with buckets, a sponsored teddy bear parachute jump, a sponsored 48-hour leapfrog, a man sleeping in a coffin on a pub roof, abseiling accountants, and the longest chain of can ring-pulls around Wembley Stadium. And in 1992 even the animals joined in with a sponsored Dogathon involving pooches all over the country raising money for people by being sponsored to stay, to sit, to lie down, to slim or compete as a superdog.

Nine records for the Guinness Book of Records have been made, including 5,050 press-ups on one arm in five hours, the making of the largest canoe raft in the world, and a record for the most London tube stations visited in 24 hours.

Where the Money Goes
In 1990 *Telethon* helped charities all over the country:
• Scottish TV gave the Stillbirth and Neonatal Death Society £500 towards the cost of a Family Bereavement Room. The Scotscraig Originals Dance Festival received £1,500 for their Wheelchair Dance Team.
• Granada TV gave £1,350 for the deaf/blind to have a special Christmas Holiday Weekend.
• Yorkshire TV gave £600 to Special Gymnastics in North Yorkshire to enable disabled and special needs children to use gym equipment.
• TSW gave £1,000 to the ADS Bridgeport Day Centre towards travelling costs for dementia sufferers.
• TVS gave £1,850 to the Council for Community Service to put together a directory of agencies which can support people after rape or sexual assault.
• Tyne Tees gave £13,000 to Tyneside Women's Employment and Training Centre for a training scheme to help women to return to work, and £500 to the Derwent Disabled Club for a ribber and linker for their knitting machine.
• Anglia TV gave £500 to the SHARP Single Homeless and Roofless Project to set up a soup kitchen and £1,000 to the British Diabetic Association for a retinal eye screening camera.
• Border TV gave the Governors

Grove Special School £6,000 to provide a soft play area for their children and £2,500 to the Bendrigg Trust to buy a special climbing tower for children with disabilities.
• Central TV gave the WRVS £500 to provide clothes for the disadvantaged and £500 to the Dudley branch of Arthritis Care for photocopying costs of their newsletter.
• Channel TV gave Shelter £10,000 to expand their service to the homeless.
• Grampian TV gave £2,000 to Grampian Regional Special Olympics to fund a winter olympics for disabled children.
• HTV Wales gave £5,000 to Wallich Clifford Community to convert their ground floor and make it wheelchair accessible and £350 to the Brownies in Glyncoch to buy uniforms for their disadvantaged girls.
• HTV West gave £400 to the Retinitis Pigmentosa Society to buy a reading aid for the visually impaired and £3,000 to the Stoke Park Hospital Special Needs Unit towards the cost of installing a 'light stimulation room'.
• Thames and LWT gave the Soldiers' Sailors' and Airmen's Families Association £1,500 to celebrate the 106th birthday of an ex-serviceman and their own anniversary which fell on the same day.
• Ulster TV gave the Association for Spina Bifida and Hydrocephalus £1,000 to buy lightweight wheelchairs and over £7,000 to the Ulster Cancer Foundation for their TASK project which aims to stop teenagers smoking.

In 1992, some of the organisations to benefit from grants made by the Independent Broadcasting Telethon Trust nationally include: the Spinal Injuries Association, Sand Schizophrenia, Women's Aid Federation, the National Children's Home, Relate, Friedrich's Ataxia Group, RNIB, the Brittle Bones Society, the National Council for One Parent Families, the Motor Neurone Disease Association, Age Concern, the Pre-School Playgroups Association and Cot Death Research.

Anne-Marie Sapsted

NSPCC CHILDREN'S ROYAL VARIETY PERFORMANCE

Some of Britain's best-loved television stars took to the stage of London's Dominion Theatre on Spring Bank Holiday Monday to raise funds for the NSPCC. Daniela Soave reviews the event

When comedian Rod Hull hit upon the idea of initiating a children's version of the Royal Variety Performance 14 years ago, little did he realise what an impact it would have. After the success of the first show, which raised £55,000, it was decided to make the occasion an annual event and it is now a firm favourite with children and adults alike.

Like its older relation, The Children's Royal Variety Performance is not only entertaining, but provides much-needed cash for a deserving charity – in this case, the National Society for the Prevention of Cruelty to Children.

The 1992 show is notable because it marked a departure in format from the familiar style of a variety performance. This was entirely due to the ingenuity of writer and producer Tudor Davies, who stepped into the breach when regular producer Kevin Bishop had prior commitments. With a cast that included Frank Bruno, Matthew Kelly, Pauline Quirke, Linda Robson, Sylvester McCoy, Brian Conley, Michaela Strachan, Lisa Maxwell, Edd the Duck, Barbara Windsor, Andi Peters, Rosemarie Ford, Bernard Cribbins, Royal Ballet dancer Stephen Jefferies and pop groups Right Said Fred and Take That, Davies decided to create a script that would employ the best of their talents, and so the hard work began.

'I had about four months to conceive the show, write it and produce it,' he explains. 'It was quite a departure because it had a story and so was a break from tradition. It was a magical, musical journey which tried to capture children's imaginations. I wanted something that was intelligent and brave and challenging, something that children would find entertaining.'

Instead of a series of unrelated

The cast of the Children's Royal Variety Show

acts, the action begins with an explosion, when a wizard, played by Sylvester McCoy, appears and conjures up a young boy, whom he sends into a fantasy world in search of a story to tell. Thus Davies was able to weave in characters such as Hans Christian Andersen, Thumbelina and the Ugly Duckling.

'I am against sitting children down in front of the television with *Masters of the Universe*.' says Davies. 'I wanted to convey the magic of books and I am glad to say it worked, because I had wonderful reactions from kids and adults alike. The show succeeded because it had elements of theatre and pantomime, which worked well given its theme.'

The task of producing such a complex format was more difficult for Davies and the performers alike. Normally, rehearsals concentrate on ensuring the smooth running of the show because the individual performers are already familiar with their repertoire. With Tudor Davies's concept, however, the acts had

Pauline Quirke as an unlikely ballerina

to become involved at a much earlier stage because they had lines to memorise and scenes to learn.

'I expected a lot more of people but they were delighted to be doing something different, instead of just being wheeled on and off,' he says. 'I don't wish to name names but after the event I had a lot of letters from performers who hadn't been able to donate their time, saying they wished they'd done it, if only they'd known it was going to be different.

'It was a double-edged sword because it was hard to hook people but they did the job absolutely beautifully. Matthew Kelly, as narrator, was wonderful. He really held it together on stage.'

For the NSPCC, organisation for the 1992 event began as soon as the curtains had closed on the 1991 show. For the past five years, Celia Joseph has been involved in the administrative side, looking for the theatre in which to stage the event, liaising with the BBC, putting together the committee and selling advertising. While the BBC looks after the production and woos celebrities, it is up to Celia and her team to generate as much income as possible through donations, sponsorships, souvenir brochures, advertising and ticket sales, so that the event achieves its potential.

'The 1992 show raised £180,000 all told,' she says. 'Vauxhall Motors of Luton gave a generous sponsorship fee, which we plough into the child protection scheme in Luton, and the rest of the money raised goes to the London child protection branch.'

There is also the added revenue from video sales and the 1992 edition should run and run because of its timeless storyline. It makes sense, because otherwise, as Tudor Davies says, 'We spend so much time and love on that one performance and then it's over.'

For Davies, all the hard work that went into creating the 1992 performance was well and truly worth it. As well as enthralling viewers and raising funds, it was a creative gift for him. 'To be handed the Children's Royal Variety Show and be told I could do what I liked with it was a dream come true.'

Daniela Soave

CHILDREN IN NEED

Each year the BBC's annual fund-raiser for children's charities raises millions of pounds for distribution to a wide range of worthy causes. Anne-Marie Sapsted reports on some of the events which made up this year's *Children in Need* appeal and finds out where past funds have been directed

BBC Photograph Library

Few people realise it, but the BBC's *Children in Need* appeal is not a recent phenomenon. It is in fact 65 years old. The first appeal was broadcast on Christmas Day 1927 and was billed in *Radio Times* as 'The BBC Christmas Fund for Children'. That first radio broadcast lasted five minutes and raised £1,143. Converted into presents or holidays, the money helped a variety of underprivileged and disabled children.

Despite the War, the appeal carried on, was popular and growing slowly but surely more successful. In 1951 the appeal became known as 'Children in Need of Help' and when *Children's Hour* was dropped, it became part of the BBC's regular *Week's Good Cause* series. In 1955 came its first television slot. Between 1927 and 1979, £630,898 was raised, and then in 1980 the first full-scale TV appeal was launched with Terry Wogan, Sue Lawley and Esther

Rantzen. More than £1 million was raised in an evening...and the rest is history. By 1991 it had become the UK's first broadcast appeal to raise more than £100 million since its inception.

Though 1992's total of just over £11¹/₂ million was well down on more than £17 million raised on the night the previous year, Terry Wogan spoke for everyone when he said after the show: 'In such difficult economic times, this is a terrific figure, a tribute to the energy of thousands of fund-raisers and it just goes to show how generous the British public still is.'

Thousands of people, both young and old, all over the country have been involved over the years in fund-raising activities ranging from the sedate to the silly to the sensational. These have included hundreds of ideas, including cartwheel contests, custard pie throwing, snail racing, jelly bathing, onion peeling, head shaving, bedroom tidying, silences, yodelling, and even a zombie lookalike competition.

One for All and All for One

The *Children in Need* appeal is unique in the BBC's calendar, according to executive producer Nick Handel, in that it's 'all hands to the pump', bringing together all the regional and network television and radio stations into one huge BBC show. The production involves hundreds of technicians all over the UK and is at least as complicated, if not more so, as General Election coverage. From the Corporation's point of view it is also a day on which the doors are thrown open at broadcasting premises all over the country, so that the public can not only come and support the appeal, but watch the BBC at work.

'This year, we really were pushing technology to its limits,' remembers Nick Handel. 'It was certainly the most adventurous technologically. We tried to involve all the 13 regions by handing over to them every hour.' One of the most ambitious events was a trans-UK jazz band performing live. With an orchestra in London and singer Marian Montgomery, each of the regions had a celebrated musician ready to perform. It went out live and was the first time the group had played together.

But there was the occasional technical hitch. Television Centre lost one and a half hours' rehearsal time in the afternoon because of a power cut. Then while Sue Cook was interviewing Right Said Fred in the studio later that evening, the lights went out again. For about a minute, the picture showed TV

Richard Fairbrass of Right Said Fred meets Pudsey Bear

Centre bathed in lights while Sue gamely struggled on with her interview, then the working lights were restored and the singer's bald head could be dimly seen through the gloom. It prompted Terry Wogan to comment that it was the best interview he'd ever seen in the dark on live television!

Other feats of technical wizardry included a region against region *It's a Knockout* competition and the Pudsey Bear Olympics where region battled against region for the Pudsey Bear Olympic Trophy in events like the long-distance karaoke competition where Wales and Northern Ireland fielded their best Cliff Richard and Elvis impersonators.

Radio Times Running for Fun

This year's appeal got off to an early and very active start with the *Radio*

Times Run. It began in Manchester at the beginning of November and was started by Sebastian Coe, one of the world's greatest-ever middle distance runners, now an MP. He launched Steve Cram, still the world mile record-holder, and a team of top British athletes on a relay which took them to all parts of the country. The run finished on *Children in Need* night at Television Centre with Linford Christie, Britain's Olympic gold medallist running the last leg. Wherever it stopped Steve Cram invited the public to pay £1 and run a mile with him. No-one was counting the seconds or even the minutes, walking was allowed and it was the taking part which was the most important thing.

Runners were joined along the

Steve Cram, who took part in the *Radio Times* Run, with the *Children in Need* presenters

way by Sally Gunnell, Britain's 400m hurdles Olympic gold medallist, Yvonne Murray, European 3,000m champion, Steve Backley, world javelin record-holder, Kriss Akabusi, Olympic 400m hurdles bronze medallist and Peter Elliott, Seoul Olympics 1500m silver medallist. Sharing the burden of running 60 miles a day with Steve Cram was a team of six other national and international athletes including

Tanni Grey, winner of four gold medals at the recent Paralympic Games in Barcelona. The round-UK relay covered Scotland, Northern Ireland, Wales, Cornwall, the Midlands, and all BBC local regions, which each staged its own Fun Run.

Radio Plays its Part

Radio 1 offered listeners the chance to bid for dinner with Right Said Fred. Radio 2 produced Pudsey Bear Paw Print Kits and offered a prize for the best display, with Debbie Greenwood touring the country looking at entries. Radio 3 invited five composers to write a song which was premiered in front of a live audience. The song scores were auctioned for the appeal. Radio 4 again offered listeners the chance to contribute to *Thought for the Day,* and Radio Drama directors moved to the other side of the microphone to join actress Anna Massey in a murder mystery *The Dead Room.* Radio 5 had daily coverage of the *Radio Times* Run and regular news of the Fast Forward Discos.

Around the Regions

Pebble Mill, home of the BBC in the West Midlands became a pirates' den for the day. East Midlands coverage came from one of Nottinghamshire's newest attractions 'The World of Robin Hood' on the edge of Sherwood Forest.

The Eastern Counties show came from Norwich's newly re-opened Theatre Royal with a host of stars. In the Northeast, there was full coverage of the Great North Toddle, an event designed for under-fives and their families.

Welsh viewers were encouraged to make home videos and submit them with the best shown on the night. There was a sponsored canoe race and an auctioning of a specially carved 3ft 6in Welsh love spoon.

Northern Irish viewers had their own special brand of entertainment and were treated to the appearance of a new commentator, Linda Martin, winner of 1992's Eurovision Song Contest. BBC South had the spectacular setting of *HMS Victory* in Portsmouth, with the Royal

Marines band, and the Hampshire Fire Brigade challenged the cast of *London's Burning* to a dramatic fire-fighting competition.

BBC West meanwhile went out and about round the pubs and clubs, offices and playing fields to watch viewers making money for the appeal. In Scotland, viewers were treated to displays by the Royal Scottish Orchestra Junior Chorus, the Dance School of Scotland and Strathclyde Youth Orchestra Jazz Sextet, and a water ski show and Pudsey Bear lookalike competition from Loch Lomond.

It Was All Right on the Night

Highlights of the main show included the surprise appearance of the former Prime Minister Lady Thatcher as mystery guest in a *What's My Line?* competition between BBC regions. With her voice distorted for the game and in response to questions, she denied being a sex symbol, but admitted to being a little overweight. This brought suggestions that she might be Cyril Smith, Lords Healey or Howe or even Norman Lamont. Later she admitted in conversation with Terry Wogan that life in the Lords was quiet and lacking in sparkle compared to the House of Commons, and that despite her grand title she preferred being known as plain Maggie.

A host of celebrities turned out. Frank Bruno challenged Noel Edmonds to 'grab a grand' and there were appearances by the cast of *Birds of a Feather* and *Casualty*. The stars of the West End show *Five Guys Named Mo* opened cabaret hour, which also included the cast of the new West End show, *Annie Get Your Gun*. But the undoubted stars of the evening were a team of news presenters led by Peter Snow of General Election swingometer fame in their version of *King of the Swingers* from *The Jungle Book*. John Cole, Nicholas Witchell, Michael Buerk and Jill Dando provided a creditable backing group.

Children of Courage and Achievement

In one of the highlights of the programme, Esther Rantzen and Gavin Campbell celebrated the achievements of some special youngsters.

• Paul Crummy from Northern Ireland, a 12-year-old born with a congenital abnormality affecting his lower limbs which led to amputation of both feet. After the operation Paul won a fund-raising award for his sponsored walk which raised nearly £3,000 for a Belfast hospital.

• Martina Williams from Birmingham, a courageous 12-year-old who fought off a dog which attacked her and her grandmother and who has since joined a scheme to help children who have been bitten by dogs to overcome their fears.

• Young conservationist Caroline Fawcett from Lincolnshire who at 12 has created and paid for a nine-acre nature reserve on her parents' smallholding which is open to the public (with access for the disabled) – she also gives talks and slide-shows.

• Three Doncaster crime-busters, Lisa Telford aged nine, Marie Telford and Mark Noble, both 11, who tracked a masked, armed robber to his home, called police and gave evidence in court which led to his conviction.

• Charlotte Slater, an 11-year-old from Lancashire who after undergoing pioneering surgery to remove a tumour from behind her nose has discovered a talent for gymnastics.

Where Does the Money Go?

Last year, the *Children in Need* appeal had more than 9,000 requests for a share in the total of over £20 million which was finally raised. Each appeal was carefully considered and more than 5,500 grants were made following the recommendations of nine regional advisory committees.

The money has gone to a wide range of projects, including organisations helping to combat child abuse, counselling for families affected by Aids/HIV and conductive education for children with cerebral palsy. Administration costs are paid for out of the interest earned on donations.

One of the largest grants went to the Friends for the Young Deaf, the national charity which is actively managed by deaf people. They have received £260,870 spread over three years to run an innovative programme of recreational and educational activities all over the country to bring together hearing and hard-of-hearing children.

One of the smallest grants went to the Inkberrow Village Bowling Club, near Worcester, where £100 was given to buy a set of bowling woods for a teenager with muscular dystrophy.

Other grants included the following:

• Craigavon Integrated Play in County Armagh, Northern Ireland, was awarded £15,000 to build a 'Starship Enterprise' outdoor play module for disabled and able-bodied children.

• The Mix in Finchley, London, which has a performing arts project called 'Safe Places' exploring issues related to bullying and child abuse, received £1,640.

• The British Ski Club for the Disabled in Yeovil, Somerset, received £5,600 to enable children with disabilities to enjoy the thrill of skiing with their able-bodied friends.

• The Explorers Parent Resource Centre in Bristol received £245 to purchase a Rompa portable 'bubble' unit which produces an ever-changing stream of multi-coloured bubbles in order to stimulate residual sight in children with partial or very little sight.

• The Clarendon Shelter in Londonderry provides refuge for women and children fleeing domestic violence and received £1,900 to provide outings and toys for children at the shelter.

• The Rainbow Trust in Leatherhead, Surrey, which offers support to families whose children have life-threatening or terminal illnesses, received £17,000 towards the cost of a mobile domiciliary worker.

• The Scottish Child and Family Alliance in Edinburgh was awarded £137,478 to pioneer development work which aims to improve services for children and families in Scotland affected by Aids/HIV.

• The Somali Bridging Project in Cardiff received £166,418 over three years to pay for staff to help refugee children from war-torn Somalia to adjust to life in Britain.

Anne-Marie Sapsted

Special Features

In this chapter, the old meets the new – as BBC Radio celebrated its 70th birthday, satellite TV introduced us to new channels and a wider range of programmes, while dramatically increasing its audience. Broadcaster Robert Robinson recalls the golden years of the wireless, and BBC Radio's Media Correspondent Torin Douglas reports on satellite TV.

Douglas also reviews the outcome of the ITV franchises battle, and the programmes viewers can expect from the new channels.

Radio Times readers can recall their favourite covers of the year, as the magazine's editor Nicholas Brett selects his own Top Ten.

Special Features

70 YEARS OF BBC RADIO

Broadcaster Robert Robinson recalls the golden years of the wireless, 70 years after the first sounds of BBC Radio came crackling over the airwaves

I've got this terrible habit of being flippant just to cheer things up, and when the girl reporter said, 'You seem to do a lot of stuff for the BBC' I replied, 'Oh, mustn't let poor Nelly starve', and she said solemnly, 'Is Nelly the name of your wife?' So I ought to have known better than to try it again when she said, 'How long have you been broadcasting?' and I replied, 'Must have been in short trousers when I started'. This time she said – even more solemnly – 'Were you a child star?'

Never learn, do you, I said to myself as I put the phone down. Bantering with journalists gets you exactly what you deserve – you come out on the page sounding like one of those talking litter-bins that's been wired up wrong. But while I was tut-tutting something suddenly came to me.

The journalist was closer to the truth than I'd given her credit for. I *was* a child star, well, as near as dammit, because during the war when they read the news the announcers would tell you their names before they began – something to do with letting you know the studio hadn't been overrun by the enemy, since it was believed no Kraut would be so ill-bred as to pretend he was Alvar Lidell. And from being just anonymous voices the announcers became very famous, and lo and behold one of

ITMA – Tommy Handley, Sydney Keith, Horace Percival and Jack Train in November 1942

The BBC recording car visits the 43rd (Wessex) Division in Germany in August 1945

Dick Barton Special Agent performed by Noel Johnson, Alex McCrindle and John Mann in 1946

them would begin, 'Here is the news, and this is Robert Robinson reading it'.

Well, actually, as a schoolboy I didn't much care for being impersonated in this way, since the announcers sounded like very pure men who had started life as Freddie Bartholomew, a child actor of nauseous rectitude, growing up into middle-aged chaps with fat bottoms who wore blazers and never used swear words (this awful prejudice must have lingered on in my mind, for when I came to write a detective novel I called the butler Dimbleby).

The only time The Wireless really made me famous was when my birthday was read out on *Children's Hour* and all of us listening at the party were so awestruck by the mere fact of someone ordinary being *actually mentioned* on The Wireless that those who weren't being sick in the fireplace jumped on to the table and skidded about in the green jellies. The Wireless was a fantasy world that existed in another universe behind the fretwork on your Philco. It was inhabited by men and women whose genteel enunciation never slipped – Commander King Hall, Aunt Elizabeth, Stuart Hibberd, Professor

Joad, never came out quite like anyone on your side of the wireless set. Voices that sounded other than formidably middle-class were, you felt, allowed out under strict licence: Mr Middleton, the original

gardening expert, was plainly a respectable member of the lower orders who had been permitted half a day off to talk about manure. 'A bucketful here and a bucketful there', he would moo gloomily, 'does the world of good'. And then you imagined him returning to Bagfox Grange on his cheap-day ticket, slipping through the green baize door into the servants' hall.

The other-worldliness of The Wireless was reinforced by the names of the places the voices came from. Of course, all the English ones originated from somewhere referred to as The Studio, the name suggesting a half-timbered bungalow within easy reach of Box Hill. But there were other places with names like Kalundborg, Hilversum, Helsingfors, which had no known location except their position on the dial – as mad to think of visiting such mythical outposts of The Wireless as of taking a jaunt to Erewhon or Atlantis. In this strange dimension, unrehearsed spontaneous behaviour was never expected, and when – just very occasionally – the *Children's Hour* actors were overcome with mirth, my mother would say, in a tone that combined plain disbelief with guilty delight, 'Good-

Jean Metcalfe and Cliff Michelmore, presenters of the Sunday two-way *Family Favourites* programme, which was broadcast jointly by the BBC and the British Forces Network from London and Hamburg

ness, they're actually laughing in The Studio!'

Oh, how very different from the workaday world of Radio, where, in later years, old Timpson and I would bang away at the *Today* typewriters, communicating in those surly grunts that earned us our nickname the Brothers Grim. A matter-of-fact world, where I endlessly consider how the contestants survive the smelly back quarters of the studio where we generate *Brain of Britain*. Or wonder why, when I'm recording a programme, I often hear a noise overhead as of a bunch of mutinous nuns walling up their Mother Superior.

Sometimes when I've been nipping down the bleak stone staircase to the sub-basement in Broadcasting House to get to grips with *Ad Lib* or *Stop the Week* I wonder if there might yet be an unexcavated office somewhere in the building where ladies in suede bootees are still getting their sweets on 'points', and Stuart Hibberd is instructing a new announcer called Mary Malcolm (as indeed she once told me he did) on the correct way of

Henry Hall's Guest Night with Gracie Fields in October 1950

signing off at the end of the day. 'You say "Goodnight", then you pause, and then you say "Goodnight" again.' 'But why the pause,' asked Mary, 'and then the second "Goodnight"?' Hibberd looked complacently at her. 'To allow the listeners to say "Goodnight" to *you*.'

Radio is here and now. But The Wireless was somewhere else.

Robert Robinson

RADIO MILESTONES
1922-1992

14 November 1922
The first daily BBC transmissions from 2LO in the Strand

28 September 1923
The first *Radio Times* is published. Newspapers fear competition from radio news and say they should be paid to carry radio programming information because it isn't interesting

1 January 1927
JCW Reith is the Director General as the BBC is established by Royal Charter for ten years

Brian Johnston demonstrates the BBC's portable outside broadcast amplifying equipment in 1959

12 March 1932
The first broadcast from Broadcasting House is by Henry Hall and the BBC Dance Orchestra

19 December 1932
The Empire Service is inaugurated, broadcasting from Daventry on short wave. It is later to be renamed the World Service

1 September 1939
Two days before war is declared, the Home Service replaces national and regional programmes

18 June 1940
Churchill's 'This was their finest hour', broadcast from a fortified Broadcasting House – itself a landmark and an enemy target

29 July 1945
The Light Programme begins and regional broadcasting resumes

29 September 1946
The Third Programme begins, including the first performance of Britten's *Festival Overture*

2 May 1955
The first VHF transmitting station

opens, at Wrotham, providing Home, Light and Third programmes to the south-east

30 September 1967
Radio 1 arrives in response to the 'pirates'. Tony Blackburn, aged 24, is the first DJ on the new network. Existing networks are renamed Radios 2, 3 and 4

8 November 1967
Radio Leicester opens as the first BBC Local Radio station

3 April 1978
Regular House of Commons broadcasts begin

27 January 1979
Radio 2 becomes the first UK network to offer 24-hour broadcasting

27 August 1990
Bruno Brookes hosts the first show on Radio 5. Using the old mediumwave frequency of Radio 2, it has a remit for sporting and young people's programming

21 January 1992
Radio Berkshire joins the local network

Ten O'Clock, the news programme, which went out on the BBC Home Service. Foreground (from left): Roy Jenkins MP, David Price MP and Hardiman Scott (political correspondent). Background (from left): Lord Lindgren, Richard Baker (presenter) and Douglas Smith (newsreader)

BBC Photograph Library

ITV FRANCHISES

Following the changes in ITV franchises which took effect on 1 January 1993, BBC Radio's Media Correspondent Torin Douglas, reports on what viewers can expect from the new channels

For viewers in the southern half of England, the first few days of January 1993 must have come as something of a shock. Instead of the familiar presenters and local programmes of Thames, TVS and Television South West, they were confronted by three newcomers – Carlton, Meridian and Westcountry.

Elsewhere in Britain, the surprise was confined to breakfast time, where viewers found TV-am replaced by GMTV, and the David Frost Sunday morning programme transplanted to BBC1.

But where was *This Week*, a fixture in the ITV network for the best part of 35 years? What had happened to the Sunday evening religious programmes, like *Highway*, replaced by blockbuster movies? And why had they mucked about with *News at Ten*?

The first day of January saw the start of a new era in commercial television. Not just a few new ITV companies – that had happened before, in 1968 (when Thames, LWT, Yorkshire and others began life) and in 1972-3 (which saw the arrival of Central, TVS, TSW and TV-am). This time, the whole system was changing, courtesy of Mrs Thatcher and the 1990 Broadcasting Act, which was designed to bring more competition and choice into commercial television.

The 1993 ITV companies won their licences not because they were judged the most likely to offer the best service to viewers but on the basis they had offered the most money to the Government. In some cases, that wasn't very much. Central Television and Scottish TV both deduced they had no challengers and bid just £2,000 a year. At the other end of the scale, GMTV and Carlton both bid over £40 million a year to see off TV-am and Thames.

There were exceptions. In some cases the largest bid had been set aside, because the Independent Television Commission was not satisfied with a group's programme or business plans. LWT and Granada were saved because their challengers failed to pass the ITC's quality hurdle.

This also proved the downfall of TVS and TSW. They were the highest bidders in their areas, and their programmes naturally passed the quality test. But the ITC and its advisers judged their business plans unsound – in effect, they had bid too much. TSW challenged the decision in the courts, all the way to the House of Lords. It lost.

In this blind auction of franchises, a company's track record counted for nothing, complained Richard Dunn, chief executive of Thames Television. Once the flagship of ITV, Thames had been responsible for some of the country's best and most popular programmes during its 25 years as the London contractor. Some of its programmes, like *This Week*, had lasted even longer, having been started by two of the original ITV companies, ABC and Rediffusion, which merged to form Thames in 1968.

As well as *This Week*, Thames was responsible for *The World at War, This is Your Life, Minder, The Sweeney, Rumpole of the Bailey, Hollywood, Edward & Mrs Simpson, The Naked Civil Servant*, Benny Hill, Tommy Cooper and countless top-rating situation comedies. Jeremy Isaacs, its former programme director who later became the first chief executive of

Channel 4 and then general director of the Royal Opera House, said it had been harshly treated. 'Thames was a great television company – I use the word advisedly – and it will be missed.'

If fewer tears were shed at the demise of the three other stations, it was because their record stretched back only ten years, having won their positions on the network in the last franchise race. Two – TVS and TSW – had inflicted similar defeats (and redundancies) on their predecessors, Southern and Westward, while TV-am, as the first breakfast station, had been forced into wholesale management and programme changes before achieving profitability.

own programmes, or swapped them for those made by other ITV companies, the new licence-holders like Carlton and Meridian have been set up as 'publisher-broadcasters', commissioning programmes from independent producers rather than making them in-house. This means they need far fewer staff and much smaller premises. The huge, purpose-built studios which the Independent Broadcasting Authority demanded of ITV companies at the start of the 80s are no longer needed in the 90s.

Programme-making techniques have changed in the last ten years. The power of the production unions has been broken – as it has in Fleet Street – and most TV drama

Leo McKern as Rumpole

Minder, one of Thames TV's most popular programmes

To the individuals whose jobs were lost as a result of their companies' loss of franchise – whether after 25 years, or ten or less – the shock was considerable. In most cases, the prospect of finding other, similar posts was slim. In previous franchise changes, the incoming company had tended to offer jobs to most of its predecessor's employees, leaving only the management in need of new posts. This time it was not so cosy.

Unlike the ITV companies of the past, which made virtually all their

can be shot on location, or in small-scale studios hired by the day or week. The programme 'factories' of yesteryear – though chock full of expensive, high quality equipment – are no longer the most efficient way of producing television.

Dozens of independent production companies have become established, nurtured by Channel 4, making highly regarded programmes more cheaply than the broadcasters themselves. And if the BBC and ITV companies had not planned to put more of their

Carlton TV / John Brown

Head over Heels – Sally Geoghegan as Catherine and Kathy Kiera Clarke as Bernadette

production into this independent sector, they suddenly found themselves required to do so by the government.

During the negotiations over the Broadcasting Bill, the Home Office decreed that a quarter of all production on ITV and BBC Television was to be made by independent producers. Mrs Thatcher, in a famous phrase, had described ITV as 'the last bastion of restrictive practices' and the independent producers – and the franchise auction – were to be the weapons with which it would be stormed.

Thus it wasn't only the losing companies in the franchise battle which had to suffer job losses. Several of the companies that won the new licences only did so by making heavy cuts in staff, both before putting in their bids and since. LWT, Granada, Yorkshire, Tyne Tees, HTV and others have jointly shed hundreds of staff as part of radical restructuring programmes to release money for their multi-million pound-bids. But those cuts are small compared with those at Thames, which had to cut its workforce from 1,600 to 140 as a result of losing its broadcasting licence.

Thames is not going out of business, and will continue to make programmes, becoming Britain's largest independent producer. Viewers outside London may not

have noticed Thames's absence – particularly since ITV no longer starts each programme with the logo and identity tune of the company which made it. Some of its most popular series are still being made for ITV, including *The Bill*, which is now being shown three times a week, *This is Your Life*, *Minder* and *Mr Bean*.

But there is no place for *This Week* or the holiday programme *Wish You Were Here* or dozens of other series that Thames made each year.

Instead, the new network controllers who run ITV's national programme output are looking to the new ITV licence-holders (all of whom made extravagant promises in their franchise applications) and to a wide range of independent producers for the programmes that will make up the national peak-time schedule.

Carlton and Meridian both have several networked series in the ITV line-up for the first few months of 1993. Carlton has commissioned three new drama series, including *Head Over Heels*, set in the rock'n' roll era of 50s London; a seven-part factual series on sex called *The Good Sex Guide*; and *Comedy Playhouse*, featuring eight separate half-hour situation comedies, any of which may be turned into a series later in the year.

Meridian has commissioned several comedy shows from one of its shareholders, SelecTV, which makes *Lovejoy* and *Birds of a Feather*. Michael Palin and Tracey Ullman are starring in *A Class Act* and the writers Dick Clement and Ian La Frenais, who created *Porridge* and *Auf Wiedersehen Pet*, have produced a comedy drama series called *Full Stretch*.

But it is in their regional output that the new ITV companies have been most ambitious. In London, Carlton has developed a close relationship with the company which takes over the franchise at weekends, LWT. Despite competing head-on for advertising revenue (Thames and LWT were hardly on speaking terms), the two London licence-holders are co-operating in areas where they believe competition would be wasteful and against the viewers' interests.

They have set up a joint news company, London News Network, to provide ITV's first seven-days-a-week news service for the capital. Its flagship is an hour-long programme *London Tonight*, fronted by the former ITN newscaster Alastair Stewart. It can take live reports from all over the region, including traffic reports using the Metropolitan Police's own roadside cameras.

Meridian's licence application

A Class Act – Michael Palin and Tracey Ullman

SelecTV / Meridian Broadcasting

The cast of *Full Stretch*

was equally ambitious in terms of regional news. Whereas its predecessor TVS had two separate regional news operations, one based in Southampton, the other in Maidstone, Meridian has three. A news centre opened in Newbury covers the northern part of the region, which had been relatively neglected before. Meridian is also offering ten new regional community and documentary series.

Westcountry is using new technology to cover its region more effectively than before by setting up seven studios in key centres like Penzance, Truro and Exeter, connected by microwave links to its new centre in Plymouth. Previously, a story in Penzance would have had to be shot by 2.30pm to get on the evening news programme. Now, instead of sending the tape back by road, it can be transmitted to Plymouth instantly.

Delays caused by TSW's court battle meant the new studios were not all in operation from the start, but the ITC has said that like all the licence-holders, Westcountry will be held to its promises.

For viewers outside these three areas there has been relatively little change. Even at breakfast time, the new licence-holder GMTV has done as much as it can to make TV-am

viewers feel comfortable with its programmes, retaining some of its predecessor's presenters and a similar style and mix of programmes, complete with pastel-coloured sofas.

In peak-time, most of the familiar programmes are still there. Bulwarks of the schedule such as *Coronation Street* and *The Bill* are firmly in place. So are the detective dramas – *Inspector Morse, Poirot*, Ruth Rendell crime thrillers, *Maigret* and the latest, *A Touch of Frost* – along with *The Darling Buds of May* and light entertainment series such as *Blind Date* and the Beadle shows. In news and current affairs, *World In Action* remains on Monday nights and *News at Ten* continues 'at ten', despite a debate over whether it should be moved, so movies can be screened from 9pm to 11pm without interruption.

But signs of change can be detected. ITN altered the format of *News at Ten* just before Christmas, in an attempt to make it more accessible and popular. Some ITV companies had voiced the belief that all programmes in peak-time – including news and current affairs – would have to command audiences of at least seven million, and the ITN changes were seen as an attempt to boost audiences. Initially

the new look seemed unsuccessful. But the ratings for news are influenced by the popularity of the programmes around them and the impact of the changes can only be judged over time.

The same is true of the fundamental questions now hanging over ITV – will there be sufficient money to pay for the big audience-pulling series and will 'minority' programmes such as those in the field of documentaries, arts and children's series keep their traditional slots and budgets? Under the Broadcasting Act, the ITC no longer has the power to dictate the scheduling of particular types of programme. The traditional 'God slot' has been replaced by movies on Sunday evenings – though *Highway* will be back later in the year – and *This Week*'s successors in current affairs have been placed at 7.30pm on Thursdays, head-to-head against *EastEnders*.

Perhaps the biggest concern lies in the split between 'rich' and 'poor' ITV companies. This is no longer just a question of size. Some licence-holders like Yorkshire, Carlton and Meridian have bid very large sums – over £35 million a year – to the Treasury. Others like LWT and Granada bid low (£8-£9 million) and some (Central and Scottish) fantastically low (£2,000). All made their bids when it seemed advertising revenue would be more buoyant than it has proved and, with increased competition from Channel 4 and the satellite companies, such advertising as there is must be spread more widely and thinly.

The ITV companies may find it hard to agree how much to spend on the all-important network programmes. Some may want to cut the programme budget so they can meet their obligations to the Treasury and the ITC. In time, there could be mergers and takeovers, with large European media companies watching to see which licence-holders are vulnerable.

The full impact of the changes will not be seen for several years. Meanwhile, viewers must hope ITV's programmes live up to its promises.

Torin Douglas

MY TOP TEN COVERS

How do you choose your ten favourite *Radio Times* covers of 1992 when every one was special? It's rather like a father – albeit an extremely fertile one – being asked to judge his own babies in a beauty contest.

Every cover was thoughtfully conceived. The pregnancy was invariably long and complicated and in many cases the birth was by forceps. But the result was more than 50 bonny babies – every one different yet all bearing a striking family resemblance.

Here goes with my ten and the stories behind each of them.

Nicholas Brett
Editor of *Radio Times*

Desert Island Discs
25 January 1992
Desert Island Discs' 50th birthday was the first of many anniversaries in 1992 for *Radio Times*. Royal photographer Terry O'Neill took the snap, Armani provided the suit, and Sue Lawley played the castaway by selecting her eight favourite records. Her book was Elizabeth David's *French Provincial Cooking* – and her luxury item? An iron and ironing board for starched white sheets.

Royal Souvenir Issue
1 February 1992
There's a saying in journalism 'put a royal on the cover and put on sales'. We marked the 40th anniversary of Her Majesty The Queen's accession to the throne with a souvenir issue, choosing Dorothy Wilding's official portrait of the time as our cover image. It sold out – and outsold every other issue of *Radio Times* in 1992 except Christmas.

The General Election
4 April 1992

1992 was election year and *Radio Times* produced the scoop of the night. We got wind of the return of the swingometer, out of mothballs for the first time since 1979. Peter Snow agreed to reveal the mysterious workings of the new, improved monster and show it off on our cover. He said later of that cover: 'It makes me look even more mad than I actually am.'

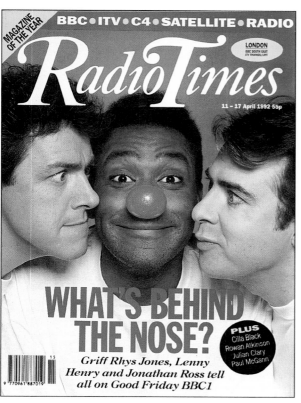

Comic Relief
11 April 1992

In 1991 *Radio Times* and its readers gave £1 million to Comic Relief and scooped up the 'Cover of the Year Award' for our Lenny Henry/Red Nose cover. So how do you top that? We asked Terry O'Neill to repeat his 91 triumph but this time to include Griff Rhys Jones and Jonathan Ross in the frame as well. Two nil!

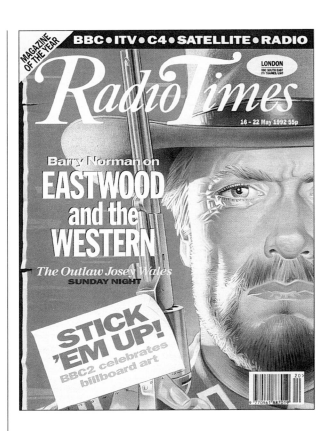

Clint Eastwood
16 May 1992
When BBC2 decided to become a patron of the arts with its national Billboard Project, it set *Radio Times* one of its toughest challenges of the year. That is until our art director Mike Clowes stepped in and dreamt up our 'Stick 'Em Up' poster-cum-cover of Clint Eastwood. It was the first of two splendid covers in 92 for top illustrator Mick Brownfield.

Paul McCartney
13 June 1992
Another anniversary – this time Paul McCartney's 50th birthday. Paul's 50? It hardly seemed possible. We felt another souvenir issue coming on. Harry Goodwin's stunning 1962, black-and-white portrait provided the perfect cover and produced one of the nicest thank-you letters we've ever received – signed Paul, aged 49 and a bit at the time of writing!

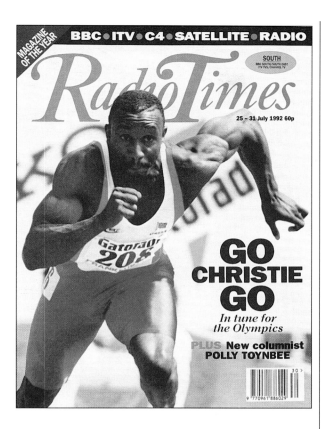

The Olympics
25 July 1992
At last! 1992 was the year we laid to rest the ancient curse of the *Radio Times* sporting cover – put a sports star on the cover and almost to a man or woman they'd break a leg, take a dive, or end up as sick as a parrot. Well, with Linford Christie we struck gold. Our special Olympics supplement was a winner with readers, too – the perfect armchair guide to Barcelona.

Star Trek
15 August 1992
The summer's traditionally when magazine sales take a dive – everyone's on holiday and there's not a lot new to watch on television. So, in our hour of need who better to turn to than 'Trekkies', those fanatical followers of all things Trek-like. It worked. Trekkies turned out in droves for our special celebration of one of the most popular television series ever made.

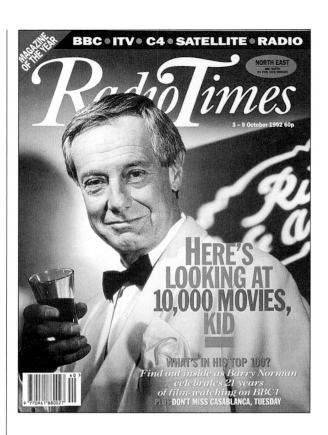

Barry Norman
3 October 1992
What are your hundred favourite movies of all time? It was party-game time when Britain's most famous movie buff and *Radio Times*'s resident film critic, Barry Norman, took the plunge and named his top hundred. We printed the list and dressed up Barry as Bogie for our super black-and-white (of course) *Casablanca* cover.

The Christmas Issue
19 December 1992
And so this is Christmas! The most important cover in the *Radio Times* year. I asked Mick Brownfield to come up with an illustration that captured the joy of Christmas, that would create a warm glow in everyone who beheld it. It would be our Christmas card to our readers. He did. Once again it was Britain's best-selling magazine of the year.

SATELLITE TELEVISION

Torin Douglas, BBC Radio's Media Correspondent, reports on the increasing popularity of satellite television. With the advent of new channels and a more extensive choice of programmes available, TV audiences are changing their viewing habits and demanding more than the four terrestrials can offer

For millions of television viewers, the thought of having only four channels to choose from is already just a memory. They are the ones with satellite or cable TV – and they are no longer a rarity. More than 8.5 million people live in homes with satellite TV – that's over 12 per cent of the population – and thousands of other viewers see the programmes in pubs and clubs.

The company providing cable in my part of west London offers no fewer than 30 channels. It seems more, because they call ITV, channel 44 and BBC1, 48. Six of them belong to BSkyB – Sky One, Sky Movies, The Movie Channel, Sky Movies Gold, Sky News and Sky Sports. There are two more sports channels, Eurosport and Screensport; another news channel, CNN; one for pop music, MTV; and the Children's Channel, which makes way for an arts channel, Performance, in the evening. These can all be received on satellite.

Others on cable include Bravo, which shows 'classic' old TV programmes and films; the Parliamentary Channel, which provides live coverage from the House of Commons and recordings of the House of Lords; the Adult Channel; Discovery, a documentaries channel; the Learning Channel; and nine foreign channels.

The newest satellite channel is UK Gold. Jointly owned by the BBC and Thames TV, it shows entertainment programmes from their extensive archives. They include soaps such as *EastEnders* and *Neighbours*; drama series like *Shoestring, Tenko* and *Miss Marple*; classic BBC serials, like *Vanity Fair*; and comedy series such as *To the Manor Born, Porridge* and *Bread*.

Penelope Keith and Peter Bowles in *To The Manor Born*

BBC Photograph Library

The arrival of UK Gold gave satellite a pre-Christmas boost. Earlier in the year, BSkyB's £304 million five-year deal with football's Premier League had given viewers a new reason for investing in a satellite dish – though a shortage of supplies in the crucial pre-season period meant sales did not rise as much as BSkyB had anticipated.

Later, spoiling tactics by Channel 4 – which bought the rights to the Italian league – and ITV – which signed up the other British league clubs to screen locally – meant the impact of the Sky Sports deal was reduced.

It was rescued for BSkyB as a commercial venture by the decision to charge viewers a subscription for Sky Sports, as it did for the movie channels. Even though most subscribers received an early-booking discount (paying £2.99 a month instead of £5.99), the income covered BSkyB's annual payments for the deal.

This is one of the keys to satellite television's success – it has tapped into a new source of revenue. The arrival of video showed that viewers were prepared to pay directly for their television programmes, renting or buying tapes – in contrast to the indirect forms of payment that fund the BBC (the licence fee) and ITV and Channel 4 (advertising). Satellite and cable TV companies have taken this principle a stage further by charging viewers a subscription for individual channels. Initially, many broadcasting experts doubted whether viewers would take to this new form of payment – after all, they complained about the licence fee, which was much lower than the annual subscription to the film channels. But it has turned out that satellite viewers *are* prepared to pay, producing a large income for BSkyB.

The sums are very straightforward. A million households paying £10 a month generate £120 million a year – and Sky's doing better than that. By last autumn, more than one and a half million households were paying to watch one or more of the movie channels, at a price of £11.99 for one or £16.99 for two.

The other key to satellite's success is its ability to offer almost limitless numbers of channels. No longer do TV stations need to be all things to all people, squeezing news, comedy, drama, sport, documentaries and music all onto one channel.

The terrestrial channels – BBC1, BBC2, ITV and Channel 4 – are likely to remain broadly based, but the satellite channels have enough airtime to specialise, serving specific groups rather than a mass audience.

During Wimbledon, the test matches, the British Open or the Olympics, the BBC may seem to devote itself to sport – but it does so knowing it aggravates a large section of the audience that has no interest in tennis, cricket, golf or athletics. It cannot cover every ball of an overseas test match, or each round of the major golf or tennis tournaments.

The satellite channels have no such limitations. Armchair sports fans know they can wallow in wall-to-wall coverage – though some would say Sky Sports stretches its coverage of the Premier League too thinly, beginning its Sunday afternoon programme a full two hours before kick-off. Its only problem – apart from acquiring the rights to these events – is the one experienced by the BBC's *Grandstand* on summer Saturdays, namely clashes between two or more top sports events.

There is, however, a problem for the viewers and the terrestrial TV channels, which cannot charge a subscription. Satellite television can now afford to buy exclusive rights to many of the top sports events, forcing viewers to buy a satellite dish and pay a subscription, or miss the live coverage. The Premier League is the first example, and it is too soon yet to judge how successful it will be. BSkyB's deal runs for five years and by 1997 many more homes will have acquired satellite television, boosting its subscription income still further.

The issue of whether viewers will be deprived of national sports events is a sensitive one. The Premier League would almost certainly not have reached agreement with Sky had not the BBC also been part of the deal, providing national coverage of match highlights in *Match of the Day* on Saturday nights.

ITV, which was outbid by Sky, accused the BBC of acting as 'Rupert Murdoch's poodle' in enabling the satellite company to win the rights. The BBC responded that it had pulled off an excellent deal for the licence-payer, who

Trevor Eve in *Shoestring*

could now watch all the Premier League goals and highlights of many of the best games.

Such arguments will grow as satellite's audience increases and more of the major sports bodies encourage the broadcasters to bid against each other for the rights to screen the top events.

Wimbledon is likely to prompt the most emotional debate, at some point during the 90s. In Germany, when Boris Becker and Steffi Graf won Wimbledon, most viewers could not watch, because the rights had been bought by a cable TV company. If Sky does the same in Britain, the Home Counties could rise in rebellion!

The sports bodies have learned a lesson, however. For all its comparative success, satellite still only reaches an eighth of the population and its audiences are measured in hundreds of thousands, not the millions that watch sport on the BBC or ITV.

Sports need the wide exposure that only national television can bring. When cricket started selling the Benson & Hedges Cup and the Refuge Assurance Sunday League to satellite stations, it discovered not only that cricket fans were unhappy, but so were the sponsors. The tiny audiences satellite delivered meant that the sponsor's name did not have the impact they had paid for – and interest in the events themselves diminished.

Before long, the Benson & Hedges Cup was back on the BBC and the Sunday League was looking for a new sponsor.

It's not only sports fans that watch satellite television. Films are still the single biggest attraction for satellite viewers. And there's an even more important group of view-ers as far as the long-term future of the new channels is concerned – children.

Homes with children are far more likely to have satellite television than households without any – a fifth of Britain's children live in homes with the new channels. Many of them have never known a time when there were only four channels and have no loyalty to the BBC or ITV. And even though the terrestrial channels are now screening more programmes for children, on Saturday and Sunday mornings as well as after school, Sky One – with *The DJ Kat Show* – and the Children's Channel take a large share of their viewing.

Viewing figures from the Broadcasters Audience Research Board (BARB) showed that last year, in homes with satellite television, 4 to 9-year-olds spent 21 per cent of their viewing time in front of Sky One (two hours, 49 minutes a week) and 10 per cent watching the Children's Channel (one hour 22 minutes per week). ITV accounted for 22 per cent of their viewing (two hours 57 minutes) and BBC1 19 per cent (two hours 33 minutes).

What's more, children in satellite homes watched 36 minutes a week more than the average child.

Viewing of satellite television seems certain to increase during 1993. In addition to football fans attracted by the Premier League, many cricket lovers will have been persuaded to buy dishes to watch Sky's coverage of the England Test series in India during January and February. (The cricket World Cup a year ago boosted dish sales by 100,000 and many Asians have been attracted to satellite not just by the cricket but by two new channels aimed at Asian viewers).

UK Gold may well attract other viewers who enjoy traditional British programmes which till now have been hard to find on satellite. As the terrestrial channels try to satisfy the demands of all viewers – from children to pensioners, sports fans to arts lovers, soap fans to news buffs – it becomes even harder, if not impossible, to please them all at the same time. Many may turn to satellite to find more of the programmes they like.

The number of homes with satellite or cable television has almost doubled in the last 18 months, according to BARB. In June 1991, when its satellite survey began, it estimated the total at 1.6 million homes. By the end of 1992, it was up to 2.9 million and Christmas sales brought the total up to 3,012,000 at 1 January 1993. BARB says that the growth has been consistent – at about 250,000 homes a quarter – and forecasts suggest this will be maintained during 1993, pulling in a million new homes by the end of the year, making four million in all.

These figures include cable television, which till recently has grown more slowly than satellite, because most parts of the country have not yet been cabled. In 1993, cable laying will speed up and the cable companies believe many viewers will prefer their system to a satellite dish. Not only is it less unsightly, they say, but it can offer many more channels, as well as inter-active services – such as home shopping and banking – and cheaper telephone calls.

Whether via cable or satellite, the number of channels on offer seems certain to grow in 1993 and so do the numbers of people watching.

Torin Douglas

Index